THE POLITICS OF WOMEN'S BODIES

THE POLITICS
OF
WOMEN'S BODIES

Sexuality, Appearance, and Behavior

Edited by

Rose Weitz
Arizona State University

New York   Oxford
OXFORD UNIVERSITY PRESS
1998

Oxford University Press

Oxford   New York
Athens   Auckland   Bangkok   Bogotá   Bombay
Buenos Aires   Calcutta   Cape Town   Dar es Salaam
Delhi   Florence   Hong Kong   Istanbul   Karachi
Kuala Lumpur   Madras   Madrid   Melbourne
Mexico City   Nairobi   Paris   Singapore
Taipei   Tokyo   Toronto   Warsaw
and associated companies in
Berlin   Ibadan

Library of Congress Cataloging-in-Publication Data
The politics of women's bodies: Sexuality, appearance, and behavior /
edited by Rose Weitz
p.   cm.
Includes bibliographical references.
ISBN 0-19-510994-5 (cloth). ISBN 0-19-510995-3 (paper)
1. Women—Psychology.   2. Women—Physiology.   3. Women—Social conditions.
4. Body, Human—Social aspects.   5. Body, Human—Political aspects.
I. Weitz, Rose. 1952–
HQ1206.P58   1998
305.42—DC21   97-9744 CIP

1 3 5 7 9 8 6 4 2
Printed in the United States of America
on acid-free paper

In memory of Anna Reba Weitz

Contents

Preface

Since the start of the modern feminist movement, many writers and scholars have examined how ideas about the female body affect women's lives. They have produced a large and diverse literature, spread across many academic disciplines and using many theoretical approaches, on topics ranging from the nature of lesbianism, to the sources of eating disorders, to the consequences of violence against women. Taken together, this literature forms the nucleus of a new field, the politics of women's bodies. To date, however, no monograph or anthology has brought this literature together and demonstrated its coherence. This book aims to cast a new light on this growing field and to bring it the attention it deserves.

Three themes unite the readings in this anthology: how ideas about women's bodies are socially constructed, how these social constructions can be used to control women's lives, and how women can resist these forces.

The social construction of women's bodies is the process through which ideas (including scientific ideas) about women's bodies develop and become socially accepted. As this anthology demonstrates, this is a political process, which reflects, reinforces, or challenges the distribution of power between men and women.

Like all political processes, the social construction of women's bodies develops through battles between groups with competing political interests and with differential access to power and resources. For example, doctors have presented their ideas about the existence, nature, and consequences of "premenstrual syndrome" (PMS) as objective medical truths. Yet those ideas reflect both a particular economic context—in which women are increasingly demanding equal treatment in the world of work—and socially determined ideas rather than objective facts regarding the frailty and dangerousness of the female body. Doctors' ability to convince the public to accept these ideas has depended both on their economic and social power and on the support they have received from women who believe they have PMS and want validation for and treatment of their symptoms.

The social construction of women's bodies often serves as a powerful tool for controlling women's lives by fostering material changes in women's lives and bodies. Again, we can use PMS as an example. The existence of this diagnostic category gives employers an excuse not to hire or promote women—regardless of whether they have PMS—on the grounds that women's menstrual cycles make them physically and emotionally unreliable. Similarly, when a woman acts or speaks in ways that others find threatening, those others may dismiss her actions or remarks as symptoms of PMS—regardless of whether the woman herself believes she experiences such a syndrome and even regardless of whether she is premenstrual. Finally, this social construction of PMS encourages medical practices (including the use of sedatives, hormones, and hysterectomies) that materially change and control women's bodies, while encouraging women to police their own behaviors more closely during their premenstrual days.

As Michel Foucault has so vividly described, a powerful array of disciplinary practices—both internalized and external—are used to produce "docile bodies" that willingly accede to their own social control. Yet women are not always passive victims of these disciplinary practices. Rather, they may actively collaborate in their creation and maintenance or actively resist these processes. For example, many women fought for the social construction of PMS because they believed it would provide medical legitimation for behaviors and emotions that were otherwise socially unacceptable, while others fought against this social construction because they believed it would restrict women's lives. Consequently, this volume looks not only at the social construction of women's bodies (including women's role in this process) but also at the possibilities for resistance.

Overview of Volume

The first section of this volume looks at the social construction of women's bodies. The first article provides a context for the rest of the anthology by providing a broad overview of the history of social ideas about women's bodies, demonstrating how changes in these ideas can challenge or reinforce women's position in society. The other articles draw on both poststructuralist and traditional social scientific theoretical traditions to provide a framework for questioning our most basic ideas about the female body, examining the political process through which these ideas develop, and exploring how and why women accept or resist these ideas.

The remainder of this volume looks in more detail at how the politics of women's bodies affects women's lives. I have somewhat arbitrarily divided these readings into three sections; the politics of sexuality, of appearance, and of bodily behavior. (Obviously, these three sections overlap. For example, to present a culturally acceptable appearance, women must engage in certain behaviors, with certain consequences for how their sexuality is perceived by others.)

The first section, on the politics of sexuality, addresses how women are socialized according to an Euro-American, heterosexual norm that emphasizes male pleasure and female restraint. One article discusses cultural attitudes toward the sexuality of African-American women and the price these women pay for those attitudes. The other articles examine how norms of heterosexual romance are taught and the social consequences suffered by those who resist these norms.

The second section explores the politics of appearance. This section looks at the myriad ways in which women throughout life are taught to adopt cultural norms regarding female appearance. It explores the ways in which these norms control and restrict women's lives, and raises questions regarding the possibilities for and limits on resistance to these norms.

The third section looks at four politically charged areas where issues of women's behavior and women's bodies intersect—menstruation, menopause, childbearing, and violence against women. These readings look at how various political interests have attempted to define women's bodies and bodily behaviors in ways that can limit women's life options and reduce their social power.

The readings included in this volume were selected to cover a wide range of topics related to women and the body. All the readings are intellectually stimulating, but written in a fashion accessible to any literate audience. The articles present theoretical concepts as well as data, but avoid the sort of convoluted "academese" and complex statistical techniques that non-academic readers might find difficult to comprehend.

To increase accessibility, I have shortened most of the articles, deleting some of the more tangential issues (deleted text is marked with ellipses). This editing also allowed me to cover many topics while restricting the book's size and, consequently, price. I also have edited the readings to regularize spelling and style.

My other goal in choosing readings was to find readings relevant to a diverse population of women, while reflecting diverse academic perspectives. Readings were selected with attention to issues of diversity with regard to class, ethnicity, age, and sexual orientation. Four of the authors included in this volume write primarily for the popular press. The rest come from anthropology, history, law, literature, philosophy, and sociology. All but four of the twenty readings were first published in the 1990s; all but the first were originally published elsewhere.

My ideas for this anthology came together during many years of teaching courses at Arizona State University on feminist theory, the sociology of women, and the politics of women's health. The Women's Studies Program at the university provided fertile ground for exploring these ideas. I especially benefited from many conversations with Georganne Scheiner and Mary Logan Rothschild, the program director. My ideas were developed further in discussions with Myra Dinnerstein, of the University of Arizona, who has been a valued collaborator and confidante, and who first suggested the idea of bringing together readings on women and the body. I would also like to thank Judith Lorber, Beth Rushing, and Wendy Simonds, who, in addition to Georganne, Mary, and Myra, read parts of the manuscript and helped me to improve it. Members of the electronic bulletin board of Sociologists for Women in Society tolerated many questions from me and provided many

xii   PREFACE

useful suggestions. My research assistants, Tanya Nieri and Bethany Gizzi, cheerfully tracked down obscure references and copyedited readings. Many others, including the anonymous reviewers of this manuscript, provided invaluable assistance by recommending topics and readings for this anthology. I cannot name them all here, but they have my gratitude nonetheless, for without their contributions this would be a far weaker book. Finally, I would like to thank my husband, Mark Pry, for his love and sense of humor, and for keeping our household running (despite the demands of his own work) while I worked on this project.

THE POLITICS OF WOMEN'S BODIES

I

THE SOCIAL
CONSTRUCTION OF
WOMEN'S BODIES

The articles in this section provide the historical and theoretical underpinnings for analyzing social ideas about women's bodies. The central theme in this section is the social construction of women's bodies. "Social construction" refers to the process through which ideas become socially accepted. As we will see, this is an intensely political process, reflecting competing groups' divergent vested interests and differential access to power.

The first article, by Rose Weitz (the editor of this volume), provides an outline history of the politics of women's bodies. This article delineates how ideas about the female body have changed over time, and the impact those changes have had on women's lives.

Judith Lorber's article, "Believing is Seeing: Biology as Ideology," attacks head on our assumptions about men's and women's natures. She argues that we can treat sex as a dichotomous variable—with male and female the two opposites—only because we choose to ignore (or hide) the evidence regarding intermediate sexes. Similarly, she argues, our assumptions about the biological differences between men and women have led us to construct a world that reinforces those very assumptions—by, for example, emphasizing the femininity and grace of women ice skaters and gymnasts while denigrating or ignoring the strength and power of women basketball players.

In "Foucault, Femininity, and the Modernization of Patriarchal Power," Sandra Lee Bartky begins by describing Michel Foucault's ideas regarding how modern society creates "docile bodies"—individuals who willingly control their bodies to conform to cultural norms. She then shows how women learn to discipline their bodies and police themselves so that they will conform to ideas based on men's desires about proper female appearance and behavior.

Finally, in "Women and Medicalization: a New Perspective," Catherine Kohler Riessman looks at the role medical ideas play in the social construction of the female body, examining how various aspects of women's lives and bodies have become defined as medical problems requiring medical intervention. She explains how illness labels can reflect social ideas, and describes why and how both women consumers and doctors have worked to label childbirth, abortion, and contraception as medical events. Finally, she discusses how this label affects women's social position and power.

1

A History of Women's Bodies

Rose Weitz

Throughout history, ideas about women's bodies have played a dramatic role in either challenging or reinforcing power relationships between men and women. We can therefore regard these ideas as political tools in an ongoing political struggle. This article presents a brief history of women's bodies, looking at how ideas about the female body have changed over time in western law and biological theory.

Beginning with the earliest written legal codes, and continuing nearly to the present day, the law typically has defined women's bodies as men's property. In ancient societies, women who were not slaves typically belonged to their fathers before marriage and to their husbands thereafter. For this reason, Babylonian law, for example, treated rape as a form of property damage, requiring a rapist to pay a fine to the husband or father of the raped woman, but nothing to the woman herself. Similarly, marriages in ancient societies typically were contracted between prospective husbands and prospective fathers-in-law, with the potential bride playing little if any role.

Women's legal status as property reflected the belief that women's bodies were inherently different from men's in ways that made women both defective and dangerous. This belief comes through clearly in the writings of Aristotle, whose ideas about women's bodies formed the basis for "scientific" discussion of this topic in the west from the fourth century B.C. through the eighteenth century (Martin 1987; Tuana 1993). Aristotle's biological theories centered around the concept of heat. According to Aristotle, only embryos that had sufficient heat could develop into fully human form. The rest became female. In other words, woman was, in Aristotle's words, a "misbegotten man" and a "monstrosity"—less than fully formed and literally half-baked. Building on this premise, Galen, a highly influential Greek doctor, later declared that women's reproductive organs were virtually identical to men's, but were located internally because female embryos lacked the heat needed for those organs to develop fully and externally. This view remained common among doctors until well into the eighteenth century.

3

Lack of heat, classical scholars argued, also produced a plethora of other deficiencies in women, including a smaller stature, a frailer constitution, a less developed brain, and emotional and moral weaknesses that could endanger any men who fell under women's spell. These ideas later would resonate with ideas about women embedded in Christian interpretations of Mary and Eve. Christian theologians argued that Eve caused the fall from divine grace and the expulsion from the Garden of Eden by succumbing when the snake tempted her with the forbidden fruit. This "original sin" occurred, these theologians argued, because women's nature made them inherently more susceptible to sexual desire and other passions of the flesh, blinding them to reason and morality and making them a constant danger to men's souls. Mary avoided the pitfalls of passion only by remaining virginal. Such ideas later would play a large role in fueling the witchcraft hysteria in early modern Europe and colonial America. Women formed the vast majority of the tens of thousands of people executed as witches during these centuries because both Protestants and Catholics assumed that women were less intelligent than men, more driven by sexual passions, and hence more susceptible to the Devil's blandishments (Barstow 1994).

By the eighteenth century, women's legal and social position in the western world had changed little. When the famous English legal theorist, Sir William Blackstone, published his encyclopedic codification of English law in 1769, non-slave women's legal status still remained closer to that of property than to that of non-slave men. According to Blackstone, "By marriage, the husband and wife are one person in the law; that is, the very being and legal existence of the woman is suspended during the marriage, or at least is incorporated into that of her husband under whose wing, protection and cover she performs everything" (1904, 432). In other words, upon marriage a woman experienced "civil death," losing any rights as a citizen, including the right to own or bestow property, make contracts or sue for legal redress, hold custody of minor children, or keep any wages she earned. Moreover, as her "protector," a husband had a legal right to beat his wife if he believed it necessary, as well as a right to her sexual services. These principles would form the basis of marital law in the United States from its founding.

Both in colonial America and in the United States for its first eighty-nine years, slave women *were* property. Moreover, both the law and contemporary scientific writings often described African-American women (and men) as animals, rather than humans. Consequently, neither slave women nor slave men held any rights of citizenship. By the same token, female African-American slaves were completely subject to their white masters. Rape was common, both as a form of "entertainment" for white men and as a way of breeding more slaves, since the children of slave mothers were automatically slaves, regardless of their fathers' race. Nor did African-American women's special vulnerability to rape end when slavery ended.

Both before and after the Civil War, the rape of African-American women was explained, if not justified, by an ideology that defined African-Americans, including African-American women, as animalistically hypersexual, and thus responsible for their own rapes (Gilman 1985; Giddings 1995). For example, an article published by a white southern woman on March 17, 1904 in a popular periodical, the *Independent,* declared:

> Degeneracy is apt to show most in the weaker individuals of any race; so Negro women evidence more nearly the popular idea of total depravity than the men do. They are so nearly lacking in virtue that the color of a Negro woman's skin is generally taken (and quite correctly) as a guarantee of her immorality. . . . I sometimes read of a virtuous Negro woman, hear of them, but the idea is absolutely inconceivable to me.

These ideas about sexuality, combined with ideas about the inherent inferiority of African Americans, are vividly reflected in the 1861 Georgia penal code. That code left it up to the court whether to fine or imprison men who raped African-American women, recommended two to twenty years' imprisonment for white men convicted of raping white women, and mandated the death penalty for African-American men convicted of raping white women (Roberts 1990, 60). Moreover, African-American men typically were lynched before being brought to trial if suspected of raping a white woman, while white men were rarely convicted for raping white women and probably never convicted for raping African-American women.

For both free and slave women in the United States, the legal definition of women's bodies as men's property experienced its first serious challenges during the nineteenth century. In 1839, Mississippi passed the first Married Women's Property Act. Designed primarily to protect family farms and property from creditors rather than to expand the rights of women (Speth 1982), the law gave married women the right to retain property they owned before marriage and wages they earned outside the home. By the end of the nineteenth century, similar laws had been passed in all the states.

Also during the nineteenth century, both white and African-American women won the right to vote in Wyoming, Utah, Colorado, and Idaho, and a national suffrage campaign took root. Beginning with Oberlin College in 1833, a growing number of colleges began accepting women students, including free African-American women, with more than five thousand women graduating in 1900 alone (Flexner 1974, 232). At the same time, the industrial revolution prompted growing numbers of women to seek paid employment. By 1900, the U.S. census listed more than five million women as gainfully employed outside the home (Flexner 1974, 250). This did not reflect any significant changes in the lives of African-American women—who had worked as much as men when slaves and who often worked full-time post-slavery (Jones 1985)—but was a major change for white women.

Each of these changes challenged the balance of power between men and women in American society. In response to these challenges, a counterreaction quickly developed. This counterreaction combined new "scientific" ideas with older definitions of women's bodies as ill or fragile to argue that white middle-class women were unable to sustain the responsibilities of political power or the burdens of education or employment.

Ideas about middle-class women's frailty drew heavily on the writings of Charles Darwin, who had published his groundbreaking *On the Origin of Species* in 1872 (Tuana 1993). As part of his theory of evolution, Darwin argued that males compete for sexual access to females, with only the fittest succeeding and reproducing. As a result, males continually evolve toward greater "perfection." Females, on the other hand, need not compete for males, and therefore are not subject to the same process of natural selection. Consequently, in any species, males are more evolved than females. In addition, Darwin argued, females must expend so much energy on reproduction that they retain little energy for either physical or mental development. As a result, women remain subject to their emotions and passions: nurturing, altruistic, and child-like, but with little sense of either justice or morality.

Darwin's theories meshed well with Victorian ideas about middle-class white women's sexuality, which depicted women as the objects of male desire, emphasized romance and downplayed female sexual desire, and reinforced a sexual double standard. Middle-class women were expected to have passionate and even romantic attachments to other women, but these attachments were assumed to be emotional, rather than physical. Most women who had "romantic friendships" with other women were married to men, and only those few who adopted male clothing or behavior were considered lesbians (Faderman 1981). Lesbianism became more broadly identified and stigmatized only in the early twentieth century, when women's entry into higher education and the workforce enabled some women to survive economically without marrying, and lesbianism therefore became a threat to male power.

With women's increasing entry into education and employment, ideas about the physical and emotional frailty of women—with their strong echoes of both Christian and Aristotelian disdain for women and their bodies—were adopted by nineteenth-century doctors as justifications for keeping women uneducated and unemployed. So, for example:

> The president of the Oregon State Medical Society, F. W. Van Dyke, in 1905, claimed that hard study killed sexual desire in women, took away their beauty, and brought on hysteria, neurasthenia [a mental disorder], dyspepsia [indigestion], astigmatism [a visual disorder], and dysmenorrhea [painful menstruation]. Educated women, he added, could not bear children with ease because study arrested the development of the pelvis at the same time it increased the size of the child's brain, and therefore its head. The result was extensive suffering in childbirth by educated women (Bullough and Voght 1984, 32).

Belief in the frailty of middle-class women's bodies similarly fostered the epidemic rise during the late nineteenth century in gynecological surgery (Barker-Benfield 1976; Longo 1984). Many doctors routinely performed surgery to remove healthy ovaries, uteruses, or clitorises, from women who experienced an extremely wide range of physical and mental symptoms— including symptoms such as rebelliousness or malaise which reflected women's constrained social circumstances more than their physical health. These operations were not only unnecessary but dangerous, with mortality rates of up to thirty-three percent (Longo 1984).

Paradoxically, at the same time that scientific "experts" emphasized the frailty of middle-class white women, they emphasized the robustness of poorer women, both white and nonwhite. As Jacqueline Jones (1985, 15) explains:

> Slaveholders had little use for sentimental platitudes about the delicacy of the female constitution. . . . There were enough women like Susan Mabry of Virginia, who could pick 400 or 500 pounds of cotton a day (150 to 200 pounds was considered respectable for an average worker) to remove from a master's mind all doubts about the ability of a strong, healthy woman field worker. As a result, he conveniently discarded his time-honored Anglo-Saxon notions about the type of work best suited for women.

Similar attitudes applied to working-class white women. Thus, Dr. Lucien Warner, a popular medical authority, could in 1874 explain how middle-class women were made frail by their affluence, while "the African negress, who toils beside her husband in the fields of the south, and Bridget [the Irish maid], who washes and scrubs and toils in our homes at the north, enjoy for the most part good health, with comparative immunity from uterine disease" (cited in Ehrenreich and English 1973, 12–13).

At any rate, despite the warnings of medical experts, women continued to enter both higher education and the paid workforce. However, although education clearly benefited women, entering the workforce endangered the lives and health of many women due to hazardous working conditions.

Although male workers could hope to improve their working conditions through union agitation, this tactic was far less useful for women, who more often worked in non-unionized jobs, were denied union membership, or were not interested in joining unions. As a result, some feminists began lobbying for protective labor laws that would set maximum working hours for women, mandate rest periods, and so on (Erickson, 1982). In 1908, the U.S. Supreme Court first upheld such a law in *Muller v. Oregon*. Unfortunately, it soon became clear that protective labor laws hurt women more than they helped, by bolstering the idea that female workers were inherently weaker than male workers.

Twelve years after the *Muller* decision, in 1920, most female U.S. citizens finally won the right to vote in national elections. (Most Asian-born and Native American women, however, were ineligible for citizenship, and most African-American women—like African-American men—were prevented from voting through legal and illegal means.) Unfortunately, suffrage largely marked the close of decades of feminist activism rather than the start of any broader reforms in women's legal, social, or economic positions.

By the 1960s, women's status had hardly changed. For example, although the fourteenth amendment (passed in 1868) guaranteed equal protection under the law for all U.S. citizens, not until 1971, in *Reed v. Reed*, did the Supreme Court rule that differential treatment based on sex was illegal. Similarly, based still on Blackstone's interpretation of women's legal position and the concept of women as men's property, until the 1970s courts routinely refused to prosecute wife batterers unless they killed their wives, and not until 1984 did any court convict a man for raping a woman to whom he was married and with whom he still legally resided.

Recognition of these and other inequities led to the emergence of a new feminist movement beginning in the second half of the 1960s (Evans 1979). In its earliest days, this movement adopted the rhetoric of liberalism and the civil rights movement, arguing that women and men were morally and intellectually equal and that women's bodies were essentially similar to men's bodies. The (unsuccessful) attempts to pass the Equal Rights Amendment, which stated that "equality of rights under the law shall not be denied or abridged by the United States or any state on account of sex," reflected this strain of thinking about gender.

The goal of these liberal feminists was to achieve equality with men within existing social structures—for example, to get men to assume a fair share of child-care responsibilities. Soon, however, some feminists began questioning whether achieving equality within existing social structures would really help women, or whether women would be served better by radically restructuring society to create more humane social arrangements—for example, establishing communal living arrangements in which child care could be more broadly shared rather than trying to allocate child-care responsibilities more equitably within a nuclear family. Along with this questioning of social arrangements came questions about the reality not only of sex differences but also of the categories "male" and "female."

In contrast, a more recent strand of feminist thought, known as "cultural feminism," has re-emphasized the idea of inherent differences between men and women. Unlike those who made this argument in the past, however, cultural feminists argue that women's bodies (as well as their minds and moral values) are *superior* to men's. From this perspective, women's ability to create human life makes women (especially mothers) innately more pacifistic, loving, moral, creative, and life-affirming than men (e.g., Daly 1978). For the same reason, some feminists, such as Susan Griffin (1978), now argue that women also have an inherently deeper connection than men to nature and to ecological concerns. (Ironically, many in the antiabortion movement and on the far right use rhetoric similar to that of cultural feminists to argue that women belong at home.)

Despite the differences among feminists in ideology and tactics, all share the goal of challenging accepted ideas about women's bodies and social position. Not surprisingly, as the modern feminist movement has grown, a backlash has developed that has attempted to reinforce more traditional ideas

(Faludi 1991). This backlash has taken many forms, including (1) increasing pressure on women to control the shape of their bodies, (2) attempts to define premenstrual and postmenopausal women as ill, and (3) the rise of the anti-abortion and "fetal rights" movements.

Throughout history, women have experienced social pressures to maintain acceptable appearances. However, as Susan Faludi (1991), Naomi Wolf (1991), and many others have demonstrated, the backlash against modern feminism seems to have increased these pressures substantially. For example, the average weight of both Miss America winners and *Playboy* centerfolds has decreased steadily since 1978, even though the average height has increased (Wiseman et al. 1992). Current appearance norms call for women to be not only painfully thin, but muscular and buxom—qualities that can occur together only if women spend vast amounts of time on exercise, money on cosmetic surgery, and emotional energy on diet (Seid 1989).

The backlash against feminism also has affected women's lives by stimulating calls for the medical control of premenstrual women. Although first defined in the 1930s, the idea of a "premenstrual syndrome" (PMS) did not garner much attention either inside or outside medical circles until the 1970s. Since then, innumerable popular and medical articles have argued that to function at work or school, women with PMS need medical treatment to control their anger and discipline their behaviors. Similarly, many doctors now believe that menopausal women need drugs to maintain their sexual attractiveness and to control their behavior and emotions.

Finally, the backlash against feminism has restricted women's lives by encouraging the rise of the antiabortion and "fetal rights" movements. Prior to the twentieth century, abortion was generally considered both legally and socially acceptable, although dangerous. By the mid-twentieth century, abortion had become a safe medical procedure, but was legal only when deemed medically necessary. Doctors were deeply divided, however, regarding when it was necessary, with some performing abortions only to preserve women's lives and others doing so to preserve women's social, psychological, or economic well-being (Luker 1984). To protect themselves legally, beginning in the 1960s, those doctors who favored more lenient indications for abortion, along with women who considered abortion a right, lobbied heavily for broader legal access to abortion. This lobbying culminated in 1973 when the U.S. Supreme Court ruled, in *Roe v. Wade*, that abortion was legal in most circumstances. However, subsequent legislative actions and Court decisions (including the 1976 Hyde Amendment and the Supreme Court's 1989 decision in *Webster v. Reproductive Health Services*), have reduced legal access to abortion substantially, especially for poor and young women.

Embedded in the legal battles over abortion is a set of beliefs about the nature of women and of the fetus (Luker 1984). On one side stand those who argue that unless women have an absolute right to control their own bodies, including the right to abortion, they will never attain fully equal status in society. On the other side stand those who argue that the fetus is fully human and that women's rights to control their bodies must be subjugated to the fetus's right to life.

This latter belief also underlies the broader social and legal pressure for "fetal rights." For example, pregnant women around the country—almost all of them nonwhite and poor—have been arrested for abusing alcohol or illegal drugs while pregnant, on the grounds that they had no right to expose their fetuses to harmful substances. Others—again, mostly poor and nonwhite— have been forced to have cesarean sections against their will. In these cases, the courts have ruled that fetuses' interests are more important than women's right to determine what will happen to their bodies—in this case, the right to refuse invasive, hazardous surgery—and that doctors know better than mothers what is in a fetus's best interests. Still other women have been denied jobs by employers who have argued that hazardous work conditions might endanger a pregnant worker's fetus; these employers have ignored evidence that the same conditions would also damage men's sperm and thus any resulting fetuses.

In sum, throughout history, ideas about women's bodies have centrally affected the strictures within which women live. Only by looking at the embodied experiences of women, as well as at how those experiences are socially constructed, can we fully understand women's lives, women's position in society, and the possibilities for resistance against that position.

References

Barker-Benfield, G. J. 1976. *The Horrors of the Half-Known Life: Male Attitudes Towards Women and Sexuality in Nineteenth-Century America*. New York: Harper.

Barstow, Anne Llewellyn. 1994. *Witchcraze: A New History of the European Witch Hunts*. San Francisco: Pandora.

Blackstone, Sir William. 1904. *Commentaries on the Laws of England in Four Books*. vol. 1 edited by George Sharswood. Philadelphia: Lippincott.

Bullough, Vern and Martha Voght. 1984. Women, menstruation, and nineteenth-century medicine. In *Women and Health in America: Historical Readings*, edited by Judith Walzer Leavitt. Madison: University of Wisconsin Press.

Daly, Mary. 1978. *Gyn/Ecology: The Metaethics of Radical Feminism*. Boston: Beacon.

Darwin, Charles. 1872. *On the Origin of Species*. Akron, OH: Werner.

Ehrenreich, Barbara, and Deirdre English. 1973. *Complaints and Disorders: The Sexual Politics of Sickness*. Old Westbury, NY: Feminist Press.

Erickson, Nancy S. 1982. Historical background of "protective" labor legislation: Muller v. Oregon. In *Women and the Law: A Social Historical Perspective*. Vol. 2, edited by D. Kelly Weisberg. Cambridge, MA: Schenkman.

Evans, Sara M. 1979. *Personal Politics: The Roots of Women's Liberation in the Civil Rights Movement and the New Left*. New York: Vintage.

Faderman, Lillian. 1981. *Surpassing the Love of Men: Romantic Friendship and Love Between Women from the Renaissance to the Present*. New York: William Morrow.

Faludi, Susan. 1991. *Backlash: The Undeclared War Against American Women*. New York: Crown.

Flexner, Eleanor. 1974. *Century of Struggle: The Women's Rights Movement in the United States*. New York: Atheneum.

Giddings, Paula. 1995. The last taboo. In *Words of Fire: An Anthology of African-American Feminist Thought*, edited by Beverly Guy-Sheftall. New York: New Press.

Gilman, Sander. 1985. Black bodies, white bodies: Toward an iconography of female sexuality in late nineteenth-century art, medicine, and literature. In *"Race," Writing, and Difference*, edited by Henry Louis Gates. Chicago: University of Chicago Press.

Griffin, Susan. 1978. *Woman and Nature: The Roaring Inside Her*. New York: Harper.

Jones, Jacqueline. 1985. *Labor of Love, Labor of Sorrow: Black Women, Work, and the Family from Slavery to the Present*. New York: Basic.

Longo, Lawrence D. 1984. The rise and fall of Battey's operation: A fashion in surgery. In *Woman and Health in America*, edited by Judith Walzer Leavitt. Madison: University of Wisconsin Press.

Luker, Kristin. 1984. *Abortion and the Politics of Motherhood*. Berkeley: University of California Press.

Martin, Emily. 1987. *The Woman in the Body: A Cultural Analysis of Reproduction*. Boston: Beacon.

Roberts, Dorothy E. 1990. The future of reproductive choice for poor women and women of color. *Women's Rights Law Reporter* 12(2):59–67.

Seid, Roberta Pollack. 1989. *Never Too Thin: Why Women Are at War with Their Bodies*. Englewood Cliffs, NJ: Prentice Hall.

Speth, Linda E. 1982. The Married Women's Property Acts, 1839–1865: Reform, reaction, or revolution? In *Women and the Law: A Social Historical Perspective*. Vol. 2, edited by D. Kelly Weisberg. Cambridge, MA: Schenkman.

Tuana, Nancy. 1993. *The Less Noble Sex: Scientific, Religious, and Philosophical Conceptions of Woman's Nature*. Bloomington: Indiana University Press.

Wiseman, Claire V., James J. Gray, James E. Mosimann, and Anthony H. Ehrens. 1992. Cultural expectations of thinness in women: An update. *International Journal of Eating Disorders* 11:85–89.

Wolf, Naomi. 1991. *The Beauty Myth: How Images of Beauty Are Used Against Women*. New York: William Morrow.

2

Believing Is Seeing
Biology as Ideology

JUDITH LORBER

Until the eighteenth century, Western philosophers and scientists thought that there was one sex and that women's internal genitalia were the inverse of men's external genitalia: the womb and vagina were the penis and scrotum turned inside out (Laqueur 1990). Current Western thinking sees women and men as so different physically as to sometimes seem two species. The bodies, which have been mapped inside and out for hundreds of years, have not changed. What has changed are the justifications for gender inequality. When the social position of all human beings was believed to be set by natural law or was considered God-given, biology was irrelevant; women and men of different classes all had their assigned places. When scientists began to question the divine basis of social order and replaced faith with empirical knowledge, what they saw was that women were very different from men in that they had wombs and menstruated. Such anatomical differences destined them for an entirely different social life from men.

In actuality, the basic bodily material is the same for females and males, and except for procreative hormones and organs, female and male human beings have similar bodies (Naftolin and Butz 1981). Furthermore, as has been known since the middle of the nineteenth century, male and female genitalia develop from the same fetal tissue, and so infants can be born with ambiguous genitalia (Money and Ehrhardt 1972). When they are, biology is used quite arbitrarily in sex assignment. Suzanne Kessler (1990) interviewed six medical specialists in pediatric intersexuality and found that whether an infant with XY chromosomes and anomalous genitalia was categorized as a boy or a girl depended on the size of the penis—if a penis was very small, the child was categorized as a girl, and sex-change surgery was used to make an artificial

Reprinted by permission of Sage Publications. Originally published in *Gender & Society* (vol. 7, issue 4) pp. 568–81. Copyright 1993 by Sage Publications.

vagina. In the late nineteenth century, the presence or absence of ovaries was the determining criterion of gender assignment for hermaphrodites because a woman who could not procreate was not a complete woman (Kessler 1990, 20).

Yet in Western societies, we see two discrete sexes and two distinguishable genders because our society is built on two classes of people, "women" and "men." Once the gender category is given, the attributes of the person are also gendered: Whatever a "woman" is has to be "female"; whatever a "man" is has to be "male." Analyzing the social processes that construct the categories we call "female and male," "women and men," and "homosexual and heterosexual" uncovers the ideology and power differentials congealed in these categories (Foucault 1978). This article will use two familiar areas of social life—sports and technological competence—to show how myriad physiological differences are transformed into similar-appearing, gendered social bodies. My perspective goes beyond accepted feminist views that gender is a cultural overlay that modifies physiological sex differences. That perspective assumes either that there are two fairly similar sexes distorted by social practices into two genders with purposefully different characteristics or that there are two sexes whose essential differences are rendered unequal by social practices. I am arguing that bodies differ in many ways physiologically, but they are completely transformed by social practices to fit into the salient categories of a society, the most pervasive of which are "female" and "male" and "women" and "men."

Neither sex nor gender are pure categories. Combinations of incongruous genes, genitalia, and hormonal input are ignored in sex categorization, just as combinations of incongruous physiology, identity, sexuality, appearance, and behavior are ignored in the social construction of gender statuses. Menstruation, lactation, and gestation do not demarcate women from men. Only some women are pregnant and then only some of the time; some women do not have a uterus or ovaries. Some women have stopped menstruating temporarily, others have reached menopause, and some have had hysterectomies. Some women breast-feed some of the time, but some men lactate (Jaggar 1983, 165 fn). Menstruation, lactation, and gestation are individual experiences of womanhood (Levesque-Lopman 1988), but not determinants of the social category "woman," or even "female." Similarly, "men are not always sperm-producers, and in fact, not all sperm producers are men. A male-to-female transsexual, prior to surgery, can be socially a woman, though still potentially (or actually) capable of spermatogenesis" (Kessler and McKenna [1978] 1985, 2).

When gender assignment is contested in sports, where the categories of competitors are rigidly divided into women and men, chromosomes are now used to determine in which category the athlete is to compete. However, an anomaly common enough to be found in several women at every major international sports competition are XY chromosomes that have not produced male anatomy or physiology because of a genetic defect. Because these women are women in every way significant for sports competition, the prestigious International Amateur Athletic Federation has urged that sex be determined by simple genital inspection (Kolata 1992). Transsexuals would pass this test, but it took a lawsuit for Renée Richards, a male-to-female transsexual, to be able to play tournament tennis as a woman, despite his male sex chromosomes (Richards 1983). Oddly, neither basis for gender categorization—chromosomes nor genitalia—has anything to do with sports prowess (Birrell and Cole 1990).

In the Olympics, in cases of chromosomal ambiguity, women must undergo "a battery of gynecological and physical exams to see if she is 'female enough' to compete. Men are not tested" (Carlson 1991, 26). The purpose is not to categorize women and men accurately, but to make sure men don't enter women's competitions, where, it is felt, they will have the advantage of size and strength. This practice sounds fair only because it is assumed that all men are similar in size and strength and different from all women. Yet in Olympics boxing and wrestling matches, men are matched within weight classes. Some women might similarly successfully compete with some men in many sports. Women did not run in marathons until about twenty years ago. In twenty years of marathon competition, women have reduced their finish times by more than one-and-one-half hours; they are expected to run as fast as men in that race by 1998 and might catch up with men's running times in races of other lengths within the next 50 years because they are increasing their fastest speeds more rapidly than are men (Fausto-Sterling 1985, 213–18).

The reliance on only two sex and gender categories in the biological and social sciences is as epistemologically spurious as the reliance on chromosomal or genital tests to group athletes. Most research designs do not investigate whether physical skills or physical abilities are really more or less common in women and men (Epstein 1988). They start out with two social categories ("women," "men"), assume they are biologically different ("female," "male"), look for similarities among them and differences between them, and attribute what they have found for the social categories to sex differences (Gelman, Collman, and Maccoby 1986). These designs rarely question the categorization of their subjects into two and only two groups, even though they often find more significant within-group differences than between-group differences (Hyde 1990). The social construction perspective on sex and gender suggests that instead of starting with the two presumed dichotomies in each category—female, male; woman, man—it might be more useful in gender studies to group patterns of behavior and only then look for identifying markers of the people likely to enact such behaviors.

What Sports Illustrate

Competitive sports have become, for boys and men, as players and as spectators, a way of constructing a masculine identity, a legitimated outlet for violence and aggression, and an avenue for upward mobility (Dunning 1986;

Kemper 1990, 167–206; Messner 1992). For men in Western societies, physical competence is an important marker of masculinity (Fine 1987; Glassner 1992; Majors 1990). In professional and collegiate sports, physiological differences are invoked to justify women's secondary status, despite the clear evidence that gender status overrides physiological capabilities. Assumptions about women's physiology have influenced rules of competition; subsequent sports performances then validate how women and men are treated in sports competitions.

Gymnastic equipment is geared to slim, wiry, prepubescent girls and not to mature women; conversely, men's gymnastic equipment is tailored for muscular, mature men, not slim, wiry, prepubescent boys. Boys could compete with girls, but are not allowed to; women gymnasts are left out entirely. Girl gymnasts are just that—little girls who will be disqualified as soon as they grow up (Vecsey 1990). Men gymnasts have men's status. In women's basketball, the size of the ball and rules for handling the ball change the style of play to "a slower, less intense, and less exciting modification of the 'regular' or men's game" (Watson 1987, 441). In the 1992 Winter Olympics, men figure skaters were required to complete three triple jumps in their required program; women figure skaters were forbidden to do more than one. These rules penalized artistic men skaters and athletic women skaters (Janofsky 1992). For the most part, Western sports are built on physically trained men's bodies:

> Speed, size, and strength seem to be the essence of sports. Women *are* naturally inferior at "sports" so conceived.
>
> But if women had been the historically dominant sex, our concept of sport would no doubt have evolved differently. Competitions emphasizing flexibility, balance, strength, timing, and small size might dominate Sunday afternoon television and offer salaries in six figures (English 1982, 266, emphasis in original).

Organized sports are big businesses and, thus, who has access and at what level is a distributive or equity issue. The overall status of women and men athletes is an economic, political, and ideological issue that has less to do with individual physiological capabilities than with their cultural and social meaning and who defines and profits from them (Messner and Sabo 1990; Slatton and Birrell 1984). Twenty years after the passage of Title IX of the U.S. Civil Rights Act, which forbade gender inequality in any school receiving federal funds, the goal for collegiate sports in the next five years is 60 percent men, 40 percent women in sports participation, scholarships, and funding (Moran 1992).

How access and distribution of rewards (prestigious and financial) are justified is an ideological, even moral, issue (Birrell 1988, 473–76, Hargreaves 1982). One way is that men athletes are glorified and women athletes ignored in the mass media. Messner and his colleagues found that in 1989, in TV sports news in the United States, men's sports got 92 percent of the coverage and women's sports 5 percent, with the rest mixed or gender-neutral (Messner, Duncan, and Jensen 1993). In 1990, in four of the top-selling newspapers in the United States, stories on men's sports outnumbered those on women's sports 23 to 1. Messner and his colleagues also found an implicit hierarchy in naming, with women athletes most likely to be called by first names, followed by black men athletes, and only white men athletes routinely referred to by their last names. Similarly, women's collegiate sports teams are named or marked in ways that symbolically feminize and trivialize them—the men's team is called Tigers, the women's Kittens (Eitzen and Baca Zinn 1989).

Assumptions about men's and women's bodies and their capacities are crafted in ways that make unequal access and distribution of rewards acceptable (Hudson 1978; Messner 1988). Media images of modern men athletes glorify their strength and power, even their violence (Hargreaves 1986). Media images of modern women athletes tend to focus on feminine beauty and grace (so they are not really athletes) or on their thin, small, wiry, androgenous bodies (so they are not really women). In coverage of the Olympics,

> loving and detailed attention is paid to pixie-like gymnasts; special and extended coverage is given to graceful and dazzling figure skaters; the camera painstakingly records the fluid movements of swimmers and divers. And then, in a blinding flash of fragmented images, viewers see a few minutes of volleyball, basketball, speed skating, track and field, and alpine skiing, as television gives its nod to the mere existence of these events (Boutilier and SanGiovanni 1983, 190).

Extraordinary feats by women athletes who were presented as mature adults might force sports organizers and audiences to rethink their stereotypes of women's capabilities, the way elves, mermaids, and ice queens do not. Sports, therefore, construct men's bodies to be powerful: women's bodies to be sexual. As Connell (1987, 85) says,

> The meanings in the bodily sense of masculinity concern, above all else, the superiority of men to women, and the exaltation of hegemonic masculinity over other groups of men which is essential for the domination of women.

In the late 1970s, as women entered more and more athletic competitions, supposedly good scientific studies showed that women who exercised intensely would cease menstruating because they would not have enough body fat to sustain ovulation (Brozan 1978). When one set of researchers did a yearlong study that compared 66 women—21 who were training for a marathon, 22 who ran more than an hour a week, and 23 who did less than an hour of aerobic exercise a week—they discovered that only 20 percent of the women in any of these groups had "normal" menstrual cycles every month (Prior et al. 1990). The dangers of intensive training for women's fertility therefore were exaggerated as women began to compete successfully in arenas formerly closed to them.

Given the association of sports with masculinity in the United States, women athletes have to manage a contradictory status. One study of women college basketball players found that although they "did athlete" on the court, "pushing, shoving, fouling, hard running, fast breaks, defense, obscenities and sweat" (Watson 1987, 441), they "did woman" off the court, using the locker room as their staging area:

> While it typically took fifteen minutes to prepare for the game, it took approx-imately fifteen minutes after the game to shower and remove the sweat of an athlete, and it took another thirty minutes to dress, apply make-up and style hair. It did not seem to matter whether the players were going out into the public or getting on a van for a long ride home. Average dressing time and rituals did not change (Watson 1987, 443).

Another way women manage these status dilemmas is to redefine the activity or its result as feminine or womanly (Mangan and Park 1987). Thus women bodybuilders claim that "flex appeal is sex appeal" (Duff and Hong 1984, 378).

Such a redefinition of women's physicality affirms the ideological subtext of sports that physical strength is men's prerogative and justifies men's physical and sexual domination of women (Hargreaves 1986, Messner 1992, 164–72; Olson 1990; Theberge 1987; Willis 1982). When women demonstrate physical strength, they are labeled unfeminine:

> It's threatening to one's takeability, one's rapeability, one's femininity, to be strong and physically self-possessed. To be able to resist rape, not to communicate rapeability with one's body, to hold one's body for uses and meanings other than that can transform what *being a woman means* (MacKinnon 1987, 122, emphasis in original).

Resistance to that transformation, ironically, was evident in the policies of American women physical education professionals throughout most of the twentieth century. They minimized exertion, maximized a feminine appear-ance and manner, and left organized sports competition to men (Birrell 1988, 461–62; Mangan and Park 1987).

Dirty Little Secrets

As sports construct gendered bodies, technology constructs gendered skills. Meta-analyses of studies of gender differences in spatial and mathematical ability have found that men have a large advantage in ability to mentally rotate an image, a moderate advantage in a visual perception of horizontality and verticality and in mathematical performance, and a small advantage in ability to pick a figure out of a field (Hyde 1990). It could be argued that these advantages explain why, within the short space of time that computers have become ubiquitous in offices, schools, and homes, work on them and with them has become gendered: Men create, program, and market computers, make war and produce science and art with them; women microwire them in computer factories and enter data in computerized offices; boys play games, socialize, and commit crimes with computers; girls are rarely seen in computer clubs, camps, and classrooms. But women were hired as computer programmers in the 1940s because

> the work seemed to resemble simple clerical tasks. In fact, however, programming demanded complex skills in abstract logic, mathematics, electrical circuitry, and machinery, all of which . . . women used to perform in their work. Once programming was recognized as "intellectually demanding," it became attractive to men (Donato 1990, 170).

A woman mathematician and pioneer in data processing, Grace M. Hopper, was famous for her work on programming language (Perry and Greber 1990, 86). By the 1960s, programming was split into more and less skilled specialties, and the entry of women into the computer field in the 1970s and 1980s was confined to the lower-paid specialties. At each stage, employers invoked women's and men's purportedly natural capabilities for the jobs for which they were hired (Cockburn 1983, 1985; Donato 1990; Hartmann 1987; Hartmann, Kraut, and Tilly 1986; Kramer and Lehman 1990; Wright et al. 1987; Zimmerman 1983).

It is the taken-for-grantedness of such everyday gendered behavior that gives credence to the belief that the widespread differences in what women and men do must come from biology. To take one ordinarily unremarked scenario: In modern societies, if a man and woman who are a couple are in a car together, he is much more likely to take the wheel than she is, even if she is the more competent driver. Molly Haskell calls this taken-for-granted phenomenon "the dirty little secret of marriage: the husband-lousy-driver syndrome" (1989, 26). Men drive cars whether they are good drivers or not because men and machines are a "natural" combination (Scharff 1991). But the ability to drive gives one mobility; it is a form of social power.

In the early days of the automobile, feminists co-opted the symbolism of mobility as emancipation: "Donning goggles and dusters, wielding tire irons and tool kits, taking the wheel, they announced their intention to move beyond the bounds of women's place" (Scharff 1991, 68). Driving enabled them to campaign for women's suffrage in parts of the United States not served by public transportation, and they effectively used motorcades and speaking from cars as campaign tactics (Scharff 1991, 67–88). Sandra Gilbert also notes that during World War I, women's ability to drive was physically, mentally, and even sensually liberating:

> For nurses and ambulance drivers, women doctors and women messengers, the phenomenon of modern battle was very different from that experienced by entrenched combatants. Finally given a chance to take the wheel, these post-Victorian girls raced motorcars along foreign roads like adventurers exploring new

lands, while their brothers dug deeper into the mud of France. . . . Retrieving the wounded and the dead from deadly positions, these once-decorous daughters had at last been allowed to prove their valor, and they swooped over the wastelands of the war with the energetic love of Wagnerian Valkyries, their mobility alone transporting countless immobilized heroes to safe havens (1983, 438–39).

Not incidentally, women in the United States and England got the vote for their war efforts in World War I.

Social Bodies and the Bathroom Problem

People of the same racial ethnic group and social class are roughly the same size and shape—but there are many varieties of bodies. People have different genitalia, different secondary sex characteristics, different contributions to procreation, different orgasmic experiences, different patterns of illness and aging. Each of us experiences our bodies differently, and these experiences change as we grow, age, sicken, and die. The bodies of pregnant and non-pregnant women, short and tall people, those with intact and functioning limbs and those whose bodies are physically challenged are all different. But the salient categories of a society group these attributes in ways that ride roughshod over individual experiences and more meaningful clusters of people.

I am not saying that physical differences between male and female bodies don't exist, but that these differences are socially meaningless until social practices transform them into social facts. West Point Military Academy's curriculum is designed to produce leaders, and physical competence is used as a significant measure of leadership ability (Yoder 1989). When women were accepted as West Point cadets, it became clear that the tests of physical competence, such as rapidly scaling an eight-foot wall, had been constructed for male physiques—pulling oneself up and over using upper-body strength. Rather than devise tests of physical competence for women, West Point provided boosters that mostly women used—but that lost them test points—in the case of the wall, a platform. Finally, the women themselves figured out how to use their bodies successfully. Janice Yoder describes this situation:

> I was observing this obstacle one day, when a woman approached the wall in the old prescribed way, got her fingertips grip, and did an unusual thing: she walked her dangling legs up the wall until she was in a position where both her hands and feet were atop the wall. She then simply pulled up her sagging bottom and went over. She solved the problem by capitalizing on one of women's physical assets: lower-body strength (1989, 530).

In short, if West Point is going to measure leadership capability by physical strength, women's pelvises will do just as well as men's shoulders.

The social transformation of female and male physiology into a condition of inequality is well illustrated by the bathroom problem. Most buildings that have gender-segregated bathrooms have an equal number for women and for men. Where there are crowds, there are always long lines in front of women's bathrooms but rarely in front of men's bathrooms. The cultural, physiological, and demographic combinations of clothing, frequency of urination, menstruation, and child care add up to generally greater bathroom use by women than men. Thus, although an equal number of bathrooms seems fair, equity would mean more women's bathrooms or allowing women to use men's bathrooms for a certain amount of time (Molotch 1988).

The bathroom problem is the outcome of the way gendered bodies are differentially evaluated in Western cultures: Men's social bodies are the measure of what is "human." Gray's *Anatomy*, in use for 100 years, well into the twentieth century, presented the human body as male. The female body was shown only where it differed from the male (Laqueur 1990, 166–67). Denise Riley says that if we envisage women's bodies, men's bodies, and human bodies "as a triangle of identifications, then it is rarely an equilateral triangle in which both sexes are pitched at matching distances from the apex of the human" (1988, 197). Catharine MacKinnon also contends that in Western society, universal "humanness" is male because

> virtually every quality that distinguishes men from women is already affirmatively compensated in this society. Men's physiology defines most sports, their needs define auto and health insurance coverage, their socially defined biographies define workplace expectations and successful career pattens, their perspectives and concerns define quality in scholarship, their experiences and obsessions define merit, their objectification of life defines art, their military service defines citizenship, their presence defines family, their inability to get along with each other—their wars and rulerships—define history, their image defines god, and their genitals define sex. For each of their differences from women, what amounts to an affirmative action plan is in effect, otherwise known as the structure and values of American society (1987, 36).

The Paradox of Human Nature

Gendered people do not emerge from physiology or hormones but from the exigencies of the social order, mostly, from the need for a reliable division of the work of food production and the social (not physical) reproduction of new members. The moral imperatives of religion and cultural representations reinforce the boundary lines among genders and ensure that what is demanded, what is permitted, and what is tabooed for the people in each gender is well-known and followed by most. Political power, control of scarce resources, and, if necessary, violence uphold the gendered social order in the face of resistance and rebellion. Most people, however, voluntarily go along with their society's prescriptions for those of their gender status because the norms and expectations get built into their sense of worth and identity as a certain kind of human being and because they believe their society's way is the natural way. These beliefs emerge from the imagery that pervades the way we think, the way we see and hear and speak, the way we fantasize, and the way we feel. There is no core or bedrock human nature below these endlessly looping processes of the social production of sex and gender, self and other, identity and psyche, each of which is a "complex cultural construction" (Butler 1990, 36). The paradox of "human nature" is that it is always a manifestation of cultural meanings, social relationships, and power politics—"not biology, but culture, becomes destiny" (Butler 1990, 8).

Feminist inquiry has long questioned the conventional categories of social science, but much of the current work in feminist sociology has not gone beyond adding the universal category "women" to the universal category "men." Our current debates over the global assumptions of only two categories and the insistence that they must be nuanced to include race and class are steps in the direction I would like to see feminist research go, but race and class are also global categories (Collins 1990; Spelman 1988). Deconstructing sex, sexuality, and gender reveals many possible categories embedded in the social experiences and social practices of what Dorothy Smith calls the "everyday/everynight world" (1990, 31–57). These emergent categories group some people together for comparison with other people without prior assumptions about who is like whom. Categories can be broken up and people regrouped differently into new categories for comparison. This process of discovering categories from similarities and differences in people's behavior or responses can be more meaningful for feminist research than discovering similarities and differences between "females" and "males" or "women" and "men" because the social construction of the conventional sex and gender categories already assumes differences between them and similarities among them. When we rely only on the conventional categories of sex and gender, we end up finding what we looked for—we see what we believe, whether it is that "females" and "males" are essentially different or that "women" and "men" are essentially the same.

References

Birrell, Susan J. 1988. Discourses on the gender/sport relationship: From women in sport to gender relations. In *Exercise and Sport Science Reviews*, Vol. 16, edited by Kent Pandolf. New York: Macmillan.

Birrell, Susan J., and Sheryl L. Cole. 1990. Double fault: Renee Richards and the construction and naturalization of difference. *Sociology of Sport Journal* 7:1–21.

Boutilier, Mary A., and Lucinda SanGiovanni. 1983. *The Sporting Woman*. Champaign, IL: Human Kinetics.

Brozan, Nadine. 1978. Training linked to disruption of female reproductive cycle. *New York Times*, 17 April.

Butler, Judith. 1990. *Gender Trouble: Feminism and the Subversion of Identity*. New York and London: Routledge & Kegan Paul.

Carlson, Alison. 1991. When is a woman not a woman? *Women's Sport and Fitness* March, 24–29.

Cockburn, Cynthia. 1983. *Brothers: Male Dominance and Technological Change*. London: Pluto.

————. 1985. *Machinery of Dominance: Women, Men, and Technical Know-How*. London: Pluto.

Collins, Patricia Hill. 1990. *Black Feminist Thought: Knowledge, Consciousness, and the Politics of Empowerment*. Boston: Unwin Hyman.

Connell, R. W. 1987. *Gender and Power*. Stanford, CA: Stanford University Press.

Donato, Katharine M. 1990. Programming for change? The growing demand for women systems analysts. In *Job Queues, Gender Queues: Explaining Women's Inroads into Male Occupations*, edited by Barbara F. Reskin and Patricia A. Roos. Philadelphia: Temple University Press.

Duff, Robert W., and Lawrence K. Hong. 1984. Self-images of women bodybuilders. *Sociology of Sport Journal* 2:374–80.

Dunning, Eric. 1986. Sport as a male preserve: Notes on the social sources of masculine identity and its transformations. *Theory, Culture, and Society* 3:79–90.

Eitzen, D. Stanley, and Maxine Baca Zinn. 1989. The deathleticization of women: The naming and gender marking of collegiate sport teams. *Sociology of Sport Journal* 6:362–70.

English, Jane. 1982. Sex equality in sports. In *Femininity, Masculinity, and Androgyny*, edited by Mary Vetterling-Braggin. Boston: Littlefield, Adams.

Epstein, Cynthia Fuchs. 1988. *Deceptive Distinctions: Sex, Gender, and the Social Order*. New Haven, CT: Yale University Press.

Fausto-Sterling, Anne. 1985. *Myths of Gender: Biological Theories about Women and Men*. New York: Basic Books.

Fine, Gary Alan. 1987. *With the Boys: Little League Baseball and Preadolescent Culture*. Chicago: University of Chicago Press.

Foucault, Michel. 1978. *The History of Sexuality: An Introduction*. Translated by Robert Hurley. New York: Pantheon.

Gelman, Susan A., Pamela Collman, and Eleanor E. Maccoby. 1986. Inferring properties from categories versus inferring categories from properties: The case of gender. *Child Development* 57:396–404.

Gilbert, Sandra M. 1983. Soldier's heart: Literary men, literary women, and the Great War. *Signs: Journal of Women in Culture and Society* 8:422–50.

Glassner, Barry. 1992. Men and muscles. In *Men's Lives*, edited by Michael S. Kimmel and Michael A. Messner. New York: Macmillan.

Hargreaves, Jennifer A., ed. 1982. *Sport, Culture, and Ideology*. London: Routledge & Kegan Paul.

————. 1986. Where's the virtue? Where's the grace? A discussion of the social production of gender relations in and through sport. *Theory, Culture, and Society* 3:109–21.

Hartman, Heidi I., ed. 1987. *Computer Chips and Paper Clips: Technology and Women's Employment*. Vol. 2. Washington, DC: National Academy Press.

Hartmann, Heidi I., Robert E. Kraut, and Louise A. Tilly, eds. 1986. *Computer Chips and Paper Clips: Technology and Women's Employment*. Vol. 1. Washington, DC: National Academy Press.

Haskell, Molly. 1989. Hers: He drives me crazy. *New York Times Magazine*, 24 September, 26, 28.

Hudson, Jackie. 1978. Physical parameters used for female exclusion from law enforcement and athletics. In *Women and Sport: From Myth to Reality*, edited by Carole A Oglesby. Philadelphia: Lea and Febiger.

Hyde, Janet Shibley. 1990. Meta-analysis and the psychology of gender differences. *Signs: Journal of Women in Culture and Society* 16:55–73.

Jaggar, Alison M. 1983. *Feminist Politics and Human Nature.* Totowa, NJ: Rowman & Allanheld.

Janofsky, Michael. 1992. Yamaguchi has the delicate and golden touch. *New York Times*, 22 February.

Kemper, Theodore D. 1990. *Social Structure and Testosterone: Explorations of the Socio-biosocial Chain.* New Brunswick, NJ: Rutgers University Press.

Kessler, Suzanne J. 1990. The medical construction of gender: Case management of intersexed infants. *Signs: Journal of Women in Culture and Society* 16:3–26.

Kessler, Suzanne J., and Wendy McKenna. [1978] 1985. *Gender: an Ethnomethodological Approach.* Chicago: University of Chicago Press.

Kolata, Gina. 1992. Track federation urges end to gene test for femaleness. *New York Times*, 12 February.

Kramer, Pamela E., and Sheila Lehman. 1990. Mismeasuring women: A critique of research on computer ability and avoidance. *Signs: Journal of Women in Culture and Society* 16:158–72.

Laqueur, Thomas. 1990. *Making Sex: Body and Gender from the Greeks to Freud.* Cambridge, MA: Harvard University Press.

Levesque-Lopman, Louise. 1988. *Claiming Reality: Phenomenology and Women's Experience.* Totowa, NJ: Rowman & Littlefield.

MacKinnon, Catherine. 1987. *Feminism Unmodified.* Cambridge, MA: Harvard University Press.

Majors, Richard. 1990. Cool pose: Black masculinity in sports. In *Sport, Men, and the Gender Order: Critical Feminist Perspectives,* edited by Michael A. Messner and Donald F. Sabo. Champaign, IL: Human Kinetics.

Mangan, J. A., and Roberta J. Park. 1987. *From Fair Sex to Feminism: Sport and the Socialization of Women in the Industrial and Post-industrial Eras.* London: Frank Cass.

Messner, Michael A. 1988. Sports and male domination: The female athlete as contested ideological terrain. *Sociology of Sport Journal* 5:197–211.

———. 1992. *Power at Play: Sports and the Problem of Masculinity.* Boston: Beacon Press.

Messner, Michael A., Margaret Carlisle Duncan, and Kerry Jensen. 1993. Separating the men from the girls: The gendered language of television sports. *Gender & Society* 7:121–37.

Messner, Michael A., and Donald F. Sabo, eds., 1990. *Sport, Men, and the Gender Order: Critical Feminist Perspectives.* Champaign, IL: Human Kinetics.

Molotch, Harvey. 1988. The restroom and equal opportunity. *Sociological Forum* 3:128–32.

Money, John and Anke A. Ehrhardt. 1972. *Man & Woman, Boy & Girl.* Baltimore, MD: Johns Hopkins University Press.

Moran, Malcolm. 1992. Title IX: A 20-year search for equity. *New York Times* Sports Section, 21–23 June.

Naftolin, F., and E. Butz, eds. 1981. Sexual dimorphism. *Science* 211:1263–1324.

Olson, Wendy. 1990. Beyond Title IX: Toward an agenda for women and sports in the 1990s. *Yale Journal of Law and Feminism* 3:105–51.

Perry, Ruth, and Lisa Greber. 1990. Women and computers: An introduction. *Signs: Journal of Women in Culture and Society* 16:74–101.

Prior, Jerilynn C., Yvette M. Yigna, Martin T. Shechter, and Arthur E. Burgess. 1990. Spinal bone loss and ovulatory disturbances. *New England Journal of Medicine* 323:1221–27.

Richards, Renée, with Jack Ames. 1983. *Second Serve*. New York: Stein and Day.

Riley, Denise. 1988. *Am I that name? Feminism and the category of women in history*. Minneapolis: University of Minnesota Press.

Scharff, Virginia. 1991. *Taking the Wheel: Women and the Coming of the Motor Age*. New York: Free Press.

Slatton, Bonnie, and Susan Birrel. 1984. The politics of women's sport. *Arena Review* 8 (July).

Smith, Dorothy E. 1990. *The Conceptual Practices of Power: A Feminist Sociology of Knowledge*. Toronto: University of Toronto Press.

Spelman, Elizabeth. 1988. *Inessential Woman: Problems of Exclusion in Feminist Thought*. Boston: Beacon Press.

Theberge, Nancy. 1987. Sport and women's empowerment. *Women Studies International Forum* 10:387–93.

Vecsey, George. 1990. Cathy Rigby, unlike Peter, did grow up. *New York Times* Sports Section, 19 December.

Watson, Tracey. 1987. Women athletes and athletic women: The dilemmas and contradictions of managing incongruent identities. *Sociological Inquiry* 57:431–46.

Willis, Paul. 1982. Women in sport in ideology. In *Sport, Culture, and Ideology*, edited by Jennifer A. Hargreaves. London: Routledge & Kegan Paul.

Wright, Barbara Drygulski, Myra Marx Ferree, Gail O. Mellow, Linda H. Lewis, Maria-Luz Daza Samper, Robert Asher, and Kathleen Claspell, eds. 1987. *Women, Work, and Technology: Transformations*. Ann Arbor: University of Michigan Press.

Yoder, Janice D. 1989. Women at West Point: Lessons for token women in male-dominated occupations. In *Women: A Feminist Perspective*, edited by Jo Freeman. 4th ed. Palo Alto, CA: Mayfield.

Zimmerman, Jan, ed. 1983. *The Technological Woman: Interfacing with Tomorrow*. New York: Praeger.

3

Foucault, Femininity, and the Modernization of Patriarchal Power

Sandra Lee Bartky

I.

In a striking critique of modern society, Michel Foucault (1979) has argued that the rise of parliamentary institutions and of new conceptions of political liberty was accompanied by a darker counter-movement, by the emergence of a new and unprecedented discipline directed against the body. More is required of the body now than mere political allegiance or the appropriation of the products of its labor: the new discipline invades the body and seeks to regulate its very forces and operations, the economy and efficiency of its movements.

The disciplinary practices Foucault describes are tied to peculiarly modern forms of the army, the school, the hospital, the prison, and the manufactory; the aim of these disciplines is to increase the utility of the body, to augment its forces:

> What was then being formed was a policy of coercions that act upon the body, a calculated manipulation of its elements, its gestures, it behavior. The human body was entering a machinery of power that explores it, breaks it down and rearranges it. A "political anatomy," which was also a "mechanics of power," was being born; it defined how one may have a hold over others' bodies, not only so that they may do what one wishes, but so that they may operate as one wishes, with the techniques, the speed and the efficiency that one determines. Thus, discipline produces subjected and practiced bodies, "docile" bodies (1979, 138).

Originally published in *Feminism and Foucault: Reflections on Resistance*, edited by Irene Diamond and Lee Quinby. Copyright 1988 by Irene Diamond and Lee Quinby. Reprinted with the permission of Northeastern University Press.

The production of "docile bodies" requires that an uninterrupted coercion be directed to the very processes of bodily activity, not just their result; this "micro-physics of power" fragments and partitions the body's time, its space, and its movements (Foucault 1979, 28).

The student, then, is enclosed within a classroom and assigned to a desk he cannot leave; his ranking in the class can be read off the position of his desk in the serially ordered and segmented space of the classroom itself. Foucault (1979, 147) tells us that "Jean-Baptiste de la Salle dreamt of a classroom in which the spatial distribution might provide a whole series of distinctions at once, according to the pupil's progress, worth, character, application, cleanliness and parent's fortune." The student must sit upright, feet upon the floor, head erect; he may not slouch or fidget; his animate body is brought into a fixed correlation with the inanimate desk.

The minute breakdown of gestures and movements required of soldiers at drill is far more relentless:

> Bring the weapon forward. In three stages. Raise the rifle with the right hand, bringing it close to the body so as to hold it perpendicular with the right knee, the end of the barrel at eye level, grasping it by striking it with the right hand, the arm held close to the body at waist height. At the second stage, bring the rifle in front of you with the left hand, the barrel in the middle between the two eyes, vertical, the right hand grasping it at the small of the butt, the arm outstretched, the triggerguard resting on the first finger, the left hand at the height of the notch, the thumb lying along the barrel against the molding. At the third stage . . . (Foucault 1979, 153).[1]

These "body-object articulations" of the soldier and his weapon, the student and his desk, effect a "coercive link with the apparatus of production." We are far indeed from older forms of control that "demanded of the body only signs or products, forms of expression or the result of labor" (Foucault 1979, 153).

The body's time, in these regimes of power, is as rigidly controlled as its space: the factory whistle and the school bell mark a division of time into discrete and segmented units that regulate the various activities of the day. The following timetable, similar in spirit to the ordering of my grammar school classroom, is suggested for French "écoles mutuelles" of the early nineteenth century:

> 8:45 entrance of the monitor, 8:52 the monitor's summons, 8:56 entrance of the children and prayer, 9:00 the children go to their benches, 9:04 first slate, 9:08 end of dictation, 9:12 second slate, etc. (Foucault 1979, 150).

Control this rigid and precise cannot be maintained without a minute and relentless surveillance.

Jeremy Bentham's design for the Panopticon, a model prison, captures for Foucault the essence of the disciplinary society. At the periphery of the

Panopticon, a circular structure; at the center, a tower with wide windows that opens onto the inner side of the ring. The structure on the periphery is divided into cells, each with two windows, one facing the windows of the tower, the other facing the outside, allowing an effect of backlighting to make any figure visible within the cell. "All that is needed, then, is to place a supervisor in a central tower and to shut up in each cell a madman, a patient, a condemned man, a worker or a schoolboy" (Foucault 1979, 200). Each inmate is alone, shut off from effective communication with his fellows, but constantly visible from the tower. The effect of this is "to induce in the inmate a state of conscious and permanent visibility that assures the automatic functioning of power"; each becomes to himself his own jailer (Foucault 1979, 201). This "state of conscious and permanent visibility" is a sign that the tight, disciplinary control of the body has gotten a hold on the mind as well. In the perpetual self-surveillance of the inmate lies the genesis of the celebrated "individualism" and heightened self-consciousness that are hallmarks of modern times. For Foucault (1979, 228), the structure and effects of the Panopticon resonate throughout society: Is it surprising that "prisons resemble factories, schools, barracks, hospitals, which all resemble prisons"?

Foucault's account in *Discipline and Punish* of the disciplinary practices that produce the "docile bodies" of modernity is a genuine *tour de force*, incorporating a rich theoretical account of the ways in which instrumental reason takes hold of the body with a mass of historical detail. But Foucault treats the body throughout as if it were one, as if the bodily experiences of men and women did not differ and as if men and women bore the same relationship to the characteristic institutions of modern life. Where is the account of the disciplinary practices that engender the "docile bodies" of women, bodies more docile than the bodies of men? Women, like men, are subject to many of the same disciplinary practices Foucault describes. But he is blind to those disciplines that produce a modality of embodiment that is peculiarly feminine. To overlook the forms of subjection that engender the feminine body is to perpetuate the silence and powerlessness of those upon whom these disciplines have been imposed. Hence, even though a liberatory note is sounded in Foucault's critique of power, his analysis as a whole reproduces that sexism which is endemic throughout Western political theory.

We are born male or female, but not masculine or feminine. Femininity is an artifice, an achievement, "a mode of enacting and reenacting received gender norms which surface as so many styles of flesh" (Butler 1985, 11). In what follows, I shall examine those disciplinary practices that produce a body which in gesture and appearance is recognizably feminine. I consider three categories of such practices: those that aim to produce a body of a certain size and general configuration; those that bring forth from this body a specific repertoire of gestures, postures, and movements; and those that are directed toward the display of this body as an ornamented surface. I shall examine the nature of these disciplines, how they are imposed, and by whom. I shall probe the effects of the imposition of such discipline on female identity and subjectivity. In the final section I shall argue that these disciplinary practices must be understood in the light of the modernization of patriarchal domination, a modernization that unfolds historically according to the general pattern described by Foucault.

II.

Styles of the female figure vary over time and across cultures: they reflect cultural obsessions and preoccupations in ways that are still poorly understood. Today, massiveness, power, or abundance in a woman's body is met with distaste. The current body of fashion is taut, small-breasted, narrow-hipped, and of a slimness bordering on emaciation; it is a silhouette that seems more appropriate to an adolescent boy or a newly pubescent girl than to an adult woman. Since ordinary women have normally quite different dimensions, they must of course diet.

Mass-circulation women's magazines run articles on dieting in virtually every issue. The *Ladies' Home Journal* of February 1986 carries a "Fat Burning Exercise Guide," while *Mademoiselle* offers to "Help Stamp Out Cellulite" with "Six Sleek-Down Strategies." After the diet-busting Christmas holidays and, later, before summer bikini season, the titles of these features become shriller and more arresting. The reader is now addressed in the imperative mode: Jump into shape for summer! Shed ugly winter fat with the all-new Grapefruit Diet! More women than men visit diet doctors, while women greatly outnumber men in such self-help groups as Weight Watchers and Overeaters Anonymous—in the case of the latter, by well over 90 percent (Millman 1980, 46).

Dieting disciplines the body's hungers: appetite must be monitored at all times and governed by an iron will. Since the innocent need of the organism for food will not be denied, the body becomes one's enemy, an alien being bent on thwarting the disciplinary project. Anorexia nervosa, which has now assumed epidemic proportions, is to women of the late twentieth century what hysteria was to women of an earlier day: the crystallization in a pathological mode of a widespread cultural obsession (Bordo 1985–86). A survey taken recently at UCLA is astounding: of 260 students interviewed, 27.3 percent of women but only 5.8 percent of men said they were "terrified" of getting fat; 28.7 percent of women but only 7.5 percent of men said they were obsessed or "totally preoccupied" with food. The body images of women and men are strikingly different as well: 35 percent of women but only 12.5 percent of men said they felt fat though other people told them they were thin. Women in the survey wanted to weigh ten pounds less than their average weight; men felt they were within a pound of their ideal weight. A total of 5.9 percent of women and no men met the psychiatric criteria for anorexia or bulimia (*USA Today* 1985).

Dieting is one discipline imposed upon a body subject to the "tyranny of slenderness"; exercise is another (Chernin 1981). Since men as well as women exercise, it is not always easy in the case of women to distinguish what is done for the sake of physical fitness from what is done in obedience to the requirements of femininity. Men as well as women lift weights and do yoga, calisthenics, and aerobics, though "jazzercise" is largely a female pursuit. Men and women alike engage themselves with a variety of machines, each designed to call forth from the body a different exertion: there are Nautilus machines, rowing machines, ordinary and motorized exercycles, portable hip and leg cycles, belt massagers, trampolines, treadmills, and arm and leg pulleys. However, given the widespread female obsession with weight, one suspects that many women are working out with these apparatuses in the health club or at the gym with an aim in mind and in a spirit quite different from men's.

But there are classes of exercises meant for women alone, these designed not to firm or reduce the body's size overall, but to resculpture its various parts on the current model. M. J. Saffon (1981), "international beauty expert," assures us that his twelve basic facial exercises can erase frown lines, smooth the forehead, raise hollow cheeks, banish crow's feet, and tighten the muscles under the chin. There are exercises to build the breasts and exercises to banish "cellulite," said by "figure consultants" to be a special type of female fat. There is "spot-reducing," an umbrella term that covers dozens of punishing exercises designed to reduce "problem areas" like thick ankles or "saddlebag" thighs. The very idea of "spot-reducing" is both scientifically unsound and cruel, for it raises expectations in women that can never be realized—the pattern in which fat is deposited or removed is known to be genetically determined.

It is not only her natural appetite or unreconstructed contours that pose a danger to woman: the very expressions of her face can subvert the disciplinary project of bodily perfection. An expressive face lines and creases more readily than an inexpressive one. Hence, if women are unable to suppress strong emotions, they can at least learn to inhibit the tendency of the face to register them. Sophia Loren (1984, 57) recommends a unique solution to this problem: a piece of tape applied to the forehead or between the brows will tug at the skin when one frowns and act as a reminder to relax the face. The tape is to be worn whenever a woman is home alone.

III.

There are significant gender differences in gesture, posture, movement, and general bodily comportment: women are far more restricted than men in their manner of movement and in their spatiality. In her classic paper on the subject, Iris Young (1980) observes that a space seems to surround women in imagination that they are hesitant to move beyond: this manifests itself both in a reluctance to reach, stretch, and extend the body to meet resistances of matter in motion—as in sport or in the performance of physical tasks—and in a typically constricted posture and general style of movement. Woman's space is not a field in which her bodily intentionality can be freely realized but an enclosure in which she feels herself positioned and by which she is confined (Wex 1979). The "loose woman" violates those norms: her looseness is manifest not only in her morals, but in her manner of speech and quite literally in the free and easy way she moves.

In an extraordinary series of over two thousand photographs, many candid shots taken in the street, the German photographer Marianne Wex (1979) has documented differences in typical masculine and feminine body posture. Women sit waiting for trains with arms close to the body, hands folded together in their laps, toes pointing straight ahead or turned inward, and legs pressed together. The women in these photographs make themselves small and narrow, harmless; they seem tense; they take up little space. Men, on the other hand, expand into the available space; they sit with legs far apart and arms flung out at some distance from the body. Most common in these sitting male figures is what Wex calls the "proffering position": the men sit with legs thrown wide apart, crotch visible, feet pointing outward, often with an arm and a casually dangling hand resting comfortably on an open, spread thigh.

In proportion to total body size, a man's stride is longer than a woman's. The man has more spring and rhythm to his step; he walks with toes pointed outward, holds his arms at a greater distance from his body, and swings them farther; he tends to point the whole hand in the direction he is moving. The woman holds her arms closer to her body, palms against her sides; her walk is circumspect. If she has subjected herself to the additional constraint of high-heeled shoes, her body is thrown forward and off balance: the struggle to walk under these conditions shortens her stride still more.

But women's movement is subjected to a still finer discipline. Feminine faces, as well as bodies, are trained to the expression of deference. Under male scrutiny, women will avert their eyes or cast them downward; the female gaze is trained to abandon its claim to the sovereign status of seer. The "nice" girl learns to avoid the bold and unfettered staring of the "loose" woman who looks at whatever and whomever she pleases. Women are trained to smile more than men, too. In the economy of smiles, as elsewhere, there is evidence that women are exploited, for they give more than they receive in return; in a smile elicitation study, one researcher found that the rate of smile return by women was 93 percent, by men only 67 percent (Henley 1977, 176). In many typical women's jobs, graciousness, deference, and readiness to serve are part of the work; this requires the worker to fix a smile on her face for a good part of the working day, whatever her inner state (Hochschild, 1983). The economy of touching is out of balance, too: men touch women more often and on more parts of the body than women touch men: female secretaries, factory workers, and waitresses report that such liberties are taken routinely with their bodies (Henley 1977, 108).

Feminine movement, gesture, and posture must exhibit not only constriction, but grace and a certain eroticism restrained by modesty: all three. Here is field for the operation of a whole new training: a woman must stand with stomach pulled in, shoulders thrown slightly back and chest out, this to display her bosom to maximum advantage. While she must walk in the confined fashion appropriate to women, her movements must, at the same time, be combined with a subtle but provocative hip-roll. But too much display is taboo: women in short, low-cut dresses are told to avoid bending over at all, but if they must, great care must be taken to avoid an unseemly display of breast or rump. From time to time, fashion magazines offer quite precise instructions on the proper way of getting in and out of cars. These instructions combine all three imperatives of women's movements: a woman must not allow her arms and leg to flail about in all directions, she must try to manage her movements with the appearance of grace—no small accomplishment when one is climbing out of the back seat of a Fiat—and she is well-advised to use the opportunity for a certain display of leg.

All the movements we have described so far are self-movements; they arise from within the woman's own body. But in a way that normally goes unnoticed, males in couples may literally steer a woman everywhere she goes: down the street, around corners, into elevators, through doorways, into her chair at the dinner table, around the dance floor. The man's movement "is not necessarily heavy and pushy or physical in an ugly way; it is light and gentle but firm in the way of the most confident equestrians with the best-trained horses" (Henley 1977, 149).

IV.

We have examined some of the disciplinary practices a woman must master in pursuit of a body of the right size and shape that also displays the proper styles of feminine motility. But woman's body is an ornamented surface too, and there is much discipline involved in this production as well. Here, especially in the application of makeup and the selection of clothes, art and discipline converge, though, as I shall argue, there is less art involved than one might suppose.

A woman's skin must be soft, supple, hairless, and smooth; ideally, it should betray no sign of wear, experience, age, or deep thought. Hair must be removed not only from the face but from large surfaces of the body as well, from legs and thighs, an operation accomplished by shaving, buffing with fine sandpaper, or applying foul-smelling depilatories. With the new high-leg bathing suits and leotards, a substantial amount of pubic hair must be removed too. The removal of facial hair can be more specialized. Eyebrows are plucked out by the roots with a tweezers. Hot wax is sometimes poured onto the mustache and cheeks and then ripped away when it cools. The woman who wants a more permanent result may try electrolysis: this involves the killing of a hair root by the passage of an electric current down a needle that has been inserted into its base. The procedure is painful and expensive.

The development of what one "beauty expert" calls "good skincare habits" requires not only attention to health, the avoidance of strong facial expressions, and the performance of facial exercises, but the regular use of skin-care preparations, many to be applied more often than once a day: cleansing lotions (ordinary soap and water "upsets the skin's acid and alkaline balance"), wash-off cleansers (milder than cleansing lotions), astringents, toners, makeup removers, night creams, nourishing creams, eye creams, moisturizers, skin balances, body lotions, hand creams, lip pomades, suntan lotions, sunscreens, and facial masks. Provision of the proper facial mask is complex: there are sulfur masks for pimples; oil or hot masks for dry areas; if these fail, then tightening masks; conditioning masks; peeling masks; cleansing masks made of herbs, cornmeal, or almonds; and mudpacks. Black women may wish to use "fade creams" to "even skin tone." Skincare preparations are never just sloshed onto the skin, but applied according to precise rules: eye cream is dabbed on gently in movements toward, never away from, the nose; cleansing cream is applied in outward directions only, straight down the nose and up and out on the cheeks (Klinger and Rowes 1978).

The normalizing discourse of modern medicine is enlisted by the cosmetics industry to gain credibility for its claims. Dr. Christian Barnard lends his enormous prestige to the Glycel line of "cellular treatment activators"; these contain "glycosphingolipids" that can "make older skin behave and look like younger skins" (ads in *Chicago Magazine*, March 1986, pp. 10, 18, 43, and 62). The Clinique computer at any Clinique counter will select a combination of preparations just right for you. Ultima II contains "procollagen" in its anti-aging eye cream that "provides hydration" to "demoralizing lines." "Biotherm" eye cream dramatically improves the "biomechanical properties of the skin" (*Chicago Magazine*, March 1986). The Park Avenue clinic of Dr. Zizmor, "chief of dermatology at one of New York's leading hospitals," offers not only such medical treatment as derma-brasion and chemical peeling, but "total deep skin cleansing" as well (ad in *Essence* magazine, April 1986, 25).[2]

Really good skincare habits require the use of a variety of aids and devices: facial steamers, faucet filters to collect impurities in the water, borax to soften it, a humidifier for the bedroom, electric massagers, backbrushes, complexion brushes, loofahs, pumice stones, and blackhead removers. I will not detail the implements or techniques involved in the manicure or pedicure.

The ordinary circumstances of life as well as a wide variety of activities cause a crisis in skincare and require a stepping-up of the regimen as well as an additional laying-on of preparations. Skincare discipline requires a specialized knowledge: a woman must know what to do if she has been skiing, taking medication, doing vigorous exercise, boating, or swimming in chlorinated pools; or if she has been exposed to pollution, heated rooms, cold, sun, harsh weather, the pressurized cabins on airplanes, saunas or steam rooms, fatigue, or stress. Like the schoolchild or prisoner, the woman mastering good skincare habits is put on a timetable: Georgette Klinger requires that a shorter or longer period of attention be paid to the complexion at least four times a day (Klinger and Rowes 1978, 137–40). Haircare, like skincare, requires a similar investment of time, the use of a wide variety of preparations, the mastery of a set of techniques, and, again, the acquisition of a specialized knowledge.

The crown and pinnacle of good haircare and skincare is, of course, the arrangement of the hair and the application of cosmetics. Here the regimen of haircare, skincare, manicure, and pedicure is recapitulated in another mode. A woman must learn the proper manipulation of a large number of devices—the blow dryer, styling brush, eyelash curler, and mascara brush. And she must learn to apply a wide variety of products—foundation, toner, covering stick, mascara, eyeshadow, eyegloss, blusher, lipstick, rouge, lip gloss, hair dye, hair rinse, hair lightener, hair "relaxer," and so on.

In the language of fashion magazines and cosmetics ads, making up is typically portrayed as an aesthetic activity in which a woman can express her individuality. In reality, while cosmetic styles change every decade or so, and while some variation in makeup is permitted depending on the occasion, making up the face is, in fact, a highly stylized activity that gives little rein to self-expression. Painting the fact is not like painting a picture; at best, it might be described as painting the same picture over and over again with minor variations. Little latitude is permitted in what is considered appropriate makeup for the office and for most social occasions; indeed, the woman who used cosmetics in a genuinely novel and imaginative way is liable to be seen not as an artist but as an eccentric. Furthermore, since a properly made-up face is, if not a card of entree, at least a badge of acceptability in most social and professional contexts, the woman who chooses not to wear cosmetics at all faces sanctions of a sort that will never be applied to someone who chooses not to paint a watercolor.

V.

Are we dealing in all this merely with sexual *difference?* Scarcely. The disciplinary practices I have described are part of the process by which the ideal body of femininity—and hence the feminine body-subject—is constructed; in doing this, they produce a "practiced and subjected" body, that is, a body on which an inferior status has been inscribed. A woman's face must be made up, that is to say, made over, and so must her body: she is ten pounds overweight; her lips must be made more kissable, her complexion dewier, her eyes more mysterious. The "art" of makeup is the art of disguise, but this presupposes that a woman's face, unpainted, is defective. Soap and water, a shave, and routine attention to hygiene may be enough for *him*; for *her* they are not. The strategy of much beauty-related advertising is to suggest to women that their bodies are deficient; but even without such more or less explicit teaching, the media images of perfect female beauty that bombard us daily leave no doubt in the minds of most women that they fail to measure up. The technologies for femininity are taken up and practiced by women against the background of a pervasive sense of bodily deficiency; this accounts for what is often their compulsive or even ritualistic character.

The disciplinary project of femininity is a "setup": it requires such radical and extensive measures of bodily transformation that virtually every woman who gives herself to it is destined in some degree to fail. Thus, a measure of shame is added to a woman's sense that the body she inhabits is deficient: she ought to take better care of herself; she might after all have jogged that last mile. Many women are without the time or resources to provide themselves with even the minimum of what such a regimen requires, for example, a decent diet. Here is an additional source of shame for poor women, who must bear what our society regards as the more general shame of poverty. The burdens poor women bear in this regard are not merely psychological, since conformity to the prevailing standards of bodily acceptability is a known factor in economic mobility.

The larger disciplines that construct a "feminine" body out of a female one are by no means race- or class-specific. There is little evidence that women of color or working-class women are in general less committed to the incarnation of an ideal femininity than their more privileged sisters: this is not to deny the many ways in which factors of race, class, locality, ethnicity, or personal taste can be expressed within the kinds of practices I have described. The rising young corporate executive may buy her cosmetics at Bergdorf-Goodman, while the counter-server at McDonald's gets her at KMart; the one may join an expensive "upscale" health club, while the other may have to make do with the $9.49 GFX Body-Flex II Home Gym advertised in the *National Enquirer*: both are aiming at the same general result.

In the regime of institutionalized heterosexuality, woman must make herself "object and prey" for the man: it is for him that these eyes are limpid pools, this cheek baby-smooth (de Beauvoir 1968, 642). In contemporary patriarchal culture, a panoptical male connoisseur resides within the consciousness of most women: they stand perpetually before his gaze and under his judgment. Woman lives her body as seen by another, by an anonymous patriarchal Other. We are often told that "women dress for other women." There is some truth in this: who but someone engaged in a project similar to my own can appreciate the panache with which I bring it off? But women know for whom this game is played: they know that a pretty young woman is likelier to become a flight attendant than a plain one, and that a well-preserved older woman has a better chance of holding onto her husband than one who has "let herself go."

Here it might be objected that performance for another in no way signals the inferiority of the performer to the one for whom the performance is intended: the actor, for example, depends on his audience but is in no way inferior to it; he is not demeaned by his dependency. While femininity is surely something enacted, the analogy to theater breaks down in a number of ways. First, as I argued earlier, the self-determination we think of as requisite to an artistic career is lacking here: femininity as spectacle is something in which virtually every woman is required to participate. Second, the precise nature of the criteria by which women are judged, not only the inescapability of judgment itself, reflects gross imbalances in the social power of the sexes that do not mark the relationship of artists and their audiences. An aesthetic of femininity, for example, that mandates fragility and a lack of muscular strength produces female bodies that can offer little resistance to physical abuse, and the physical abuse of women by men, as we know, is widespread. It is true that the current fitness movement has permitted women to develop more muscular strength and endurance than was heretofore allowed; indeed, images of women have begun to appear in the mass media that seem to eroticize this new muscularity. But a woman may by no means develop more muscular strength than her partner; the bride who would tenderly carry her groom across the threshold is a figure of comedy, not romance.

Under the current "tyranny of slenderness" women are forbidden to become large or massive; they must take up as little space as possible. The very contours a woman's body takes on as she matures—the fuller breasts and rounded hips—have become distasteful. The body by which a woman feels herself judged and which by rigorous discipline she must try to assume is the body of early adolescence, slight and unformed, a body lacking flesh or substance, a body in whose very contours the image of immaturity has been inscribed. The requirement that a woman maintain smooth and hairless skin carries further the theme of inexperience, for an infantilized face must accompany her infantilized body, a face that never ages or furrows its brow in thought. The face of the ideally feminine woman must never display the marks of character, wisdom, and experience that we so admire in men.

To succeed in the provision of a beautiful or sexy body gains a woman attention and some admiration but little real respect and rarely any social power. A woman's effort to master feminine body discipline will lack importance just because she does it: her activity partakes of the general depreciation of everything female. In spite of unrelenting pressure to "make the most of what she has," women are ridiculed and dismissed for their interest in such "trivial" things as clothes and makeup. Further, the narrow identification of woman with sexuality and the body in a society that has for centuries displayed profound suspicion toward both does little to raise her status. Even the most adored female bodies complain routinely of their situation in ways that reveal an implicit understanding that there is something demeaning in the kind of attention they receive. Marilyn Monroe, Elizabeth Taylor, and Farrah Fawcett have all wanted passionately to become actress-artists—and not just "sex objects."

But it is perhaps in their more restricted motility and comportment that the inferiorization of women's bodies is most evident. Women's typical body language, a language of relative tension and constriction, is understood to be a language of subordination when it is enacted by men in male status hierarchies. In groups of men, those with higher status typically assume looser and more relaxed postures: the boss lounges comfortably behind the desk, while the applicant sits tense and rigid on the edge of his seat. Higher-status individuals may touch their subordinates more than they themselves get touched; they initiate more eye contact and are smiled at by their inferiors more than they are observed to smile in return (Henley 1977). What is announced in the comportment of superiors is confidence and ease, especially ease of access to the Other. Female constraint in posture and movement is no doubt overdetermined: the fact that women tend to sit and stand with legs, feet, and knees close or touching may well be a coded declaration of sexual circumspection in a society that still maintains a double standard, or an effort, albeit unconscious, to guard the genital area. In the latter case, a woman's tight and constricted posture must be seen as the expression of her need to ward off real or symbolic sexual attack. Whatever proportions must be assigned in the final display to fear or deference, one thing is clear: woman's body language speaks eloquently, though silently, of her subordinate status in a hierarchy of gender.

VI.

If what we have described is a genuine discipline—a system, in Foucault's words (1979, 222), of "micro-power" that is "essentially non-egalitarian and asymmetrical"—who then are the disciplinarians? Who is the top sergeant in the disciplinary regime of femininity? Historically, the law has had some responsibility for enforcement: in times gone by, for example, individuals who appeared in public in the clothes of the other sex could be arrested. While cross-dressers are still liable to some harassment, the kind of discipline we are considering is not the business of the police or the courts. Parents and teachers, of course, have extensive influence, admonishing girls to be demure and ladylike, to "smile pretty," to sit with their legs together. The influence of the media is pervasive, too, constructing as it does an image of the female body as spectacle, nor can we ignore the role played by "beauty experts" or by emblematic public personages such as Jane Fonda and Lynn Redgrave.

But none of these individuals—the skincare consultant, the parent, the policeman—does in fact wield the kind of authority that is typically invested in those who manage more straightforward disciplinary institutions. The disciplinary power that inscribes femininity on the female body is everywhere and it is nowhere; the disciplinarian is everyone and yet no one in particular. Women regarded as overweight, for example, report that they are regularly admonished to diet, sometime by people they scarcely know. These intrusions are often softened by reference to the natural prettiness just waiting to emerge: "People have always said that I had a beautiful face, and 'if you'd only lose weight you'd be really beautiful' " (Millman 1980, 80). Here, "people"— friends and casual acquaintances alike—act to enforce prevailing standards of body size.

Foucault tends to identify the imposition of discipline upon the body with the operation of specific institutions, for example, the school, the factory, the prison. To do this, however, is to overlook the extent to which discipline can be institutionally *unbound* as well as institutionally bound.[3] The anonymity of disciplinary power and its wide dispersion have consequences that are crucial to a proper understanding of the subordination of women. The absence of a formal institutional structure and of authorities invested with the power to carry out institutional directives creates the impression that the production of femininity is either entirely voluntary or natural. The several senses of "discipline" are instructive here. On the one hand, discipline is something imposed on subjects of an "essentially non-egalitarian and asymmetrical" system of authority. Schoolchildren, convicts, and draftees are subject to discipline in this sense. But discipline can be sought voluntarily as well—for example, when an individual seeks initiation into the spiritual discipline of Zen Buddhism. Discipline can, of course, be both at once: the volunteer may seek the physical and occupational training offered by the army without the army's ceasing in any way to be the instrument by which he and other members of his class are kept in disciplined subjection. Feminine bodily discipline has this dual character: on the one hand, no one is marched off for electrolysis at gunpoint, nor can we fail to appreciate the initiative and ingenuity displayed by countless women in an attempt to master the rituals of beauty. Nevertheless, insofar as the disciplinary practices of femininity produce a "subjected and practiced," an inferiorized, body, they must be understood as aspects of a far larger discipline, an oppressive and inegalitarian system of sexual subordination. This system aims at turning women into the docile and compliant companions of men just as surely as the army aims to turn its raw recruits into soldiers.

Now the transformation of oneself into a properly feminine body may be any or all of the following: a rite of passage into adulthood, the adoption and celebration of a particular aesthetic, a way of announcing one's economic level and social status, a way to triumph over other women in the competition for men or jobs, or an opportunity for massive narcissistic indulgence (Bartky 1982). The social construction of the feminine body is all these things, but at its base it is discipline, too, and discipline of the inegalitarian sort. The absence of formally identifiable disciplinarians and of a public schedule of sanctions only disguises the extent to which the imperative to be "feminine" serves the interest of domination. This is a lie in which all concur: making up is merely artful play; one's first pair of high-heeled shoes is an innocent part of growing up, not the modern equivalent of foot-binding.

Why aren't all women feminists? In modern industrial societies, women are not kept in line by fear of retaliatory male violence; their victimization is not that of the South African black [under the former system of apartheid]. Nor will it suffice to say that a false consciousness engendered in women by patriarchal ideology is at the basis of female subordination. This is not to deny that women are often subject to gross male violence or that women and men alike are ideologically mystified by the dominant gender arrangements. What I wish to suggest instead is that an adequate understanding of women's oppression will require an appreciation of the extent to which not only women's lives but their very subjectivities are structured within an ensemble of systematically duplicitous practices. The feminine discipline of the body is a case in point: the practices that construct this body have an overt aim and character far removed, indeed, radically distinct, from their overt function. In this regard, the system of gender subordination, like the wage-bargain under capitalism, illustrates in its own way the ancient tension between what-is and what-appears: the phenomenal forms in which it is manifested are often quite different from the real relations that form its deeper structure.

VII.

The lack of formal public sanctions does not mean that a woman who is unable or unwilling to submit herself to the appropriate body discipline will face no sanctions at all. On the contrary, she faces a very severe sanction indeed in a world dominated by men: the refusal of male patronage. For the heterosexual woman, this may mean the loss of badly needed intimacy; for both heterosexual women and lesbians, it may well mean the refusal of a decent livelihood.

As noted earlier, women punish themselves too for the failure to conform. The growing literature on women's body size is filled with wrenching confessions of shame from the overweight:

> I felt clumsy and huge. I felt that I would knock over furniture, bump into things, tip over chairs, not fit into VW's especially when people were trying to crowd into the back seat. I felt like I was taking over the whole room. . . . I felt disgusting and like a slob. In the summer I felt hot and sweaty and I knew people saw my sweat as evidence that I was too fat.

> I feel so terrible about the way I look that I cut off connection with my body. I operate from the neck up. I do not look in mirrors. I do not want to spend time buying clothes. I do not want to spend time with makeup because it's painful for me to look at myself (Millman 1980, 80, 195).

> I can no longer bear to look at myself. . . . Whenever I have to stand in front of a mirror to comb my hair I tie a large towel around my neck. Even at night I slip my nightgown on before I take off my blouse and pants. But all this has only made it worse and worse. It's been so long since I've really looked at my body (Chernin 1981, 53).

The depth of these women's shame is a measure of the extent to which all women have internalized patriarchal standards of bodily acceptability. A fuller examination of what is meant here by "internalization" may shed light on a question posed earlier: Why isn't every woman a feminist?

Something is "internalized" when it gets incorporated into the structure of the self. By "structure of the self" I refer to those modes of perception and of self-perception that allow a self to distinguish itself both from other selves and from things that are not selves. I have described elsewhere (Bartky 1982) how a generalized male witness comes to structure woman's consciousness of herself as a bodily being. This, then, is one meaning of "internalization." The sense of oneself as a distinct and valuable individual is tied not only to the sense of how one is perceived, but also to what one knows, especially to what one knows how to do; this is a second sense of "internalization." Whatever its ultimate effect, discipline can provide the individual upon whom it is imposed with a sense of mastery as well as a secure sense of identity. There is a certain contradiction here: while its imposition may promote a larger disempowerment, discipline may bring with it a certain development of a person's powers. Women, then, like other individuals, have a stake in the perpetuation of their skills, whatever it may have cost to acquire them and quite apart from the question of whether, as a gender, they would have been better off had they never had to acquire them in the first place. Hence, feminism, especially a genuinely radical feminism that questions the patriarchal construction of the female body, threatens women with a certain de-skilling, something people normally resist: beyond this, it calls into question that aspect of personal identity that is tied to the development of a sense of competence.

Resistance from this source may be joined by a reluctance to part with the rewards of compliance; further, many women will resist the abandonment of an aesthetic that defines what they take to be beautiful. But there is still another source of resistance, one more subtle, perhaps, but tied once again to questions of identity and internalization. To have a body felt to be "feminine"—a body socially constructed through the appropriate practices—is in most cases crucial to a woman's sense of herself as female and, since persons currently can *be* only as male or female, to her sense of herself as an existing individual. To possess such a body may also be essential to her sense of herself as a sexually desiring and desirable subject. Hence, any political project that aims to dismantle the machinery that turns a female body into a feminine one may well be apprehended by a woman as something that threatens her with desexualization, if not outright annihilation.

The categories of masculinity and femininity do more than assist in the construction of personal identities; they are critical elements in our informal social ontology. This may account to some degree for the otherwise puzzling phenomenon of homophobia and for the revulsion felt by many at the sight of female bodybuilders; neither the homosexual nor the muscular woman can be assimilated easily into the categories that structure everyday life. The radical feminist critique of femininity, then, may pose a threat not only to a woman's sense of her own identity and desirability but to the very structure of her social universe.

Of course, many women *are* feminists, favoring a program of political and economic reform in the struggle to gain equality with men. But many "reform," or liberal, feminists (indeed, many orthodox Marxists) are committed to the idea that the preservation of a woman's femininity is quite compatible with her struggle for liberation (Markovic 1976). These thinkers have rejected a normative femininity based upon the notion of "separate spheres" and the traditional sexual division of labor, while accepting at the same time conventional standards of feminine body display. If my analysis is correct, such a feminism is incoherent. Foucault has argued that modern bourgeois democracy is deeply flawed in that it seeks political micropowers that lie beyond the realm of what is ordinarily defined as the "political." "The man described for us whom we are invited to free," he says, "is already in himself the effect of a subjection much more profound than himself" (Foucault 1979, 30). If, as I have argued, female subjectivity is constituted in any significant measure in and through the disciplinary practices that construct the feminine body, what Foucault says here of "man" is perhaps even truer of "woman." Marxists have maintained from the first the inadequacy of a purely liberal feminism: we have reached the same conclusion through a different route, casting doubt at the same time on the adequacy of traditional Marxist prescriptions for women's liberation as well. Liberals call for equal rights for women, traditional Marxists for the entry of women into production on an equal footing with men, the socialization of housework, and proletarian revolution; neither calls for the deconstruction of the categories of masculinity and femininity. [Some radical feminists such as Wittig (1976), however, have called for just such a deconstruction.] Femininity as a certain "style of the flesh" will have to be surpassed in the direction of something quite different— not masculinity, which is in many ways only its mirror opposite, but a radical and as yet unimagined transformation of the female body.

VIII.

Foucault (1979, 44) has argued that the transition from traditional to modern societies has been characterized by a profound transformation in the exercise of power, by what he calls "a reversal of the political axis of individualization." In older authoritarian systems, power was embodied in the person of the monarch and exercised upon a largely anonymous body of subjects; violation of the law was seen as an insult to the royal individual. While the methods employed to enforce compliance in the past were often quite brutal, involving gross assaults against the body, power in such a system operated in a haphazard and discontinuous fashion; much in the social totality lay beyond its reach.

By contrast, modern society has seen the emergence of increasingly invasive apparatuses of power: these exercise a far more restrictive social and psychological control than was heretofore possible. In modern societies, effects of power "circulate through progressively finer channels, gaining access to individuals themselves, to their bodies, their gestures and all their daily actions" (Foucault 1980, 151). Power now seeks to transform the minds of those individuals who might be tempted to resist it, not merely to punish or imprison their bodies. This requires two things: a finer control of the body's time and of its movements—a control that cannot be achieved without ceaseless surveillance and a better understanding of the specific person, of the genesis and nature of his "case." The power these new apparatuses seek to exercise requires a new knowledge of the individual: modern psychology and sociology are born. Whether the new modes of control have charge of correction, production, education, or the provision of welfare, they resemble one another; they exercise power in a bureaucratic mode—faceless, centralized, and pervasive. A reversal has occurred: power has now become anonymous, while the project of control has brought into being a new individuality. In fact, Foucault believes that the operation of power constitutes the very subjectivity of the subject. Here, the image of the Panopticon returns: knowing that he may be observed from the tower at any time, the inmate takes over the job of policing himself. The gaze that is inscribed in the very structure of the disciplinary institution is internalized by the inmate: modern technologies of behavior are thus oriented toward the production of isolated and self-policing subjects (Dews 1984, 77).

Women have their own experience of the modernization of power, one that begins later but follows in many respects the course outlined by Foucault. In important ways, a woman's behavior is less regulated now than it was in the past. She has more mobility and is less confined to domestic space. She enjoys what to previous generations would have been an unimaginable sexual liberty. Divorce, access to paid work outside the home, and the increasing secularization of modern life have loosened the hold over her of the traditional family and, in spite of the current fundamentalist revival, of the church. Power in these institutions was wielded by individuals known to her. Husbands and fathers enforced patriarchal authority in the family. As in the ancient regime, a woman's body was subject to sanctions if she disobeyed. Not Foucault's royal individual but the Divine Individual decreed that her desire be always "unto her husband," while the person of the priest made known to her God's more specific intentions concerning her place and duties. In the days when civil and ecclesiastical authority were still conjoined, individuals formally invested with power were charged with the correction of recalcitrant women whom the family had somehow failed to constrain.

By contrast, the disciplinary power that is increasingly charged with the production of a properly embodied femininity is dispersed and anonymous; there are no individuals formally empowered to wield it; it is, as we have seen, invested in everyone and in no one in particular. This disciplinary power is peculiarly modern: it does not rely upon violent or public sanctions, nor does it seek to restrain the freedom of the female body to move from place to place. For all that, its invasion of the body is well-nigh total: the female body enters "a machinery of power that explores it, breaks it down and rearranges it" (Foucault 1979, 138). The disciplinary techniques through which the "docile bodies" of women are constructed aim at a regulation that is perpetual and exhaustive—a regulation of the body's size and contours, its appetite, posture, gestures and general comportment in space, and the appearance of each of its visible parts.

As modern industrial societies change and as women themselves offer resistance to patriarchy, older forms of domination are eroded. But new forms arise, spread, and become consolidated. Women are no longer required to be chaste or modest, to restrict their sphere of activity to the home, or even to realize their properly feminine destiny in maternity: normative femininity is coming more and more to be centered on woman's body—not its duties and obligations or even its capacity to bear children, but its sexuality, more precisely, its presumed heterosexuality and its appearance. There is, of course, nothing new in women's preoccupation with youth and beauty. What is new is the growing power of the image in a society increasingly oriented toward the visual media. Images of normative femininity, it might be ventured, have replaced the religiously oriented tracts of the past. New too is the spread of this discipline to all classes of women and its deployment throughout the life cycle. What was formerly the specialty of the aristocrat or courtesan is now the routine obligation of every woman, be she a grandmother or a barely pubescent girl.

To subject oneself to the new disciplinary power is to be up-to-date, to be "with it"; as I have argued, it is presented to us in ways that are regularly disguised. It is fully compatible with the current need for women's wage labor, the cult of youth and fitness, and the need of advanced capitalism to maintain high levels of consumption. Further, it represents a saving in the economy of enforcement: since it is women themselves who practice this discipline on and against their own bodies, men get off scott-free.

The woman who checks her makeup half a dozen times a day to see if her foundation has caked or her mascara has run, who worries that the wind or the rain may spoil her hairdo, who looks frequently to see if her stockings have bagged at the ankle or who, feeling fat, monitors everything she eats, has become, just as surely as the inmate of the Panopticon, a self-policing subject, a self committed to a relentless self-surveillance. This self-surveillance is a form of obedience to patriarchy. It is also the reflection in woman's consciousness of the fact that *she* is under surveillance in ways that *he* is not, that whatever else she may become, she is importantly a body designed to please or to excite. There has been induced in many women, then, in Foucault's words (1979, 201), "a state of conscious and permanent visibility that assures the automatic functioning of power." Since the standards of female bodily acceptability are impossible to realize fully, requiring as they do a virtual transcendence of nature, a woman may live much of her life with a pervasive feeling of bodily deficiency. Hence a tighter control of the body has gained a new kind of hold over the mind.

Foucault often writes as if power constitutes the very individuals upon whom it operates:

> The individual is not to be conceived as a sort of elementary nucleus, a primitive atom, a multiple and inert material on which power comes to fasten or against which it happens to strike. . . . In fact, it is already one of the prime effects of power that certain bodies, certain gestures, certain discourses, certain desires, come to be identified and constituted as individuals (Foucault 1980, 98).

Nevertheless, if individuals were wholly constituted by the power-knowledge regime Foucault describes, it would make no sense to speak of resistance to discipline at all. Foucault seems sometimes on the verge of depriving us of a vocabulary in which to conceptualize the nature and meaning of those periodic refusals of control that, just as much as the imposition of control, mark the course of human history.

Peter Dews (1984, 92) accuses Foucault of lacking a theory of the "libidinal body," that is, the body upon which discipline is imposed and whose bedrock impulse toward spontaneity and pleasure might perhaps become the locus of resistance. Do women's "libidinal" bodies, then, not rebel against the pain, constriction, tedium, semistarvation, and constant self-surveillance to which they are currently condemned? Certainly they do, but the rebellion is put down every time a woman picks up her eyebrow tweezers or embarks upon a new diet. The harshness of a regime alone does not guarantee its rejection, for hardships can be endured if they are thought to be necessary or inevitable.

While "nature," in the form of a "libidinal" body, may not be the origin of a revolt against "culture," domination (and the discipline it requires) are never imposed without some cost. Historically, the forms and occasions of resistance are manifold. Sometimes, instances of resistance appear to spring from the introduction of new and conflicting factors into the lives of the dominated: the juxtaposition of old and new and the resulting incoherence or "contradiction" may make submission to the old ways seem increasingly unnecessary. In the present instance, what may be a major factor in the relentless and escalating objectification of women's bodies—namely, women's growing independence—produces in many women a sense of incoherence that calls into question the meaning and necessity of the current discipline. As women (albeit a small minority of women) begin to realize an unprecedented political, economic, and sexual self-determination, they fall ever more completely under the dominating gaze of patriarchy. It is this paradox, not the "libidinal body," that produces, here and there, pockets of resistance.

In the current political climate, there is no reason to anticipate either widespread resistance to currently fashionable modes of feminine embodiment or joyous experimentation with new "styles of the flesh"; moreover, such novelties would face profound opposition from material and psychological sources identified earlier in this essay (see section VII). In spite of this, a number of oppositional discourses and practices have appeared in recent years. An increasing number of women are "pumping iron," a few with little concern for the limits of body development imposed by current canons of femininity. Women in radical lesbian communities have also rejected hegemonic images of femininity and are struggling to develop a new female aesthetic. A striking feature of such communities is the extent to which they have overcome the oppressive identification of female beauty and desirability with youth: here, the physical features of aging—"character" lines and graying hair—not only do not diminish a woman's attractiveness, they may even enhance it. A popular literature of resistance is growing, some of it analytical and reflective, like Kim Chernin's (1981) *The Obsession*, some oriented toward practical self-help, like Marcia Hutchinson's (1985) *Transforming Body Image: Learning to Love the Body You Have*. This literature reflects a mood akin in some ways to that other and earlier mood of quiet desperation to which Betty Friedan (1963) gave voice in *The Feminine Mystique*. Nor should we forget that a mass-based women's movement is in place in this country that has begun a critical questioning of the meaning of femininity, if not yet in the corporeal presentation of self, then in other domains of life. We women cannot begin the re-vision of our own bodies until we learn to read the cultural messages we inscribe upon them daily and until we come to see that even when the mastery of the disciplines of femininity produces a triumphant result, we are still only women.

Notes

An earlier version of this paper was read to the Southwestern Philosophical Society, November 1985. Subsequent versions were read to the Society of Women in Philosophy, March 1986, and to the American Philosophical Association, May 1986. Many people in discussions at those meetings offered incisive comments and criticisms. I would like to thank in particular the following persons for their critiques of earlier drafts of this paper: Nancy Fraser, Alison Jaggar, Jeffner Allen, Laurie Shrage, Robert Yanal, Martha Gimenez, Joyce Trebilcot, Rob Crawford, and Iris Young.

1. Foucault is citing an eighteenth-century military manual, "Ordonnance du Ier janvier 1766 . . . , title XI, article 2."
2. I am indebted to Laurie Shrage for calling this to my attention and for providing most of these examples.
3. I am indebted to Nancy Fraser for the formulation of this point.

References

Bartky, Sandra Lee. 1982. Narcissism, femininity and alienation. *Social Theory and Practice* 8:127–43.

Bordo, Susan. 1985–86. Anorexia nervosa: Psychopathology as the crystallization of culture. *Philosophical Forum* 17:73–104.

Butler, Judith. 1985. Embodied identity in de Beauvoir's *The Second Sex*. Paper presented at the American Philosophical Association, Pacific Division, March 22, 1985.

Chernin, Kim. 1981. *The Obsession: Reflections on the Tyranny of Slenderness*. New York: Harper and Row.

de Beauvoir, Simone. 1968. *The Second Sex*. New York: Bantam Books.

Dews, Peter. 1984. Power and subjectivity in Foucault. *New Left Review* 144 (March-April):17.

Foucault, Michel. 1979. *Discipline and Punish: The Birth of the Prison*. New York: Vintage.

———. *Power/Knowledge: Selected Interviews and Other Writings, 1972–1977* (ed. Colin Gordon). Brighton, U.K.: 1980.

Friedan, Betty. 1963. *The Feminine Mystique*. New York: Norton.

Henley, Nancy. 1977. *Body Politics*. Englewood Cliffs: N.J.: Prentice-Hall.

Hochschild, Arlie. 1983. *The Managed Heart: The Commercialization of Human Feeling*. Berkeley: University of California Press.

Hutchinson, Marcia. 1985. *Transforming Body Image: Learning to Love the Body You Have*. Trumansburg, N.Y.: Crossing Press.

Klinger, Georgette, and Barbara Rowes. 1978. *Georgette Klinger's Skincare*. New York: William Morrow.

Loren, Sophia. 1984. *Women and Beauty*. New York: William Morrow.

Markovic, Mihailo. 1976. Women's liberation and human emancipation. In *Women and Philosophy*, edited by Carol C. Gould and Marx W. Wartofsky. New York: G. P. Putnam.

Millman, Marcia. 1980. *Such a Pretty Face: Being Fat in America*. New York: W. W. Norton.

Saffon, M. J. 1981. *The 15-Minute-A-Day Natural Face Lift*. New York: Warner Books.

USA Today. May 30, 1985.

Wex, Marianne. 1979. *Let's Take Back Our Space: "Female" and "Male" Body Language as a Result of Patriarchal Structures*. Berlin: Frauenliteraturverlag Hermine Fees.

Wittig, Monique. 1976. *The Lesbian Body*. New York: Avon Books.

Young, Iris. 1980. Throwing like a girl: A phenomenology of feminine body comportment, motility, and spatiality. *Human Studies* 3:137–56.

4

Women and Medicalization
A New Perspective

Catherine Kohler Riessman

Illness expands by means of two hypotheses. The first is that every form of social deviation can be considered an illness. Thus, if criminal behavior can be considered an illness, then criminals are not to be condemned or punished but to be understood (as a doctor understands), treated, cured. The second is that every illness can be considered psychologically. Illness is interpreted as, basically, a psychological event, and people are encouraged to believe that they get sick because they (unconsciously) want to, and that they can cure themselves by the mobilization of will; that they can choose not to die of the disease. These two hypotheses are complementary. As the first seems to relieve guilt, the second reinstates it. Psychological theories of illness are a powerful means of placing the blame on the ill. Patients who are instructed that they have, unwittingly, caused their disease are also made to feel that they have deserved it.

Susan Sontag, 1979

It is widely acknowledged that illness has become a cultural metaphor for a vast array of human problems. The medical model is used from birth to death in the social construction of reality. Historically, as a larger number of critical events and human problems have come under the "clinical gaze"

Originally published as "Women and Medicalization: A New Perspective," Catherine K. Riessman *Social Policy* (Summer, 1983) pp. 3–18. *Social Policy*, published by Social Policy Corporation, New York, NY 10036.

(Foucault 1973), our experience of them has been transformed. For women in particular, this process has had far-reaching consequences.

Feminist health writers have emphasized that women have been the main targets in the expansion of medicine. These scholars have analyzed how previous religious justifications for patriarchy were transformed into scientific ones (Ehrenreich and English 1979). They have described how women's traditional skills for managing birth and caring for the sick were expropriated by psychomedical experts at the end of the nineteenth century (Ehrenreich and English 1973). Feminist writers have described the multiple ways in which women's health in the contemporary period is being jeopardized by a male controlled, technology-dominated medical care system (Dreifus 1978; Frankfort 1972; Ruzek 1978; Seaman 1972). These critics have been important voices in changing women's consciousness about their health. They have identified the sexual politics embedded in conceptions of sickness and beliefs about appropriate care. In addition, they have provided the analytic basis for a social movement that has as its primary goal the reclaiming of knowledge about and control over women's bodies.

However, in their analyses, feminists have not always emphasized the ways in which women have simultaneously gained and lost with the medicalization of their life problems. Nor have the scholars always noted the fact that women actively participated in the construction of the new medical definitions, nor discussed the reasons that led to their participation. Women were not simply passive victims of medical ascendancy. To cast them solely in a passive role is to perpetuate the very kinds of assumptions about women that feminists have been trying to challenge.

This paper will extend the feminist critique by emphasizing some neglected dimensions of medicalization and women's lives. I will argue that both physicians and women have contributed to the redefining of women's experience into medical categories. More precisely, I will suggest that physicians seek to medicalize experience because of their specific beliefs and economic interests. These ideological and material motives are related to the development of the profession and the specific market conditions it faces in any given period. Women collaborate in the medicalization process because of their own needs and motives, which in turn grow out of the class-specific nature of their subordination. In addition, other groups bring economic interests to which both physicians and women are responsive. Thus a consensus develops that a particular human problem will be understood in clinical terms. This consensus is tenuous because it is fraught with contradictions for women, since, as stated before, they stand both to gain and to lose from this redefinition.

I will explore this thesis by examining . . . childbirth [and] reproductive control. . . .

The Medicalization Framework

The term *medicalization* refers to two interrelated processes. First, certain behaviors or conditions are given medical meaning—that is, defined in terms of health and illness. Second, medical practice becomes a vehicle for eliminating or controlling problematic experiences that are defined as deviant, for the purpose of securing adherence to social norms. Medicalization can occur on various levels: conceptually, when a medical vocabulary is used to define a problem; institutionally, when physicians legitimate a program or a problem; or on the level of doctor-patient interaction, when actual diagnosis and treatment of a problem occurs (Conrad and Schneider 1980b).

Historically, there has been an expansion of the spheres of deviance that have come under medical social control (Ehrenreich and Ehrenreich 1978; Freidson 1970; Zola 1972). Various human conditions such as alcoholism, opiate addiction, and homosexuality—which at one time were categorized as "bad"—have more recently been classified as "sick" (Conrad and Schneider 1980a). Currently, more and more of human experience is coming under medical scrutiny, resulting in what Illich (1976) has called "the medicalization of life." For example, it is now considered appropriate to consult physicians about sexuality, fertility, childhood behavior, and old-age memory problems. It is important to note that the medical profession's jurisdiction over these and other human conditions extends considerably beyond its demonstrated capacity to "cure" them (Freidson 1970).

There is disagreement about what causes medicalization. Some have assumed that the expansion of medical jurisdiction is the outcome of "medical imperialism"—an effort on the part of the profession to increase its power (Illich 1976). Others have argued that an increasingly complex technical and bureaucratic society has led to a reluctant reliance on scientific experts (Zola 1972, 1975). Other scholars have stressed the ways in which the medical establishment, in its thrust to professionalize, organized to create and then control markets (Larson 1977). In order for the occupational strategy of this emerging professional class to succeed, it was necessary to control the meaning of things, including interpretations of symptoms and beliefs about health care. Stated differently, professional dominance could be achieved only if people could be convinced of the medical nature of their problems and the appropriateness of medical treatment for them. Thus physicians, as part of an occupational strategy, created conditions under which their advice seemed appropriate (Starr 1982).

In spite of the disagreement about what motivates medicalization, there is a consensus that it has mixed effects. Greater humanitarianism, tolerance, and other benefits associated with "progress" may be more likely with medical definitions than with criminal ones. Yet medical labeling also has negative social consequences. Far from reducing stigma, the label of illness may create deviance. For example, the career of a psychiatric patient begins with a diagnosis of schizophrenia. As a result, family and friends perceive and interpret the patient's behavior in light of the illness, even after the acute symptoms subside (Mills 1962). Another consequence of medicalization is that the shroud of medical language mystifies human problems, and thus removes them from public debate (Conrad and Schneider 1980a). A deskilling of the populace takes place when experts manage human experiences. The application of medical definitions makes it more likely that medical remedies will be applied, thereby increasing the risk of iatrogenic disease. In addition, both the meaning and interpretation of an experience is transformed when it is seen as a disease or syndrome (Freidson 1970). For example, the meaning of murder is significantly altered when the label of "sociopathic personality" is used to account for the behavior. In this way, moral issues tend not be faced and may not even be raised (Zola 1975). Finally and most important, awareness of the social causes of disease is diminished with medicalization. As Stark and Flitcraft (1982) state:

> Medicine attracts public resources out of proportion to its capacity for health enhancement, because it often categorizes problems fundamentally social in origin as biological or personal deficits, and in so doing smothers the impulse for social change which could offer the only serious resolution.

Medicalization is a particularly critical concept because it emphasizes the fact that medicine is a social enterprise, not merely a scientific one. A biological basis is neither necessary nor sufficient for an experience to be defined in terms of illness. Rather, illness is constructed through human action—that is, illness is not inherent in any behavior or condition, but conferred by others. Thus, medical diagnosis becomes an interpretive process through which illnesses are constructed (Mishler 1981). . . .

Finally, the medicalization framework emphasizes that the power of physicians to define illness and monopolize the provision of treatment is the outcome of a political process. It highlights the ways in which medicine's constructions of reality are related to the structure of power at any given historical period. The political dimension inherent in medicalization is underscored when we note that structurally dependent populations—children, old people, racial minorities, and women—are subject disproportionately to medical labeling. For example, children's behavior is medicalized under the rubric of juvenile delinquency and hyperkinesis (Conrad and Schneider 1980a). Old people's mental functioning is labeled organic brain syndrome or senility. Racial minorities, when they come in contact with psychiatrists, are more likely than whites to be given more severe diagnoses for comparable symptoms and to receive more coercive forms of medical social control, such as psychiatric hospitalization (Gross et al. 1969). Women, as I will argue, are more likely than men to have problematic experiences defined and treated medically. In each of these examples, it is important to note that the particular group's economic and social powerlessness legitimates its "protection" by medical authorities. Of course, physicians act on behalf of the larger society, thus further reinforcing existing power relations.

Although medicalization theory has emphasized power, it has tended to minimize the significance of class. Historically, as I will suggest, the medicalization of certain problems was rooted in specific class interests. Physicians and women from the dominant class joined together—albeit out of very different motives—to redefine certain human events into medical categories. Women from other class groups at times embraced and at other times resisted these class-based definitions of experience.

In sum, the medicalization framework provides useful analytic categories for examining the medicalization of women's problems as a function of (1) the interests and beliefs of physicians; (2) the class-specific needs of women; and (3) the "fit" between these, resulting in a consensus that redefines a human experience as a medical problem. As stated before, I will use this framework to explore childbirth [and] reproductive control. . . . Clearly, because of space considerations, it is impossible to discuss each example in depth. Instead, I hope to provide a fresh look at each problem and lay out the issues as I perceive them at this point.

Childbirth

Today, pregnancy and birth are considered medical events. This was not always the case. Moreover, there is nothing inherent in either condition that necessitates routine medical scrutiny. In fact, birth is an uncomplicated process in roughly 90 percent of cases (Wertz and Wertz 1979). In order to understand the medicalization of childbirth, it must be analyzed as the outcome of a complex sociopolitical process in which both physicians and women participated.

In mid-nineteenth-century America, virtually anyone could be a doctor. As a result, there was an oversupply of healers—a series of competing sects with varying levels of training. These included "regular" college-trained physicians, physicians trained by apprenticeship, homeopaths, botanic physicians, male accoucheurs, midwives, and other healers (Drachman 1979). The "regular" physicians—white, upper-class males—struggled to achieve professional dominance as boundaries between professional and lay control shifted. It is important to emphasize that this group sought control over the healing enterprise at a time when they were not more effective than their competitors in curing disease. As Larson (1977) has noted, the diffusion of knowledge about scientific discoveries in microbiology that revolutionized medical care occurred only after medicine successfully gained control over the healing market. Thus, in the absence of superior skill, it was necessary to convert public perceptions. In order to gain "cultural authority" (Starr 1982) over definitions of health and disease and over the provision of health services, "regular" doctors had to transform general human skills into their exclusive craft. Social historians of medicine have documented the political activities that succeeded in guaranteeing a closed shop for "regular"doctors in late nineteenth- and early twentieth-century America (Reverby and Rosner 1979; Walsh 1977).

A central arena for the struggle over professional dominance was childbirth. In colonial America, this event was handled predominantly by female midwives who, assisted by a network of female relatives and friends, provided emotional support and practical assistance to the pregnant woman both during the actual birth and in the weeks that followed. Over a period of more than a century, "social childbirth" was replaced (Wertz and Wertz 1979). The site of care shifted from the home to the hospital. The personnel who gave care changed from female midwives to male physicians. The techniques changed from noninterventionist approaches to approaches relying on technology and drugs. As a consequence, the meaning of childbirth for women was transformed from a human experience to a medical-technical problem.

A crucial historical juncture in the medicalization of childbirth occurred in the second decade of the twentieth century. In 1910, about 50 percent of all reported births were attended by midwives. The medical profession and the laity generally believed that the midwife—essentially a domestic worker—was an adequate birth attendant. Nature was thought to control the process of birth. As a result, there was little to be done in case of difficulty. The teaching of obstetrics in medical schools was minimal, and direct experience with birth by medical students was rare (Kobrin 1966).

Beginning around 1910, a contest began between the emerging specialty of obstetrics, the general practitioner, and the midwife. Although seemingly about issues of science and efficacy, this struggle was also about class and race. Obstetricians were from the dominant class, whereas midwives were mostly immigrant and Black women. Struggling to differentiate themselves from general practitioners, obstetricians fought to upgrade the image of their field. They searched for a respectable science to legitimate their work. They argued that normal pregnancy and parturition were an exception rather than the rule. Because they believed that birth was a pathological process, obstetricians often used surgical interventions as well as instruments such as high forceps previous to sufficient dilation. These approaches, used routinely and often unnecessarily, frequently had deleterious effects on both mother and child. Over a period of several decades, obstetricians were successful in persuading both their physician colleagues and the general public of the "fallacy of normal pregnancy," and therefore of the need for a "science" of obstetrical practice. Their political activities, coupled with changing demographic trends, resulted in the demise of midwifery (Kobrin 1966).

It is important to note that the medical management of childbirth did not result in greater safety for women, at least in the short run. The evidence suggests that both maternal and infant mortality rates actually rose during the period between 1915 and 1930 when midwives' attendance at birth abruptly declined (Wertz and Wertz 1979). In the long run, there has been a steady decline in death rates, which has coincided with modern childbirth practice. However, it is not clear how much of this decline is due to improved environmental circumstances and nutrition and how much to medical care.

In light of these facts, what motivated women to go along with the medicalization of childbirth? Because childbirth is an event that occurs without complications in most cases, it is tempting to emphasize the many losses that accompanied its medicalization. In modern birth, the woman is removed from familiar surroundings, from kin and social support, and subjected to a series of technical procedures—many of which are dehumanizing and others of which carry significant health risks (Rothman 1982; Shaw 1974). A woman's experience of birth is alienated because the social relations and instrumentation of the medical setting remove her control over the experience (Young 1984). Because of these negative consequences of modern birth, there is a tendency to romanticize the midwife and pretechnological childbirth and fail to consider the contradictory nature of the process.

Women participated in the medicalization of childbirth for a complex set of reasons. First, nineteenth-century women wanted freedom from the pain, exhaustion, and lingering incapacity of childbirth. Pregnancy every other year was the norm for married women, and this took a significant toll on the reproductive organs. Contraception was not a viable alternative, for reasons I will discuss shortly. For working-class women, the problems of maternity were intensified by harsh working and housing conditions. The letters of early twentieth-century working class women vividly portray the exhaustion of motherhood (Davies 1978). Albeit for different reasons, women from different class groups experienced birth as a terrifying ordeal (Dye 1980).

In the early decades of the twentieth century, relief from the pain of childbirth was promised with "twilight sleep," a combination of morphine and scopolamine, which European physicians had begun to use. Historical analysis of the twilight sleep movement in the United States reveals that it was women who demanded it, frequently pitting themselves against the medical profession who both resented lay interference and feared the dangers of the drug (Leavitt 1980). These women—middle- and upper-class reformers with a progressive ideology—wanted to alter the oppressive circumstances of women's lives. Thus, the demand for anesthesia in childbirth was part of a larger social movement. Pregnancy was no longer seen as a condition to be endured with fatalism and passivity (Smith-Rosenberg and Rosenberg 1973). As Miller (1979) argues, people believed that civilization had increased the subjective experience of pain in childbirth, and that anesthesia would once again make childbirth natural. The upper class experienced greater pain than working-class women, who were thought to be more like primitive peoples. People believed that upper-class women had been particularly warped by civilization. (The corset also may have distorted their internal organs.) In other words, pain had accompanied the progress of civilization. If freed from painful and exhausting labor, women could (the reformers felt) more fully participate in democratic society (Miller 1979).

Second, because of declining fertility in upper- and middle-class women at the end of the nineteenth century, the meaning of birth was particularly significant to them. Because childbirth was a less frequent event, concern about fetal death was greater. In addition, women were fearful because it was common to have known someone who had died in childbirth (Dye 1980). Thus, well-to-do women wanted to be attended by doctors not only because they were of higher social status compared to midwives but also because they possessed the instruments and surgical techniques that might be beneficial in cases of prolonged labor, toxemia, fetal distress, and other abnormal conditions. Of course, physicians used these fears to gain control over the entire market, including routine births.

Thus, the demise of midwifery and the resultant medicalization of childbirth were consequences of forces within the women's community as well as from outside it. Furthermore, it was a class-specific process. Well-to-do women wanted to reduce the control that biology had over their lives. They wanted freedom from pain. Because of their refinement, medical ideology of the period insisted that well-do-do women were more delicate and hence more likely to experience pain and complications. By contrast, working-class women were believed to be inherently stronger (Cott 1972). Perhaps as a way of resisting these ideological assumptions, well-to-do women wanted control over the birthing process—the right to decide what kind of labor and delivery they would have. The contradiction was that the method these women demanded—going to sleep—put them out of control (Leavitt 1980).

Obstetricians also wanted control. They believed that birth was a pathological process and that "scientific birth" would result in greater safety for affluent women especially. In addition, it was in the interest of physicians to capture the childbirth market, because this event provided a gateway to the family, and hence the entire healing market (Wertz and Wertz 1979). Physicians were particularly anxious to attend the births of well-to-do women, because the social status of these women lent legitimacy and respectability to the shift from midwifery to obstetrics (Drachman 1979). In order to control childbirth, physicians needed drugs and technology to appear indispensable (Miller 1979). Therefore, they went along with twilight sleep, at least for a time. The irony for women was that this approach to the pain of childbirth served to distance women from their bodies and redefine birth as an event requiring hospitalization and physician attendance (Leavitt 1980).

Currently, the medicalization of childbirth is taking new forms. First, there is the strikingly high rate of cesarean deliveries—21.2% of American babies as of 1994 (Ventura et al., 1994). Although some of these are necessary for maternal health as well as infant survival, evidence suggests that many caesareans are unnecessary (O'Driscoll and Foley 1983). In view of medicalization, it is important to point out that the potential need for a cesarean places childbirth squarely and exclusively in the hands of the physician. Vaginal delivery, by contrast, can be the province of nonphysician experts, such as nurse-midwives.

Second, there is a trend to make the birth experience more humane, for both mother and baby. Hospitals are developing "birthing rooms" and other alternatives to the usual delivery room atmosphere of steel tables, stirrups, and bright lights. After birth, maternal-infant contact is permitted so as to foster "bonding." Pediatricians believe that a critical period exists for the development of an optimal relationship between mother and newborn

(Klaus and Kennell 1976). Thus, pediatricians are joining obstetricians in medicalizing the childbirth experience. By defining what should be (and therefore what is) deviant, pediatricians create social norms for parenting.

The contradiction is that the recent changes in the hospital environment of birth have both helped and hurt women. Birthing rooms and early contact between mother and newborn are a welcome change from previous oppressive obstetrical and pediatric practices (which poor women still face because these reforms are more characteristic of elite hospitals than of public ones). Yet the contemporary feminist critique of childbirth practice has been cut short by these reforms. As in many reform movements, larger issues are silenced. Challenges to the medical domination of pregnancy and demands for genuine demedicalization have been co-opted by an exclusive focus on the birth environment. Even when "natural" childbirth occurs in birthing rooms, birth is still defined medically, is still under the control of physicians, and still occurs in hospitals (Rothman 1981).

Moreover, the social meaning of parenting changes when scientific rationales such as "bonding" and "attachment" are used to justify mothers being near their babies after giving birth (Arney 1980). In addition, sex roles are reinforced when it is mothers and not fathers who need to be "bonded" to their infants.

Reproductive Freedom

Abortion

Today, abortion is treated as a medical event. Yet in previous historical periods, it was defined in nonmedical terms. Physicians brought specific professional and class interests to the abortion issue in the nineteenth century. To realize their interests, they needed to alter public beliefs about the meaning of unwanted pregnancy. Well-to-do women formed an alliance with doctors in this redefinition process because of their own needs.

As Mohr (1978) documents, abortion before quickening (the perception of fetal movement) was widely practiced in the mid-nineteenth century and was not seen as morally or legally wrong. Information on potions, purgatives, and quasi-surgical techniques was available in home medical manuals. As autoabortive instruments came on the market, women became skillful in performing their own abortions, and they shared information with one another. In addition, midwives, herbal healers, and other "irregular" doctors established lucrative practices in the treatment of "obstructed menses." It is estimated that by 1878 one in five pregnancies was intentionally aborted. The growing frequency of abortion was particularly evident in the middle and upper classes (Mohr 1978).

"Regular" physicians were central figures in redefining abortion as a social problem. The practice of abortion was leading to a declining birth rate, especially among the middle and upper classes who feared that this could lead to "race suicide" (Smith-Rosenberg and Rosenberg 1973). One physician warned that abortion was being used "to avoid the labor of caring for and rearing children" (Silver as quoted in Mohr 1978). In other words, women were shirking the responsibilities of their seemingly biologically determined role.

Mohr (1978) argues that physicians led the moral crusade against abortion not so much out of these antifeminist feelings, but primarily in order to restrict the practice of medicine. They wanted to get rid of competitors ("irregulars" and "doctresses") and gain a monopoly over the practice of medicine. By altering public opinion and persuading legislators, they succeeded in establishing their code of ethics (which specifically excluded abortion) as the basis for professional practice. These actions limited the scope of medicine's competitors, especially women doctors whose practices were devoted to the care of female complaints. By the late 1870s, anti-abortion statutes were on the books. Professional dominance was further strengthened in the 1880s when physicians became more organized. They used the scientific paradigm to force more and more folk practitioners from the field.

It is interesting to note the social relations at work in the nineteenth-century abortion struggle. First, the "regulars"—upper- and middle-class men—had natural allies in the state legislators, who were also men from prosperous families. Second, patriarchal class interests in general and nativism in particular provided the racist and sexist ideology for the anti-abortion movement. Physicians, legislators, and other well-to-do men wanted their women to reproduce the species, or, more specifically, the dominant class of the species. These groups, fearing the increasing numbers of the foreign-born, were concerned that the upper classes would be outbred. Finally, the conflict between the "regular" doctors and their competitors was not only about issues of science and professional control but also about the issues of class and patriarchy. The "irregular" doctors were, in general, not from families of the dominant class. In addition, these practitioners were more likely to be female. Thus social characteristics provided the rationale for exclusion, further reinforcing patriarchal class relations.

Women's participation in the anti-abortion crusade of the 1870s also was class-specific. Feminists of the period—well-to-do women—came out against abortion, arguing instead for voluntary motherhood. These early feminists recommended periodic or permanent abstinence as methods of birth control because they did not approve of contraceptive devices (Gordon 1976).

It is obvious that women lost significant freedoms when abortion was defined as a medical procedure and ruled illegal. Yet, from the perspective of the sexual politics of late-nineteenth-century America, it is significant that women favored abstinence over abortion. Abstinence was a more radical response to the power relations in the patriarchal family than a pro-abortion stance would have been.

Well-to-do women of the late nineteenth century had a level of hostility toward sex, both because it brought unwanted and dangerous pregnancy and because it was a legally prescribed wifely duty. Even more important,

Gordon (1976) argues that these women resented the particular kind of sexual encounter that was characteristic of American Victorian society: intercourse dominated by the husband's needs and neglecting what might bring pleasure to a woman. Men's style of lovemaking repelled women. They felt that men were oversexed and violent. Furthermore, because men visited prostitutes, marital sex for women not infrequently resulted in venereal disease. Under these conditions, a woman's right to refuse was central to her independence and personal integrity.

In sum, the termination of an unwanted pregnancy underwent a series of changing definitions: it went from a human problem to a topic of medical concern to a crime. With the 1973 Supreme Court decision [in Roe v. Wade], it was remedicalized, but this time with the support of the medical profession. Physicians no longer needed this issue to advance their sovereignty.

Contraception

In the twentieth century, well-to-do women joined physicians again in the medicalization of reproduction with the issue of contraception. These women struggled to define a "new sense of womanhood" that did not require sexual passivity, maternity, domesticity, and the absence of ambition. In order to achieve these goals feminists overcame their scruples against artificial contraception. Importantly, women ultimately won the battle of reproductive freedom. Technology to limit family size was developed in response to the social demand for it (Gordon 1976).

But as women gained from this newly won independence, they also lost. Birth control technology is not without problems, both in its female centricity and its risk. Furthermore, as Gordon argues, the professionalism and medicalization of birth control stripped it of its political content. As a result of its definition as a health issue, contraception became somewhat separate from the larger social movement that gave rise to the demand for birth control in the first place. Finally, the battle over medicalization was lost again when birth control methods went in the direction of high technology. The pill, the IUD, and injectable contraceptives are forever in the hands of medicine, because access to these drugs and devices is legally controlled. In contrast, the low-technology barrier methods—the condom, cervical cap, or diaphragm—require little medical intervention or control.

These historical examples underscore the fact that women's experience was a site for the initial medicalization effort. Medicine "staked claims" for childbirth, abortion, and birth control and secured them as "medical turf" by altering public beliefs and persuading the state of the legitimacy of their claim (cf. Conrad and Schneider 1980a). Physicians used science as the rationale for professional dominance. As I have suggested, women's participation in the redefinition of each experience was the result of complex historical and class-specific motives, and they not only gained but lost with the medicalization of each area. . . .

The Fit Between Women's Interests and Physicians' Interests

These examples illustrate a general point about medical social control: there are times when the interests of women from the middle and upper classes are served by the therapeutic professions, whose political and economic interests are in turn served by transforming these women's complaints into illnesses. In other words, both historically and currently, there has tended to be a "fit" between medicine's interest in expanding its jurisdiction and the need of women to have their experience acknowledged. I have emphasized that this "fit" has been tension-filled and fraught with contradictions for women, who have both gained and lost with each intrusion medicine has made into their lives.

While necessary, the particular interests of women and physicians do not alone explain the expansion of the clinical domain. Other communities also influence what occurs in the doctor's office. In the context of a capitalist economy and a technologically dominated medical care system, large profits accompany each redefinition of human experience into medical terms, since more drugs, tests, procedures, equipment, and insurance coverage are needed. As mentioned before, specific medical industries have played a direct role in influencing both physicians' and women's perceptions of reproductive control, premenstrual syndrome, and weight. Yet it is important to emphasize that corporations, in their effort to maximize profits, work *through* both physicians and women.

Implicit in my analysis is the assumption that women's experience has been medicalized more than men's. Yet it could be argued instead that medicine has encroached into men's lives in a different but equal fashion. For example, medicine has focused on childhood hyperactivity and the adult addictions—problems more common in males than females (Conrad and Schneider 1980a). Occupational medicine has tended to focus on male jobs. In particular, "stress management" programs are targeting male executives. However, while not to diminish these examples, I believe that women's lives have undergone a more total transformation as a result of medical scrutiny. Medicalization has resulted in the construction of medical meanings of *normal* functions in women—experiences the typical woman goes through, such as menstruation, reproduction, childbirth, and menopause. By contrast, routine experiences that are uniquely male remain largely unstudied by medical science and, consequently, are rarely treated by physicians as potentially pathological. For example, male hormonal cycles and the male climacteric remain largely unresearched. Less is known about the male reproductive system than about that of the female. Male contraceptive technology lags far behind what is available for women. Baldness in men has not yet been defined as a medical condition needing treatment, even though an industry exists to remedy the problem of hair loss. Men's psychological lives have not been subjected to psychiatric scrutiny nearly to the degree that women's emotions have been studied. As a result, male violence, need for power, and overrationality are not defined as pathological conditions. Perhaps only impotence has been subject to the same degree of medical scrutiny as women's problems.

Why has women's experience been such a central focus for medicalization? In addition to the complex motives that women bring to each particular health issue, physicians focus on women as a primary market for expansion for a number of reasons. First, there is a good match between women's biology and medicine's biomedical orientation. External markers of biological processes exist in women (menstruation, birth, lactation, and so forth), whereas they are more hidden in men. Given modern medicine's biomedical orientation, these external signs make women easy targets for medical encroachment. A different medical paradigm (one that viewed health as the consequence of harmony between the person and the environment, for example) might have had less basis for focusing on women.

Second, women's social roles make them readily available to medical scrutiny. Women are more likely to come in contact with medical providers because they care for children and are the "kin keepers" of the family (Rossi 1980). In concrete terms, women are more likely to accompany sick children and aged relatives to the doctor.

Third, women have greater exposure to medical labeling because of their pattern of dealing with their own symptoms, as well as medicine's response to that pattern. Women make more visits to physicians than men, although it is not clear whether this is due to the medicalization of their biological functions, "real" illness, behavior when ill, or cultural expectations (Nathanson 1977). When they visit the doctor for any serious illness, they are more likely than men to be checked for reproductive implications of the illness. They are more subject to regular checks of their reproductive systems, in the form of yearly pap smears or gynecological exams. Importantly, whenever they visit the doctor there is evidence that they receive more total and extensive services—in the form of lab tests, procedures, drug prescriptions, and return appointments—than do men with the same complaints and sociodemographic risk factors (Verbrugge and Steiner 1981). Thus, a cycle of greater medical scrutiny of women's experiences is begun with each visit to the doctor.

Finally, women's structural subordination to men has made them particularly vulnerable to the expansion of the clinical domain. In general, male physicians treat female patients. Social relations in the doctor's office replicate patriarchal relations in the larger culture, and this all proceeds under the guise of science. (Patriarchal control is most evident when physicians socialize young women regarding appropriate sexual behavior, perhaps withholding contraceptive advice, or lecturing them about the dangers of promiscuity). For all these reasons, it is not surprising that women are more subject to medical definitions of their experience than men are. In these ways, dominant social interests and patriarchal institutions are reinforced.

As a result, women are especially appropriate markets for the expansion of medicine. They are suitable biologically, socially, and psychologically. The message that women are expected to be dependent on male physicians to manage their lives is reinforced by the pharmaceutical industry in drug advertisements and by the media in general. Yet it is far too simple to portray the encroachment of medicines as a conspiracy—by male doctors and the "medical industrial complex"—to subordinate women further. Although some have argued that medicine is the scientific equivalent of earlier customs like marriage laws and kinship rituals that controlled women by controlling their sexuality, such an analysis is incomplete. As I have stressed, medicalization is more than what doctors do, although it may be through doctors that the interests of other groups are often realized. Nor does a conspiracy theory explain why, for the most part, women from certain class groups have been willing collaborators in the medicalization process. Rather than dismissing these women as "duped," I have suggested some of the complex motives that have caused certain classes of women to participate with physicians in the redefinition of particular experiences.

In addition, a conspiracy theory does not explain why medicalization has been more virulent in some historical periods and in some medical specialties than in others. For example, gynecologists initially trivialized menopausal discomfort, only to reclaim it later for treatment [as premenstrual syndrome]. At the same time that gynecologists were unwilling to acknowledge the legitimacy of women's complaints, the developing specialty of psychiatry moved in with the psychogenic account. I have argued that these shifts and interprofessional rivalries over turf are explained by internal issues facing each specialty at particular points in history. Thus, an analysis of the market conditions faced by physicians in general, and certain specialties in particular, is necessary to explain the varying response of medicine to women's problems.

Further research is needed to capture more fully the historical aspect of these shifts in medical perception. Such an analysis needs to focus in depth on specific events in women's experience and trace their medicalization in historical and class context: the issues brought in turn by groups of women, by the particular medical specialties, by the pharmaceutical industry, and by the "fit" between these that resulted in a redefinition. A conspiracy theory fails to capture the nuances of this complex process.

Conclusion

The medicalization of human problems is a contradictory reality for women. It is part of the problem and of the solution. It has grown out of and in turn has created a series of paradoxes. As women have tried to free themselves from the control that biological processes have had over their lives, they simultaneously have strengthened the control of a biomedical view of their experience. As women visit doctors and get symptom relief, the social causes of their problems are ignored. As doctors acknowledge women's experience and treat their problems medically, problems are stripped of their political content and popular movements are taken over. Because of these contradictions, women in different class positions have sought and resisted medical control.

I have argued that the transformation of such human experiences as childbirth, reproduction, premenstrual problems, weight, and psychological distress into medical events has been the outcome of a reciprocal process involving both physicians and women. Medicine, as it developed as a profession, was repeatedly redefined. The interest of physicians in expanding jurisdiction into new areas coincided with the interest of certain class groups in having their experience in those areas understood in new terms. In other words, physicians created demand in order to generate new markets for their services. They also responded to a market that a class of women created. . . .

As Conrad and Schneider (1980a) note, the potential for medicalization increases as science discovers the subtle physiological correlates of human behavior. A wealth of knowledge is developing about women's physiology. As more becomes known, the issue will be how to acknowledge the complex biochemical components that are related to menstruation, pregnancy, weight, and the like without allowing these conditions to be distorted by scientific understanding. The issue will be to gain understanding of our biology, without submitting to control in the guise of medical "expertise." The answer is not to "suffer our fate" and return exclusively to self-care, as Illich (1976) recommends, thereby turning our backs on discoveries and treatments that may ease pain and suffering. To "demedicalize" is not to deny the biological components of experience but rather to alter the ownership, production, and use of scientific knowledge. . . .

In sum, women's health is faced by a series of challenges. We need to expose the "truth claims" (Bittner 1968) of medical entrepreneurs who will seek to turn new areas of experience into medical events, and instead introduce a healthy skepticism about professional claims. We need to develop alternatives to the masculinist biomedical view and place women's health problems in the larger context of their lives. Specifically, it is not at all clear what form pregnancy, menstruation, weight, sexuality, aging, or other problems would take in a society "that allowed women to normally and routinely express anger, drive, and ambition, a society in which women felt more empowered" (Harrison 1982). We need to reconceptualize our whole way of thinking about biology and explore how "natural" phenomena are, in fact, an outgrowth of the social circumstances of women's lives (Hubbard 1981).

In the meantime, because we will continue to need health care, the challenge will be to alter the terms under which care is provided. In the short term, we need to work for specific reforms and gain what we can while, at the same time, acknowledging the limitation of reform. As I have argued, reform is not what we want in the long run. For certain problems in our lives, real demedicalization is necessary; experiences such as routine childbirth, menopause, or weight in excess of cultural norms should not be defined in medical terms, and medical-technical treatments should not be seen as appropriate solutions to these problems. For other conditions where medicine may be of assistance, the challenge will be to differentiate the beneficial treatments from those that are harmful and useless. The real challenge is to use existing medical knowledge selectively and to extend knowledge with new paradigms so as to improve the quality of our lives.

References

Arney, William R. 1980. Maternal-infant bonding: The politics of falling in love with your child. *Feminist Studies* 6:547–570.

Bittner, Egon. 1968. The structure of psychiatric influence. *Mental Hygiene* 52:423–30.

Conrad, Peter, and Joseph W. Schneider. 1980a. *Deviance and Medicalization: From Badness to Sickness.* St. Louis: C. V. Mosby.

———. 1980b. Looking at levels of medicalization: A comment on Strong's critique of the theses of medical imperialism. *Social Science and Medicine* 14A:75–79.

Cott, Nancy F., ed. 1972. *Root of Bitterness: Documents of the Social History of American Women.* New York: E. P. Dutton.

Davies, Marjorie L. 1978. *Maternity: Letters from Working Women.* New York: Norton.

Drachman, V. G. 1979. The Loomis Trial: Social mores and obstetrics in the mid-nineteenth century. In *Health Care in America: Essays in Social History,* edited by Susan E. Reverby and David Rosner. Philadelphia: Temple University Press.

Dreifus, Claudia, ed. 1978. *Seizing Our Bodies: The Politics of Women's Health.* New York: Vintage.

Dye, Nancy S. 1980. History of childbirth in America. *Signs* 97:97–108.

Ehrenreich, Barbara, and John Ehrenreich. 1978. Medicine and social control. In *The Cultural Crisis of Modern Medicine,* edited by J. Ehrenreich. New York: Monthly Review Press.

Ehrenreich, Barbara, and Deidre English. 1973. *Complaints and Disorders: The Sexual Politics of Sickness.* Old Westbury: Feminist Press.

———. 1979. *For Her Own Good: 150 Years of the Experts' Advice to Women.* Garden City: Anchor.

Foucault, Michel. 1973. *The Birth of the Clinic: An Archeology of Medical Perception.* New York: Pantheon.

Freidson, Eliot. 1970. *Profession of Medicine.* New York: Dodd, Mead.

Frankfort, Ellen. 1972. *Vaginal Politics.* New York: Quadrangle Books.

Gordon, Linda. 1976. *Woman's Body, Woman's Right: A Social History of Birth Control in America.* New York: Penguin.

Gross, H. S., M. R. Herbert, G. L. Knatterud, and L. Donner. 1969. The effect of race and sex on the variation of diagnosis and disposition in a psychiatric emergency room. *Journal of Nervous and Mental Disease* 148:638–43.

Harrison, Michelle. 1982. *Self-Help for Premenstrual Syndrome.* Cambridge: Matrix Press.

Hubbard, R. 1981. "The Politics of Women's Biology." Lecture given at Hampshire College.

Illich, Ivan. 1976. *Medical Nemesis: The Expropriation of Health.* New York: Pantheon.

Klaus, Marshall H., and John H. Kennell. 1976. *Maternal-Infant Bonding: The Impact of Early Separation or Loss on Family Development.* St. Louis: C. V. Mosby.

Kobrin, Francis E. 1966. The American midwife controversy: A crisis of professionalization. *Bulletin of the History of Medicine* 40:350–63.

Larson, Magali S. 1977. *The Rise of Professionalism: A Sociological Analysis.* Berkeley: University of California Press.

Leavitt, Judith W. 1980. Birthing and anesthesia: The debate over twilight sleep. *Signs* 6:147–64.

Miller, L. G. 1979. Pain, parturition, and the profession: Twilight sleep in America. In *Health Care in America: Essays in Social History,* edited by Susan E. Reverby and David Rosner. Philadelphia: Temple University Press.

Mills, E. 1962. *Living with Mental Illness: A Study of East London.* London: Routledge and Kegan Paul.

Mishler, Elliot G. 1981. The social construction of illness. In *Social Context of Health, Illness, and Patient Care,* edited by Elliot G. Mishler, Lorna R. AmaraSingham, Stuart T. Hauser, Samuel D. Osherson, Nancy E. Waxler, and Ramsay Liem. Cambridge: Cambridge University Press.

Mohr, John C. 1978. *Abortion in America: The Origins and Evolution of National Policy, 1800–1900.* New York: Oxford University Press.

Nathanson, Constance. 1975. Illness and the feminine role: A theoretical review. *Social Science and Medicine* 9:57–62.

O'Driscoll, K., and M. Foley. 1983. Correlation of decrease in perinatal mortality and increase in caesarean section rates. *Obstetrics and Gynecology* 61:1–5.

Reverby, Susan E., and David Rosner, eds. 1979. *Health Care in America: Essays in Social History.* Philadelphia: Temple University Press.

Rossi, Alice. 1980. Life span theories and women's lives. *Signs* 6:4–32.

Rothman, Barbara Katz. 1981. Awake and aware, or false consciousness: The cooptation of childbirth reform in America. In *Childbirth: Alternative to Medical Control,* edited by Sherry Romalis. Austin: University of Texas Press.

———. 1982. *In Labor: Women and Power in the Birthplace.* New York: Norton.

Ruzek, Sheryl B. 1978. *The Women's Health Movement: Feminist Alternatives to Medical Control.* New York: Praeger.

Seaman, B. 1972. *Free and Female.* New York: Coward, McCann, and Geoghegan.

Shaw, Nancy S. 1974. *Forced Labor: Maternity Care in the United States.* New York: Pergamon.

Smith-Rosenberg, Carroll and Charles Rosenberg. 1973. The female animal: Medical and biological views of woman and her role in nineteenth-century America. *Journal of American History* 60:332–55.

Sontag, Susan. 1979. *Illness as Metaphor.* New York: Vintage.

Stark, Evan, and Anne Flitcraft. 1982. Medical therapy as repression: The case of battered women. *Health and Medicine* 1:29–32.

Starr, Paul. 1982. *The Social Transformation of American Medicine.* New York: Basic Books.

Ventura, S. J., J. A. Martin, T. J. Mathews, and S. C. Clarke. Advance report of final natality statistics, 1994. *Monthly Vital Statistics Report* 44 (11):71.

Verbrugge, Lois M., and R. P. Steiner. 1981. Physician treatment of men and women patients: Sex bias or appropriate care? *Medical Care* 19:609–32.

Walsh, Mary R. 1977. *Doctors Wanted: No Women Need Apply.* New Haven, CT: Yale University Press.

Wertz, Richard W., and Dorothy C. Wertz. 1979. *Lying In: A History of Childbirth in America.* New York: Free Press.

Young, Iris M. 1984. Pregnant embodiment: Subjectivity and alienation. *Journal of Medicine and Philosophy* 9:45–62.

Zola, Irving K. 1972. Medicine as an institution of social control. *Sociological Review* 20:487–504.

———. 1975. In the name of health and illness: On some socio-political consequences of medical influence. *Social Science and Medicine* 9:83–87.

II

THE POLITICS
OF SEXUALITY

Sexuality is an integral part of everyone's life. Even those who are celibate generally retain sexual feelings, whether of longing or of revulsion, and still define themselves in terms of their sexual history and sexual orientation. Moreover, sexual activity provides a broad canvas on which individuals express their personality and values. For these reasons, both individuals and societies have found that controlling women's sexuality is an effective way to control women's lives.

The articles in this section address the links between women's bodies, women's sexuality, and the control of women's lives. In "From the 'Muscle Moll' to the 'Butch' Ballplayer: Mannishness, Lesbianism, and Homophobia in U.S. Women's Sports," Susan K. Cahn traces the history of women's participation in sports from the early twentieth century through the 1960s to show how attitudes toward women's sports both reflected and reinforced social ideas about proper female sexuality and the proper place of women in American society. She shows how, prior to the 1930s, critics of women's sports argued that, by encouraging unrestrained emotional excitement and exuberant physical activity, athletics could lead women to lose control over their heterosexual desires. Conversely, in later years, in response to the loosening of family bonds and traditional female roles that resulted from both the Great Depression and the Second World War, critics argued that athletics could lead women to lose their attractiveness to men or their interest in heterosexual relationships. These fears and stereotypes served to keep women out of sports and to stigmatize those whose interests or appearance did not fit dominant cultural standards.

Janet Lee's article, "Menarche and the (Hetero)sexualization of the Female Body," uses women's narratives regarding their early experiences with menstruation to show how these experiences socialize women to think of their bodies and sexuality in ways demanded by American culture. Through these experiences, women learn to think of their bodies as contaminating and embarrassing. They become alienated from their bodies—learning to think of the changes in their bodies as something happening to them rather than something they are doing, and learning to think of their appearance and sexuality as things designed for men's viewing and pleasure rather than things they themselves can take pleasure in. Similarly, young women at menarche learn to fear both that they will not be attractive to men and that they will attract unwanted male attention. Lee ends her article with a discussion of how women resist these cultural pressures, by, for example, using their stories to reframe their experiences and using the cultural restrictions on menstruating women to their advantage.

The article by Linda Christian-Smith, "Young Women and Their Dream Lovers: Sexuality in Adolescent Fiction," examines the role modern teenage romance novels have played in socializing women to adopt culturally-demanded heterosexual goals. These books, whose popularity grew enormously beginning in the 1980s, teach young women to emphasize romance and to restrict their sexual desires and activities solely to romantic heterosexual relationships. In addition, the books teach young women that they are responsible for keeping heterosexual relationships from leading to the genital sexual encounters that boys routinely demand, and that female sexual desire can emerge only in response to male desire. In so doing, these books reinforce the gendered distribution of power in our society, by encouraging girls to define their selves, bodies, and sexuality through their romantic relationships with boys.

Finally, bell hooks's article, "Selling Hot Pussy: Representations of Black Female Sexuality in the Cultural Marketplace," looks at cultural ideas about African-American women's bodies and sexuality. She shows how, consistently, Western culture has depicted African-American women as both expendable and animalistically hypersexual. She then demonstrates how these ideas continue to pervade contemporary representations of African-American female sexuality, from Richard Wright's novels to Tina Turner's performances to the presentation of African-American fashion models.

5

From the "Muscle Moll" to the "Butch" Ballplayer

Mannishness, Lesbianism, and Homophobia in U.S. Women's Sports

Susan K. Cahn

In 1934, *Literary Digest* subtitled an article on women's sports, "Will the Playing Fields One Day Be Ruled by Amazons?" The author, Fred Wittner, answered the question affirmatively and concluded that as an "inevitable consequence" of sport's masculinizing effect, "girls trained in physical education today may find it more difficult to attract the most worthy fathers for their children" (1934, 43). The image of women athletes as mannish, failed heterosexuals represents a thinly veiled reference to lesbianism in sport. At times, the homosexual allusion has been indisputable, as in a journalist's description (Murray n.d.) of the great athlete Babe Didrikson as a "Sapphic, Brobdingnagian woman" or in television comedian Arsenio Hall's more recent (1988) witticism, "If we can put a man on the moon, why can't we put one on Martina Navratilova?" More frequently, however, popular commentary on lesbians in sport has taken the form of indirect references, surfacing through denials and refutations rather than open acknowledgment. When in 1955 an *Ebony* magazine article on African-American track stars insisted that "off track, girls are entirely feminine. Most of them like boys, dances, club affairs," the reporter answered the implicit but unspoken charge that athletes, especially Black women in a "manly" sport, were masculine manhaters, or lesbians.

The figure of the mannish lesbian athlete has acted as a powerful but unarticulated "bogey woman" of sport, forming a silent foil for more positive, corrective images that attempt to rehabilitate the image of women athletes and resolve the cultural contradiction between athletic prowess and femininity. As

Originally published as Susan K. Cahn, *Feminist Studies*, Vol. 19, No. 2 (Summer 1993): 343–68. Reprinted by permission of the publisher, University of Maryland, College Park, MD 20742.

a stereotyped figure in U.S. society, the lesbian athlete forms part of everyday cultural knowledge. Yet historians have paid scant attention to the connection between female sexuality and sport.[1] This essay explores the historical relationship between lesbianism and sport by tracing the development of the stereotyped "mannish lesbian athlete" and examining its relation to the lived experience of mid-twentieth-century lesbian athletes.

I argue that fears of mannish female sexuality in sport initially centered on the prospect of unbridled heterosexual desire. By the 1930s, however, female athletic mannishness began to connote heterosexual failure, usually couched in terms of unattractiveness to men, but also suggesting the possible absence of heterosexual interest. In the years following World War II, the stereotype of the lesbian athlete emerged full-blown. The extreme homophobia and the gender conservatism of the postwar era created a context in which longstanding linkages among mannishness, female homosexuality, and athletes cohered around the figure of the mannish lesbian athlete. . . .

Amazons, Muscle Molls, and the Question of Sexual (Im)mortality

The athletic woman sparked interest and controversy in the early decades of the twentieth century. In the United States and other Western societies, sport functioned as a male preserve, an all-male domain in which men not only played games together but also demonstrated and affirmed their manhood (Dunning 1986; Kimmel 1987; Mangan and Park 1987; Mrozek 1983). The "maleness" of sport derived from a gender ideology which labeled aggression, physicality, competitive spirit, and athletic skill as masculine attributes necessary for achieving true manliness. This notion found unquestioned support in the dualistic, polarized concepts of gender which prevailed in Victorian America. However, by the turn of the century, women had begun to challenge Victorian gender arrangements, breaking down barriers to female participation in previously male arenas of public work, politics, and urban nightlife. Some of these "New Women" sought entry into the world of athletics as well. On college campuses students enjoyed a wide range of intramural sports through newly formed Women's Athletic Associations. Off-campus women took up games like golf, tennis, basketball, swimming, and occasionally even wrestling, car racing, or boxing. As challengers to one of the defining arenas of manhood, skilled female athletes became symbols of the broader march of womanhood out of the Victorian domestic sphere into once prohibited male realms.

The woman athlete represented both the appealing and the threatening aspects of modern womanhood. In a positive light, she captured the exuberant spirit, physical vigor, and brazenness of the New Woman. The University of Minnesota student newspaper proclaimed in 1904 that the athletic girl was the "truest type of All-American coed" (1904–5 Scrapbooks of Anne Maude Butner, Butner Papers, University of Minnesota Archives, Minneapolis). Several years later, *Harper's Bazaar* labeled the unsportive girl as "not strictly up to date" (Mange 1910, 246), and *Good Housekeeping* noted that the "tomboy" had come to symbolize "a new type of American girl, new not only physically, but mentally and morally" (de Koven 1912, 150).

Yet, women athletes invoked condemnation as often as praise. Critics ranged from physicians and physical educators to sportswriters, male athletic officials, and casual observers. In their view, strenuous athletic pursuits endangered women and threatened the stability of society. They maintained that women athletes would become manlike, adopting masculine dress, talk, and mannerisms. In addition, they contended, too much exercise would damage female reproductive capacity. And worse yet, the excitement of sport would cause women to lose control, conjuring up images of frenzied, distraught co-eds on the verge of moral, physical, and emotional breakdown. These fears collapsed into an all-encompassing concept of "mannishness," a term signifying female masculinity.

The public debate over the merits of women's athletic participation remained lively through the 1910s and 1920s. Implicit in the dispute over "mannishness" was a longstanding disagreement over the effect of women's athletic activities on their sexuality. Controversy centered around two issues, damage to female reproductive capacity and the unleashing of heterosexual passion. Medical experts and exercise specialists disagreed among themselves about the effects of athletic activity on women's reproductive cycles and organs. Some claimed that athletic training interfered with menstruation and caused reproductive organs to harden or atrophy; others insisted that rigorous exercise endowed women with strength and energy which would make them more fit for bearing and rearing children. Similarly, experts vehemently debated whether competition unleashed nonprocreative, erotic desires identified with male sexuality and unrespectable women, or, conversely, whether invigorating sport enhanced a woman's feminine charm and sexual appeal, channeling sexual energy into wholesome activity.

Conflicting opinion on sexual matters followed closely along the lines of a larger dispute which divided the world of women's sport into warring camps. Beginning in the 1910s, female physical educators and male sport promoters squared off in a decades-long struggle over the appropriate nature of female competition and the right to govern women's athletics (Gerber 1975; Himes 1986; Hult 1985). The conflict was a complicated one, involving competing class and gender interests played out in organizational as well as philosophical battles. It was extremely important in shaping women's sports for more than fifty years. Although historians of sport have examined the broad parameters of the conflict, they have paid less attention to the competing sexual perspectives advanced by each side.

Physical educators took a cautious approach on all matters of sexuality, one designed to safeguard vulnerable young athletes and to secure their own professional status as respectable women in the male-dominated worlds of academia and sport. Heeding dire warnings about menstrual dysfunction, sterility, and inferior offspring, educators created policies to curtail strenuous competition and prohibit play during menstruation. They worried equally about the impact of sport on sexual morality. Alleging that competition would induce "powerful impulses" leading girls into a "temptation to excess" and the "pitfall of overindulgence," educators and their allies pressured popular sport promoters to reduce the competitive stimulation, publicity, and physical strain thought to endanger the sexuality of their female charges (Inglis 1910; Paret 1900, 1567; Sargent 1913).

Popular sport organizations like the Amateur Athletic Union agreed that unregulated female competition posed psychological and moral dangers. But AAU officials countered protectionist physical education policies with a nationalist, eugenic stance which argued that strenuous activity under proper guidance would actually strengthen reproductive organs, creating a vigorous cadre of mothers to produce a generation of stalwart American sons (e.g., MacFadden 1929; Steers 1932). Although making some concessions to demands for modesty and female supervision, in the long run AAU leaders and commercial sport promoters also rejected educators' emphasis on sexual control. Sponsors of popular sport found that sexual hype, much more than caution, helped to attract customers and mute charges of mannishness. In working-class settings and in more elite sports like swimming, an ideal of the "athlete as beauty queen" emerged. Efforts to present the female athlete as sexually attractive and available mirrored the playful, erotic sensibility present in the broader commercial leisure culture of the early twentieth century (Erenberg 1981; Freedman and D'Emilio 1988; Peiss 1986).

The class and gender lines in this dispute were complicated by overlapping constituencies. Female educators adhered closely to middle-class, even Victorian, notions of respectability and modesty. But their influence spread beyond elite private and middle-class schools into working-class public schools and industrial recreation programs. And male promoters, often themselves of the middle-class, continued to control some school sport and, outside the schools, influenced both working-class and elite sports. Moreover, Black physical educators advanced a third point of view. Although few in number, early-twentieth-century African-American physical education instructors generally aligned themselves with popular promoters in favor of competition and interscholastic sports. Yet their strong concern with maintaining respectability created some sympathy for the positions advanced by white leaders of women's physical education (Arnett 1921; Dunham 1924; Ellis 1939; Roberts 1927).

On all sides of the debate, however, the controversy about sport and female sexuality presumed heterosexuality. Neither critics nor supporters suggested that "masculine" athleticism might indicate or induce same-sex love. When experts warned of the amazonian athlete's possible sexual transgressions, they linked the physical release of sport with a loss of heterosexual *control*, not *inclination*. The most frequently used derogatory term for women athletes was "Muscle Moll." In its only other usages, the word "moll" referred to either the female lovers of male gangsters or to prostitutes. Both represented disreputable, heterosexually deviant womanhood.

By contrast, medical studies of sexual "deviance" from the late nineteenth and early twentieth centuries quite clearly linked "mannishness" to lesbianism, and in at least two cases explicitly connected female homosexuality with boyish athleticism (Chauncey 1989, 90–91; Ellis 1915, 250; Wise 1883, 88). It is curious then that in answering charges against the mannish Muscle Moll, educators and sport promoters of this period did not refer to or deny lesbianism. However, the "mannish lesbian" made little sense in the heterosexual milieu of popular sports. Promoters encouraged mixed audiences for women's athletic events, often combining them with men's games, postgame dances and musical entertainment, or even beauty contests. The image of the athlete as beauty queen and the commercial atmosphere that characterized much of working-class sport ensured that the sexual debate surrounding the modern female athlete would focus on her heterosexual charm, daring, or disrepute. The homosocial environment of women's physical education left educators more vulnerable to insinuations that their profession was populated by "mannish" types who preferred the love of women. However, the feminine respectability and decorum cultivated by the profession provided an initial shield from associations with either the mannish lesbian or her more familiar counterpart, the heterosexual Muscle Moll.

The Muscle Moll as Heterosexual Failure: Emerging Lesbian Stereotypes

In the 1930s, however, the heterosexual understanding of the mannish "amazon" began to give way to a new interpretation which educators and promoters could not long ignore. To the familiar charge that female athletes resembled men, critics added the newer accusation that sport-induced mannishness disqualified them as candidates for heterosexual romance. In 1930, an *American Mercury* medical reporter decried the decline of romantic love, pinning the blame on women who entered sport, business, and politics. He claimed that such women "act like men, talk like men, and think like men." The author explained that "women have come closer and closer to men's level," and, consequently, "the purple allure of distance has vamoosed" (Nathan 1930). Four years later, the *Ladies Home Journal* printed a "Manual on the More or Less Subtle Art of Getting a Man" which listed vitality, gaiety, vivacity, and good sportsmanship—qualities typically associated with women athletes and formerly linked to the athletic flapper's heterosexual appeal—as "the very qualities that are likely to make him consider anything but marriage" (Moats 1934). Although the charges didn't exclusively focus on athletes, they implied that female athleticism was contrary to heterosexual appeal, which appeared to rest on women's difference from and deference to men.

The concern with heterosexual appeal reflected broader sexual transformations in U.S. society. Historians of sexuality have examined the multiple forces which reshaped gender and sexual relations in the first few decades of the twentieth century. Victorian sexual codes crumbled under pressure from an assertive, boldly sexual working-class youth culture, a women's movement which defied prohibitions against public female activism, and the growth of a new pleasure-oriented consumer economy. In the wake of these changes, modern ideals of womanhood embraced an overtly erotic heterosexual sensibility. At the same time, medical fascination with sexual "deviance" created a growing awareness of lesbianism, now understood as a form of congenital or psychological pathology. The medicalization of homosexuality in combination with an antifeminist backlash in the 1920s against female autonomy and power contributed to a more fully articulated taboo against lesbianism. The modern heterosexual woman stood in stark opposition to her threatening sexual counterpart, the "mannish" lesbian (Freedman and D'Emilio 1988; Simmons 1989).

By the late 1920s and early 1930s, with a modern lesbian taboo and an eroticized definition of heterosexual femininity in place, the assertive, muscular female competitor aroused increasing suspicion. It was at this moment that both subtle and direct references to the lesbian athlete emerged in physical education and popular sport. Uncensored discussions of intimate female companionship and harmless athletic "crushes" disappear from the record, pushed underground by the increasingly hostile tone of public discourse about female sexuality and athleticism. Fueled by the gender antagonisms and anxieties of the Depression, the public began scrutinizing women athletes—known for their appropriation of masculine games and styles—for signs of deviance.

Where earlier references to "amazons" had signaled heterosexual ardor, journalists now used the term to mean unattractive, failed heterosexuals. Occasionally, the media made direct mention of athletes' presumed lesbian tendencies. A 1933 *Redbook* article, for example, casually mentioned that track and golf star Babe Didrikson liked men just to horse around with her and not "make love," adding that Babe's fondness for her best girlfriends far surpassed her affection for any man (Marston 1933, 60). The direct reference was unusual; the lesbian connotation of mannishness was forged primarily through indirect links of association. The preponderance of evidence appears in public exchanges between opponents and advocates of women's sport

After two decades of celebrating the female collegiate athlete, yearbooks at co-ed colleges began to ridicule physical education majors and Women's Athletic Association (WAA) members, portraying them as hefty, disheveled, and ugly. A 1937 Minnesota *Gopher* yearbook sarcastically titled its presentation on the WAA "Over in No Man's Land." Finding themselves cast as unattractive prudes or mannish misfits, physical educators struggled to revise their image. They declared the muscle-bound, manhating athlete a relic of the past, supplanted by "lovely, feminine charming girls" whose fitness, suppleness, and grace merely made them "more beautiful on the dance floor that evening" (Mooney 1937; Sefton 1937).

Similar exchanges appeared in popular magazines. After *Literary Digest* published Fred Wittner's assertion (1934, 42) that "worthy fathers" would not find trained women athletes attractive mates, AAU official Ada Taylor

Sackett issued a rebuttal which reassured readers that because athletic muscles resembled "those of women who dance all night," women in sport could no doubt "still attract a worthy mate" (1934, 43). When critics maligned athletic femininity, they suggested that athletes were literally un-becoming women: unattractive females who abdicated their womanhood and fell under sexual suspicion. When defenders responded with ardent assertions that women athletes did indeed exhibit interest in men, marriage, and motherhood, it suggested that they understood "mannish" to mean "not-heterosexual."

The Butch Ballplayer: Midcentury Stereotypes of the Lesbian Athlete

Tentatively voiced in the 1930s, these accusations became harsher and more explicit under the impact of wartime changes in gender and sexuality and the subsequent panic over the "homosexual menace." In a post-World War II climate markedly hostile to nontraditional women and lesbians, women in physical education and in working-class popular sports became convenient targets of homophobic indictment.

World War II opened up significant economic and social possibilities for gay men and women. Embryonic prewar homosexual subcultures blossomed during the war and spread across the midcentury urban landscape. Bars, nightclubs, public cruising spots, and informal social networks facilitated the development of gay and lesbian enclaves. But the permissive atmosphere did not survive the war's end. Waving the banner of Cold War political and social conservatism, government leaders acted at the federal, state, and local levels to purge gays and lesbians from government and military posts, to initiate legal investigations and prosecutions of gay individuals and institutions, and to encourage local police crackdowns on gay bars and street life. The perceived need to safeguard national security and to reestablish social order in the wake of wartime disruption sparked a "homosexual panic" which promoted the fear, loathing, and persecution of homosexuals (Bérubé 1990; D'Emilio 1983; Freedman and D'Emilio 1988).

Lesbians suffered condemnation for their violation of gender as well as sexual codes. The tremendous emphasis on family, domesticity, and "traditional" femininity in the late 1940s and 1950s reflected postwar anxieties about the reconsolidation of a gender order shaken by two decades of depression and war. As symbols of women's refusal to conform, lesbians endured intense scrutiny by experts who regularly focused on their subjects' presumed masculinity. Sexologists attributed lesbianism to masculine tendencies and freedoms encouraged by the war, linking it to a general collapsing of gender distinctions which, in their view, destabilized marital and family relations (Breines 1986; Penn 1991).

Lesbians remained shadowy figures to most Americans, but women athletes—noted for their masculine bodies, interests, and attributes—were visible representatives of the gender inversion often associated with homosexuality.

Physical education majors, formerly accused of being unappealing to men, were increasingly charged with being uninterested in them as well. The 1952 University of Minnesota *Gopher* yearbook snidely reported: "Believe it or not, members of the Women's Athletic Association are normal" and found conclusive evidence in the fact that "at least one . . . of WAA's 300 members is engaged" (p. 257). And on May 10, 1956, a newspaper account in the *Texan* regarding the University of Texas Sports Association (UTSA) women's sports banquet led off with the headline, "UTSA Gives Awards," followed by a subheading "Gayness Necessary." The second headline referred to a guest speaker's talk on positive attitudes, entitled "The Importance of Being Debonair," but the lesbian allusion was unmistakable and I believe fully intentional.[2]

The lesbian stigma began to plague popular athletes too, especially working-class sports noted for their masculine toughness. The pall of suspicion did not completely override older associations with heterosexual deviance. When a *Collier's* 1947 article (Lagemann) on the Red Heads, a barnstorming women's basketball team, exclaimed "It's basketball—not a striptease!" the author alluded to both the heterosexual appeal and the hint of disrepute long associated with working-class women athletes. But the dominant postwar voice intimated a different type of disrepute. Journalists continued to attack the mannish athlete as ugly and sexually unappealing, implying that this image could only be altered through proof of heterosexual "success."

The career of Babe Didrikson, which spanned the 1920s to the 1950s, illustrates the shift. In the early 1930s the press had ridiculed the tomboyish track star for her "hatchet face," "door-stop jaw," and "button-breasted" chest. After quitting track, Didrikson dropped out of the national limelight, married professional wrestler George Zaharias in 1938, and then staged a spectacular athletic comeback as a golfer in the late 1940s and 1950s. Fascinated by her personal transformation and then, in the 1950s, moved by her battle with cancer, journalists gave Didrikson's comeback extensive coverage and helped make her a much-loved popular figure. In reflecting on her success, however, sportswriters spent at least as much time on Didrikson's love life as her golf stroke. Headlines blared, "Babe is a lady now: The world's most amazing athlete has learned to wear nylons and cook for her huge husband," and reporters gleefully described how "along came a great big he-man wrestler and the Babe forgot all her man-hating chatter" (Andersen 1945; Gallico 1960; Farmer 1947; Martin 1947).

Postwar sport discourse consistently focused on women's sexual as well as athletic achievements. As late as 1960, a *New York Times Magazine* headline asked, "Do men make passes at athletic lasses?" Columnist William B. Furlong answered no for most activities, concluding that except for a few "yes" sports like swimming, women athletes "surrendered" their sex. The challenge for women athletes was not to conquer new athletic feats, which would only further reduce their sexual appeal, but to regain their womanhood through sexual surrender to men.

Media coverage in national magazines and metropolitan newspapers typically focused on the sexual accomplishments of white female athletes, but postwar observers and promoters of African-American women's sport also confronted the issue of sexual normalcy. In earlier decades, neither Black nor white commentary on African-American athletes expressed a concern with "mannish" lesbianism. The white media generally ignored Black athletes. Implicitly, however, stereotypes of Black females as highly sexual, promiscuous, and unrestrained in their heterosexual passions discouraged the linkage between mannishness and lesbianism. Racist gender ideologies further complicated the meaning of mannishness. Historically, European-American racial thought characterized African-American women as aggressive, coarse, passionate, and physical—the same qualities assigned to manliness in sport (Carby 1987; Collins 1990; Giddings 1984). Excluded from dominant ideals of womanhood, Black women's success in sport could be interpreted not as an unnatural deviation but, rather, as the natural result of their reputed closeness to nature, animals, and masculinity.[3]

Within Black communities, strong local support for women's sport may also have weakened the association between sport and lesbianism. Athletes from Tuskegee Institute's national championship track teams of the late 1930s and 1940s described an atmosphere of campus-wide enthusiastic support. They noted that although a male student might accuse an athlete of being "funny" if she turned him down for a date, in general lesbianism was not a subject of concern in Black sport circles (personal interviews, Alice Coachman Davis, Lula Hymes Glenn, and Leila Perry Glover, 1992). Similarly, Gloria Wilson (pseudonym, personal interview, 1988) found that she encountered far less uneasiness about lesbianism on her Black semipro softball team in the late 1950s and 1960s than she did in the predominantly white college physical education departments she joined later. She explained that the expectation of heterosexuality was ingrained in Black women to the point that "anything outside of that realm is just out of the question." While recalling that her teammates "had no time or patience for 'funnies,'" Wilson noted that the issue rarely came up, in large part because most team members were married and therefore "didn't have to prove it because then, too, their men were always at those games. They were very supportive."

Although Black athletes may have encountered few lesbian stereotypes at the local level, circumstances in the broader society eventually pressed African American sport promoters and journalists to address the issue of mannish sexuality. The strong association of sports and lesbianism developed at the same time as Black athletes became a dominant presence in American sport culture. Midcentury images of sport, Blackness, masculinity, and lesbianism circulated in the same orbit in various combinations. There was no particular correlation between Black women and lesbianism; however, the association of each with mannishness and sexual aggression potentially linked the two. In the late 1950s, Black sport promoters and journalists joined others in taking up the question of sexual "normalcy." One Black newspaper (*Baltimore Afro-American*) in 1957 described tennis star Althea Gibson as a childhood "tomboy" who "later in life . . . finds herself victimized by complexes." The article did not elaborate on the nature of Gibson's "complex," but lesbianism is inferred in the linkage between "tomboys" and psychological illness. This connotation becomes clearer by looking at the defense of Black women's sport. Echoing *Ebony*'s avowal (1955, 28, 32) that "entirely feminine" Black female track stars "like boys, dances, club affairs," in 1962 Tennessee State University track coach Ed Temple asserted in the *Detroit News*, "None of my girls have any trouble getting boyfriends. . . . We don't want amazons."

Constant attempts to shore up the heterosexual reputation of athletes can be read as evidence that the longstanding reputation of female athletes as mannish women had become a covert reference to lesbianism. By midcentury, a fundamental reorientation of sexual meanings fused notions of femininity, female eroticism, and heterosexual attractiveness into a single ideal. Mannishness, once primarily a sign of gender crossing, assumed a specifically lesbian-sexual connotation. In the wake of this change, the strong cultural association between sport and masculinity made women's athletics ripe for emerging lesbian stereotypes. This meaning of athletic mannishness raises [the] further question: What impact did the stereotype have on women's sport? . . .

Sport and the Heterosexual Imperative

The image of the mannish lesbian athlete had a direct effect on women competitors, on strategies of athletic organizations, and on the overall popularity of women's sport. The lesbian stereotype exerted pressure on athletes to demonstrate their femininity and heterosexuality, viewed as one and the same. Many women adopted an apologetic stance toward their athletic skill. Even as they competed to win, they made sure to display outward signs of femininity in dress and demeanor. They took special care in contact with the media to reveal "feminine" hobbies like cooking and sewing, to mention current boyfriends, and to discuss future marriage plans (Del Rey 1978).

Leaders of women's sport took the same approach at the institutional level. In answer to portrayals of physical education majors and teachers as social rejects and prudes, physical educators revised their philosophy to place heterosexuality at the center of professional objectives. In the late 1930s, they invited psychologists to speak at national professional meetings about problems of sexual adjustment. Such experts described the "types of people who are unadjusted to heterosexual cooperative activity" and warned women in physical education to "develop a prejudice *against* segregation of the sexes" (National Amateur Athletic Federation—Women's Division 1938). Told that exclusively female environments caused failed heterosexual development, physical educators who had long advocated female separatism in sport were pressed to promote mixed-sex groups and heterosexual "adjustment."

Curricular changes implemented between the mid-1930s and mid-1950s institutionalized the new philosophy. In a paper on postwar objectives, Mildred A. Schaeffer (1945) explained that physical education classes should help women "develop an interest in school dances and mixers and a desire to voluntarily attend them." To this end, administrators revised coursework to emphasize beauty and social charm over rigorous exercise and health. They exchanged old rationales of fitness and fun for promises of trimmer waistlines, slimmer hips, and prettier complexions. At Radcliffe, for example, faculty redesigned health classes to include "advice on dress, carriage, hair, skin, voice, and any factor that would tend to improve personal appearance and thus contribute to social and economic success" (Physical Education Director, no date). Intramural programs replaced interclass basketball tournaments and weekend campouts for women with mixed-sex "co-recreational" activities like bowling, volleyball, and "fun nights" of ping-pong and shuffleboard. Some departments also added co-educational classes to foster "broader, keener, more sympathetic understanding of the opposite sex" (Department of Physical Education 1955).[4] Department heads cracked down on "mannish" students and faculty, issuing warnings against "casual styles" which might "lead us back into some dangerous channels" (Ashton 1957). They implemented dress codes which forbade slacks and men's shirts or socks, adding as well a ban on "boyish hair cuts" and unshaven legs. For example, the 1949–50 Physical Training Staff Handbook at the University of Texas stated (p. 16), "Legs should be kept shaved," while restrictions on hair and dress are spelled out in the staff minutes and physical education handbooks for majors at the universities of Wisconsin, Texas, and Minnesota. . . .

Popular sport promoters adopted similar tactics. Marshalling sexual data like they were athletic statistics, a 1954 AAU poll sought to sway a skeptical public with numerical proof of heterosexuality—the fact that 91 percent of former female athletes surveyed had married (Andersen 1954). Publicity for the midwestern All-American Girls Baseball League (AAGBL) included statistics on the number of married players in the league. In the same vein, the women's golf tour announced that one-third of the pros were married, and the rest were keeping an eye peeled for prospects who might "lure them from the circuit to the altar" (All-American Girls Baseball League Records, Pennsylvania State University Libraries; *Saturday Evening Post* 1954).

The fear of lesbianism was greatest where a sport had a particularly masculine image and where promoters needed to attract a paying audience. Professional and semipro basketball and softball fit the bill on both accounts. Athletic leaders tried to resolve the problem by "proving" the attractive femininity of athletes. Softball and basketball tournaments continued to feature beauty pageants. Although in earlier times such events celebrated the "sexiness" of the emancipated modern woman, in later decades they seemed to serve a more defensive function. The AAU's magazine, the *Amateur Athlete*, made sure that at least one photograph of the national basketball tournament's beauty "queen and her court" accompanied the photo of each year's championship team. Behind the scenes, teams passed dress and conduct codes. For example, the All-American Girls Baseball League's 1951 Constitution prohibited players from wearing men's clothing or getting "severe" haircuts. That this was an attempt to secure the heterosexual image of athletes was made even clearer when league officials announced that AAGBL policy prohibited the recruitment of "freaks" and "Amazons" (Markey n.d.; Feminine Sluggers 1952).

In the end, the strategic emphasis on heterosexuality and the suppression of "mannishness" did little to alter the image of women in sport. The stereotype of the mannish lesbian athlete grew out of the persistent common-sense equation of sport and masculinity. Opponents of women's sport reinforced this belief when they denigrated women's athletic efforts and ridiculed skilled athletes as "grotesque," "mannish," or "unnatural." Leaders of women's sport unwittingly contributed to the same set of ideas when they began to orient their programs around the new feminine heterosexual ideal. As physical education policies and media campaigns worked to suppress lesbianism and marginalize athletes who didn't conform to dominant standards of femininity, sports officials embedded heterosexism into the institutional and ideological framework of sport. The effect extended beyond sport to the wider culture, where the figure of the mannish lesbian athlete announced that competitiveness, strength, independence, aggression, and physical intimacy among women fell outside the bounds of womanhood. As a symbol of female deviance, she served as a powerful reminder to all women to toe the line of heterosexuality and femininity or risk falling into a despised category of mannish (not-women) women. . . .

Notes

I would like to thank Birgitte Soland, Maureen Honish, Kath Weston, George Chauncey, Jr., and Nan Enstad for their criticisms, encouragement, and editorial advice on earlier versions of this essay.

1. Among the works that do consider the issue of homosexuality are Lenskyj (1986), Zipter (1988), and Bennett (1982). On the relationship between male homosexuality and sport, see Pronger (1990).
2. Although the term "gay" as a reference to homosexuals occurred only sporadically in the mass media before the 1960s, it was in use as a slang term among some homosexual men and lesbians as early as the 1920s and quite commonly by the 1940s.
3. Elizabeth Lunbeck (1987) notes a similar pattern in her discussion of medical theories of the "hypersexual" white female. Because psychiatrists assumed that Black women were naturally "oversexed," when defining the medical condition of hypersexuality, they included only young white working-class women whose sexual ardor struck physicians and social workers as unnaturally excessive.
4. For curricular changes, I examined physical education records at the universities of Wisconsin, Texas, and Minnesota, Radcliffe College, Smith College, Tennessee State University, and Hampton University.

References

Andersen, Roxy. 1945. Fashions in feminine sport. *Amateur Athlete*, March.

———. 1954. Statistical survey of former women athletes. *Amateur Athlete*, September.

Arnett, Ruth. 1921. Girls need physical education. *Chicago Defender*, 10 December.

Ashton, Dudley. 1957. Recruiting future teachers. *Journal of Health, Physical Education, and Recreation* 28 (October):49.

Baltimore Afro-American. 1957. 29 June, Magazine Section, 1.

Bennett, Roberta. 1982. Sexual labeling as social control: Some political effects of being female in the gym. *Perspectives* 4:40–50.

Bérubé, Alan. 1990. *Coming Out Under Fire: The History of Gay Men and Women in World War Two*. New York: Free Press.

Breines, Wini. 1986. The 1950s: Gender and some social science. *Sociological Inquiry* 56 (Winter):69–92.

Carby, Hazel. 1987. *Reconstructing Womanhood: The Emergence of the Afro-American Woman Novelist*. New York: Oxford University Press.

Chauncey, George Jr. 1989. From sexual inversion to homosexuality: Medicine and the changing conceptualization of female deviance. In *Passion and Power: Sexuality in History*, edited by Kathy Peiss and Christina Simmons. Philadelphia: Temple University Press.

Collins, Patricia Hill. 1990. *Black Feminist Thought: Knowledge, Consciousness, and the Politics of Empowerment*. Boston: Unwin Hyman.

D'Emilio, John. 1983. *Sexual Politics, Sexual Communities: The Making of a Homosexual Minority in the United States, 1940–1970*. Chicago: University of Chicago Press.

de Koven, Anna. 1912. The athletic woman. *Good Housekeeping*, August.

Del Rey, Patricia. 1978. The apologetic and women in sport. In *Women and Sport*, edited by Carole Oglesby. Philadelphia: Lea & Febiger.

Department of Physical Education, University of California, Los Angeles. 1955. Coeducational classes. *Journal of Health, Physical Education, and Recreation* 26 (February):18.

Detroit News. 1962. 31 July, sec. 6, p. 1.

Dunham, Elizabeth. 1924. Physical education for women at Hampton Institute. *Southern Workman* 53 (April):167.

Dunning, Eric. 1986. Sport as a male preserve: Notes on the social sources of masculine identity and its transformation. In *Quest for Excitement: Sport and Leisure in the Civilizing Process*, edited by Eric Dunning and Norbert Elias. New York: Basil Blackwell.

Ebony. 1955. Fastest women in the world. June:28.

Ellis, A. W. 1939. The status of health and physical education for women in negro colleges and universities. *Journal of Negro Education* 8 (January):58–63.

Ellis, Havelock. 1915. *Sexual Inversion*. Vol. 2 of *Studies in the Psychology of Sex*. 3rd rev. ed. Philadelphia: F.A. Davis.

Erenberg, Lewis. 1981. *Steppin' Out: New York Nightlife and the Transformation of American Culture, 1890–1930*. Westport: Greenwood Press.

Farmer, Gene. 1947. What a Babe! *Life*, June.

Feminine Sluggers. 1952. *People and Places* 8 (12), reproduced in AAGBL Records.

Freedman, Estelle, and John D'Emilio. 1988. *Intimate Matters: A History of Sexuality in America*. New York: Harper & Row.

Furlong, William B. 1960. Venus wasn't a shotputter. *New York Times Magazine*, 28 August.

Gallico, Paul. 1960. *Houston Post*, 22 March.

Gerber, Ellen W. 1975. The controlled development of collegiate sport for women, 1923–36. *Journal of Sport History* 2 (Spring):1–28.

Giddings, Paula. 1984. *When and Where I Enter: The Impact of Black Women on Race and Sex in America*. New York: William & Morrow.

Himes, Cindy L. 1986. *The Female Athlete in American Society, 1860–1940*. Ph.D. diss., University of Pennsylvania.

Hult, Joan. 1985. The governance of athletics for girls and women. *Research Quarterly for Exercise and Sport* April:64–77.

Inglis, William. 1910. Exercise for girls. *Harper's Bazaar*, March.

Kimmel, Michael S. 1987. The contemporary 'crisis' of masculinity in historical perspective. In *The Making of Masculinities: The New Men's Studies*, edited by Harry Brod. Boston: Allen & Unwin.

Lagemann, John Lord. 1947. Red heads you kill me! *Collier's*, 8 February, 64.

Lenskyj, Helen. 1986. *Out of Bounds: Women, Sport, and Sexuality*. Toronto: Women's Press.

Lunbeck, Elizabeth. 1987. "A new generation of women:" Progressive psychiatrists and the hypersexual female. *Feminist Studies* 13 (Fall):513–43.

MacFadden, Bernard. 1929. Athletics for women will help save the nation. *Amateur Athlete* 4 (February-July):7.

Mangan, J. A., and Roberta J. Park, eds. 1987. *From "Fair Sex" to Feminism: Sport and the Socialization of Women in the Industrial and Post-Industrial Eras*. London: Frank Cass.

Mange, Violet W. 1910. Field hockey for women. *Harper's Bazaar*, April.

Markey, Morris. No date. Hey Ma, you're out! 1951 Records of the AAGBL.

Marston, William. 1933. How can a woman do it? *Redbook*, September.

Martin, Pete. 1947. Babe Didrikson takes off her mask. *Saturday Evening Post*, 20 September.

Moats, A. 1934. He hasn't a chance. *Ladies Home Journal*, December.

Mooney, Gertrude. 1937. The benefits and dangers of athletics for the high school girl. Department of Physical Training for Women Records (Health Ed. folder), box 3R251. Barker Texas History Center, University of Texas, Austin.

Mrozek, Donald J. 1983. *Sport and the American Mentality, 1880–1910*. Knoxville: University of Tennessee Press.

Murray, Jim. no date. 1970s column in *Austin American Statesman*, Zaharias scrapbook, Barker Texas History Center, University of Texas, Austin.

Nathan, George. 1930. Once there was a princess. *American Mercury*, February.

National Amateur Athletic Federation—Women's Division. 1938. Newsletter no. 79 (1 June 1938), from Department of Women's Physical Education, University of Wisconsin Archives.

Paret, J. Parmley. 1900. Basket-ball for young women. *Harper's Bazaar*, October.

Peiss, Kathy. 1986. *Cheap Amusements: Working Women and Leisure in Turn- of-the-Century New York*. Philadelphia: Temple University Press.

Penn, Donna. 1991. The meanings of lesbianism in post-war America. *Gender and History* 3:190–203.

Physical Education Director. No date. Official Reports, Kristin Powell's collected materials on Radcliffe Athletics, Radcliffe College Archives, acc. no. R87.

Pronger, Brian. 1990. *The Arena of Masculinity: Sport, Homosexuality, and the Meaning of Sex.* New York: St. Martin's Press.

Roberts, Amelia. 1927. Letter to *Chicago Defender*, 12 March, sec. 2, p. 7.

Sackett, Ada T. 1934. Beauty survives sport. *Literary Digest* 117:43.

Sargent, Dudley A. 1913. Are athletics making girls masculine? *Ladies Home Journal*, March.

Saturday Evening Post. 1954. Next to marriage, we'll take golf. 23 January.

Schaeffer, Mildred A. 1945. Desirable objectives in post-war physical education. *Journal of Health and Physical Education* 16:446–47.

Sefton, Alice Allene. 1937. Must women in sports look beautiful? *Journal of Health and Physical Education* 8:481.

Simmons, Christina. 1989. Modern sexuality and the myth of Victorian repression. In *Passion and Power: Sexuality in History*, edited by Kathy Peiss and Christina Simmons. Philadelphia: Temple University Press.

Steers, Fred. 1932. Spirit. *Amateur Athlete* October:7.

Wise, P. M. 1883. Case of sexual perversion. *Alienist and Neurologist* 4:88.

Wittner, Fred. 1934. Shall the ladies join us? *Literary Digest*, 19 May.

Zipter, Yvonne. 1988. *Diamonds are a Dyke's Best Friend.* Ithaca: Firebrand Books.

6

Menarche and the (Hetero)sexualization of the Female Body

JANET LEE

In high school I wanted to be a beatnik. I too wanted to go on the road, but I could never figure out what would happen if, travelling in Mexico in 1958, I got my period. Were you supposed to carry a supply of Kotex with you? How many could you carry? If you took all you needed, there wouldn't be any room for all those nice jugs of wine in Jack Kerouac's car. The only beatnik I know who even considered this question was Diana diPrima in *Memoirs of a Beatnik*. She describes her first big orgy, the one with the works, including Allen Ginsburg. As she takes a deep breath and decided to plunge in, so to speak, she pulls out her Tampax and flings it across the room where somehow it gets irretrievably lost. A grand moment, that. Do I hear you thinking, How gross? Or, How irrelevant? Gross, yes, irrelevant, no. And that's the point. Having to worry about the gross mess becomes a part of life from puberty on (Dimen 1986, 32–33).

Menstruation is a biological act fraught with cultural implications, helping to produce the body and women as cultural entities. The body is a "text" of culture; it is a symbolic form upon which the norms and practices of society

Originally published as Janet Lee, "Menarche and the (Hetero)sexualization of the Female Body," *Gender & Society* 8(3):343–62. Copyright © 1994 by Sage Publications. Reprinted by permission of Sage Publications.

are inscribed (Bartky 1992; Bordo 1989; Haug 1987). Male desire and policy have been scripted onto the female body at the same time that "woman" has been overdetermined and overrepresented in contemporary art, social science and politics, as well as scientific and medical discourses. In this article I share stories of the body in an analysis of the menarche (or first period) experiences of ordinary women who participated in an ongoing oral and written history project. It is primarily through the body that women are inserted, and insert themselves, into the hierarchical ordering of the sexual.

I explore menarche as a central aspect of body politics since it is loaded with the ambivalence associated with being a woman in Western society today. Menarche represents the entrance into womanhood in a society that devalues women through cultural scripts associated with the body. Overwhelmingly, messages associated with menarche in a wide range of cultural and historical contexts are ambivalent (Buckley and Gottlieb 1988; Delaney, Lupton, and Toth 1988; Golub 1983, 1992; Lander 1988). Even those women who have reflected on this experience with positive thoughts and memories have been found to articulate its negative and shameful aspects (Hays 1987; Jackson 1992; Koff, Rierdan, and Jacobson 1981; Martin 1987; Weideger 1976; Whisnant and Zegans 1975). To talk of menstruation in contemporary Western culture is to articulate its secretive, emotionally laden, and shame-filled aspects (Thorne 1993). . . .

While women's bodies are produced discursively within misogynist societies (Bartky 1992; Foucault 1978; Scott 1992), women's everyday experiences negotiating adolescence are concretely lived in ways that not only internalize and maintain such discourses, but also actively resist them through appropriation and/or the integration of more positive discourses of the body (Martin 1987). . . . Narratives of women's memories of menarche highlight this interactive nature of discourse and agency; when women remember their first menses, their memories are framed by many competing discourses, having become subjects through the sifting and making meaning out of their experiences.

My methodological focus is phenomenological. I explore the meanings women attribute to menarche, what they think and feel, and the significance of this event as represented in what they say and write. I analyzed forty narratives (twenty-eight oral and twelve written narratives), listening and reading for interpretations of menarche embedded within the everyday, lived experience of women. . . . Participants were volunteers who had agreed to participate as word of the project spread through presentations made in classes, flyers in a local physician's office, and through contact with colleagues, students, and friends and the Extended Education Office at Oregon State University.

This local sample was Eurocentric, including thirty white women, three Jews, two African Americans, one biracial woman, three Asian Americans, two Mexican Americans, and three women each from Nepal, Malaysia, and Iran. Since three-quarters of the participants were white, reflecting the general lack of racial and ethnic diversity in Oregon, where this study was done, I must emphasize its limitations and the dangers of over-generalization. The age range spanned from 18 to 80 years. Five women identified themselves as lesbians and three as bisexuals, although none said they identified as such during early adolescence. Nineteen of the participants are working class and twenty-one are middle class, all residing in the Willammette Valley and south and central Oregon.

I suggest here that menarche is an important time when young women become inserted and insert themselves into the dominant patterns of sexuality. As a crucial signifier of reproductive potential and thus embodied womanhood, menarche becomes intertwined with sexuality. Certain orifices and their secretions take on sexual significance and menarche marks a simultaneous entry into adult womanhood and adult female sexualization. I will share excerpts from the narratives to illustrate themes associated with female sexualization at menarche, exploring the ways these women relate to the female body and menstrual blood. I focus on issues of contamination and alienation, and the relationship between menarche, boys, and developing bodies. Finally, I will discuss issues of consciousness and resistance, exploring ways women have coped with menarche in their everyday lives.

Contaminating Bodies

Historically and cross-culturally, menstrual blood has been considered both magical and poisonous, and menstrual taboos have structured and restricted women's lives (Buckley and Gottlieb 1988; Golub 1992). Since women are associated with the body, earth, and nature, and men with the abstract powers of reason, women's bodies connote words like *earthy, fleshy,* and *smelly,* reminding humans of their mortality and vulnerability. Dorothy Dinnerstein (1976) captures this in her discussion of the deep-seated cultural perceptions of the female body as corrupting, contaminating, unclean, and sinful. On the one hand, woman is associated with life, while on the other, her bleeding and oozing body is met with disgust, reminiscent of earthly vulnerabilities. Male bodies are not so symbolically marked with such connotations; men are more easily able to imagine their bodies free of such constraints, and they are allowed to project their fears and hatred onto women's flesh. Cultural contexts provide mythologies and images of disgust for women's bleeding that are deeply internalized into the psyche, encouraging women to hate their bodies and men to hate things they recognize as feminine in themselves (Ussher 1989).

Repeatedly, women in this study stated that their monthly bleeding made them feel ambivalent about their bodies, menarche being clouded by negativity. Almost half the sample specifically mentioned "the curse" as a term they and others had used to describe menstruation. Edith, a 66-year-old mother and grandmother emphasized the gloom associated with menarche:

> It's so long ago . . . I guess it was mid-winter, and waking after dozing to sleep, briefly, having had a "funny" tummy ache, to a sticky, nasty, uncomfortable feeling

between my legs; slightly smelly too, if I really think deeply, ugh. . . . There was this dark, clammy gloominess and sort of "dread" accompanying it.

Others also stated that their first menstrual blood made them feel dirty and unclean, ashamed and fearful. Bertha, a Jewish woman in her forties, remembered her menarche as similar to "a feeling I used to feel when I was young and wet my pants. . . . It was a feeling of having soiled myself." Such feelings affect women's sense of self and worth, establishing female bodies and sexuality as bad and corrupting. These memories of shame and embarrassment were shared by Northstar, a Chinese-American woman in her late twenties who grew up in Taiwan:

> I feel I have a big diaper. I feel everyone can see me . . . very embarrassed. . . . I know sometimes when I went to my uncle's house that sometimes my aunt would forbid my uncle to take garbage out because she said that we have "women's mess" inside so men cannot carry the garbage out because there are women's pads inside.

With similar sentiment, a white working-class woman in her thirties named Anna wrote that she was "mortified," and felt she needed to hide her shame and embarrassment:

> When I first started menstruating (the very first time) I had experienced incredible stomach pains the night before. I stayed in bed all night and was the first one up in the morning. I went to the bathroom and lo and behold there was blood. I felt mortified because I knew what had happened. I felt incredibly ashamed and didn't tell anyone for a year (I used tissue paper). Now I was like my mother, a woman who had a bad smelly part of her. This, for the most part, is also how men see menstruation, as something filthy belonging to a woman that makes them mentally unstable.

The disdain associated with menstrual blood encouraged many women to go to great lengths to hide such evidence of their contamination from the potentially disapproving gaze of others. There was overwhelming evidence of women's fears of showing evidence of wearing pads or staining garments or sheets. Three-quarters of all women in the sample specifically shared a story of the embarrassment associated with staining, or a fear that it might happen to them. This illustrates how the bulge or stain becomes a visible emblem of their contamination and shame, announcing their "condition" for all to see. It also symbolizes a lapse in women's task of maintaining the taboo, concealing the evidence and preventing the embarrassment of others (Laws 1990). Seventy-four-year-old Laverne shared the following:

> A problem with menstruating at that time was the napkin pads. They were made out of absorbent cotton with a cotton mesh cover (no shields). They soaked through easily and you often stained your underwear. I always worried that my

skirt might be stained and would sometimes wear my coat in school all day long. At Girls High, it was the custom for the Seniors to wear all white every Friday. When I was a Junior, I happened to notice that one of the Seniors was wearing a thin white skirt which showed the outline of her sanitary pad, so when I had my Senior skirt made I bought rather heavy material and had a double panel put in the back.

Women tended to see themselves as becoming more visible at the same time that they felt the pressure to conceal evidence of menstruation. Many women talked about wearing baggy clothes or coats to hide evidence of menstruation. Other research has also reported such findings, with women sharing feelings of being afraid of being found out, with a strong desire to hide any traces of their period (Patterson and Hale 1985). One study found that it was only after several menstrual periods that girls would share their experiences with anyone other than their mothers (Brooks-Gunn and Ruble 1983). Similar results were found here, with several women using tissue and toilet paper for months, or hiding soiled underwear at the back of drawers and closets.

The most intense and poignant stories of contamination came from childhood survivors of violence. Of the 10 women who shared experiences of incest or child sexual abuse, all connected the violation of their bodies to menarche as a contaminating experience and said that they felt their bodies were dirty and shameful. Hannah, a young, white lesbian spoke poignantly of the way her feelings about her contaminated body as a survivor coincided with her feelings about her menstrual flow:

> The abuse made me feel awful. It colored everything, so much of what I did, how I felt about my body and my self-esteem. . . . I felt really dirty and you know because I was on my period, and I would cramp more and I just felt dirty, I felt icky, I felt horrible, like people could smell me and I just felt subhuman. . . . I felt kind of shameful to be around men and I don't want to be around people and I don't want people to know at all. . . . I hated the feeling of flowing, I hated just that warm feeling whenever. . . . I felt as if it was something dirty, something horrible coming out and I wanted to not flow as much as possible and if I got really active I would flow more and I didn't want to flow. I just wanted it to stop.

Child sexual abuse survivors' words illustrate the way the vulnerabilities associated with women's emerging sexuality (and in these cases, the exploitation of what these little girls' bodies signified in the context of a society that exploits female sexuality) become integrated so that the body becomes and is experienced by girls as something acted upon, used, and soiled.

Alienated Bodies

Many of the women interviewed experienced menarche as something that was happening to them, as something outside of themselves and frequently referred to as "it," giving an illusion of a self that was fragmented. Overwhelmingly, women used the passive voice to describe menarche. Examples include: "I couldn't believe it was happening to me," "we called it 'the visitor,'" "I got it when I was fourteen," "I remember exactly when it started," "this monthly event," and (my favorite) "when it came I was at home."

Karin, a 22-year-old white woman, shared the following:

> I mean she [her sister] had no problem with it. I don't know if she was happy about it but she was on good terms with it. . . . I guess I'm not really in control of it because I just felt like it happened to me, I didn't ask for it, it just suddenly happened.

Similarly, Barbara, a 19-year-old lesbian, also clearly illustrates this sense of bodily alienation: "It was unknown and I really didn't understand it and it was something I couldn't control so it seemed kind of abstract and not within me."

With their passive construction and image, these quotes suggest a fragmentation between self and body, a sense of menarche as something a woman has to cope with, adjust to, and manage. Menarche is something that seems to appear from the outside, invading the self. Such findings were also reported by Martin (1987), who wrote of the women she interviewed as seeing menstruation as something that happened to them, rather than seeing the process as being a part of them. While she explained this in terms of the medicalization of the female body and the way a scientifically based society produces images of human bodies as machines, I suggest that there is more at work here, since many women framed menarche as happening "to them" in the context of their emerging understandings of sexuality. Charlotte, a white bisexual mother in her late thirties, shared her feelings about this fragmentation and lack of control, illustrating how menarche is intimately connected to feelings about sexual alienation and objectification (the "it" is her first period):

> When it came, I was a high school exchange student in Europe, staying with the family of a friend. I felt like I was out of control, that something was happening to me that I couldn't stop. I bled terribly all over the sheets and was horribly embarrassed telling my friend's aunt (especially since I didn't know the right words, menstruation is hardly one of the common vocabulary words you have to learn). I remember distinctly being embarrassed because this blood seemed like an emblem of my sexuality, like somehow it indicated that I might run out and have sex, yet really I felt like it was all happening to someone else, not me, like I was watching myself in a movie and now was this sexual being.

The passive, indirect, fragmented language of menarche and menstruation is about sexual objectification and alienation. This sense of bodily alienation is entwined with women's object status in patriarchal societies that allow men subjectivity but construct femininity as a mirror through which men see themselves as human (Irigaray 1985). Adolescence and the

[handwritten: individualism affects all this]

journey from girlhood to womanhood involve forms of self-silencing whereby girls become preoccupied with how they are perceived by others (Brown and Gilligan 1992; Gilligan, Lyons, and Hanmer 1990). Femininity means moving from assertive actor to developing woman, learning to respond to the world indirectly through the filter of relationships. Women are encouraged to accommodate male needs, understand themselves as others see them, and feel pleasure through their own bodily objectification, especially being looked at and identified as objects of male desire (Connell 1987). Again, the voice of a survivor, this time Susan, is especially poignant in illustrating this objectification:

> Becoming a woman kind of opened the avenues which I think I unconsciously kind of knew that men would start looking at me more which was, I think, a little bit scary in a sense. I mean I was confused, I think I wanted to be accepted by the male gender, but yet with this experience [incest] it was a frightening thing because, it wasn't even me, it was like my body, and it was happening to my body. . . . It was no longer my mind or who I was, I mean it was like I was nothing. But yet my body was something, a sex object or something and I couldn't have said it, I didn't think that my body was like a sex object. I mean I couldn't clarify what was a norm, but, to look back now, that is what it was, my body was a sex object and the menstruation process was, just defined it that much more that I was a woman. . . . You know what I am saying? Because I related the menstrual cycle, I connected it directly with all this. . . . So there is a connection there, one part of me, I wanted to be that woman for the opposite sex, because it was kind of like expected of me, you know, that I be pleasing to look at and starting that menstrual cycle was my direct link with that, wow, I am a woman. But then there is this bad incident that I don't think had a lot of negative influence on that, but yet it must have somehow, you know, been buried there.

Anxious Bodies

Adolescence is a difficult and vulnerable time when girls focus attention on their bodies (Koff 1983; Koff, Rierdan, and Silverstone 1978; Rierdan and Koff 1980; Ussher 1989) in the context of a culture that demands perfect female bodies (Brownmiller 1984; Coward 1985). In a study that asked pre- and postmenarcheal girls to draw pictures of women, Koff found that girls who had experienced menarche drew considerably more sexually differentiated bodies. She writes about how girls come to experience themselves as more sexually mature at menarche: "It appears that regardless of the actual physical changes that are taking place, the girl at menarche anticipates and experiences a reorganization of her body image in the direction of greater sexual maturity and feminine differentiation" (1983, 83).

For many women, the increasing focus on their bodies was associated with painful cramps or even severe dysmenorrhea or painful periods. For example, Mehra, a young Iranian woman, spoke of how she noticed her body more at this time: "Yes, I felt like I paid more attention to my body, how it looked, felt, but also about where the pain comes from. . . . I would focus on that because of the pain." Some, like Laurence, a 20-year-old Malaysian student, started tuning into their body at menarche, becoming more self-conscious generally: "Yes, I guess mentally I became more aware of my body and what you would say 'the journey to womanhood,' yeah, and I became more self-conscious when I had my period. . . . I did become more self-conscious."

Others, like Robin, a young, lesbian, biracial woman, were aware that other people treated their bodies differently, and felt that this contributed to their interpretations of menarche:

> Then they [her brothers] started becoming critical of the way I dressed, and my hair and the way I spoke . . . and criticizing and saying you need to go over that way and you need to start wearing skirts and you need to start doing your hair, and you need to care about what you look like and not talk like this or that. So, I think there was a definite change in how they saw me. . . . I think it did set inside their heads "she is woman, I mean, she is not a boy. Yeah, she is different, other."

For most women, anxieties about their developing bodies at menarche concerned the way these bodies looked and might be interpreted by others, rather than how they looked or felt to themselves. Breast development seemed especially fraught with such anxiety. When recounting their first period stories, many women described their feelings toward their breasts, emphasizing how menarche is so often framed within the discourse of the sexual. Although enlarging breasts and hips are visual representations of femaleness, they are also highly constituted in our culture as objects of male desire (to be gazed at), and contribute to the experience of menarche as connected to the process of sexualization. As Haug et al. (1987, 139) suggest, "female breasts are never innocent." The excerpt below from Madeleine, a white woman in her thirties, illustrates the anxiety and self-consciousness associated with the developing body at menarche; a body that is being increasingly viewed as sexual, and, given the patriarchal context, a body that is becoming increasingly objectified:

> I remember when I was in 6th grade and this boy called me "stuffy," in other words he was accusing me of stuffing my bra, because I wore a sweater that was, you know, more fitted than the day before and I was developing very early as a 6th grader and I didn't like my body at all, in fact I had a breast reduction when I was in 10th grade. . . . But so, I had a lot of hang-ups about that and they were very painful to me and so it just, my boobs were just so big that, I mean, I am still busty and I mean, they are huge and I was a small person and they got in my way [long laugh] and I really hated them. . . . I just remember feeling that I was going to grow up and the only thing that I would be good for was something like a Playboy bunny or something really you know . . . disgusting or just to be a housewife which was like a fate worse than death. . . . So, I guess that maybe that's why I felt so angry about my period because I associated it with these feelings about my boobs, you know.

At menarche, women say that their physical bodies are becoming problematic; women report that their breasts are too small or too big, hips tend to become enemy sites, and there is the overwhelming fear of fat. These reports spanned generations as Florence, an 80-year-old Jewish woman remembered feeling "ugly and fat," just as did 18-year-old Marie, who, when asked how she felt about her body, responded: "I had a really low self-esteem about my physical appearance and stuff . . . it was pretty heavy dislike." Ambivalence is a good word to describe the feeling that many women report since, while many felt okay about their developing bodies (especially in the context of competition with female friends and the relief from the embarrassment that goes along with being undeveloped—of not "measuring up," so to speak), these were accompanied by strong negative experiences of self-consciousness and embarrassment, and the internalization of ambivalence about women's flesh and sexuality. The relationship here between menarche and sexuality is illustrated by several women who commented that friends of theirs whose bodies had developed early were somehow seen as promiscuous, even though they were just young girls with no active sexual relationships. The use of the term "precocious puberty" in the literature to describe girls with early puberty and onset of menarche is also an example of this issue. Robin shares the following:

> Oh, there was one person I knew who had it before any of us you know . . . this is really terrible, but I think that I thought that she was just a little more ahead of us sexually. I am positive the woman wasn't sexual, but I knew that was a part of getting older, and I knew that getting older meant having sex, and I think seeing someone else with their period made me feel that they were a lot further ahead than I was. . . . I am sure they probably weren't having sex, I don't know, but I saw them as more promiscuous.

Bodies and Boys

Women also make a clear association between menarche and changing relationships with boys through the language of the body. Many were distressed that their camaraderie with boys dissipated. They felt they could no longer be "one of the boys" or their friendships became infused with the sexual tensions of early adolescence and its budding compulsory heterosexuality. Barbara, a strong athlete during adolescence, illustrates this:

> Yeah, I think it was in the sense that it [her menarche] separated me from the boys, and so I felt like I was going to have to dress up and just drop sports by the wayside because now it was like some way of being notified that well, you have had your fun as a tomboy but it is time to really do what you are "supposed" to do.

Women worried about what boys might think, if boys noticed them, if they didn't. Sixty-two-year-old Rowena remembered distinctly how her behavior changed. She wrote, "I began to 'be careful' at school, to not act 'too smart' although I continued to get straight A's. That was stupid."

Women remembered being embarrassed around boys, and especially remembered the teasing and crude comments about menstruation. Urmila, in her twenties and raised in Nepal, shared her memories of such teasing:

> Maybe they [boys] don't understand it, so the only way of doing it is by laughing, making fun . . . they just laugh, making it feel for the girls that they do know, so it sort of makes them dominant and makes the girls feel like "oh, my goodness, I have done something wrong."

Women reported that they learned early that they must hide all evidence of menstruation from boys and men, brothers and fathers. This set up a self-consciousness for girls who were used to playing with boys. Crystal, a young, white, bisexual woman, summed this up best: "When I didn't have my period I didn't mind playing with the guys, but when I did, I was afraid someone would see me, like something might leak through or things like that."

In terms of potential sexual relationships with boys, the risk of pregnancy that sets in at menarche influences family dynamics. Research suggests that parents tend to see their daughter's emerging sexuality as more problematic than their son's, with early sexual maturation being associated with greater independence and achievement from parents for boys, and to a lesser extent for girls (Fine 1988; Hill and Lynch 1983; Ussher 1989). Hill and Holmbeck (1987) found that menarche was accompanied by intense family turmoil for a large number of the girls in their sample, with daughters reporting more parental control in the first six months after menarche than at any other time. The comments of Elizabeth, a white woman in her forties who grew up in a Catholic home with thirteen brothers and sisters, are illustrative of this:

> When I hit my adolescent years our relationship [with her mother] really split because my mother all of a sudden was very suspicious of everything I did. . . . I still remember her just all of a sudden, a suspicion about me, maybe I was becoming sexual.

In predictable ways the double standard of sexual conduct plays itself out as boys are encouraged to sow their wild oats and girls are chastised for similar behavior, resulting in closer monitoring. "I was told by my mother that I was a lady now, so that I had to act like one, and not play with the boys anymore," recalled Darlene, a white working-class woman in her forties. She followed this statement with:

> I started to cry, I said, "I'm not ready to be a lady and I like playing with the boys." I guessed the reason I couldn't play with them anymore is that they would smell me too and know my horrible secret. I felt dirty, humiliated, and angry.

Finally, the remarks of 77-year-old Gerta, a widow and retired teacher, illustrate the responsibilities of potential sexual relations that girls have to assume at menarche:

During the "curse," as we termed it, I was concerned about odor and spotting. My mother made it clear that now necking and petting could have serious results if we went "all the way"—which could happen if emotions got out of hand.

Consciousness and Resistance

To study menarche is to study the female body as it is contextualized through the sociopolitical constructs of specific societies. In this study, the words that women used to describe menarche are those that symbolize the relationship of women to their bodies in a misogynist society: fear, shame, embarrassment, humiliation, preoccupation, mess, hassle, and so on; however, running through these stories are also tales of consciousness, agency, and resistance. Women are not merely acted upon, nor are they merely powerless pawns embedded in the discursive struggles that determine existence. While these discourses do frame the body, the woman in the body does resist, as Martin (1987) has suggested. Women show their resistance to the destructive and alienating discourses associated with menarche through insight and analysis, through telling their stories, and through the many ways that women have learned to cope. Some spoke of increasing solidarity with girls, of using menstruation as a way to manipulate and get their way; many spoke of having done or having a desire to do things differently when their own daughters start to menstruate. It is to these forms of consciousness and resistance that I now turn.

Telling the Story

Since this project involved participants who were volunteers, the women's voices I share here are all those who wanted to have the opportunity to tell their stories. Usually, when the tape had been switched off and women were leaving, they would comment on the benefits of speaking about something that they had never really spoken of in any public way before, something that was an important experience in their lives, but which the society in which they lived, as well as academia, has tended to ignore. "I don't know if it's making any real sense, but it is starting to make more sense to me when I talk about it" was a comment often heard.

For many, the telling of their stories took the form of ongoing analysis and commentary on those experiences, speaking or writing with insight into body politics and the effects of those politics on women's everyday lives. Kay, a white mother and student in her thirties, wrote the following, nicely illustrating this consciousness and insightful analysis:

First, in fifth or sixth grade, at my elementary school, we were separated from the boys and shown a film about menstruation. Next we were given a packet which contained some kind of feminine hygiene products and propaganda. We considered this whole affair hilarious, embarrassing, and yet it took the place of what could be considered a puberty ritual for us girls. We never knew what the boys talked about or what they were told about us, reproductively, etc. But I always somehow felt that they had been given some important secret that day, that we, as girls, were not privy to, and that this was just some kind of weird, divisive act on the part of the administration to distract and codify us. I suppose that sounds like a true paranoid at work, or perhaps hindsight talking, eh? But it's true I did feel that way. . . . I also believe that most of what I experienced, or did not experience, were [sic] consistent with much of the cultural conditioning that women receive from the media and the medical establishment.

Many women revealed a form of resistance in the contradictory voices used to tell their stories. Women moved between the anxious, hesitant, and fearful disclosure complete with multiple "umms" and "you knows" to the staging of their stories as a series of adventures, gaining control over the experience and framing it in hindsight as ridiculous. In so doing, they claimed control over events, appropriating them and defusing the pain and anguish. This emphasizes the sometimes contradictory ways gender is negotiated, discourses of resistance being crucial components of this negotiation. Virginia, a 38-year-old white student, illustrates this as she jokes about the story of her first period, laughing and describing the event as a funny experience:

So I was 10 years old and didn't understand any of it. In fact I misunderstood most of it. What I remember about it from the book was that somehow the menstrual blood came out on the outside of your lower abdomen somehow like it seeped through your skin! [laugh] . . . and so here's the book telling me that these napkins don't show and I'm holding them up to my stomach and saying, yeah, right [laugh], that is going to show, you can't tell me that is not going to show. . . . So I told my mother and it was like "oh," she did seem rather pleased but it wasn't like the kind of pleased where if I got a really good grade or you know, gotten the solo in the school play [laugh]. . . . She pulls out the Kotex kit and that is when I begin to connect, this is what it is, it doesn't come out of your stomach!

Hannah, an incest survivor, spoke very poignantly about her first menses. Despite her sadness she tells funny stories of menarche, her humor helping her gain control over her pain:

I saw blood in my underwear and it was like I just sat on the toilet [laugh] and I am like "mom." She comes in and she was like, "What? Well honey, congratulations, you are a little lady now." I am like, "Say what?!!" I was cramping really bad and I was given medication. It was to get me regulated. . . . I remember lying on the floor and my mom, she used to have bad cramps because she had a tipped uterus, so my grandfather used to buy her a pint of alcohol because they didn't have medication then, and she would drink it and she would pass out and she would be out for a day, so my mom gave me some brandy because she thought it would solve it! [laugh] Well, after I had the brandy I just started to york it, I was throwing up left and right, so it seems like after that time every period I ever had I would throw up!

Acceptances, Coping, and Appropriation

For some women, especially those at midlife and beyond, there was a general sense of acceptance or resignation to the politics of menarche that was apparent in the narratives. I had never thought of this as a form of resistance until I read Emily Martin's discussion of acceptance, lament, and nonaction as a way of responding to women's reproductive restrictions (Martin 1987, 184–86); yet these ways of coping and surviving are important, and they also subvert the masculinist idea of resistance as oppositional action and behavior. When asked about the specifics of their menarche, many women responded with such comments as "people didn't talk about such things back then," "it was just something I had to endure," "that's the way it was back then." The comments of Alex, an 80-year-old white woman, were typical:

> And in those days we didn't have the sanitary napkins we have today, or even now the Tampax and so on, but you always had that laundry to do. That was just not very pleasant, but it was a thing you did. I mean, that was the way it went.

This acceptance did not always take the form of resignation. Many women, such as Yvonne, an African-American woman in her thirties, were angry that they had had to endure certain experiences. "I was pissed" was among Yvonne's comments. Some tempered their frustrations with observations such as "Well, that's just the way it was then you see." The important point is that these were survival and coping mechanisms.

Louie, age 73, talked about the hardships associated with menstruation before the onset of disposable sanitary supplies. She remembers being in a tight spot with no menstrual cloths: "I had a jackknife and I cut up one of my blankets for pads and used those." Women of all ages reported using toilet paper, tissue, and underwear to help them hide their bleeding and cope with their first menses. Some hid evidence, some threw it away, some washed it out when no one was around. Many worked out ways to avoid going to a grocery store where they might be recognized, and others modified their clothes and activities to avoid embarrassment.

Many women told stories of using menstruation as a way to manipulate and have some control over situations. A Mexican-American woman in her thirties was not alone in sharing how she avoided showers in school by telling the teacher she had her period, and also telling her boyfriend the same to avoid sexual contact. Gerta spoke for many as she wrote:

> As far as school was concerned—during Physical Education, we were benched for three days. CLUB members [those girls who had already started their periods] often considered this a plus as we were not required to wear gym attire.

Bonding and Solidarity

Some women found that the experience of menarche helped girls identify and bond with each other, providing support and solidarity. Amy, an African-American student and mother, told how she had pretended to have her period for several months before she actually experienced it in order to feel accepted by her friends. She said: "I was happy because I didn't have to lie anymore, now I was one of the girls. . . . It was important for me to be accepted as one of the group, it was a significant event for that reason." Gerta, almost 40 years Amy's senior, talked about how friends who had "joined the Club" were closer and held in a higher regard by other girls. For many women, then, first menses was an ambivalent time; it was framed by negativity, but at the same time, symbolic of maturation; it brought status. This was usually acted out in the context of sisters and peers, where girls wanted very much to be included in the group. As Thorne (1993) suggests, the "popular" girls set the stage; if they were perceived as having started their period, then this development was seen as desirable. Since this status is intertwined with their sexual status, it is complex: girls do not want to start too soon and be seen as too advanced or promiscuous, but they do not want to start last and be branded a less mature child. Timing is definitely of the essence.

The importance such a personal event held within girls' groups was illustrated by Robin, who reported that she was obsessed with the idea of starting her period and looked forward to the drama of it all: "Blood would run down your leg and you would have to run out of class!" She was not daunted by this thought and said, "I wanted very much for it to begin at school. . . . Just for the attention I guess. . . . It was a social thing. All my friends were going to get their period and I wanted to be social."

While most girls suffered the embarrassment of menarche alone, some reported how friends had supported and helped them. Laurence, a young Malaysian woman, spoke of the support and solidarity received from friends when she started her period while away at boarding school:

> It was during choir practice, we were just singing and I felt something weird and so a girl said "you have a little stain on your skirt." The girls' side of the choir was really restless and the guys had no idea what was happening. A bunch of girls, about three of them my close friends, escorted me to the bathroom and everything happened, they got me the pads, told me what to do, everything.

Others also talked and wrote about friends and older sisters who helped them figure out what was happening to their bodies, as well as helped them access and use menstrual products. Karin emphasized how she felt closer to her friends after she started her period:

> I think it kind of brought me closer to girls in a certain way because when you talk about things that are personal it really kind of strengthens your friendships I think, and I think it makes it a very intimate friendship. So I realize that [with] some of my girlfriends I was really closer, I felt very close to them.

Changing the Scripts

For many women, the framing of womanhood at menarche occurred within the context of the complex dynamic of their relationship with their mothers.

Scholars have suggested (and the data here certainly support this) that since girls rely on their mothers at menarche, they report either increased conflict or closeness, depending on the relationship and communication patterns before puberty (Brooks-Gunn and Petersen 1983; Danza 1983; Orbach 1986). Mothers often socialize their daughters into the same restrictions associated with femininity that they have endured, ensuring that their daughters will fit into society and maintaining a shared compliance in the development of a submissive femininity and gendered sexual identity. Girls may grow to resent their mothers for their role in this at the same time that they may fear becoming what they perceive their mothers have become; however, there is much evidence here to suggest that these patterns are being disrupted. Many of the women who had negative experiences with their mothers at menarche also said that they would never want that to happen to their own daughters, and several went on to tell stories of positive experiences of menarche with adolescent children. Nonetheless, several women also emphasized that even though they had prepared their children and made it a positive experience, their daughters still felt some shame and embarrassment. The values of the culture are strong; children are not raised in a vacuum and quickly internalize the negative messages associated with menstruation.

Judy, a Japanese American in her twenties, shared her desire for a better experience for any future daughters:

> If I have daughters of my own in the future, I will tell them more positive things about periods, such as that it's not something you should be ashamed of or something dirty. I would make sure that they'll have some knowledge about menstruation before it starts because, when my period started, I didn't have any knowledge why women have [a] period or how it starts or anything.

Ann, a white mother of two daughters and a grandmother, spoke with regret that she acted very much like her own mother and was not able to give information and help her daughters feel good about their first menses. She is, however, committed to undoing this piece of family history with her granddaughter:

> My mother neglected telling me and I neglected telling my girls and I wouldn't want that to happen to my granddaughter . . . because I wouldn't want it to come from an outside source like from girls at school. I feel that my daughter really should do this, but like I said, if she doesn't I am prepared to do it for her.

Conclusion

Although women's bodies have been the object of derogation and admiration, women themselves have not had the power to control how their bodies might look, act, and feel. Menarche is an event that symbolizes both reproductive and sexual potential and centers attention on the body. Since "woman" is over-represented through the practices and values of sexuality, menarche takes on loaded meanings that have consequences for women and their everyday lives, scripting relations of power into the discourses and practices that surround women's bodies. The women who participated in the study remembered menarche as an important experience and, for most, this experience provoked anxiety, reminding them of their contaminating natures and encouraging them to hide evidence of their bleeding, while focusing attention on the sexualized body and changing relationships with others. Bodies are contextualized in a society that devalues and trivializes women; however, while adult women have internalized the stigma and shame associated with having bodies that bleed and all that this entails in terms of restrictions on body, mind, and soul, they have responded as active agents, and have resisted these discourses through a variety of means. They continue to resist them as they reminisce about their first menses, viewing their experiences retrospectively, framing and reframing them, hoping to neutralize the pain, perhaps taking back their power.

Menarche is a physiological happening, framed by the biomedical metaphors of current scientific knowledge, yet also a gendered sexualized happening, a transition to womanhood as objectified other. What is crucial here is that this juncture, menarche, is a site where girls become women and gender relations are reproduced. Such relations are about power and its absence; power to define the body and live in it with dignity and safety; power to move through the world with credibility and respect. May this be in our futures.

References

Bartky, Sandra. 1992. Foucault, femininity, and the modernization of patriarchal power. In *Feminist Philosophies: Problems, Theories and Applications*, edited by Janet J. A. Kourany, James J. P. Sterba, and Rosemarie R. Tong. Englewood Cliffs, NJ: Prentice-Hall.

Bordo, Susan R. 1989. The body and the reproduction of femininity: A feminist appropriation of Foucault. In *Gender/body/knowledge: A Feminist Reconstruction of Being and Knowing*, edited by Alice M. Jaggar and Susan R. Bordo. New Brunswick, NJ: Rutgers University Press.

Brooks-Gunn, Jeanne, and Anne C. Petersen. 1983. The experience of menarche from a developmental perspective. In *Girls at Puberty*, edited by Jeanne Brooks-Gunn and Anne C. Petersen. New York: Plenum.

Brooks-Gunn, Jeanne, and Diane N. Ruble. 1983. Dysmenorrhea in adolescence. In *Menarche: The Transition from Girl to Woman*, edited by Sharon Golub. Lexington, MA: D. C. Heath.

Brown, Lyn Mikel, and Carol Gilligan. 1992. *Meeting at the Crossroads: Women's Psychology and Girls' Development*. Cambridge, MA: Harvard University Press.

Brownmiller, Susan. 1984. *Femininity*. New York: Ballantine.

Buckley, Thomas, and Alma Gottlieb. 1988. *Blood Magic: The Anthropology of Menstruation*. Berkeley: University of California Press.

Connell, R. W. 1987. *Gender and power*. Stanford, CA: Stanford University Press.

Coward, Rosalind. 1985. *Female Desires: How They Are Sought, Bought, and Packaged*. New York: Grove Press.

Danza, Roberta. 1983. Menarche: Its effects on mother-daughter and father-daughter interactions. In *Menarche: the Transition from Girl to Woman*, edited by Sharon Golub. Lexington, MA: D. C. Heath.

Delaney, Janice, Mary Jane Lupton and Emily Toth. 1988. *The Curse: The Cultural History of Menstruation*. Urbana: University of Illinois.

Dimen, Muriel. 1986. *Surviving Sexual Contradiction: A Startling and Different Look at a Day in the Life of a Contemporary Professional Woman*. New York: Macmillan.

Dinnerstein, Dorothy. 1976. *The Mermaid and the Minotaur: Sexual Arrangements and Human Malaise*. New York: Harper & Row.

Fine, Michelle. 1988. Sexuality, schooling, and adolescent females: The missing discourse of desire. *Harvard Educational Review* 58:29–53.

Foucault, Michel. 1978. *The History of Sexuality: An Introduction*. Translated by Robert Hurley. New York: Pantheon.

Gilligan, Carol, Nona P. Lyons, and Trudy J. Hanmer, eds. 1990. *Making Connections: The Relational Worlds of Adolescent Girls at Emma Willard School*. Cambridge, MA: Harvard University Press.

Golub, Sharon, ed. 1983. *Menarche: The Transition from Girl to Woman*. Lexington, MA: D. C. Heath.

———. 1992. *Periods: From Menarche to Menopause*. Newbury Park, CA: Sage.

Haug, Frigga. 1987. *Female Sexualization*. London: Verso.

Hays, Terence E. 1987. Menstrual expression and menstrual attitudes. *Sex Roles* 16:605–14.

Hill, John P., and Grayson N. Holmbeck. 1987. Familial adaptation to biological change during adolescence. In *Biological-Psychological Interactions of Early Adolescence*, edited by Richard M. Lerner and Terryl T. Foch. Hillside, NJ: Lawrence Erlbaum.

Hill, John P., and Mary Ellen Lynch. 1983. The intensification of gender-related role expectations during early adolescence. In *Girls at Puberty*, edited by Jeanne Brooks-Gunn and Anne C. Petersen. New York: Plenum.

Irigaray, Luce. 1985. *Speculum of the Other Woman*. Ithaca, NY: Cornell University Press.

Jackson, Beryl B. 1992. Black women's responses to menarche and menopause. In *Menstrual Health in Women's Lives*, edited by Alice J. Dan and Linda L. Lewis. Urbana: University of Illinois Press.

Koff, Elissa. 1983. Through the looking glass of menarche: What the adolescent girl sees. In *Menarche: The Transition from Girl to Woman*, edited by Sharon Golub. Lexington, MA: D. C. Heath.

Koff, Elissa, Jill Rierdan, and S. Jacobson. 1981. The personal and interpersonal significance of menarche. *Journal of the American Academy of Child Psychiatry* 20:148–58.

Koff, Elissa, Jill Rierdan, and Ellen Silverstone. 1978. Changes in representation of body image as a function of menarcheal status. *Developmental Psychology* 14:635–42.

Lander, Louise. 1988. *Images of Bleeding: Menstruation as Ideology*. New York: Orlando Press.

Laws, Sophie. 1990. *Issues of Blood*. London: Macmillan.

Martin, Emily. 1987. *The Woman in the Body: A Cultural Analysis of Reproduction*. Boston: Beacon Press.

Orbach, Susie. 1986. *Hunger Strike*. London: Faber and Faber.

Patterson, Ellen T., and Ellwyn S. Hale. 1985. Making sure: Integrating menstrual care practices into activities of everyday living. *Advances in Nursing Science* 7:18–31.

Rierdan, Jill, and Elissa Koff. 1980. Representation of the female body by early and late adolescent girls. *Journal of Youth and Adolescence* 9:339–96.

Scott, Joan W. 1992. Experience. In *Feminists Theorize the Political*, edited by Judith Butler and Joan W. Scott. New York: Routledge.

Thorne, Barrie. 1993. *Gender Play: Girls and Boys in School*. New Brunswick, NJ: Rutgers University Press.

Ussher, Jane. 1989. *The Psychology of the Female Body*. New York: Routledge.

Weideger, Paula. 1976. *Menstruation and Menopause: The Physiology and Psychology: The Myth and Reality*. New York: Knopf.

Whisnant, Lynn, and Leonard Zegans. 1975. A study of attitudes towards menarche in white, middle-class American adolescent girls. *American Journal of Psychiatry* 132:809–14.

7

Young Women and Their Dream Lovers
Sexuality in Adolescent Fiction

LINDA K. CHRISTIAN-SMITH

Almost two weeks since she'd met him and she was still thinking about Seth. . . . What if she could be in the car with Seth again? Everything would be different. He'd drive her home. She'd talk intelligently. Amusingly. Seriously. At her house, she'd say, "Thanks for the ride." "My pleasure," he'd say. He'd lean toward her and kiss her. "Finn, I'm so crazy about you. . . . I never knew a girl like you." . . . And he'd kiss her again . . . and again . . . .
(Mazer 1979, 52)

In this episode from Norma F. Mazer's *Up in Seth's Room* (1979) teenage Finn Rousseau indulges in romantic fantasies about tall, dark, and handsome Seth. Sweet dreams of desire pervade Finn's thoughts almost to the exclusion of everything else. This scenario is repeated endlessly in a new genre of adolescent fiction, the teenage romance novel. Finn's romantic reverie encapsulates the feelings of many young women today as they seek their dream lovers between the covers of a book. The concept of romance fiction written for teens dates back to the 1940s and 1950s, when Betty Cavanna, Maureen Daly, and Rosamond du Jardin wrote books focusing on young women's first love experience. A new version of the teen romance novel was developed through

Originally published as Linda K. Christian-Smith. 1991. "Young women and their dream lovers: Sexuality in adolescent fiction." pp. 206–25 in Janice M. Irvine (ed.), *Sexual Cultures and the Construction of Adolescent Identities*. Philadelphia, PA: Temple University Press. Copyright 1994 by Linda K. Christian-Smith. Reprinted by permission of Temple University Press.

market research by Scholastic Inc. and appeared in school book clubs and bookstores in 1980 (Roman and Christian-Smith 1988). This fiction's rise to international readership in only twelve years parallels recent wide-ranging economic, political, and social changes in the United States (Christian-Smith 1993).

It may seem incredible that these novels of first love should gain popularity in the last two decades, when many aspects of young women's lives have changed considerably. Increased access to education, better-paying jobs, and more political power is many a young woman's legacy from decades of struggles by feminists and other politically progressive groups. (Woman are still among the poor and unemployed. See Stallard, Ehrenreich, and Sklar 1983). However, there is a dark side to this legacy, since many young women also confront the realities of early pregnancy, sexually transmitted infections (STIs), a job structure segmented by gender, class, race, and sexuality, and an intense national debate over the control of women's bodies. Teen romance fiction's popularity makes a great deal of sense in light of these realities, especially current concerns over young women's sexuality. According to Steven Seidman (1991), sexuality has been a prominent feature of the many "purity campaigns" that have swept the United States since the 1970s. Expanding sexual choices and preferences throughout the twentieth century have recently led to demands from many sectors for greater control of sexuality. The current campaign against AIDS and the representation of sexuality as a domain of danger have reconnected sex to love, with increased emphasis on romance and monogamy.

Many of the purity campaigns are further directed at the growing numbers of teenagers involved in sexuality at a younger age. Sharon Thompson's (1984) research demonstrates that sex and romance are very much on the minds of young women. To understand young women's sexuality, one must first examine romance. Romance not only refers to the emotional and caring aspects of a special human relationship but also involves patterns of power between people, especially between women and men.

At first glance, a teen romance fiction appears to be an innocent tale of girl meets boy, but romance fiction concerns not only hearts and flowers, but hearts and minds. Like other books for young readers, teen romance novels shape young women's femininity and secure their consent to the dominant organization of society (Christian-Smith 1990; Rose 1984). Yet these books have other dimensions that allow readers to reflect on their developing sexualities by becoming the heroine (Walkerdine 1984). In this chapter I explore these two dimensions of teen romance novel reading by analyzing a sample of thirty-four romance novels (listed in Appendix A) that are highly recommended by the books and journals [that] librarians and teachers use when selecting books for students. [See Christan-Smith (1990) for additional discussion of sampling procedures.] . . . I recount the way teen romance novels construct sexual differences and channel young women's fantasies and desires toward heterosexuality. . . .

Procedures

This textual analysis of a sample of thirty-four adolescent romance novels written between 1942 and 1982[1] is grounded in semiotic methodology and in Michel Foucault's work on sexuality, discourse formation, and power (Haug 1987; McRobbie 1978; Seidler 1987). My aim is to specify how power relations work in and through these romance novels to form sexual discourses. . . .

In his *History of Sexuality*, Foucault (1980) claims that sexuality concerns knowledge, power, the body, and enacted sexual practices. Sexuality is also constructed through discursive practices, particularly literature. Foucault's important contribution lies in the insight that sexuality involves the incorporation of increasingly wide areas of knowledge. This knowledge concerns definitions of "proper" sexuality and the regulation of sexual practices. Of prime importance is the "deployment of sexuality," which refers to the position sexuality occupies within the network of institutions where sexual practices occur. The primary elements in this network are families that "anchor sexuality and provide it with a permanent support" (1980, 108).

Power is central to Foucault's views on sexuality. Power relations define what is legitimate or secret sexual knowledge and practices. Power operates by designating sites of pleasure and "appropriate" objects of desire. Hence, power operates at the very fundamental levels of identity and meaning.

Although Foucault's work is useful for analyzing sexuality in teen romance fiction, it must be extended in several respects. Foucault's concept of power does not shed light on the particular power relations between and among the sexes or on the everyday experience of sexuality within relationships. Romance is not included in Foucault's notion of sexuality, but romance is where sexual meanings are established; it is the primary means of preparing young women for their positions in heterosexuality. . . .

This discussion provides a backdrop for how sexual meanings are constructed in romance fiction. In the context of the novels, sexuality refers to girls' acquisition of knowledge about their bodies and their relation to them. Connected to this relation are the practices surrounding the use of the body, prohibitions and constraints, and pleasure and desire. Power enters the picture in the form of girls' struggles to control their bodies and to define what sexuality means to them. Together these factors constitute the code of sexuality in the novels. The key elements of this code are the following:

1. Romance is the only proper context for sexuality.
2. Sexuality is defined as heterosexuality.
3. Genital sexuality is mostly reserved for adults.
4. Girls respond to boys' sexual overtures but do not initiate any of their own.

5. Sexual definitions reside within a network of power based in romance and the family.

6. Resistance to genital practices is encouraged.

I was able to group teen romance fiction into three periods according to the forms of sexual expression found in individual novels and the ways in which sexuality was treated over time. The periods are: period 1, 1942–59; period 2, 1963–79; and period 3, 1980–82. (I was not able to locate any teen romance novels written between 1960 and 1962; hence the gap in time between periods 1 and 2.) In novels written in the 1940s and the 1950s sexuality is limited to kissing, with heroines guarding their "reputations." Fiction written between 1963–79 features boys' pressures toward intercourse and heroines' resistance to these pressures. The novels from 1980 to 1982 mostly limit sexuality to kissing; however, heroines are less passive regarding sexual desire. The periodization is a way of accounting for changes in sexuality in this sample of romance fiction. (Space does not permit analysis of all thirty-four novels.)

Sealed with a Kiss

Like Sleeping Beauty, heroines' sexuality is awakened by boys. In the novels, girls interpret their sexuality in terms of romance, which establishes feelings and emotions as its proper content. Romance has a double-edged quality where sexuality is concerned. It controls the forms of and occasions for sexuality and gives heroines some way of controlling boys' sexual demands. Each period contributes to the establishment of linkages between romance and sexuality by privileging romance as the only legitimate context for sexual expression. In periods 1 and 3, sexual expression is mostly limited to chaste kissing and hugging within steady relationships. White middle-class Jane Howard of *The Boy Next Door* (Cavanna 1956) demands that Ken Sanderson go through the rituals of romance before he can kiss her. In the period 3's *Princess Amy* (Pollowitz 1981), white working-class Amy Painter is outraged at being kissed by white middle-class Guy Wetherington. This reaction can only be understood within the larger context that links sexuality with romance. The kiss as a sign of love is evident in all three periods, where romances are, as the song goes, "sealed with a kiss." In *Practically Seventeen* (Pollowitz 1981) the sometime romance of Tobey Heydon and Brose Gilman is finally confirmed when Brose gives Tobey his class ring and seals their relationship with a kiss on the hand. Halfway through *Seventeenth Summer* (Daly 1968, 59) Angie Morrow experiences her first kiss: "In the movies they always shut their eyes but I didn't. In the loveliness of the next moment I think I grew up. . . . Jack kissed me and his lips were as smooth and baby soft as a new raspberry." The first kiss signals growing up; it facilitates the awakening of girls' sexual feelings and gives them a particular form.

The kiss as the symbol of love is also found in period 2 fiction. In *Up in Seth's Room* (Mazer 1979), Seth's kiss signifies for Finn his commitment, even though the text is very clear that he does not love her. Similarly, in *Drop-Out* (Eyerly 1963) Donnie Muller interprets Mitch Donelson's first kiss as a token of love, and it is therefore welcomed. This linking of sexuality with love is especially strong when sexuality includes intercourse.

In the novels boys are presented as the only legitimate objects of girls' desire. In *Wait for Marcy* (du Jardin 1950) fifteen-year-old white middle-class Marcy initially lacks interest in boys and prefers the companionship of her female friends. Her parents are concerned that she develop in the "normal direction" (p. 14). Heterosexuality is constructed as the natural and unquestioned form of sexuality in the novels of periods 1 and 3 and is unconditionally endorsed in period 2 despite the presence of two novels about love relationships between girls, *Ruby* (Guy 1976) and *Hey, Dollface* (Hautzig 1978). The critical power of this emerging sexual discourse is undercut at several points because the girls' relationships are already foregrounded in heterosexuality and are constantly measured against it and found lacking. In *Hey, Dollface*, Val seeks the advice of her mother and her teacher, Miss Udry, concerning her feelings for Chloe. Her mother believes that lesbian relationships are substitutes for some inability to attract men (p. 64), whereas Miss Udry views lesbians desire as a phase in "normal" sexual development (pp. 86–87). Homophobia is strong in both novels but is most pronounced in *Ruby*. The relationship between African-American middle-class Ruby and Daphne has attracted the attention of Ed Books, a schoolmate. He confronts Ruby and Daphne: " 'I knew something was wrong with you. Dykes is your thing.' He put his hand to his forever swollen crotch. 'You want to feel the real thing? Here, I'll let you feel it' " (p. 58). Here the "real thing" represented by the penis becomes a larger symbol of "proper" desire and male control over heroines' sexuality. The subsequent attempts by Daphne's mother to compel her "to go straight," as well as Ruby's father's reconsidering his ban on dating boys, help to establish heterosexuality as the prevailing sexual discourse.

Genital relationships do not occur with frequency in the novels, and nowhere are they sanctioned between adolescents. However, they find reluctant recognition in some novels from periods 1 and 3, such as *My Darling, My Hamburger* (Zindel 1969) and *I'll Always Remember You . . . Maybe* (Pevsner 1981). What partially legitimates intercourse is that it is the outcome of long-term relationships that have all the hallmarks of "trial marriages." However, the novels as a whole favor a "wait until we are married" attitude and reinforce this perspective through their treatment of sexuality. First, sexual intercourse is presented as a dangerous practice that must be strictly controlled. In *Drop Out* (Eyerly 1963, 68), Donnie's neighbor Mrs. O'Meara warns her that "sex is like a kitten they can take out of a little box to play with, then put back when they're through. Too late they discover they've got a tiger on their hands." Sex is compared to "dynamite" that "you don't turn . . . on and off like a radio" in *Mr. and Mrs. Bo Jo Jones* (Head 1967, 62). This novel and *My Darling, My Hamburger* use the stock device of the heroine's pregnancy as a consequence of intercourse. In both novels the protagonist, July Greher and Liz Carstensen, feel guilty and see their pregnancies as a punishment for teen intercourse.

Although some interest in and knowledge of sex is allowed in later romance fiction, in the end the novels define girls' sexuality as distinctly nongenital. Another thread running through the novels is that girls should follow boys' cues and not take the lead. Heroines' lives are marked by continuous waiting. They wait to be asked for dates, and most important they wait to be kissed. These heroines have good reasons for their concern over being perceived as too forward, for in their world proper femininity requires a certain passiveness, with their ability to take the initiative restricted to carefully defined situations.

This pattern is evident in all periods. Jean Jarrett of *Jean and Johnny* (Cleary 1959) is chastised by her sister Sue for telephoning a boy and appearing to be "too eager and too available" to him. Similarly, in *Paintbox Summer* (Cavanna 1949) Kate Vale accuses her friend Misty of "throwing herself" at boys and behaving in an "improper" manner. In *Up a Road Slowly* (Hunt 1966) Julie Trilling is very attracted to her childhood friend Danny Trevort but is reluctant to show him how she feels. Not until Danny has kissed her and confessed his love is Julie able to share her feelings. "Coming on too strong" is a prime concern of Jennie Webster in *California Girl* (Quin-Harkin 1981). For over a hundred pages the reader waits along with Jennie for that first kiss, which finally happens toward the end of the novel.

Furthermore, the topic of heroines' sexual pleasures is rarely discussed in specifically sexual terms. Heroines' sexuality is presented as expressive and as responsive to boys. The language used avoids the concrete and specific in favor of the vague and evocative:

> Jane's heart began to hammer curiously, and she felt almost frightened (Cavanna 1956, 26).

> Something deep within me stirred and a throbbing warmth surged through my whole body until the very tips of my fingers tingled (Daly 1968, 53).

> I felt the warmth of his hand. . . . The touch had created a tiny tingle of electricity that reached the insides of my heart (Conklin 1981, 34).

The novels avoid the distinctly physical aspects of heroines' sexuality, primarily dwelling on psychological aspects. *My First Love and Other Disasters* (Pascal 1979), which is the only novel analyzed that directly discusses male erection, has nothing to say about any accompanying genital responses in heroines. Although it is certainly true that the psychological is an important aspect of sexual response, downplaying physiological components removes this dimension as a legitimate aspect of heroines' sexuality.

The silence surrounding heroines' sexual pleasure is especially apparent in novels where intercourse occurs. In *Mr. and Mrs. Bo Jo Jones* (Head 1967, 9) all the reader learns is that July is "humiliated," "shattered," and "furious" with herself and Bo Jo afterwards. When Paul Leonard in *I'll Always Remember You . . . Maybe* (Pevsner 1981) goes off to college, he decides to sever the relationship with his steady girlfriend, Darien Holmes. Darien is reluctant to agree to this, holding on to the hope that Paul will change his mind. During Christmas visit, Paul sees Darien, and they renew the sexual side of the relationship. The way in which this episode is treated once again shows a reluctance to treat girls as active in their own sexual pleasure.

> As he began kissing me again, the word *savagely* that Genie [Darien's friend] and I used to howl over when we read gothics aloud went through my mind. It didn't seem funny at all now. And if Paul's love-making was more urgent this time, that was only natural, considering that we'd been separated for so long. The important thing was that we were back together. The next time or the next he'd be more relaxed and tender . . . the way he used to be (Pevsner 1981, 113).

Darien's responses are lost through the focus on Paul's actions, and the passive character of the heroine is once again reinforced.

My Darling, My Hamburger (Zindel 1969) is one of the few novels in which a heroine expresses her desire for a boy. Liz's note to Sean saying, "I want you" (p. 44), is the most direct statement of feminine desire in the entire sample. The sexual tension between Liz Carstensen and Sean Collins supposedly culminates in the night of the Winter Starlight Dance when Liz and Sean are stranded with a flat tire at Marine Park. I say "supposedly," since Liz's oblique remark to Sean that she is "not in a hurry to go home anymore" (p. 68) stands as the only textual clue to what may transpire. That intercourse has occurred is confirmed some chapters later when Liz finds herself pregnant. By leaving out Liz's actions, the text silences Liz at an important point in the novel. Liz here assumes a certain passivity, seemingly worn down by another of her fights with her parents and Sean's continual sexual pressure. Hence, the power of her initial desire for Sean has been totally lost by the time this episode occurs. An important aspect of the heroine's sexuality is subverted by a common convention of romance fiction: the weary capitulation of the heroine to the masterful hero. . . .

These novels demonstrate the contradictory position that sexuality occupies in heroines' lives. Heroines may have desires, but their desires are to be held in check. Otherwise, they run the risk of familial censure and all the consequences that censure implies. Sexual desire has another consequence for heroines that has not yet been discussed: it makes them vulnerable to sexual exploitation.

In all the novels, sexuality is confined to clearly defined life stages. When girl meets boy and falls in love, the occasional chaste kiss and hug is permitted; beyond this, however, girls' sexuality creates alarm in the world of the romance novel. The first kiss stands as a sign of a heroine passing from girl to woman; sexual intercourse is not afforded an equal status. Despite this, intercourse plays an important role in consolidating heroines' sexual identities through the stands they must take, especially in period 2.

As I have indicated, genital sexuality poses great difficulty for heroines. They find themselves caught between adherence to a dominant sexual code forbidding teenage intercourse and the new sexual demands placed on them by boyfriends. Parents who subscribe to traditional forms of sexual expression apply additional pressure. This pressure culminates in heroines' resistance to both boyfriend and parents. A good example is found in Ursula Le Guin's *Very Far Away from Anywhere Else* (1976), where the romance between Owen Griffiths and Natalie Field takes an unexpected turn. On an outing to the beach a kiss threatens to turn into something more. Owen's decision that intercourse should be the next step in their relationship results from media representations of proper gender relations and peer pressure: "Man Plus Woman Equals Sex. Nothing else. No unknowns in the equation. Who needs unknowns?" (p. 43). For Natalie, just being with Owen is enough, and she is quick to remind him of this to forestall any further sexual advances. The stand that Natalie takes confirms her belief that sexuality has no role in her life at this time and that a sexual relationship may jeopardize her future plans for a professional music career.

Sexual conflict has a hidden dimension in romance fiction. *My First Love and Other Disasters* (Pascal 1979) and *Up in Seth's Room* (Mazer 1979) demonstrate its actual content: control of heroines' bodies and definition of their sexual pleasure. In the first novel, Jim Freeman is the boy of Victoria Martin's dreams—blond, tan, and athletic. Victoria's summer job as a mother's helper on Fire Island allows her to realize her dreams, for Jim will be working there as well. Her fantasies are, however, shattered when Jim applies tremendous pressure for a sexual relationship on the very first date. Victoria immediately interprets the conflict as involving power and control: " 'I don't want you to do that,' I say, and it's really crazy because here it is, my body, and he's annoyed that he can't do what he wants to it. Unreal. And he really is annoyed, like it was his" (p. 102). Victoria's remarks have little effect on Jim. As they leave the beach, Jim continues to kiss her and stops only when they part for the night. The next evening at The Monkey (the local teen club), Jim wastes no time before inviting Victoria to go out and sit with him on the pier. At her refusal, Jim flares up, remarking, "You have a lot of growing up to do" (p. 137), and turns to dance with another girl. Jim infantilizes Victoria in an attempt to instill doubt in her mind regarding the validity of her actions.

This discrediting of the heroine's feelings and right to control her body is also evident in *Up in Seth's Room*. Seth Warnecke pressures Finn Rousseau to sleep with him. This shatters Finn's feelings regarding the special quality of their romance and reveals Seth's lack of respect for her opinions. Finn's resistance only makes matters worse, causing a breach in their relationship. Some time later, Seth explains that his relentless pressure was a male tactic to counteract what he interpreted to be Finn's empty and meaningless protestations:

> "I always figured the thing to do was try, just keep trying. You know. If at first you don't succeed . . . that's the male creed."
> "That's a poem," she said. "I don't understand. What does it mean?"
> "It means that the macho thing to do with a girl is never take no for an answer. Just keep trying. Wear her down one way or another." (p. 190)

Although Finn is finally able to convince Seth of the validity of her position, the novel leaves the reader with the impression that at some future date Finn will be involved in a genital relationship. There is never any question of Finn's or any other heroine's eventual incorporation of this form of sexuality. Finn's decision to forgo intercourse represents a stage in her sexual development and is not viewed as a lifetime restraint on her sexual conduct. Timing has been the issue in this and other novels. This indicates how the novels link sexuality with power, control, and knowledge.

Sexuality, power, and knowledge are connected by privileging romance as the set of relations in which heroines' sense of their own sexuality arises and where their knowledge of sexuality is acquired. Heroines' heads throb (Pascal 1979), stomachs feel fluttery (du Jardin 1943), faces burn, palms sweat (Pollowitz 1981), and the girls feel tingly all over (Conklin 1981), only after that special boy has sealed his love with a kiss. In all the novels, girls' sexuality is dormant up to the moment of romantic specialness. Sexual pleasure begins with romance and is ultimately shaped and controlled by this same set of relations. At the juncture of the moments of romance and specialness, the heroine becomes sexually aware and is subjected to the male power and control underlying sexuality. This represents the heroine's incorporation into the power relations underlying heterosexuality. The formal control of romance by boyfriends is consolidated through their positions as definers of girls' sexuality. This control is buttressed by the books' insistence that boys are the only legitimate objects of girls' desires. The resistance of heroines in so many period 2 novels provides a clear glimpse of the systems of power and control implicit in the code of sexuality within the entire sample. Heroines' sexuality is portrayed as dangerous, especially when biological reproduction is linked to sexuality. The resistance of heroines to boys' sexual advances tends to defuse the danger of their own sexuality and to mold that sexuality into patterns the very opposite of boys': passive, controlled, and nongenital. Through this process, sexual desire is held in check, leaving love as its substitute. Sex then becomes the domain of masculinity, a domain to which girls have access, but legitimately only through a romance with a boy. . . .

Readers and Their Dream Lovers

Heroines and young women readers are taught several things about sexuality through teen romance fiction. They are taught that women's sexuality is dangerous, that sexual desire must be properly channeled, and that the proper channel is heterosexual romance. Other lessons heroines learn by heart concern their roles as enforcers of the traditional code of sexuality that limits sexual expression to chaste kissing. Heroines also learn that their bodies are the site of many struggles for control; boyfriends, parents, and the girls themselves all contend for ultimate control. They learn that the relation between sexuality and procreation is much closer for women than it is for men because almost every instance of intercourse results in pregnancy. They learn that biology is destiny. The novels reinforce the old double standard that is rooted in a rigid gender division. Heroines learn that sexuality means heterosexuality. The emphasis on one sexual orientation perpetuates the idea that sexuality is a unitary phenomenon rather than a process marked by a plurality of definitions (Caplan 1987). Another important lesson is that women should demonstrate a low level of sexual desire and should appear passive, a lesson related to the Victorian view that an adult woman's sexuality is "passionless" (Cott 1978). However, romance fiction contains strong undercurrents: heroines strain against this passionlessness and endeavor to control their own sexuality. Michele Barrett (1980) contends that sexuality has a political character in that it involves the unequal power relations between women and men. The romance novels I have analyzed certainly exemplify this . . .

As these readers turn pages of their romance novels, their consent to traditional views on sexuality is negotiated. The rise of teen romance fiction's popularity is bound to the growing conservatism of the Right in the United States and to the expansion of its traditional views on sexuality. The Right's purity campaigns are aimed at restricting sexual choice and tying sex to love, romance, and monogamy (Seidman 1991, 195). These are the very themes of teen romance fiction. Teen romance novels are read during adolescence, when sexuality is of utmost concern to young women. Although teen romance reading is a vehicle for making sense of their sexuality, it is deeply implicated in reconciling young women to traditional places in the world.

Note

1. The thirty-four books are novels highly recommended by twelve sources that librarians and teachers use when selecting books. Some of these are *School Library Journal, Alan Review*, and the *Junior High School Library Catalog*. An initial sample of well over one hundred books was checked against several of these sources to determine if a book was recommended by two sources. The remaining books were once against evaluated. Those recommended by an additional source formed the final sample of thirty-four books. See Christian-Smith (1990) for additional discussion of sampling procedures and of other aspects of these novels.

References

Caplan, Pat, ed. 1987. *The Cultural Construction of Sexuality*. New York: Tavistock.
Christian-Smith, Linda K. 1990. *Becoming a Woman Through Romance*. New York: Routledge and Kegan Paul.

Christian-Smith, Linda K., ed. 1993. *Texts of Desire: Essays on Fiction, Femininity, and Schooling*. London: Falmer Press.

Cott, Nancy F. 1978. Passionlessness: An interpretation of Victorian sexual ideology. *Signs: Journal of Women in Culture and Society* 4:219–36.

Foucault, Michel. 1980. *The History of Sexuality*. New York: Vintage Books.

Haug, Frigga. 1987. *Female Sexualization: A Collective Work of Memory*, translated by Erica Carter. London: Verso.

McRobbie, Angela. 1978. *Jackie: An Ideology of Adolescent Femininity*. Stenciled occasional paper. Birmingham, UK: Centre for Contemporary Cultural Studies.

Roman, Leslie, and Linda K. Christian-Smith, eds. 1988. *Becoming Feminine: The Politics of Popular Culture*. New York: Falmer Press.

Rose, Jacqueline. 1984. *The Case of Peter Pan*. London: Macmillan.

Rosenblatt, Louise. 1978. *The Reader, the Text, the Poem: The Transactional Theory of the Literary Work*. Carbondale: Southern Illinois University Press.

Seidler, Victor. 1987. Reason, desire, and male sexuality. In *The Cultural Construction of Sexuality*, edited by Pat Caplan. New York: Tavistock.

Seidman, Steven. 1991. *Romantic Longings*. New York: Routledge and Kegan Paul.

Stallard, Karin, Barbara Ehrenreich, and Holly Sklar. 1983. *Poverty in the American Dream: Women and Children First*. Boston: South End Press.

Thompson, Sharon. 1984. The search for tomorrow: On feminism and the reconstruction of teen romance. In *Pleasure and Danger: Exploring Female Sexuality*, edited by Carole S. Vance. Boston: Routledge and Kegan Paul.

Walkerdine, Valerie. 1984. Some day my prince will come: Young girls and the preparation for adolescent sexuality. In *Gender and Generation*, edited by Angela McRobbie and Mica Nava. London: Macmillan.

Appendix A

The Thirty-four Teen Romance Novels

Benson, Sally. [1942] 1969. *Junior Miss*. New York: Pocket Books.

Cavanna, Betty. 1946. *Going on Sixteen*. New York: Scholastic Books.

———. 1949. *Paintbox Summer*. New York: Westminster Press.

———. 1956. *The Boy Next Door*. New York: William Morrow.

Cleary, Beverly. 1959. *Jean and Johnny*. New York: Pocket Books.

———. 1963. *Sister of the Bride*. New York: Dell

Conklin, Barbara. 1981. *P. S. I Love You*. New York: Bantam.

Conford, Ellen. 1981. *Seven Days to a Brand-new Me*. New York: Atlantic, Little, Brown.

Daly, Maureen. [1942] 1968. *Seventeenth Summer*. New York: Simon and Schuster.

Du Jardin, Rosamond. 1943. *Practically Seventeen*. New York: Scholastic Books.

———. 1950. *Wait for Marcy*. New York: Scholastic Books.

Emery, Anne. 1952. *Sorority Girl*. Philadelphia: Westminster Press.

Eyerly, Jeanette. 1963. *Drop-Out*. New York: Berkley Books.

Freedman, Benedict and Nancy Freedman. 1947. *Mrs. Mike*. New York: Berkley Books.

Gauch, Patricia. 1979. *Fridays*. New York: Pocket Books.

Guy, Rosa. 1973. *The Friends*. New York: Holt.

———. 1976. *Ruby*. New York: Viking.

Hautzig, Deborah. 1978. *Hey, Dollface*. New York: William Morrow.
Head, Ann. 1967. *Mr. and Mrs. Bo Jo Jones*. New York: New American Library.
Hunt, Irene. 1966. *Up a Road Slowly*. New York: Grosset and Dunlap.
L'Engle, Madeleine. 1965. *Camilla*. New York: Delacorte.
Le Guin, Ursula. 1976. *Very Far Away from Anywhere*. New York: Bantam.
Lyle, Katie L. 1973. *I Will Go Barefoot All Summer for You*. New York: Dell.
Mazer, Norma F. 1979. *Up in Seth's Room*. New York: Dell.
Pevsner, Stella. 1980. *Cute Is a Four-Letter Word*. New York: Archway Books.
———. 1981. *I'll Always Remember You . . . Maybe*. New York: Pocket Books.
Ogilvie, Elizabeth. 1956. *Blueberry Summer*. New York: Scholastic Books.
Pascal, Francine. 1979. *My First Love and Other Disasters*. New York: Viking.
Pollowitz, Melinda. 1981. *Princess Amy*. New York: Bantam..
Quin-Harkin, Janet. 1981. *California Girl*. New York: Bantam.
Stolz, Mary. 1956. *The Day and the Way We Met*. New York: Harper and Row.
Summers, James L. 1953. *Girl Trouble*. New York: Scholastic Books.
Wilkinson, Brenda. 1981. *Ludelle and Willie*. New York: Bantam.
Zindel, Paul. 1969. *My Darling, My Hamburger*. New York: Bantam.

8

Selling Hot Pussy

Representations of Black Female Sexuality
in the Cultural Marketplace

BELL HOOKS

Friday night in a small midwestern town—I go with a group of artists and professors to a late night dessert place. As we walk past a group of white men standing in the entry way to the place, we overhear them talking about us, saying that my companions, who are all white, must be liberals from the college, not regular "townies," to be hanging out with a "nigger." Everyone in my group acts as though they did not hear a word of this conversation. Even when I call attention to the comments, no one responds. It's like I am not only not talking, but suddenly, to them, I am not there. I am invisible. For my colleagues, racism expressed in everyday encounters—this is our second such experience together—is only an unpleasantness to be avoided, not something to be confronted or challenged. It is just something negative disrupting the good time, better to not notice and pretend it's not there.

As we enter the dessert place they all burst into laughter and point to a row of gigantic chocolate breasts complete with nipples—huge edible tits. They think this is a delicious idea—seeing no connection between this racialized image and the racism expressed in the entryway. Living in a world where white folks are no longer nursed and nurtured primarily by black female caretakers, they do not look at these symbolic breasts and consciously think about "mammies." They do not see this representation of chocolate breasts as a sign of displaced longing for a racist past when the bodies of black women were a commodity, available to anyone white who could pay the price. I look at these dark breasts and think about the representation of black female bodies in popular culture. Seeing them, I think about the connection between contemporary representations and the types of images popularized

Reprinted from bell hooks's *Black Looks: Race and Representtion*, with permission from the publisher, South End Press, 116 Saint Botolph Street, Boston, MA 02115.

from slavery on. I remember Harriet Jacobs' (1973) powerful exposé of the psychosexual dynamics of slavery in *Incidents in the Life of a Slave Girl*. I remember the way she described that "peculiar" institution of domination and the white people who constructed it as a "cage of obscene birds."

Representations of black female bodies in contemporary popular culture rarely subvert or critique images of black female sexuality which were part of the cultural apparatus of 19th-century racism and which still shape perceptions today. Sander Gilman's (1985) essay, "Black Bodies, White Bodies: Toward an Iconography of Female Sexuality in Late Nineteenth-Century Art, Medicine, and Literature," calls attention to the way black presence in early North American society allowed whites to sexualize their world by projecting onto black bodies a narrative of sexualization disassociated from whiteness. Gilman documents the development of this image, commenting that "by the eighteenth century, the sexuality of the black, male and female, becomes an icon for deviant sexuality." He emphasizes that it is the black female body that is forced to serve as "an icon for black sexuality in general."

Most often attention was not focused on the complete black female on display at a fancy ball in the "civilized" heart of European culture, Paris. She is there to entertain guests with the naked image of Otherness. They are not to look at her as a whole human being. They are to notice only certain parts. Objectified in a manner similar to that of black female slaves who stood on auction blocks while owners and overseers described their important, salable parts, the black women whose naked bodies were displayed for whites at social functions had no presence. They were reduced to mere spectacle. Little is known of their lives, their motivations. Their body parts were offered as evidence to support racist notions that black people were more akin to animals than other humans. When Sarah Bartmann's body was exhibited in 1810, she was ironically and perversely dubbed "the Hottentot Venus." Her naked body was displayed on numerous occasions for five years. When she died, the mutilated parts were still subject to scrutiny. Gilman stressed that: "The audience which had paid to see her buttocks and had fantasized about the uniqueness of her genitalia when she was alive could, after her death and dissection, examine both." Much of the racialized fascination with Bartmann's body concentrated attention on her buttocks. . . .

Although contemporary thinking about black female bodies does not attempt to read the body as a sign of "natural" racial inferiority, the fascination with black "butts" continues. In the sexual iconography of the traditional black pornographic imagination, the protruding butt is seen as an indication of a heightened sexuality. Contemporary popular music is one of the primary cultural locations for discussions of black sexuality. In song lyrics, "the butt" is talked about in ways that attempt to challenge racist assumptions that suggest it is an ugly sign of inferiority, even as it remains a sexualized sign. The popular song, "Doin' the Butt," fostered the promotion of a hot new dance favoring those who could most protrude their buttocks with pride and glee. A scene in Spike Lee's film *School Daze* depicts an all-black party where everyone is attired in swimsuits dancing—doing the butt. It is one of the most compelling moments in the film. The black "butts" on display are unruly and outrageous. They are not the still bodies of the female slave made to appear as mannequin. They are not a silenced body. Displayed as playful cultural nationalist resistance, they challenge assumptions that the black body, its skin color and shape, is a mark of shame. Undoubtedly the most transgressive and provocative moment in *School Daze*, this celebration of buttocks either initiated or coincided with an emphasis on butts, especially the buttocks of women, in fashion magazines. Its potential to disrupt and challenge notions of black bodies, specifically female bodies, was undercut by the overall sexual humiliation and abuse of black females in the film. Many people did not see the film, so it was really the song "Doin' the Butt" that challenged dominant ways of thinking about the body which encourage us to ignore asses because they are associated with undesirable and unclean acts. Unmasked, the "butt" could be once again worshiped as an erotic seat of pleasure and excitement.

When calling attention to the body in a manner inviting the gaze to mutilate black female bodies yet again, to focus solely on the "butt," contemporary celebrations of this part of the anatomy do not successfully subvert sexist/racist representations. Just as 19th century representations of black female bodies were constructed to emphasize that these bodies were expendable, contemporary images (even those created in black cultural production) give a similar message. When Richard Wright's (1969) protest novel *Native Son* was made into a film in the 1980s, the film did not show the murder of Bigger's black girlfriend Bessie. This was doubly ironic. She is murdered in the novel and then systematically eliminated in the film. Painters exploring race as artistic subject matter in the 19th century often created images contrasting white female bodies with black ones in ways that reinforced the greater value of the white female icon. Gilman's essay colludes in this critical project: he is really most concerned with exploring white female sexuality. . . .

Bombarded with images representing black female bodies as expendable, black women have either passively absorbed this thinking or vehemently resisted it. Popular culture provides countless examples of black female appropriation and exploitation of "negative stereotypes" to either assert control over the representation or at least reap the benefits of it. Since black female sexuality has been represented in racist/sexist iconography as more free and liberated, many black women singers, irrespective of the quality of their voices, have cultivated an image which suggests they are sexually available and licentious. Undesirable in the conventional sense, which defines beauty and sexuality as desirable only to the extent that it is idealized and unattainable, the black female body gains attention only when it is synonymous with accessibility, availability; when it is sexually deviant.

Tina Turner's construction of a public sexual persona most conforms to this idea of black female sexuality. In her recent autobiography *I, Tina* (1987) she presents a sexualized portrait of herself—providing a narrative that is centrally "sexual confession." Even though she begins by calling attention to the fact that she was raised with puritanical notions of innocence and virtuous womanhood which made her reticent and fearful of sexual experience, all that follows contradicts this portrait. Since the image that has been cultivated and commodified in popular culture is of her as "hot" and highly sexed—the sexually ready and free black woman—a tension exists in the autobiography between the reality she presents and the image she must uphold. Describing her first sexual experience, Turner recalls:

> Naturally, I lost my virginity in the backseat of a car. This was the fifties, right? I think he had planned it, the little devil—he knew by then that he could get into my pants, because there's already been a lot of kissing and touching inside the blouse, and then under the skirt and so forth. The next step was obvious. And me, as brazen as I was, when it came down to finally doing the real thing, it was like: "Uh-oh, it's time." I mean, I was scared. And then it happened.
>
> Well, it hurt so bad—I think my earlobes were hurting. I was just dying, God. And he wanted to do it two or three times! It was like poking an open wound. I could hardly walk afterwards.
>
> But I did it for love. The pain was excruciating; but I loved him and he loved me, and that made the pain less—Everything was right. So it was beautiful.

Only there is nothing beautiful about the scenario Turner describes. A tension exists between the "cool" way she describes this experience, playing it off to suggest she was in control of the situation, and the reality she recounts where she succumbs to male lust and suffers sex. After describing a painful rite of sexual initiation, Turner undermines the confession by telling the reader that she felt good. Through retrospective memory, Turner is able to retell this experience in a manner that suggests she was comfortable with sexual experience at an early age, yet cavalier language does not completely mask the suffering evoked by the details she gives. However, this cavalier attitude accords best with how her fans "see" her. Throughout the biography she will describe situations of extreme sexual victimization and then undermine the impact of her words by evoking the image of herself and other black women as sexually free, suggesting that we assert sexual agency in ways that are never confirmed by the evidence she provides.

Tina Turner's singing career has been based on the construction of an image of black female sexuality that is made synonymous with wild animalistic lust. Raped and exploited by Ike Turner, the man who made this image and imposed it on her, Turner describes the way her public persona as singer was shaped by his pornographic misogynist imagination:

> Ike explained: As a kid back in Clarksdale, he'd become fixated on the white jungle goddess who romped through Saturday matinee movie serials—revealing rag-clad women with long flowing hair and names like Sheena, Queen of the Jungle, and Nyoka—particularly Nyoka. He still remembered *The Perils of Nyoka*, a fifteen-part Republic Picture serial from 1941, starring Kay Alridge in the title role and featuring a villainess named Vultura, an ape named Satan, and Clayton

Moore (later to be TV's Lone Ranger) as love interest. Nyoka, Sheena—Tina! Tina Turner—Ike's own personal Wild woman. He loved it.

Turner makes no comment about her thoughts about this image. How can she? It is part of the representation which makes and maintains her stardom.

Ike's pornographic fantasy of the black female as wild sexual savage emerged from the impact of a white patriarchally controlled media shaping his perceptions of reality. His decision to create the wild black woman was perfectly compatible with prevailing representations of black female sexuality in a white supremacist society. Of course the Tina Turner story reveals that she was anything but a wild woman; she was fearful of sexuality, abused, humiliated, fucked, and fucked over. Turner's friends and colleagues document the myriad ways she suffered about the experience of being brutally physically beaten prior to appearing on stage to perform, yet there is no account of how she coped with the contradiction (this story is told by witnesses in *I, Tina*). She was on the one hand in excruciating pain inflicted by a misogynist man who dominated her life and her sexuality, and on the other hand projecting in every performance the image of a wild tough sexually liberated woman. Not unlike the lead character in the novel *Story of O* by Pauline Reage (1965), Turner must act as though she glories in her submission, that she delights in being a slave of love. Leaving Ike, after many years of forced marital rape and physical abuse, because his violence is utterly uncontrollable, Turner takes with her the "image" he created.

Despite her experience of abuse rooted in sexist and racist objectification, Turner appropriated the "wild woman" image, using it for career advancement. Always fascinated with wigs and long hair, she created the blonde lioness mane to appear all the more savage and animalistic. Blondeness links her to jungle imagery even as it serves as an endorsement of a racist aesthetics which sees blonde hair as the epitome of beauty. Without Ike, Turner's career has soared to new heights, particularly as she works harder to exploit the visual representation of woman (and particularly black woman) as sexual savage. No longer caught in the sadomasochistic sexual iconography of black female in erotic war with her mate that was the subtext of the Ike and Tina Turner show, she is now portrayed as the autonomous black woman whose sexuality is solely a way to exert power. Inverting old imagery, she places herself in the role of dominator.

Playing the role of Aunty Entity in the film *Mad Max: Beyond the Thunderdome*, released in 1985, Turner's character evokes two racist/sexist stereotypes, that of the black "mammy" turned power-hungry and the sexual savage who uses her body to seduce and conquer men. Portrayed as lusting after the white male hero who will both conquer and reject her, Aunty Entity is the contemporary reenactment of that mythic black female in slavery who supposedly "vamped" and seduced virtuous white male slave owners. Of course the contemporary white male hero of *Mad Max* is stronger than his colonial forefathers. He does not succumb to the dangerous lure of the deadly black seductress who rules over a mini-nation whose power is based on the use of shit. Turner is the bad black woman in this film, an image she will continue to exploit.

Turner's video "What's Love Got To Do With It" also highlights the convergence of sexuality and power. Here, the black woman's body is represented as potential weapon. In the video, she walks down rough city streets, strutting her stuff, in a way that declares desirability, allure, while denying access. It is not that she is no longer represented as available; she is "open" only to those whom she chooses. Assuming the role of hunter, she is the sexualized woman who makes men and women her prey (in the alluring gaze of the video, the body moves in the direction of both sexes). This tough black woman has no time for woman bonding, she is out to "catch." Turner's fictive model of black female sexual agency remains rooted in misogynist notions. Rather than being a pleasure-based eroticism, it is ruthless, violent; it is about women using sexual power to do violence to the male Other.

Appropriating the wild woman pornographic myth of black female sexuality created by men in a white supremacist patriarchy, Turner exploits it for her own ends to achieve economic self-sufficiency. When she left Ike, she was broke and in serious debt. The new Turner image conveys the message that happiness and power come to women who learn to beat men at their own game, to throw off any investment in romance and get down to the real dog-eat-dog thing. "What's Love Got To Do With It" sung by Turner evokes images of the strong bitchified black woman who is on the make. Subordinating the idea of romantic love and praising the use of sex for pleasure as commodity to exchange, the song had great appeal for contemporary postmodern culture. It equates pleasure with materiality, making it an object to be sought after, taken, acquired by any means necessary. When sung by black women singers, "What's Love Got To Do With It" called to mind old stereotypes which make the assertion of black female sexuality and prostitution synonymous. Just as black female prostitutes in the 1940s and 1950s actively sought clients in the streets to make money to survive, thereby publicly linking prostitution with black female sexuality, contemporary black female sexuality is fictively constructed in popular rap and R&B songs solely as commodity—sexual service for money and power, pleasure is secondary.

Contrasted with the representation of wild animalistic sexuality, black female singers like Aretha Franklin and younger contemporaries like Anita Baker fundamentally link romance and sexual pleasure. Aretha, though seen as a victim of no-good men, the classic "woman who loves too much" and leaves the lyrics to prove it, also sang songs of resistance. "Respect" was heard by many black folks, especially black women, as a song challenging black male sexism and female victimization while evoking notions of mutual care and support. In a recent PBS special highlighting individual musicians, Aretha Franklin was featured. Much space was given in the documentary to white male producers who shaped her public image. In the documentary, she describes the fun of adding the words "sock it to me" to "Respect" as a powerful refrain. One of the white male producers, Jerry Wexler, offers his interpretation of its meaning, claiming that it was a call for "sexual attention of the highest order." His sexualized interpretations of the song seemed far removed from the way it was heard and celebrated in black communities. Looking at this documentary, which was supposedly a tribute to Aretha Franklin's power, it was impossible not to have one's attention deflected away from the music by the subtext of the film, which can be seen as a visual narrative documenting her obsessive concern with the body and achieving a look suggesting desirability. To achieve this end, Franklin constantly struggles with her weight, and the images in the film chronicle her various shifts in body size and shape. As though mocking this concern with her body, throughout most of the documentary Aretha appears in what seems to be a household setting, a living room maybe, wearing a strapless evening dress, much too small for her breast size, so her breasts appear like two balloons filled with water about to burst. With no idea who shaped and controlled this image, I can only reiterate that it undermined the insistence in the film that she has overcome sexual victimization and remained a powerful singer; the latter seemed more likely than the former. . . .

According to postmodern analyses of fashion, this is a time when commodities produce bodies. . . . In her essay "Fashion and the Cultural Logic of Postmodernity," Gail Faurshou (1988) explains that beauty is no longer seen as a sustained "category of precapitalist culture." Instead, "the colonization and the appropriation of the body as its own production/consumption machine in late capitalism is a fundamental theme of contemporary socialization." This cultural shift enables the bodies of black women to be represented in certain domains of the "beautiful" where they were once denied entry, i.e., high fashion magazines. Reinscribed as spectacle, once again on display, the bodies of black women appearing in these magazines are not there to document the beauty of black skin, of black bodies, but rather to call attention to other concerns. They are represented so readers will notice that the magazine is racially inclusive even though their features are often distorted, their bodies contorted into strange and bizarre postures that make the images appear monstrous or grotesque. They seem to represent an anti-aesthetic, one that mocks the very notion of beauty.

Often black female models appear in portraits that make them look less like humans and more like mannequins or robots. Currently, black models whose hair is not straightened are often photographed wearing straight wigs; this seems to be especially the case if the models' features are unconventional, i.e., if she has large lips or particularly dark skin, which is not often featured in the magazine. The October 1989 issue of *Elle* presented a short profile of designer Azzedine Alaia. He stands at a distance from a black female body holding the sleeves of her dress. Wearing a ridiculous straight hair-do, she appears naked holding the dress in front of her body. The caption reads, "THEY ARE BEAUTIFUL AREN'T THEY!" His critical gaze is on the model and not the dress. As commentary it suggests that even black women can look beautiful in the right outfit. Of course when you read the piece, this statement is not referring to the model, but is a statement Alaia makes about his clothes. In contemporary postmodern fashion sense, the black female is the best medium for the showing of clothes because her image does not detract from the outfit; it is subordinated.

Years ago, when much fuss was made about the reluctance of fashion magazines to include images of black women, it was assumed that the presence of such representations would in and of themselves challenge racist stereotypes that imply black women are not beautiful. Nowadays, black women are included in magazines in a manner that tends to reinscribe prevailing stereotypes. Darker-skinned models are most likely to appear in photographs where their features are distorted. Biracial women tend to appear in sexualized images. Trendy catalogues like *Tweeds* and *J. Crew* make use of a racialized subtext in their layout and advertisements. Usually they are emphasizing the connection between a white European and American style. When they began to include darker-skinned models, they chose biracial or fair-skinned black women, particularly with blonde or light brown long hair. The non-white models appearing in these catalogues must resemble as closely as possible their white counterparts so as not to detract from the racialized subtext. A recent cover of *Tweeds* carried this statement:

> Color is, perhaps, one of the most important barometers of character and self-assurance. It is as much a part of the international language of clothes as silhouette. The message colors convey, however, should never overwhelm. They should speak as eloquently and intelligently as the wearer. Whenever colors have that intelligence, subtlety, and nuance we tend to call them European. . . .

Given the racialized terminology evoked in this copy, it follows that when flesh is exposed in attire that is meant to evoke sexual desirability it is worn by a non-white model. As sexist/racist sexual mythology would have it, she is the embodiment of the best of the black female savage tempered by those elements of whiteness that soften this image, giving it an aura of virtue and innocence. In the racialized pornographic imagination, she is the perfect combination of virgin and whore, the ultimate vamp. The impact of this image is so intense that Iman, a highly paid black fashion model who once received worldwide acclaim because she was the perfect black clone of a white ice goddess beauty, has had to change. Postmodern notions that black female beauty is constructed, not innate or inherent, are personified by the career of Iman. Noted in the past for features this culture sees as "Caucasian"— thin nose, lips, and limbs—Iman appears in the October 1989 issue of *Vogue* "made over." Her lips and breasts are suddenly full. Having once had her "look" destroyed by a car accident and then remade, Iman now goes a step further. Displayed as the embodiment of a heightened sexuality, she now looks like the racial/sexual stereotype. In one full-page shot, she is naked, wearing only a pair of brocade boots, looking as though she is ready to stand on any street corner and turn a trick, or worse yet, as though she just walked off one of the pages of *Players* (a porn magazine for blacks). Iman's new image appeals to a culture that is eager to reinscribe the image of black woman as sexual primitive. This new representation is a response to contemporary fascination with an ethnic look, with the exotic Other who promises to fulfill racial and sexual stereotypes, to satisfy longings. This image is but an extension of the edible black tit.

Currently, in the fashion world the new black female icon who is also gaining greater notoriety, as she assumes both the persona of sexually hot "savage" and white-identified black girl, is the Caribbean-born model Naomi Campbell. Imported beauty, she, like Iman, is almost constantly visually portrayed nearly nude against a sexualized background. Abandoning her "natural" hair for blonde wigs or ever-lengthening weaves, she has great crossover appeal. Labeled by fashion critics as the black Brigitte Bardot, she embodies an aesthetic that suggests black women, while appealingly "different," must resemble white women to be considered really beautiful.

Within literature and early film, this sanitized ethnic image was defined as that of the "tragic mulatto." Appearing in film, she was the vamp that white men feared. As Julie Burchill (1986) puts it outrageously in *Girls On Film*:

> In the mature Forties, Hollywood decided to get to grips with the meaty and messy topic of multiracial romance, but it was a morbid business. Even when the girls were gorgeous white girls—multiracial romance brought tears, traumas, and suicide. The message was clear: you intelligent white men suffer enough guilt because of what your grandaddy did—you want to suffer some more! Keep away from those girls. . . .

Contemporary films portraying biracial stars convey this same message. The warning for women is different from that given men—we are given messages about the danger of asserting sexual desire. Clearly the message from *Imitation of Life* was that attempting to define oneself as sexual subject would lead to rejection and abandonment. In the film *Choose Me*, Rae Dawn Chong plays the role of the highly sexual black woman chasing and seducing the white man who does not desire her (as was first implied in *Imitation of Life*) but instead uses her sexually, beats her, then discards her. The biracial black woman is constantly "gaslighted" in contemporary film. The message her sexualized image conveys does not change even as she continues to chase the white man as if only he had the power to affirm that she is truly desirable.

European films like *Mephisto* and the more recent *Mona Lisa* also portray the almost white, black woman as tragically sexual. The women in the films can only respond to constructions of their reality created by the more powerful. They are trapped. Mona Lisa's struggle to be sexually self-defining leads her to choose lesbianism, even though she is desired by the white male hero. Yet her choice of a female partner does not mean sexual fulfillment, as the object of her lust is a drug-addicted young white woman who is always too messed up to be sexual. Mona Lisa nurses and protects her. Rather than asserting sexual agency, she is once again in the role of mammy. . . .

There are few films that explore issues of black female sexuality in ways that intervene and disrupt conventional representations. The short film *Dreaming Rivers*, by the British black film collective Sankofa, juxtaposes the idealized representation of black woman as mother with that of sexual subject. showing adult children facing their narrow notions of black female identity. The film highlights the autonomous sexual identity of a mature black woman which exists apart from her role as mother and caregiver. *Passion of Remembrance*, another film by Sankofa, offers exciting new representations of the black female body and black female sexuality. In one playfully erotic scene, two young black women, a lesbian couple, get dressed to go out. As part of their celebratory preparations they dance together, painting their lips, looking at their images in the mirror, exulting in their black female bodies. They shake to a song that repeats the refrain "let's get loose" without conjuring images of a rotgut colonized sexuality on display for the racist/sexist imagination. Their pleasure, the film suggests, emerges in a decolonized erotic context rooted in commitments to feminist and anti-racist politics. When they look in the mirror and focus on specific body parts (their full thick lips and buttocks), the gaze is one of recognition. We see their pleasure and delight in themselves.

Films by African-American women filmmakers also offer the most oppo-sitional images of black female sexuality. Seeing for a second time Kathleen Collin's film *Losing Ground*, I was impressed by her daring, the way she por-trays black female sexuality in a way that is fresh and exciting. Like *Passion of Remembrance* it is in a domestic setting, where black women face one another (in Collin's film as mother and daughter), that erotic images of black female sexuality surface outside a context of domination and exploitation. When daughter and mother share a meal, the audience watches as a radical sexual aesthetics emerges as the camera moves from woman to woman, focusing on the shades and textures of their skin, the shapes of their bodies, and the way their delight and pleasure in themselves is evident in their environment. Both black women discreetly flaunt a rich sensual erotic energy that is not directed outward, it is not there to allure or entrap; it is a powerful declaration of black female sexual subjectivity.

When black women relate to our bodies, our sexuality, in ways that place erotic recognition, desire, pleasure, and fulfillment at the center of our efforts to create radical black female subjectivity, we can make new and different representations of ourselves as sexual subjects. To do so we must be willing to transgress traditional boundaries. We must no longer shy away from the critical project of openly interrogating and exploring representations of black female sexuality as they appear everywhere, especially in popular culture. In *The Power of the Image: Essays on Representation and Sexuality*, Annette Kuhn (1985) offers a critical manifesto for feminist thinkers who long to explore gender and representation:

. . . in order to challenge dominant representations, it is necessary first of all to understand how they work, and thus where to seek points of possible productive transformation. From such understanding flows various politics and practices of oppositional cultural production, among which may be counted feminist interventions. . . . there is another justification for a feminist analysis of main-stream images of women: may it not teach us to recognize inconsistencies and contradictions within dominant traditions of representation, to identify points of leverage for our own intervention: cracks and fissures through which may be captured glimpses of what in other circumstance might be possible, visions of "a world outside the order not normally seen or thought about?"

This is certainly the challenge facing black women, who must confront the old painful representations of our sexuality as a burden we must suffer, representations still haunting the present. We must make the oppositional space where our sexuality can be named and represented, where we are sexual subjects—no longer bound and trapped.

References

Burchill, Julie. 1986. *Girls On Film*. New York: Pantheon.

Faurshou, Gail. 1988. Fashion and the cultural logic of postmodernity. In *Body Invaders*, edited by Arthur and Marilouise Kroker. Canada: New Word Perspectives.

Gilman, Sander. 1985. Black bodies, white bodies: Toward an iconography of female sexuality in late nineteenth-century art, medicine, and literature. *Critical Inquiry* 12:204–42.

Jacobs, Harriet. 1973. *Incidents in the Life of a Slave Girl*. New York: Harcourt Brace Jovanovich.

Kuhn, Annette. 1985. *The Power of the Image: Essays on Representation and Sexuality*. New York: Routledge.

Reage, Pauline. 1965. *Story of O*. New York: Grove Press.

Turner, Tina. 1987. *I, Tina: My Life Story*. New York: Avon.

Wright, Richard. 1969. *Native Son*. New York: Harper Collins.

III

THE POLITICS
OF APPEARANCE

In a society still largely controlled by men, women's appearance dramatically affects women's lives. Attractiveness serves as an indirect form of power, by increasing women's odds of obtaining the protection of powerful men—at least so long as the women's attractiveness lasts. Among other benefits, attractiveness typically brings women more marital prospects and friendships, higher salaries, and higher school grades. The articles in this section explore how norms of female attractiveness serve as a form of social control, and how women attempt to conform to or resist these norms.

One feature of the female body that attracts special attention in contemporary American culture is the breast. From *Playboy* to *The Simpsons* to religious iconography, we receive a constant stream of messages regarding men's view of the female breast. Only rarely, however, do we get a glimpse of women's relationships with their breasts. This is the topic Iris Young explores in her article, "Breasted Experience." She examines how women learn to see their breasts as objects through men's eyes, and how women may experience their breasts independently of that male gaze.

The "breasted experience" is especially problematic for women who have had mastectomies for breast cancer. In "'Perfect People': Cancer Charities," Sharon Batt shows how cancer charities have refused to allow such women to define their own experiences and instead have taught women to accept their doctors' definition of their situation. In addition, she shows how cancer charities have defined breast cancer largely as a cosmetic problem, to be "cured" through makeup, prostheses, and implants. Thus the cancer charities—supposedly established to aid cancer survivors—have acted as one more form of social control designed to reinforce women's subordinate position.

One of the ironies of our cultural norms regarding female attractiveness is that few women can satisfy those norms, and no women can do so across the lifespan. Given the sanctions against those who do not meet those norms, it is not surprising that women have turned to artificial means of conforming, from makeup and corsets to diets and, most recently, plastic surgery. In "Women and the Knife: Cosmetic Surgery and the Colonization of Women's Bodies," Kathryn Pauly Morgan explores why cosmetic surgery has become accepted and why so many women choose it. Her article lays out the contradictions between the rhetoric of cosmetic surgery as a woman-centered choice and the reality of surgery as a coerced "choice" for those who otherwise cannot conform to feminine appearance norms.

The articles by Eugenia Kaw and Marcia Ann Gillespie describe the special pain experienced by Asian-American and African-American women faced with impossible Caucasian standards of beauty. In "Medicalization of Racial Features: Asian-American Women and Cosmetic Surgery," Kaw describes the racial and gender ideologies that pressure Asian-American women to have surgery designed to make them look more Caucasian, and shows how both Asian-American women and Caucasian doctors accept these ideologies unquestioningly. Similarly, in "Mirror Mirror," Gillespie describes the special emotional and social costs paid by African-American women faced with impossible, Caucasian standards of female beauty.

As women age, even those who once could meet standards for female attractiveness find they no longer can. In the article "Jane Fonda, Barbara Bush, and Other Aging Bodies: Femininity and the Limits of Resistance," Myra Dinnerstein and Rose Weitz describe how two women, Jane Fonda and Barbara Bush, have struggled with these impossible standards. Ironically, despite their diametrically opposed appearances—Fonda with her pumped-up muscles, Bush with her heavy-set body, gray hair, and wrinkles—both describe their appearance as resistance to cultural norms. Yet their lives and the reactions of others to them demonstrate the difficulties of resistance more than its possibilities.

9

Breasted Experience
The Look and the Feeling

IRIS MARION YOUNG

. . . For many women, if not all, breasts are an important component of body self-image; a woman may love them or dislike them, but she is rarely neutral.

In this patriarchal culture, focused to the extreme on breasts, a woman, especially in those adolescent years but also through the rest of her life, often feels herself judged and evaluated according to the size and contours of her breasts, and indeed she often is. For her and for others, her breasts are the daily visible and tangible signifier of her womanliness, and her experience is as variable as the size and the shape of breasts themselves. A woman's chest, much more than a man's, is *in question* in this society, up for judgment, and whatever the verdict, she has not escaped the condition of being problematic.

In this essay I explore some aspects of the cultural construction of breasts in our male-dominated society and seek a positive women's voice for breasted experience. . . .

I. Breasts as Objects

I used to stand before the mirror with two Spalding balls under my shirt, longing to be a grown woman with the big tits of Marilyn Monroe and Elizabeth Taylor. They are called boobs, knockers, knobs; they are toys to be grabbed, squeezed, handled. In the total scheme of the objectification of women, breasts are the primary things.

A fetish is an object that stands in for the phallus—the phallus as the one and only measure and symbol of desire, the representation of sexuality. This culture fetishizes breasts. Breasts are the symbol of feminine sexuality, so the "best" breasts are like the phallus: high, hard, and pointy. Thirty years ago it

Originally published as Iris Young (1992), "Breasted experience," pp. 215–30 in Drew Leder (ed.) *The Body in Medical Thought and Practice*, Boston: Kluwer. Reprinted with permission from Kluwer Academic Publishers.

was de rigueur to encase them in wire, rubber, and elastic armor that lifted them and pointed them straight out. Today fashion has loosened up a bit, but the foundational contours remain; some figures are better than others, and the ideal breasts look like a Barbie's.

We experience our objectification as a function of the look of the other, the male gaze that judges and dominates from afar (Bartky 1979; Kaplan 1983, 23–35). We experience our position as established and fixed by a subject who stands afar, who has looked and made his judgment before he ever makes me aware of his admiration or disgust. When a girl blossoms into adolescence and sallies forth, chest out boldly to the world, she experiences herself as being looked at in a different way than before. People, especially boys, notice her breasts or her lack of them; they may stare at her chest and remark on her. If her energy radiates from her chest, she too often finds the rays deflected by the gaze that positions her from outside, evaluating her according to standards that she had no part in establishing and that remain outside her control. She may enjoy the attention and learn to draw the gaze to her bosom with a sense of sexual power. She may loathe and fear the gaze that fixes her in shock or mockery, and she may take pains to hide her chest behind baggy clothes and bowed shoulders. She may for the most part ignore the objectifying gaze, retaining nevertheless edges of ambiguity and uncertainty about her body. The way women respond to the evaluating gaze on their chests is surely as variable as the size and character of the breasts themselves, but few women in our society escape having to take some attitude toward the potentially objectifying regard of the other on her breasts. . . .

Breasts are the most visible sign of a woman's femininity, the signal of her sexuality. In phallocentric culture sexuality is oriented to the man and modeled on male desire. Capitalist, patriarchal, American, media-dominated culture objectifies breasts before a distancing gaze that freezes and masters. The fetishized breasts are valued as objects, things; they must be solid, easy to handle. Subject to the logic of phallocentric domination of nature, their value, her value as a sexual being, appears in their measurement. Is she a B-cup or a C-cup? Even when sleek athletic fashions were current, breasts were often still prominent. And today the news is that the big bosom is back (Anderson 1988; *Wall Street Journal* 1988).

What matters is the look of them, how they measure up before the normalizing gaze. There is one perfect shape and proportion for breasts: round, sitting high on the chest, large but not bulbous, with the look of firmness. The norm is contradictory, of course. If breasts are large, their weight will tend to pull them down; if they are large and round, they will tend to be floppy rather than firm. In its image of the solid object this norm suppresses the fleshy materiality of breasts, this least muscular, softest body part.[1] Magazines construct and parade these perfect breasts. They present tricks for how to acquire and maintain our own—through rigorous exercise or $50 creams (neither of which generally produces the desired effect), or tricks of what to wear and how to stand so as to appear to have them.

Like most norms of femininity, the normalized breast hardly describes an "average" around which real women's breasts cluster. It is an ideal that only a very few women's bodies even approximate; given the power of the dominant media, however, the norm is ubiquitous, and most of us internalize it to some degree, making our self-abnegation almost inevitable (Bartky 1988). Even those women whose breasts do approximate the ideal can do so only for a short period in their lives. It is a pubescent norm from which most women deviate increasingly with each passing year. Whatever her age, if she has given birth her breasts sag away from the ideal; perhaps they have lost some of their prepartum fullness and roundness, and her nipples protrude. Whether a woman is a mother or not, gravity does its work, quickly defining a woman's body as old because it is no longer adolescent. The truly old woman's body thereby moves beyond the pale. Flat, wrinkled, greatly sagging, the old woman's breasts signify for the ageist dominant culture a woman no longer useful for sex or reproduction, a woman used up. Yet there is nothing natural about such a decline in value. Some other cultures venerate the woman with wrinkled, sagging breasts; they are signs of much mothering and the wisdom of experience. From their point of view an obsession with firm, high breasts would be considered to express a desire to be immature (Ayalah and Weinstock 1979, 136).

II. Woman-centered Meaning

However alienated male-dominated culture makes us from our bodies, however much it gives us instruments of self-hatred and oppression, still our bodies are ourselves. We move and act in this flesh and these sinews, and live our pleasures and pains in our bodies. If we love ourselves at all, we love our bodies. And many women identify their breasts as themselves, living their embodied experience at some distance from the hard norms of the magazine gaze. However much the patriarchy may wish us to, we do not live our breasts only as the objects of male desire, but as our own, the sproutings of a specifically female desire.

But phallocentric culture tends not to think of a woman's breasts as hers. Woman is a natural territory; her breasts belong to others—her husband, her lover, her baby. It's hard to imagine a woman's breasts as her own, from her own point of view, to imagine their *value* apart from measurement and exchange. I do not pretend to discover a woman-centered breast experience. My conceptualization of a woman-centered experience of breasts is a construction, an imagining. . . .

From the position of the female subject, what matters most about her breasts is their feeling and sensitivity rather than how they look. The size or age of her breasts does not matter for the sensitivity of her nipples, which often seem to have a will of their own, popping out at the smallest touch, change of temperature, or embarrassment. For many women breasts are a multiple and fluid zone of deep pleasure quite independent of intercourse, though sometimes not independent of orgasm. For a phallic sexuality this is a scandal. A woman does not always experience the feeling of her breasts positively; if they are large she often feels them pulling uncomfortably on her neck and back. Her breasts are also a feeling of bodily change. She often experiences literal growing pains as her body moves from girl to woman. When she becomes pregnant, she often knows this first through changes in the feeling of her breasts, and many women have breast sensitivity associated with menstruation. When she is lactating, she feels the pull of milk letting down, which may be activated by a touch, or a cry, or even a thought.

Breasts stand as a primary badge of sexual specificity, the irreducibility of sexual difference to a common measure. Yet phallocentric sexuality tries to orient the sexual around its one and only sexual object. Active sexuality is the erect penis, which rises in its potency and penetrates the passive female receptacle. Intercourse is the true sex act, and nonphallic pleasures are either deviant or preparatory. Touching and kissing the breasts is "foreplay," a pleasant prelude after which the couple goes on to the real Thing. But in her own experience of sexuality there is a scandal: she can derive the deepest pleasure from these dark points on her chest, a pleasure maybe greater than he can provide in intercourse. Phallocentric heterosexist norms try to construct female sexuality as simply a complement to male sexuality, its mirror, or the hole—a lack that he fills. But her pleasure is different, a pleasure he can only imagine. To the degree that he can experience anything like it, it's only a faint copy of female potency. Imagine constructing the model of sexual power in breasts rather than penises. Men's nipples would have to be constructed as puny copies, just as men have constructed women's clitorides as puny copies of the penis. Of course this all presumes constructing sexuality by a common measure. Phallocentric construction of sexuality denies and represses the sensitivity of breasts.

> For what male "organ" will be set forth in derision like the clitoris?—that penis too tiny for comparison to entail anything but total devaluation, complete decathexization. Of course, there are the breasts. But they are to be classed among the secondary, or so-called secondary, characteristics. Which no doubt justifies the fact that there is so little questioning of the effects of breast atrophy in the male. Wrongly, of course (Irigaray 1985, 22–23).

Both gay men and lesbians often defy this niggardly attitude toward nipple sexuality. Gay men often explore the erotic possibilities of one another's breasts, and lesbians often derive a particular pleasure from the mutual touching of breasts.

The breasts, for many women, are places of independent pleasure. Deconstructing the hierarchical privilege of heterosexual complementarity, giving equal value to feelings of the breast diffuses the identity of sex. Our sex is not one but, as Irigaray says, plural and heterogeneous; we have sex organs all over our bodies, in many places, and perhaps none is privileged. We experience eroticism as flowing, multiple, unlocatable, not identical or in the same place (Irigaray 1985, 23–33).

The brassiere functions partly as a barrier to touch. Without it, every movement can produce a stroking of cloth across her nipples, which she may find pleasurable or distracting, as the case may be. But if the chest is a center of a person's being-in-the-world, her mode of being surely differs depending on whether her chest is open to touch, moving in the world, or confined and bordered.

Without a bra, a woman's breasts are also deobjectified, desubstantialized. Without a bra, most women's breasts do not have the high, hard, pointy look that phallic culture posits as the norm. They droop and sag and gather their bulk at the bottom. Without a bra, the fluid being of breasts is more apparent. They are not objects with one definite shape, but radically change their shape with body position and movements. Hand over the head, lying on one's back or side, bending over in front—all produce very different breast shapes. Many women's breasts are much more like a fluid than a solid; in movement, they sway, jiggle, bounce, ripple even when the movement is small.

Women never gathered in a ritual bra burning, but the image stuck. We did, though, shed the bra—hundreds of thousands, millions of us. I was no feminist when, young and impetuous, I shoved the bras back in the drawer and dared to step outside with nothing on my chest but a shirt. It was an ambiguous time in 1969. I had a wondrous sense of freedom and a little bit of defiance. I never threw the bras away; they were there to be worn on occasions when propriety and delicacy required them. Why is burning the bra the ultimate image of the radical subversion of the male-dominated order?[2] Because unbound breasts show their fluid and changing shape; they do not remain the firm and stable objects that phallocentric fetishism desires. Because unbound breasts make a mockery of the ideal of a "perfect" breast. The bra normalizes the breasts, lifting and curving the breasts to approximate the one and only breast ideal.

But most scandalous of all, without a bra, the nipples show. Nipples are indecent. Cleavage is good—the more, the better—and we can wear bikinis that barely cover the breasts, but the nipples must be carefully obscured. Even go-go dancers wear pasties. Nipples are no-nos, for they show the breasts to be active and independent zones of sensitivity and eroticism.

What would a positive experience of ourselves as breasted be in the absence of the male gaze? There are times and places where women in American society can experience hints of such an experience. In lesbian-dominated women's spaces where women can be confident that the male gaze will not invade, I have found a unique experience of women's bodies. In such women's spaces women frequently walk around, do their chores, sit around and chat naked from the waist up. Such a context deobjectifies the breasts. A woman not used to such a womanspace might at first stare, treating the breasts as objects. But the everydayness, the constant engagement of this bare-breasted body in activity de-reifies them. But they do not thereby recede, as they might when clothed. On the contrary, women's breasts are *interesting.* In a womanspace with many women walking around bare-breasted, the variability and individuality of breasts becomes salient. I would like to say that in a womanspace, without the male gaze, a woman's breasts become almost like part of her face. Like her nose or her mouth, a woman's breasts are distinctive, one sign by which one might recognize her. Like her mouth or her eyes, their aspect changes with her movement and her mood; the movement of her breasts is part of the expressiveness of her body.

III. Motherhood and Sexuality

The woman is young and timeless, clothed in blue, a scarf over her head, which is bowed over the child at her breast, discreetly exposed by her hand that draws aside her covering, and the baby's hand rests on the round flesh. This is the Christian image of peace and wholeness, the perfect circle of generation (Miles 1985). With hundreds of variations, from Florentine frescoes to the cover of dozens of books at B. Dalton's, this is a primary image of power, female power. To be purity and goodness itself, the origin of life, the source to which the living man owes his substance—this is an awesome power. For centuries identification with that power has bonded women to the patriarchal order, and while today its seductive hold on us is loosening, it still provides women a unique position with which to identify (Kristeva 1985; Suleiman 1985).

But it is bought at the cost of sexuality. The Madonna must be a virgin mother. The logic of identity that constructs being as objects also constructs categories whose borders are clear and exclusive: essence/accident, mind/body, good/bad. The logic of such oppositions includes everything, and they exclude one another by defining the other as excluded by their oneness or essence. In Western logic woman is the seat of such oppositional categorization, for patriarchal logic defines an exclusive border between motherhood and sexuality. The virgin or the whore, the pure or the impure, the nurturer or the seducer is either asexual mother or sexualized beauty, but one precludes the other.

Thus psychoanalysis, for example, regards motherhood as a substitute for sexuality. The woman desires a child as her stand-in for the penis, as her way of appropriating the forbidden father. Happily, her desires are passive, and she devotes herself completely to giving. Helene Deutsch (1985), for example, identifies normal motherhood with feminine masochism; the true woman is one who gets pleasure from self-sacrifice, the abnegation of pleasure.

Barbara Sichtermann (1986, 57) discusses this separation of motherhood and sexuality:

> Basically, women were only admitted to the realm of sexuality as guests to be dispatched off towards their "true" vocation as agents of reproduction. And reproduction was something which happened outside the realm of pleasure, it was God's curse on Eve. Women have to cover the longest part of the road to

reproduction with their bodies and yet in this way they became beings existing outside sexuality, outside the delights of orgiastic release, they became asexual mothers, the bearers of unborn children and the bearers of suffering. Breastfeeding too was of course part of this tamed, pleasureless, domesticated world of "maternal duties."

Patriarchy depends on this border between motherhood and sexuality. In our lives and desires it keeps women divided from ourselves, in having to identify with one or another image of womanly power—the nurturing, competent, selfless mother, always sacrificing, the soul of goodness; or the fiery, voluptuous vamp with the power of attraction, leading victims down the road of pleasure, sin, and danger. Why does patriarchy need this division between motherhood and sexuality? This is perhaps one of the most overdetermined dichotomies in our culture; accordingly, I have several answers to this question.

In the terms in which Kristeva (1980) puts it, for both sexes entrance into the symbolic requires repressing the original jouissance of attachment to the mother's body. A baby's body is saturated with feeling, which it experiences as undifferentiated from the caretaking body it touches; repeated pains break the connection, but its pleasure is global and multiple. Eroticism must be made compatible with civilization, submission to the law, and thus adult experience of sexuality must repress memory of this infantile jouissance. Adult meanings of eroticism thus must be divorced from mothers. Even though for both genders, sexual desire and pleasure are informed by presymbolic jouissance, this must be repressed in the particular cultural configuration that emphasizes rationality as unity, identity, thematic reference.

The dichotomy of motherhood and sexuality, I said, maps onto a dichotomy of good/bad, pure/impure. These dichotomies play in with the repression of the body itself. One kind of attachment, love, is "good" because it is entirely defleshed, spiritual. Mother love and the love of the child for the mother represent the perfection of love—eroticism entirely sublimated. Fleshy eroticism, on the other hand, goes on the other side of the border, where lies the despised body, bad, impure. The separation of motherhood and sexuality thus instantiates the culture's denial of the body and the consignment of fleshy desires to fearful temptation.

The incest taboo also accounts for the separation, as even classical Freudianism suggests. Such patriarchal propriety in women's bodies may be unconsciously motivated by a desire to gain control over himself by mastering the mother. But sexual desire for the mother must be repressed in order to prepare the man for separation from femininity and entrance into the male bond through which women are exchanged. As Dinnerstein (1977) suggests, repression of desire for the mother is also necessary to defend his masculinity against the vulnerability and mortality of the human condition.

Now to some explanations more directly related to the interests of patriarchy. By separating motherhood and sexuality men/husbands do not have to perceive themselves as sharing female sexuality with their children. The oedipal triangle has three nodes, and there are issues for the father as well as the child. The Law of the Father establishes ownership of female sexuality. The satisfactions of masculinity are in having her to minister to his ego, the complement to his desire; he has private ownership of her affections (Pateman 1988). Her function either as the phallic object or the mirror to his desire cannot be maintained if her mother love is the same as her sex love. They need to be projected onto different people or thought of as different kinds of relationships.

The separation between motherhood and sexuality within a woman's own existence seems to ensure her dependence on the man for pleasure. If motherhood is sexual, the mother and child can be a circuit of pleasure for the mother, then the man may lose her allegiance and attachment. So she must repress her eroticism with her child, and with it her own particular return to her repressed experience of jouissance, and maintain a specific connection with the man. If she experiences motherhood as sexual, she may find him dispensable. This shows another reason for repressing a connection between motherhood and sexuality in women. A woman's infantile eroticism in relation to her mother must be broken in order to awaken her heterosexual desire. Lesbian mothering may be the ultimate affront to patriarchy, for it involves a double displacement of an erotic relation of a woman to a man.

Without the separation of motherhood and sexuality, finally, there can be no image of a love that is all give and no take. I take this as perhaps the most important point. The ideal mother defines herself as giver and feeder, takes her existence and sense of purpose entirely from giving. Such a mother-giver establishes a foundation for the self-absorbed ego, the subject of modern philosophy, which many feminists have uncovered as being happily male (Schemen 1983; Flax 1983). Thus motherhood must be separated from her sexuality, her desire. She cannot have sexual desire in her mothering because this is a need, a want, and she cannot be perfectly giving if she is wanting or selfish.

In all these ways, then, patriarchy is founded on the border between motherhood and sexuality. Woman is both, essentially—the repository of the body, the flesh that he desires, owns and masters, tames and controls; and the nurturing source of his life and ego. Both are necessary functions, bolstering male ego, which cannot be served if they are together, hence the border, their reification into the hierarchical opposition of good/bad, pure/impure. The separation often splits mothers; it is in our bodies that the sacrifice that creates and sustains patriarchy is re-enacted repeatedly (Ferguson 1983). Freedom for women involves dissolving this separation.

The border between motherhood and sexuality is lived out in the way women experience their breasts and in the cultural marking of breasts. To be understood as sexual, the feeding function of the breasts must be suppressed, and when the breasts are nursing they are desexualized. A great many women in this culture that fetishizes breasts are reluctant to breastfeed because they perceive that they will lose their sexuality. They believe that nursing will alter their breasts and make them ugly and undesirable. They fear that their men will find their milky breasts unattractive or will be jealous of the babies who take their bodies. Some women who decide to breast-feed report that they themselves are uninterested in sex during that period or that they cease to think of their breasts as sexual and to take sexual pleasure in their breasts while they are nursing.[3]

Breasts are a scandal because they shatter the border between motherhood and sexuality. Nipples are taboo because they are quite literally, physically and functionally, *undecidable* in the split between motherhood and sexuality. One of the most subversive things feminism can do is affirm this undecidability of motherhood and sexuality.

When I began nursing I sat stiff in a chair, holding the baby in the crook of my arm, discreetly lifting my shirt and draping it over my breast. This was mother work, and I was efficient and gentle, and watched the time. After some weeks, drowsy during the morning feeding, I went to bed with my baby. I felt that I had crossed a forbidden river as I moved toward the bed, stretched her legs out alongside my reclining torso, me lying on my side like a cat or a mare while my baby suckled. This was pleasure, not work. I lay there as she made love to me, snuggling her legs up to my stomach, her hand stroking my breast, my chest. She lay between me and my lover, and she and I were a couple. From then on I looked forward with happy pleasure to our early-morning intercourse, she sucking at my hard fullness, relieving and warming me, while her father slept.

I do not mean to romanticize motherhood, to suggest by means of a perverted feminist reversal that through motherhood, women achieve their access to the divine or the moral. Nor would I deny that there are dangers in the eroticization of mothering—dangers to children, in particular, that derive from the facts of power more than sexuality. Mothers must not abuse their power, but this has always been so. Certainly I do not wish to suggest that all women should be mothers; there is much that would be trying about mothering even under ideal circumstances, and certainly there is much about it in our society that is oppressive. But in the experience of many women we may find some means for challenging patriarchal divisions that seek to repress and silence those experiences.

Some feminist discourse criticizes the sexual objectification of women and proposes that feminists dissociate women from the fetishized female body and promote instead an image of women as representing caring, nurturing, soothing values. American cultural feminism exhibits this move: women will retreat from, reject patriarchal definitions of sexuality and project motherly images of strength, wisdom, and nurturance as feminist virtues, or even redefine the erotic as like mother love.[4] Much French feminism is also in danger of a mere revaluation that retains this dichotomy between motherhood and sexuality, rather than exploding patriarchal definitions of motherhood (Stanton 1989).

A more radical move would be to shatter the border between motherhood and sexuality. What can this mean? Most concretely, it means pointing to and celebrating breast-feeding as a sexual interaction for both the mother and the infant (Sichtermann 1986). It means letting women speak in public about the pleasure that many report they derive from their babies and about the fact that weaning is often a loss for them (Myers and Siegel 1985). But there is a more general meaning to shattering the border, which applies even to mothers. Crashing the border means affirming that women, all women, can "have it all." It means creating and affirming a kind of love in which a woman does not have to choose between pursuing her own selfish, insatiable desire and giving pleasure and sustenance to another close to her, a nurturance that gives and also takes for itself. Whether they are mothers or not, women today are still too often cast in the nurturant role, whatever their occupation or location. This nurturant position is that of the self-sacrificing listener and stroker, the one who turns toward the wounded, needful ego that uses her as mirror and enclosing womb, giving nothing to her, and she of course is polite enough not to ask. As feminists we should affirm the value of nurturing; an ethic of caring does indeed hold promise for a more human justice, and political values guided by such an ethic would change the character of the public for the better. But we must also insist that nurturers need, that love is partly selfish, and that a woman deserves her own irreducible pleasures.

Notes

I am grateful to Sandra Bartky, Lucy Candib, Drew Leder, and Francine Rainone for helpful comments on an earlier version of this paper. Thanks to Nancy Irons for research help.

Considering the vast explosion of women's studies literature in the past two decades, there is an amazing absence of writing about women's experience of breasts, and some of what little there is does not arise from feminist sensibility. One wants to explain why it is that feminists have not written about breasts, even when there is a great deal of writing about sexuality, mothering, the body, and medical interactions with women's bodies. Why this silence about breasts, especially when, if you tell women you are writing about women's breasted experience, they begin to pour out stories of their feelings about their breasts? Women are interested in talking about their breasted bodies and interested in listening to one another. But we almost never do it conversation, let alone in writing.

In the darkness of my despair about women's own breast censorship, I uncovered a gold mine: Daphna Ayalah and Isaac Weinstock (1979), *Breasts: Women Speak About Their Breasts and Their Lives*. This is a collection of photographs of the breasts, with accompanying experiential accounts, of fifty women. Ayalah and Weinstock asked all the women the same set of questions about growing up, sexuality, aging, birthing and nursing, and so on. Thus while each woman's stories are her own and in her own words, they can be compared. The authors were careful to interview different kinds of women: old, young, and middle aged; women of color as well as white women; women who have and have not had children; lesbians as well as straight women; models; call girls; etc. This is an extraordinary book, and many of the generalizations I make about women's experience in this paper are derived from my reading of it.

1. Susan Bordo (1989) suggests that achievement society takes Western culture's denial of the body and fleshiness to extremes, projecting norms of tightness and hardness for all bodies. This is the particular contemporary cultural meaning of the demand for slenderness in both men and women, but especially women. Bordo does not mention breasts specifically in this discussion, but clearly this analysis helps us understand why media norms of breasts make this impossible demand for a "firm" breast.

2. Susan Brownmiller (1984, 45) suggests that women going braless evoke shock and anger because men implicitly think that they own breasts and that only they should remove bras.

3. Women's attitudes toward breast-feeding and its relation or lack of it to sexuality are, of course, extremely variable. Teenage mothers, for example, have a great deal more difficulty than do older mothers with the idea of breast-feeding, probably because they are more insecure about their sexuality (Yoos 1985). Ayalah and Weinstock (1979) interview many mothers specifically about their attitudes toward and experiences in breast-feeding. The reactions are quite variable, from women who report the experience of breast-feeding as being nearly religious to women who say they could not consider doing it because they thought it was too disgusting.

4. In the feminist sexuality debate, some sexual libertarians accuse those whom they debate of holding a kind of desexualized, spiritualized, or nurturant eroticism. [See Ann Ferguson (1989) for an important discussion of the way out of this debate.] I do not here wish to take sides in this debate, which I hope is more or less over. The debate certainly reveals, however, the strength of a good/bad opposition around eroticism as it plays out in our culture. Ferguson suggests that the debate sets up an opposition between pleasure and love, which is an unhelpful polarity.

References

Anderson, Jeremy Weir. 1988. Breast frenzy. *Self* December:83–89.

Ayalah, Daphna, and Isaac Weinstock. 1979. *Breasts: Women Speak About Their Breasts and Their Lives.* New York: Simon and Schuster.

Bartky, Sandra. 1979. On psychological oppression. In *Philosophy and Women,* edited by Sharon Bishop and Marjorie Weinzweig. Belmont, Calif.: Wadsworth.

———. 1988. Foucault, femininity, and the modernization of patriarchal power. In *Feminism and Foucault: Reflections on Resistance,* edited by Irene Diamond and Lee Quimby. Boston: Northeastern University Press.

Bordo, Susan. 1989. Reading the slender body. In *Body/Politics: Women and the Discourses of Science,* edited by Mary Jacobus, Evelyn Fox Keller, and Sally Shuttleworth. New York: Routledge Chapman and Hall.

Brownmiller, Susan. 1984. *Femininity.* New York: Simon and Schuster.

Deutsch, Helene. 1985. *The Psychology of Women: A Psychoanalytic Interpretation.* Vol. II. New York: Grune & Stratton.

Dinnerstein, Dorothy. 1977. *The Mermaid and the Minotaur: Sexual Arrangements and Human Malaise.* New York: Harper and Row.

Ferguson, Ann. 1983. On conceiving motherhood and sexuality: A feminist materialist approach. In *Mothering: Essays in Feminist Theory,* edited by Joyce Trebilcot. Totowa, N.J.: Rowman and Allenheld.

————. 1989. *Blood at the Root*. London: Pandora Press.

Flax, Jane. 1983. Political philosophy and the patriarchal unconscious: A psycho-analytic perspective on epistemology and metaphysics. In *Discovering Reality: Feminist Perspectives on Epistemology, Metaphysics, Methodology, and Philosophy of Science*, edited by Sandra Harding and Merrill B. Hintikka. Dordrecht, the Netherlands: D. Reidel Publishing.

Irigaray, Luce. 1985. *Speculum of the Other Woman*. Ithaca, N.Y.: Cornell University Press.

Kaplan, E. Ann. 1983. *Women and Film: Both Sides of the Camera*. New York: Methuen.

Kristeva, Julia. 1980. The father, love, and banishment. In *Desire in Language*, edited by Leon S. Roudiez. New York: Columbia University Press.

————. 1985. Sabat Mater. In *The Female Body in Western Culture*, edited by Susan Rubin Suleiman. Cambridge, Mass.: Harvard University Press.

Miles, Margaret R. 1985. The virgin's one bare breast: Female nudity and religious meaning in Tuscan early Renaissance culture. In *The Female Body in Western Culture*, edited by Susan Rubin Suleiman. Cambridge, Mass.: Harvard University Press.

Myers, Harriet H., and Paul S. Siegel. 1985. Motivation to breastfeed: A fit to the opponent-process theory? *Journal of Personality and Social Psychology* 49:188–93.

Pateman, Carole. 1988. *The Sexual Contract*. Stanford, Calif.: Stanford University Press.

Schemen, Naomi. 1983. Individualism and the objects of psychology. In *Discovering Reality: Feminist Perspectives on Epistemology, Metaphysics, Methodology, and Philosophy of Science*, edited by Sandra Harding and Merrill B. Hintikka. Dordrecht, the Netherlands: D. Reidel Publishing.

Sichtermann, Barbara. 1986. The lost eroticism of the breasts. In *Femininity: The Politics of the Personal*. Minneapolis: University of Minnesota Press.

Stanton, Donna. 1989. Difference on trial: A critique of the maternal metaphor in Cixous, Irigaray, and Kristeva. In *The Thinking Muse: Feminism and Modern French Philosophy*, edited by Jeffner Allen and Iris Marion Young. Bloomington: Indiana University Press.

Suleiman, Susan Rubin. 1985. Writing and motherhood. In *The (M)other Tongue: Essays in Feminist Psychoanalytical Interpretation*, edited by Shirley Nelson Garner, Claire Kahane, and Madelon Sprengnether. Ithaca, N.Y.: Cornell University Press.

Wall Street Journal. 1988. Forget hemlines: The bosomy look is big fashion news, 2 December, 1.

Yoos, Lorie. 1985. Developmental issues and the choice of feeding method of adolescent mothers. *Journal of Obstetrical and Gynecological Nursing* 28:68–72.

10

"Perfect People"
Cancer Charities

SHARON BATT

Some readers may be startled to learn that the overall mortality rate from carcinoma of the breast remains static. If one were to believe all the media hype, the triumphalism of the profession in published research, and the almost weekly miracle breakthroughs trumpeted by the cancer charities, one might be surprised that women are dying at all from this cancer.

—EDITORIAL, *LANCET*, FEB. 6, 1993

. . . The period of my cancer treatments was an intensely inward-looking time. I counted the days to the end of my chemotherapy and radiation treatments, and watched my athletic looks give way to pallor, weight gain and ghoulish baldness. I struggled with my fear of death. And I wondered: how could I have been so oblivious to a disease that claims the lives of so many women—5,500 in Canada and 45,000 in the U.S. in 1992; 376,000 worldwide in 1996. Breast cancer claims women at an age considered young in industrialized countries; age 62, compared with age 82 for women who die of cardiovascular disease. Many who die are women like me, who believed themselves healthy, well informed, and somewhere in the mid-region of their life. When I learned these facts, I felt tricked, as if I had stumbled into a chamber of horrors kept secret behind a veil of cheerful platitudes. *Do breast self-exams. Have regular mammograms. See your doctor at the first sign of a lump. Breast cancer can be cured!* I needed to know where these slogans had come from. . . .

Originally published in *Patient No More: The Politics of Breast Cancer* by Sharon Batt, 1994, published by Gynergy books, PO Box 2023, Charlottetown, Prince Edward Island, Canada C1A7N7.

After my diagnosis I became very curious about the [Canadian] Cancer Society. What I had assumed was a worthy organization devoted to aiding people who had cancer took on the appearance of an extremely odd beast which lumbered in incomprehensible ways. As a cancer patient, I was struck most of all by the Society's absence in my time of need. No volunteer had visited me in the hospital. After my surgery, in the long hours of waiting for chemotherapy treatments and check-ups, I sometimes perused the stacks of brochures in the hospital waiting room. Most were published in the U.S. and simply reprinted with a Canadian Cancer Society logo. For the most part they gave the standard advice on breast self-exams and explained the conventional treatments. One that caught my eye was titled "The Woman with Breast Cancer as a Single Woman." I picked it up, wondering why we singles needed our own special leaflet. Inside, a text that would do Ann Landers proud explained that a woman does not have to mention her cancer surgery to a man on a casual first date, but she would want to tell him soon, "if he is someone she cares about."

A few years later, I got another glimpse of the Cancer Society at a meeting of the National Coalition of Cancer Survivors (NCSS) in Denver. I joined the American advocacy group because I wanted to meet others with cancer and no Canadian organization existed to give voice to our concerns. The conference had a slot set aside for networking and a group of about 12 of us with breast cancer squeezed into someone's hotel room to exchange experiences.

Elaine Hill, a slender Black woman in her early 50s, gave a frank account of her frustration with the American Cancer Society. Her first disappointment with the Society had come shortly after her diagnosis. She decided she needed something more than her conversations with doctors, friends and family could provide. "I'd reached the point where I wanted to talk to another woman who had the disease." She called the American Cancer Society in her Tennessee community and explained her situation. The receptionist told her about Reach to Recovery. She could send Elaine a visitor, but she needed a doctor's referral.

Elaine was incredulous. "You mean you don't believe I have breast cancer?" she asked.

"Oh, no," said the receptionist, "You just have to have a doctor's referral."

At that point Elaine was looking for another surgeon. She didn't want the same doctor who had done her biopsy to perform the rest of her surgery and she had no physician who could make the referral. "So I struggled along without another woman to talk with, until I finally pinned down a neighbor and said to her, 'You've lived here all these years, surely you must know *one* woman with breast cancer I can talk to!' "

"And that was my first experience with Reach to Recovery."

I considered Elaine's experience little short of emotional abuse, but it wasn't the first disturbing story I'd heard about Reach to Recovery. Rose Kushner (1986) waged a long battle with the American Cancer Society over its Reach to Recovery program. The problems started in 1974 when Kushner, who was convinced that women who had mastectomies suffered long-term physical and psychological trauma, asked the Society to help her document women's reactions to breast surgery long after the operation. No way, said a Reach to Recovery rep in the ACS' Washington office. Kushner's idea ran counter to the whole philosophy of Reach to Recovery, namely, "to convince women they do not have a disabling handicap." When setting up the program, the Cancer Society had explicitly rejected the idea of a "mastectomy club" although such long-term support groups exist for people who have had bowel, bladder and larynx operations. "Having a mastectomy is not a permanent handicap," the woman informed Kushner, "and even the worst of scars can be hidden by a well-fitting prosthesis and the right clothes. So we decided we would help the woman for just a few weeks and then leave her to her own psychological recovery" (Kushner 1986, 314–15).

This made no sense to Kushner. "What good was a 'recovery' program that left women stranded after a hospital visit and a few weeks of telephone service?" she asked. Her own mastectomy, although expertly done and not a radical, left her numb for five months in the area around the incision, and so tender in other places that "any fondling from the waist up was simply out of the question." Anywhere near the left arm was "strictly no touch." And a day of Caribbean sun left her with a temporary case of lymphedema— her arm "began to develop strange swollen curves and to twist and grind" (Kushner 1986, 325). As for her psychological adjustment, she firmly believed for several years that she had no hang-ups about being one-breasted, until a fire in a hotel where she was staying forced her to admit that she could not venture out in public looking lopsided, even if her life was in danger.

I had also read an essay by the poet Audre Lorde (1980) about her encounter with a Reach to Recovery volunteer. Lorde felt "outraged and insulted" after the woman's visit to her hospital room, and "even more isolated than before." The volunteer, says Lorde, was "quite admirable and even impressive in her own right." But she did not speak to Lorde's concerns, which were not about "what man I could capture in the future, much less whether my two children would be embarrassed by me in front of their friends." Lorde's questions had to do with her chances of survival, the effects of a possibly shortened life upon her work and her priorities, whether the cancer could have been prevented, and how she could keep it from recurring. As a 44-year-old Black lesbian feminist, she did not expect the woman to be a role model but she did attempt to discuss with her the task of integrating the experience into the whole of her life. The woman glossed over her questions, chided her for not looking "on the bright side of things," and gave her a lambswool puff to fill out her bra.

The volunteer's response gathered resonance when Lorde went to her doctor's office 10 days later. This was her first trip out since coming home from the hospital and she had groomed and dressed herself very carefully. She felt beautiful and glad to be alive. She was surprised when the nurse, rather than complimenting her on how well she looked, remarked instead ("a little anxiously and not at all like a question") that she was not wearing a prosthesis. "No," said Lorde, "it doesn't really feel right."

The nurse, usually sympathetic, continued to press the point. Even if the temporary prosthesis didn't look exactly right, it was "better than nothing" and would do until she was ready for a "real form." She informed Lorde that she would "feel so much better with it on" and that they really would like her to wear something when she came for her appointments, "otherwise it's bad for the morale of the office" (Lorde 1980, 59). Lorde was outraged by this "assault on my right to define and to claim my own body."

In a newspaper article, I'd read about a Canadian Cancer Society volunteer named Darlene Betteley in Waterloo, Ontario. Darlene's story was so odd I made a detour to her modest bungalow in the community outside Toronto, to hear her full account.

After Betteley's cancer diagnosis in 1986, she had both breasts removed. A few years later, she became a Reach to Recovery volunteer. When one of the convenors (the woman who matches visitors with patients) discovered that Betteley did not wear breast prostheses, Betteley was advised that she would have to get a bustline or give up her visits. "We like our volunteers to look normal," the convenor explained.

Betteley has all the letters and newspaper clippings from the dispute neatly organized in a big blue binder. The opening page has two full-length, color photos of her, standing erect in her back yard–Before and After Surgery. "Now I ask you, Sharon," she prompts me, "Do I look normal?"

An unlikely rebel, Betteley is in her mid-50s, a mother of grown children and a devout believer. She loved making hospital visits. She enjoys people and when she recovered from her two operations she was so happy to be alive that she wanted to share her zest for life with others. She had modeled as a teenager and she still loves clothes. She took pride in her ability to dress becomingly after the two mastectomies. She had been a Reach to Recovery volunteer for over a year when her convenor, who knew she didn't wear a prosthesis, called her to "talk things over." It happened that the head convenor for Ontario had called the local convenor in search of a suitable visitor for a woman who was having a double prophylactic mastectomy. Darlene's name was suggested. Did she wear a prosthesis? the Ontario convenor wanted to know.

"No."

"Well," the provincial convenor said, "we like our volunteers to look normal."

The local convenor, a woman Betteley knew well, presented her with the senior convenor's verdict. Faced with the prospect of losing her volunteer status, Betteley almost capitulated, but something in her rose up in protest. "Why should I have to go against something I really believe?" she asked. "I am happy with myself. You have to like yourself before you can share your happiness and your love with other people."

In that case, the convenor said, Betteley could no longer make hospital visits.

"Well, there were tears and there was anger," explained Betteley, "because visiting was very important to me." She began asking questions that had never occurred to her before. "I thought, 'Does the Cancer Society have anything to do with all these companies that make prostheses? And what do they do with the money they raise?'" Betteley's daughter Cathy was particularly incensed by her mother's dismissal. Cathy worked as a personnel officer and she urged her mother to complain to the Human Rights Commission. Betteley demurred. She would rather put the whole thing behind her. "There'll be another door opening," she said, with her characteristic aplomb.

Cathy wrote a letter to the chairman of the volunteer unit at the local Cancer Society office. Betteley also wrote to the Society, explaining that "after discussions with my doctor and my husband, I decided, for my own physical comfort, not to wear a prosthesis." Cathy sent yet another letter to the editor of the local newspaper and the paper decided to run a story. At a nearby university, a sociology student was so indignant when he read the article, he fired off letters to every major newspaper in the country. The first to pick up on it was the *Globe and Mail* (MacLeod 1990). By now, Betteley had lost her reticence about speaking out. A male volunteer, she pointed out in the front page story, "is not required to shove a golf ball down his pants before meeting people." The policy, she said, was sexist ("a word I didn't even have in my vocabulary until these students brought it to mind"). "I'm wondering how many men sit on the board of the Cancer Society who need to see a woman with a bustline," she told the reporter. The *Globe and Mail* story opened the media floodgates. First the *Toronto Star* phoned for an interview, then a Florida tabloid, which ran its version of the story under the headline, "Whatta Bunch of Boobs!" The same day, reporters from her local TV station crowded into her small living room with lights and cameras while another TV crew waited in the driveway to get in. Next Betteley guested on a noon hour radio phone-in program from Montreal. "It was awesome," she recalls.

The Canadian Cancer Society's public response did little to shed light on the organization's thinking. "There is a lot of misinformation and confusion about our policy," said the local convenor, Maryann Istiloglu. "Women who are about to undergo breast surgery, or who have just had the procedure, don't want to be reminded of how they are going to end up looking," she said (MacLeod 1990). Mark Sikich, co-chairman of patient services for Betteley's local unit, explained that breast cancer patients are usually emotional after surgery. "Most patients are very concerned with body image and looking so-called normal. It's best to send someone in wearing a prosthesis." An Ontario representative said that since one aspect of a volunteer's visit was to provide a temporary prosthesis, and information about purchasing a permanent prosthesis, "To be not wearing a prosthesis herself would appear to be a contradiction of the message she is bringing." Not all Society personnel agreed. One said the policy made her angry and she would never enforce it (Mironowicz 1990). Most of the eight volunteers working for the Society's Kitchener-Waterloo office resigned after the incident.

Wear casual clothes. Must be well-fitted over the bustline. Darlene Betteley points to the offending line in the handbook she was given when she was trained as a Canadian Cancer Society volunteer. In later editions the grooming instructions were changed (*Be nicely groomed and dressed. Don't wear heavy cologne or jangly jewelry*) but the policy stood as an unwritten rule, at least in the minds of some Cancer Society officials. Other rules circumscribe the volunteer's scope for discussion. "*Never* give medical advice or interfere with the patient's relationship with the doctor," says one; "Do not be persuaded to show your scar, or look at the scar of the person you are visiting," instructs another. Among the qualifications for volunteers is "a positive attitude toward conventional treatment methods." As well, the volunteer "does not promote unconventional therapies." . . .

Elaine Hill's second experience with the Cancer Society in Tennessee was a variation on the same theme. Elaine's surgery left her with lymphedema ("milk-arm"), a permanent and debilitating result of breast surgery which is not uncommon. Both surgery and radiation can damage the circulatory system of lymph fluid in the arm so that the fluid flows down the arm but not up. One result is a lowered resistance to infection in that arm; another is swelling which can be extremely painful and impair movement. An elastic post-mastectomy sleeve is one method of damage-control, while severe cases may require a lymphedema pump.

Elaine wears a lymphedema sleeve. When I met her in Denver, she described a rejection not unlike Darlene Betteley's. People at the local branch of the ACS knew that Elaine had worked as a social worker and approached her about working as a Reach to Recovery visitor. She agreed, she says, "because I thought it was a very good thing."

Shortly before the training session started, Elaine developed lymphedema. She decided she should let the Cancer Society know about this development before the training started. "In the back of my mind," she says, "I guess I thought they would say, 'well gee, you're so great, come on and do it anyway.' Instead, they said they would get back to me." Three weeks passed without a word, so Elaine called the office. "After hemming and hawing," Elaine recalls, "the lady told me that they couldn't use me because of the sleeve. They needed 'perfect people,' people with no sign of cancer to go to talk to the women. That was their policy."

"Well, lymphedema *is* a common side effect of breast cancer surgery," Elaine responded. The woman wouldn't bite on that one, but suggested perhaps Elaine could take off the sleeve, or come in when the lymphedema got better. "I have no real hope that I can ever go without the sleeve," Elaine told her, "and I can't do exercises without the sleeve on."

Elaine didn't let on how hurt she felt (personal interview, Jan. 4, 1992). "I assured them I had no hard feelings—though I really did feel badly. I said, 'I understand, I certainly don't want to frighten anyone or raise their anxiety level.'" In fact, she felt rejected. "First I had surgery, then three months later they found cancer in the other breast so I had surgery again.

This seemed like another knock in the face—and from the American Cancer Society!"

Far from overhauling its "get-on-with-it" view of breast cancer recovery, in recent years the American Cancer Society has redefined the cosmetic problem. In 1988, the ACS launched a new initiative called Look Good, Feel Better (LGFB), in collaboration with a charitable foundation set up by cosmetics manufacturers and people employed in the beauty industry. Women having treatment are now invited to come to their local hospital for a group makeover "workshop" where they receive tips on beauty techniques and a package of free cosmetics. The idea caught fire in the U.S., spread to Australia, and soon had its copycat program in Canada, sponsored by the Canadian Cancer Society and a similar consortium from the beauty industry. . . .

The PR and marketing appeal of LGFB for the beauty industry is fairly straightforward, but the gusto with which medical professionals have taken up the cause of makeup for cancer patients warrants scrutiny. Oncology is, after all, the same specialty that rains skepticism on meditation, visualization, support groups, and other "soft" feel-good adjuncts to medical treatment. Yet in no time, with funding from the cosmetic industry's Foundation, Yale University's Comprehensive Cancer Center undertook a two-year study "to evaluate the effectiveness of Look Good, Feel Better on quality of life for women breast cancer patients undergoing chemotherapy treatment" (Aarsteinsen 1993).

The intense romance between medical experts and cosmeticians is less bizarre than it seems at first glance. The same magnet that pulled surgeons to Reach to Recovery now has oncologists stuck on Look Good, Feel Better. In the days of the Halsted radical, surgeons used to worry that terror of surgical mutilation would keep women from having a lump investigated. Bedside visits by "perfect people," they hoped, would soothe fears about surgery. These fears were firmly rooted in reality—the operation was sexually devastating, often causing permanent physical disability and frequently failing to arrest the disease—but that was of no matter. Reach to Recovery was tailored precisely to deflect these fears, not to meet the woman's deep emotional needs. Part of Reach to Recovery's current crisis stems from the fact that the Cancer Society can't figure out how to adapt the program to women who look no different after surgery than before.

Enter Look Good, Feel Better. The treatment that most often affects a breast cancer patient's appearance today is chemotherapy. Now it's the oncologist who frets that a patient might not show up for her appointment. Chemotherapy's most dramatic effect is hair loss, but the circulating poisons can also cause weight loss or weight gain and turn glowing skin into a splotchy mess. In the early stages of the disease, when most women are diagnosed, the illness itself is much less likely to affect the woman's appearance than are the treatments. Radiation, which is standard therapy after breast-conserving therapy, has some of the same effects on one's looks. Reach to Recovery gained entrée as a Cancer Society program in the late 1960s, just when the Halsted radical was going down for the last count. Now, with chem cocktails on the ropes, makeup companies are welcomed in many leading cancer centers. . . .

The Canadian Cancer Society has scheduled a review of its Reach to Recovery program for 1994, an exercise that the American Cancer Society completed two years ago. As a chance to overhaul the Society's signature service to women with breast cancer, the ACS review was an opportunity missed. The report acknowledges that the service has problems, that it needs to be updated and strengthened, but the focus of change is to align the service with the "new medical technology" in treating breast cancer. The phase-out of the radical mastectomy and the increasing number of women now having lumpectomies with radiation plus chemotherapy means that women now spend less time in the hospital and their treatment experience differs from that of the older cohort of volunteers, explains the report. Increasing cultural heterogeneity (or awareness of its importance) gets a nod and the surgeon-referral system is recognized as passé. Self-referrals and referrals by social workers and nurses are discussed as valuable ways of linking women with volunteers (Kreuter 1992, 15–16).

Nowhere does the report address the fundamental criticism that Reach to Recovery falsifies the breast cancer experience by packaging it as a cosmetic mishap, only slightly more serious than a broken fingernail. The emotional support function of Reach to Recovery, says the report, comes from the patient "interacting with a woman who has experienced what she has experienced and survived as a fully functional person," and the expected benefit is that the woman "will feel supported and will respond with hope and courage to get on with her life" (Kreuter 1992, 28). Look Good, Feel Better, like big sister Reach to Recovery, makes a fetish of looking "normal." When you are having chemotherapy treatments, sallow skin, a bald head, and facial puffiness are as normal as a flat chest after a double mastectomy. Rather than put on makeup, a woman might well prefer to stay home and sleep. Or she may want to halt her treatments.

When your life is at risk, playacting that you are well exacts an emotional price. It creates barriers of communication between the woman with cancer and those she loves. Attempting to look "beautiful," "normal," or "perfect" drains money from our bank accounts at a time when we may be unable to work. Most important, these tricks to keep surgery and baldness secret make us invisible to each other and to society at large. Astonishingly, it took activists speaking out in large numbers to alert the North American public that the "advances" of modern medicine have not lowered the death rate of women in our most prosperous societies from breast cancer. Women, and the public at large, had swallowed the lie that breast cancer is a piffling disease, easily treated and relegated to one's past.

Naomi Wolf (1991, 12–13) argues that the idea of an objective quality called "beauty" is a myth that is not about women at all. "It is about men's institutions and institutional power." The experiences of Audre Lorde, Darlene Betteley, Rose Kushner, and Elaine Hill illustrate how the beauty myth is used against women with cancer to reinforce the power of the institutions of medicine and medical technology. Inner confidence in her own beauty allowed each woman to buck the coercion. Rather than conforming to the norm of silence, they spoke out. The same assurance permits a growing number of women, like Ellen Hobbs, to live with breast cancer on their own terms, and to challenge these oppressive institutions.

The changes in my appearance when I was having cancer treatments affected me in a way that was not trivial. My altered appearance was an integral part of a profound change in my life. Just after my diagnosis, I recall glimpsing myself in the washroom mirror at the office and observing a woman with disheveled hair and wild eyes. The Madwoman of Shallot, I thought with a shock . . . and I continued out into the office without bothering to comb my hair. I was a madwoman at that moment and if it bothered my co-workers, so be it. As the months wore on, I lost my hair and became increasingly fatigued. When my friend Jeannie commented that I looked tired, I snapped in anger that I was not at all tired, I'd just been to the gym. Later I admitted to myself that her remark, meant caringly, was extremely threatening. Maybe the treatments weren't doing me any good. Maybe I was dying. My appearance was an imperfect barometer to my prospects of recovery but it was more real to me than a blood test. I also remember shocks of pleasure, like examining the contours of my bald head in the mirror and marveling at its shapeliness. These experiences, and many more, were part of reconciling myself to the changed person I was—no longer a woman whose health was "perfect."

The beauty myth subverts women's power, says Naomi Wolf (1991, 46). A woman with cancer who confronts the world with her baldness or breastlessness has tremendous power to effect change. Audre Lorde captured this in her oft-quoted image, "What would happen if an army of one-breasted women descended upon Congress and demanded that the use of carcinogenic fat-stored hormones in beef-fed cattle be outlawed?" Gradually women with cancer are beginning to harness the power Lorde held out to us. Artist Matushka used it when she revealed her mastectomy scar on the cover of the *New York Times Magazine* (August 15, 1993). With one unforgettable image, she obliterated the pretense that women look "normal" after breast surgery.

Seeing my own photo, hairless, in the newspaper gave me strength. I had faced my own human vulnerability and exposed my tenuous grip on life to others. I felt the power of my act when I arrived for a doctor's appointment and learned that a nurse had posted the article in the staff room. Again, when a stranger who heard me say my name in the post office accosted me to tell me that she had given my article to a newly diagnosed friend. And once more when a shy woman approached me at a public meeting holding the crumpled three-year-old clipping in which I had voiced her own feelings.

"There is nothing wrong, per se, with the use of prostheses, if they can be chosen freely for whatever reason after a woman has had a chance to accept her new body," says Audre Lorde (1980, 63). Nor is there any reason why a woman with cancer shouldn't wear makeup or a wig. I know women who thoroughly enjoyed a Look Good, Feel Better session, who were happy to have a free bag of expensive cosmetics to take home. (Not the least of their pleasure came from the opportunity to meet with other women with cancer.) But the intense promotion of prostheses and cosmetics, coupled with the coercive tactics used on those who eschew them, signal that these accessories are not really meant for our benefit.

The myth that medical treatments transform women with breast cancer back into "perfect people" nurtures a dependence on the medical profession and related technologies. We turn their inadequacies against ourselves, believing that if we die of the disease, it is because we failed to do breast self-exams the "right" way; or we didn't have mammograms often or soon enough; or our uncooperative bodies "failed to respond to treatment." If each woman with breast cancer understood medicine's limited ability to control the disease, our reliance on physicians, tests, and medical interventions would be enormously reduced. The power of these institutions over us would dwindle accordingly. Without the Rosy Filter, women with breast cancer would gain the right to map our own futures, within the very real constraints imposed by a life-threatening disease.

References

Aarsteinsen, Barbara. Oct. 1993. Don't make do . . . make up: The Look Good, Feel Better Program. *Chatelaine*.

Kreuter, Marshall W., Marsha Hearn, and Matthew W. Kreuter. 1992. *A National Assessment of Reach to Recovery: A Report to the Nursing and Patients Services Department*. Atlanta, GA: American Cancer Society.

Kushner, Rose. 1986. *Alternatives: New Developments in the War on Breast Cancer*. New York: Warner.

Lorde, Audre. 1980. *The Cancer Journals*. San Francisco: Spinsters Ink.

MacLeod, Robert. 1990. Cancer society aide attacks 'sexist' policy. *Globe and Mail*, Dec. 6, p. A1.

Mironowicz, Margaret. 1990. Ex-cancer patient is eager to share gained confidence. *Kitchener-Waterloo Record*, Aug. 24, p. C1.

Wolf, Naomi. 1991. *The Beauty Myth*. Toronto: Vintage.

11

Women and the Knife
Cosmetic Surgery and the Colonization of Women's Bodies

KATHRYN PAULY MORGAN

Introduction

Consider the following passages:

> If you want to wear a Maidenform Viking Queen bra like Madonna, be warned: A body like this doesn't just happen. . . . Madonna's kind of fitness training takes time. The rock star *whose muscled body was recently on tour* spends a minimum of three hours a day working out (*Toronto Star* 1990d; emphasis added).

> A lot of the contestants [in the Miss America Pageant] do not owe their beauty to their Maker but to their Re-Maker. Miss Florida's nose came courtesy of her surgeon. So did Miss Alaska's. And Miss Oregon's breasts came from the manufacturers of silicone (Goodman 1989).

> Jacobs [a plastic surgeon in Manhattan] constantly answers the call for cleavage. "Women need it for their holiday ball gowns" (*Sheboygan Press* 1985).

> We hadn't seen or heard from each other for twenty-eight years. . . . Then he suggested it would be nice if we could meet. I was very nervous about it. How much had I changed? I wanted a facelift, tummy tuck and liposuction, all in one week. (A woman, age forty-nine, being interviewed for an article on "older couples" falling in love; *Toronto Star* 1990c).

> "It's hard to say why one person will have cosmetic surgery done and another won't consider it, but generally I think people who go for surgery are more

Originally published as Kathryn Pauly Morgan. 1991. "Women and the knife: Cosmetic surgery and the colonization of women's bodies." *Hypatia* 6(3):25–53. Kathryn Pauly Morgan.

aggressive, they are the doers of the world. It's like make up. You see some women who might be greatly improved by wearing make up, but they're, I don't know, granola-heads or something, and they just refuse." (Dr. Ronald Levine, director of plastic surgery education at the University of Toronto and vice-chairman of the plastic surgery section of the Ontario Medical Association; *Toronto Star* 1990a).

Another comparable limitation [of the women's liberation movement] is a tendency to reject certain good things only in order to punish men. . . . There is no reason why a women's liberation activist should not try to look pretty and attractive (Markovic 1976).

Now look at the needles and at the knives (Figure 1). Look at them carefully. Look at them for a long time. *Imagine them cutting into your skin.* Imagine that you have been given this surgery as a gift from your loved one who read a persuasive and engaging press release from Drs. John and Jim Williams that ends by saying "The next morning the limo will chauffeur your loved one back home again, with a gift of beauty that will last a lifetime" (Williams and Williams, 1990). Imagine the beauty that you have been promised. . . .

We need a feminist analysis to understand why actual, live women are reduced and reduce themselves to "potential women" and choose to participate in anatomizing and fetishizing their bodies as they buy "contoured bodies," "restored youth," and "permanent beauty." In the face of a growing market and demand for surgical interventions in women's bodies that can and do result in infection, bleeding, embolisms, pulmonary edema, facial nerve injury, unfavorable scar formation, skin loss, blindness, crippling, and death, our silence becomes a culpable one. . . .

Not only is elective cosmetic surgery moving out of the domain of the sleazy, the suspicious, the secretively deviant, or the pathologically narcissistic, it is *becoming the norm.* This shift is leading to a predictable inversion of the domains of the deviant and the pathological, so that women who contemplate *not using* cosmetic surgery will increasingly be stigmatized and seen as deviant. . . .

Cosmetic surgery entails the ultimate envelopment of the lived temporal *reality* of the human subject by technologically created appearances that are then regarded as "the real." Youthful appearance triumphs over aged reality.

I. "Just the Facts in America, Ma'am"

As of 1990, the most frequently performed kind of cosmetic surgery is liposuction, which involves sucking fat cells out from underneath our skin with a vacuum device. This is viewed as the most suitable procedure for removing specific bulges around the hips, thighs, belly, buttocks, or chin. It is most appropriately done on thin people who want to get rid of certain bulges, and surgeons guarantee that even if there is weight gain, the bulges won't reappear since the fat cells have been permanently removed. At least twelve deaths are known to have resulted from complications such as hemorrhages and embolisms. "All we know is there was a complication and that complication

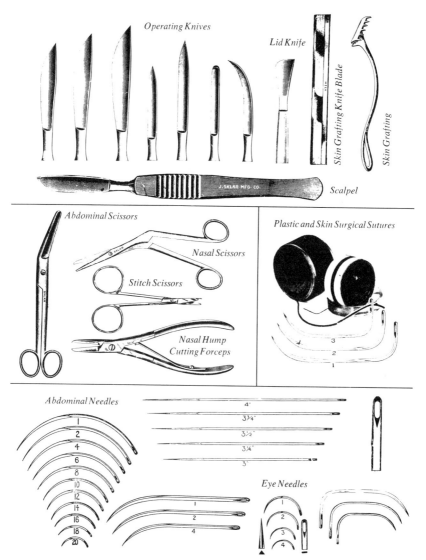

Figure 1

was death," said the partner of Toni Sullivan, age forty-three ("hardworking mother of two teenage children" says the press; *Toronto Star* 1989b). Cost: $1,000-$7,500.

The second most frequently performed kind of cosmetic surgery is breast augmentation, which involves an implant, usually of silicone. Often the silicone implant hardens over time and must be removed surgically. Over one million women in the United States are known to have had breast augmentation surgery. Two recent studies have shown that breast implants block X-rays and cast a shadow on surrounding tissue, making mammograms difficult to interpret, and that there appears to be a much higher incidence of cancerous lumps in "augmented women" (*Toronto Star* 1988). Cost: $1,500-$3,000.

"Facelift" is a kind of umbrella term that covers several sorts of procedures. In a recent Toronto case, Dale Curtis "decided to get a facelift for her fortieth birthday. . . . Bederman used liposuction on the jowls and neck, removed the skin and fat from her upper and lower lids and tightened up the muscles in the neck and cheeks. . . . 'She was supposed to get a forehead lift but she chickened out,' Bederman says" (*Toronto Star* 1989a). Clients are now being advised to begin their facelifts in their early forties and are also told that they will need subsequent facelifts every five to fifteen years. Cost: $2,500-$10,500.

"Nips" and "tucks" are cute, camouflaging labels used to refer to surgical reduction performed on any of the following areas of the body: hips, buttocks, thighs, belly, and breasts. They involve cutting out wedges of skin and fat and sewing up the two sides. These are major surgical procedures that cannot be performed in out-patient clinics because of the need for anaesthesia and the severity of possible post-operative complications. Hence, they require access to costly operating rooms and services in hospitals or clinics. Cost: $3,000-$7,000.

The number of "rhinoplasties," or nose jobs, has risen by 34 percent since 1981. Some clients are coming in for second and third nose jobs. Nose jobs involve either the inserting of a piece of bone taken from elsewhere in the body or the whittling down of the nose. Various styles of noses go in and out of fashion, and various cosmetic surgeons describe the noses they create in terms of their own surnames, such as "the Diamond nose" or "the Goldman nose" (*Sheboygan Press* 1985). Cost: $2,000-$3,000.

More recent types of cosmetic surgery, such as the use of skin-expanders and suction lipectomy, involve inserting tools, probes, and balloons under the skin either for purposes of expansion or reduction (Hirshson 1987).

Lest one think that women (who represent between 60 and 70 percent of all cosmetic surgery patients) choose only one of these procedures, heed the words of Dr. Michael Jon Bederman of the Center for Cosmetic Surgery in Toronto:

> We see working girls, dental technicians, middle-class women who are unhappy with their looks or are aging prematurely. And we see executives—both male and female. . . . Where before someone would have a tummy tuck and not have anything else done for a year, frequently we will do liposuction and tummy tuck and then the next day a facelift, upper and lower lids, rhinoplasty and *other things*. The recovery time is the same whether a person has one procedure or *the works*, generally about two weeks (*Toronto Star* 1989a; emphasis added).

In principle, there is no area of the body that is not accessible to the interventions and metamorphoses performed by cosmetic surgeons intent on creating twentieth century versions of "femina perfecta."

II. From Artifice to Artifact: The Creation of Robo Woman?

[Today, what] is designated "the natural" functions primarily as a frontier rather than as a barrier. While genetics, human sexuality, reproductive outcome, and death were previously regarded as open to variation primarily in evolutionary terms, they are now seen by biotechnologists as domains of creation and control. Cosmetic surgeons claim a role here too. For them, human bodies are the locus of challenge. As one plastic surgeon remarks:

> Patients sometimes misunderstand the nature of cosmetic surgery. It's not a shortcut for diet or exercise. *It's a way to override the genetic code* (*Toronto Star* 1990b; emphasis added).

. . . Practices of coercion and domination are often camouflaged by practical rhetorical and supporting theories that appear to be benevolent, therapeutic, and voluntaristic. Previously, for example, colonizing was often done in the name of bringing "civilization" through culture and morals to "primitive, barbaric people," but contemporary colonizers mask their exploitation of "raw materials and human labor" in the name of "development."

The beauty culture is coming to be dominated by a variety of experts, and consumers of youth and beauty are likely to find themselves dependent not only on cosmetic surgeons but on anesthetists, nurses, aestheticians, nail technicians, manicurists, dietitians, hairstylists, cosmetologists, masseuses, aroma therapists, trainers, pedicurists, electrolysists, pharmacologists, and dermatologists. All these experts provide services that can be bought; all these experts are perceived as administering and transforming the human body into an increasingly artificial and ever more perfect object. . . .

For virtually all women as women, success is defined in terms of interlocking patterns of compulsion: compulsory attractiveness, compulsory motherhood, and compulsory heterosexuality, patterns that determine the legitimate limits of attraction and motherhood.[1] Rather than aspiring to self-determined and woman-centered ideals of health or integrity, women's attractiveness is defined as attractive-to-men; women's eroticism is defined as either nonexistent, pathological, or peripheral when it is not directed to phallic goals; and motherhood is defined in terms of legally sanctioned and constrained reproductive service to particular men and to institutions such as the nation, the race, the owner, and the class—institutions that are, more often than not, male-dominated. Biotechnology is now making beauty, fertility, the appearance of heterosexuality through surgery, and the appearance of youthfulness accessible to virtually all women who can afford that technology—and growing numbers of women are making other sacrifices in their lives in order to buy access to the technical expertise.

In Western industrialized societies, women have also become increasingly socialized into an acceptance of technical knives. We know about knives that can heal: the knife that saves the life of a baby in distress, the knife that cuts out the cancerous growths in our breasts, the knife that straightens our spines, the knife that liberates our arthritic fingers so that we may once again gesture, once again touch, once again hold. But we also know about other knives: the knife that cuts off our toes so that our feet will fit into elegant shoes, the knife that cuts out ribs to fit our bodies into corsets, the knife that slices through our labia in episiotomies and other forms of genital mutilation, the knife that cuts into our abdomens to remove our ovaries to cure our "deviant tendencies" (Barker-Benfield 1976), the knife that removes our breasts in prophylactic or unnecessary radical mastectomies, the knife that cuts out our "useless bag" (the womb) if we're the wrong color and poor or if we've "outlived our fertility," the knife that makes the "bikini cut" across our pregnant bellies to facilitate the cesarean section that will allow the obstetrician to go on holiday. We know these knives well.

And now we are coming to know the knives and needles of the cosmetic surgeons—the knives that promise to sculpt our bodies, to restore our youth, to create beauty out of what was ugly and ordinary. What kind of knives are these? Magic knives. Magic knives in a patriarchal context. Magic knives in a Eurocentric context. Magic knives in a white supremacist context. What do they mean? I am afraid of these knives.

III. Listening to the Women

In order to give a feminist reading of any ethical situation we must listen to the women's own reasons for their actions (Sherwin 1984–85, 1989). It is only once we have listened to the voices of women who have elected to undergo cosmetic surgery that we can try to assess the extent to which the conditions for genuine choice have been met and look at the consequences of these choices for the position of women. Here are some of those voices:

Voice 1 (*a woman looking forward to attending a prestigious charity ball*): "There will be a lot of new faces at the Brazilian Ball" (*Toronto Star* 1989a). [Class/status symbol]

Voice 2 "You can keep yourself trim. . . . But you have no control over the way you wrinkle, or the fat on your hips, or the skin of your lower abdomen. If you are *hereditarily predestined* to stretch out or wrinkle in your face, you will. If your parents had puffy eyelids and saggy jowls, you're going to have puffy eyelids and saggy jowls" (*Toronto Star* 1989a). [Regaining a sense of control; liberation from parents; transcending hereditary predestination]

Voice 3 "Now we want a nose that makes a statement, with tip definition and a strong bridge line" (*Toronto Star* 1989a). [Domination; strength]

Voice 4 "I decided to get a facelift for my fortieth birthday after ten years of living and working in the tropics had taken its toll" (*Toronto Star* 1989a). [Gift to the self; erasure of a decade of hard work and exposure]

Voice 5 "I've gotten my breasts augmented. I can use it as a tax write-off" (*Toronto Star* 1989a). [Professional advancement; economic benefits]

Voice 6 "I'm a teacher and kids let schoolteachers know how we look and they aren't nice about it. A teacher who looks like an old bat or has a big nose will get a nickname" (*Toronto Star* 1990b). [Avoidance of cruelty; avoidance of ageist bias]

Voice 7 "I'll admit to a boob job." (Susan Akin, Miss America of 1986 quoted in Goodman 1989). [Prestige; status; competitive accomplishments in beauty contest]

Voice 8 (*forty-five-year-old grandmother and proprietor of a business*): "In my business, the customers expect you to look as good as they do" (Hirschson 1987). [Business asset; economic gain; possible denial of grandmother status]

Voice 9 "People in business see something like this as showing an overall aggressiveness and go-forwardness. *The trend is to, you know, be all that you can be*" (*Sheboygan Press* 1985). [Success; personal fulfillment]

Voice 10: (*paraphrase*): "I do it to fight holiday depression" (*Sheboygan Press* 1985). [Emotional control; happiness]

Voice 11: "I came to see Dr. X for the holiday season. I have important business parties, and the man I'm trying to get to marry me is coming in from Paris" (*Sheboygan Press* 1985). [Economic gain; heterosexual affiliation]

Women have traditionally regarded (and been taught to regard) their bodies, particularly if they are young, beautiful, and fertile, *as a locus of power* to be enhanced through artifice and, now, through artifact. In 1792, in *A Vindication of the Rights of Woman*, Mary Wollstonecraft remarked: "Taught from infancy that beauty is woman's scepter, the mind shapes itself to the body and roaming round its gilt cage, only seeks to adorn its prison." How ironic that the mother of the creator of *Frankenstein* should be the source of that quote. We need to ask ourselves whether today, involved as we are in the modern inversion of "our bodies shaping themselves to our minds," we are creating a new species of woman-monster with new artifactual bodies that function as prisons or whether cosmetic surgery for women does represent a potentially liberating field of choice.

When Snow White's stepmother asks the mirror, "Who is fairest of all?" she is not asking simply an empirical question. In wanting to continue to be "the fairest of all," she is striving, in a clearly competitive context, for a prize, for a position, for power. The affirmation of her beauty brings with it privileged heterosexual affiliation, privileged access to forms of power unavailable to the plain, the ugly, the aged, and the barren.

The Voices are seductive—they speak the language of gaining access to transcendence, achievement, liberation, and power. And they speak to a kind of reality. First, electing to undergo the surgery necessary to create youth and beauty artificially not only appears to but often actually does give a woman a sense of identity that, to some extent, she has chosen herself. Second, it offers her the potential to raise her status both socially and economically by increasing her opportunities for heterosexual affiliation (especially with white men). Third, by committing herself to the pursuit of beauty, a woman integrates her life with a consistent set of values and choices that bring her widespread approval and a resulting sense of increased self-esteem. Fourth, the pursuit of beauty often gives a woman access to a range of individuals who administer to her body in a caring way, an experience often sadly lacking in the day-to-day lives of many women. As a result, a woman's pursuit of beauty through transformation is often associated with lived experiences of self-creation, self-fulfilment, self-transcendence, and being cared for. The power of these experiences must not be underestimated.

While I acknowledge that these choices can confer a kind of integrity on a woman's life, I also believe that they are likely to embroil her in a set of interrelated contradictions. I refer to these as "Paradoxes of Choice."

IV. Three Paradoxes of Choice

In exploring these paradoxes, I appropriate Foucault's analysis of the diffusion of power in order to understand forms of power that are potentially more personally invasive than are more obvious, publicly identifiable aspects of power. In the chapter "Docile Bodies" in *Discipline and Punish*, Foucault (1979, 136–37) highlights three features of what he calls disciplinary power:

1. The *scale* of the control. In disciplinary power the body is treated individually and in a coercive way because the body itself is the *active* and hence apparently free body that is being controlled through movements, gestures, attitudes, and degrees of rapidity.

2. The *object* of the control, which involves meticulous control over the efficiency of movements and forces.

3. The *modality* of the control, which involves constant, uninterrupted coercion.

Foucault argues that the outcome of disciplinary power is the docile body, a body "that may be subjected, used, transformed, and improved" (Foucault 1979, 136). Foucault is discussing this model of power in the context of prisons and armies, but we can adapt the central insights of this notion to see how women's bodies are entering "a machinery of power that explores it, breaks it down, and rearranges it" through a recognizably political metamorphosis of embodiment (Foucault 1979, 138).[2] What is important about this notion in relation to cosmetic surgery is the extent to which it makes it possible to speak about the diffusion of power throughout Western industrialized cultures that are increasingly committed to a technological beauty imperative. It also makes it possible to refer to a set of experts—cosmetic surgeons—whose explicit power mandate is to explore, break down, and rearrange women's bodies.

Paradox One: The Choice of Conformity—Understanding the Number 10

While the technology of cosmetic surgery could clearly be used to create and celebrate idiosyncrasy, eccentricity, and uniqueness, it is obvious that this is not how it is presently being used. Cosmetic surgeons report that legions of women appear in their offices demanding "Bo Derek" breasts (*Sheboygan Press* 1985). Jewish women demand reductions of their noses so as to be able to "pass" as one of their Aryan sisters who form the dominant ethnic group (Lakoff and Scherr 1984). Adolescent Asian girls who bring in pictures of Elizabeth Taylor and of Japanese movie actresses (whose faces have already been reconstructed) demand the "Westernizing" of their own eyes and the creation of higher noses in hopes of better job and marital prospects (*Newsweek* 1985). Black women buy toxic bleaching agents in hopes of attaining lighter skin. What is being created in all of these instances is not simply beautiful bodies and faces but white, Western, Anglo-Saxon bodies in a racist, anti-Semitic context.

More often than not, what appear at first glance to be instances of choice turn out to be instances of conformity. The women who undergo cosmetic surgery in order to compete in various beauty pageants are clearly choosing to conform. So is the woman who wanted to undergo a facelift, tummy tuck, and liposuction all in one week, in order to win heterosexual approval *from a man she had not seen in twenty-eight years* and whose individual preferences she could not possibly know. In some ways, it does not matter who the particular judges are. Actual men—brothers, fathers, male lovers, male beauty "experts"—and hypothetical men live in the aesthetic imaginations of women. Whether they are male employers, prospective male spouses, male judges in the beauty pageants, or male-identified women, these modern day Parises are generic and live sometimes ghostly but powerful lives in the reflective awareness of women (Berger 1972). A woman's makeup, dress, gestures, voice, degree of cleanliness, degree of muscularity, odors, degree of hirsuteness, vocabulary, hands, feet, skin, hair, and vulva can all be evaluated, regulated, and disciplined in the light of the hypothetical often-white male viewer and the male viewer present in the assessing gaze of other women (Haug 1987). Men's appreciation and approval of achieved femininity becomes all the more invasive when it resides in the incisions, stitches, staples, and scar tissue of women's bodies as women choose to conform. And . . . women's public conformity to the norms of beauty often signals a deeper conformity to the norms of compulsory heterosexuality along with an awareness of the violence that can result from violating those norms. Hence the first paradox: that what looks like an optimal situation of reflection, deliberation, and self-creating choice often signals conformity at a deeper level.

Paradox Two: Liberation into Colonization

As argued above, a woman's desire to create a permanently beautiful and youthful appearance that is not vulnerable to the threats of externally applied cosmetic artifice or to the natural aging process of the body must be understood as a deeply significant existential project. It deliberately involves the exploitation and transformation of the most intimately experienced domain of immanence, the body, in the name of transcendence: transcendence of hereditary predestination, of lived time, of one's given "limitations." What I see as particularly alarming in this project is that what comes to have primary significance is not the real given existing woman but her body viewed as a "primitive entity" that is seen only as potential, as a kind of raw material to be exploited in terms of appearance, eroticism, nurturance, and fertility as defined by the colonizing culture.[3]

But for whom is this exploitation and transformation taking place? Who exercises the power here? Sometimes the power is explicit. It is exercised by brothers, fathers, male lovers, male engineering students who taunt and harass their female counterparts, and by male cosmetic surgeons who offer "free advice" in social gatherings to women whose "deformities" and "severe problems" can all be cured through their healing needles and knives. And the colonizing power is transmitted through and by those women whose own bodies and disciplinary practices demonstrate the efficacy of "taking care of herself" in these culturally defined feminine ways. Sometimes, however, the power may be so diffused as to dominate the consciousness of a given woman with no other subject needing to be present. . . .

In electing to undergo cosmetic surgery, women appear to be protesting against the constraints of the "given" in their embodied lives and seeking liberation from those constraints. But I believe they are in danger of retreating and becoming more vulnerable, at that very level of embodiment, to those colonizing forms of power that may have motivated the protest in the first place. Moreover, in seeking independence, they can become even more dependent on male assessment and on the services of all those experts they initially bought to render them independent.

Here we see a second paradox bound up with choice: that the rhetoric is that of liberation and care, of "making the most of yourself," but the reality is often the transformation of oneself as a woman for the eye, the hand, and the approval of the Other—the lover, the taunting students, the customers, the employers, the social peers. And the Other is almost always affected by the dominant culture, which is male-supremacist, racist, ageist, heterosexist, anti-Semitic, ableist and class-biased.[4]

Paradox Three: Coerced Voluntariness and the Technological Imperative

Where is the coercion? At first glance, women who choose to undergo cosmetic surgery often seem to represent a paradigm case of the rational chooser. Drawn increasingly from wider and wider economic groups, these women clearly make a choice, often at significant economic cost to the rest of their life, to pay the large sums of money demanded by cosmetic surgeons (since American health insurance plans do not cover this elective cosmetic surgery).

Furthermore, they are often highly critical consumers of these services, demanding extensive consultation, information regarding the risks and benefits of various surgical procedures, and professional guarantees of expertise. Generally they are relatively young and in good health. Thus, in some important sense, they epitomize relatively invulnerable free agents making a decision under virtually optimal conditions.

Moreover, on the surface, women who undergo cosmetic surgery choose a set of procedures that are, by definition, "elective." This term is used, quite straightforwardly, to distinguish cosmetic surgery from surgical intervention for reconstructive or health-related reasons (e.g., following massive burns, cancer-related forms of mutilation, etc.). The term also appears to distinguish cosmetic surgery from apparently involuntary and more pathologically transforming forms of intervention in the bodies of young girls in the form of, for example, foot-binding or extensive genital mutilation.[5] But I believe that this does not exhaust the meaning of the term "elective" and that the term performs a seductive role in facilitating the ideological camouflage of the *absence of choice*. Similarly, I believe that the word "cosmetic" serves an ideological function in hiding the fact that the changes are *noncosmetic*: they involve lengthy periods of pain, are permanent, and result in irreversibly alienating metamorphoses such as the appearance of youth on an aging body. . . .

There are two important ideological, choice-diminishing dynamics at work that affect women's choices in the area of . . . cosmetic surgery. The first of these is the *pressure to achieve perfection through technology*.

The second . . . is the *double-pathologizing of women's bodies*. The history of Western science and Western medical practice is not altogether a positive one for women. As voluminous documentation has shown, cell biologists, endocrinologists, anatomists, sociobiologists, gynecologists, obstetricians, psychiatrists, surgeons, and other scientists have assumed, hypothesized, or "demonstrated" that women's bodies are generally inferior, deformed, imperfect, and/or infantile. . . .

[Now, women are being pressured to see plainness or being ugly as a form of pathology. Consequently, there is strong pressure] to be beautiful in relation to the allegedly voluntary nature of "electing" to undergo cosmetic surgery. It is clear that pressure to use this technology is on the increase. Cosmetic surgeons report on the wide range of clients who buy their services, pitch their advertising to a large audience through the use of the media, and encourage women to think, metaphorically, in terms of the seemingly trivial "nips" and "tucks" that will transform their lives. As cosmetic surgery becomes increasingly normalized through the concept of the female "makeover" that is translated into columns and articles in the print media or made into nationwide television shows directed at female viewers, as the "success stories" are invited onto talk shows along with their "makers," and as surgically transformed women win the Miss America pageants, women who refuse to submit to the knives and to the needles, to the anesthetics and the bandages, will come to be seen as deviant in one way or another. Women who refuse to use these technologies are already becoming stigmatized as "unliberated," "not caring about their appearance" (a sign of disturbed gender identity and low self-esteem according to various health-care professionals), as "refusing to be all that they could be" or as "granola-heads."

And as more and more success comes to those who do "care about themselves" in this technological fashion, more coercive dimensions enter the scene. In the past, only those women who were perceived to be *naturally* beautiful (or rendered beautiful through relatively conservative superficial artifice) had access to forms of power and economic social mobility closed off to women regarded as plain or ugly or old. But now womanly beauty is becoming technologically achievable, a commodity for which each and every woman can, in principle, sacrifice if she is to survive and succeed in the world, particularly in industrialized Western countries. Now technology is making obligatory the appearance of youth and the reality of "beauty" for every woman who can afford it. Natural destiny is being supplanted by technologically grounded coercion, and the coercion is camouflaged by the language of choice, fulfillment, and liberation.

Similarly, we find the dynamic of the double-pathologizing of the normal and of the ordinary at work here. In the technical and popular literature on cosmetic surgery, what have previously been described as normal variations of female bodily shapes or described in the relatively innocuous language of "problem areas," are increasingly being described as "deformities," "ugly protrusions," "inadequate breasts," and "unsightly concentrations of fat cells"— a litany of descriptions designed to intensify feelings of disgust, shame, and relief at the possibility of recourse for these "deformities." Cosmetic surgery promises virtually all women the creation of beautiful, youthful-appearing bodies. As a consequence, more and more women will be labeled "ugly" and "old" in relation to this more select population of surgically created beautiful faces and bodies that have been contoured and augmented, lifted and tucked into a state of achieved feminine excellence. I suspect that the naturally "given," so to speak, will increasingly come to be seen as the technologically "primitive"; the "ordinary" will come to be perceived and evaluated as the "ugly." Here, then, is the *third paradox*: that the technological beauty imperative and the pathological inversion of the normal are coercing more and more women to "choose" cosmetic surgery.

V. Are There Any Politically Correct Feminist Responses to Cosmetic Surgery?

Attempting to answer this question is rather like venturing forth into quicksand. Nevertheless, I will discuss two very different sorts of responses that strike me as having certain plausibility: the response of refusal and the response of appropriation.[6] I regard both of these as utopian in nature.

The Response of Refusal

In her witty and subversive parable, *The Life and Loves of a She-Devil*, Fay Weldon puts the following thoughts into the mind of the cosmetic surgeon whose services have been bought by the protagonist, "Miss Hunter," for her own plans for revenge:

> He was her Pygmalion, but she would not depend upon him, or admire him, or be grateful. He was accustomed to being loved by the women of his own construction. A soft sigh of adoration would follow him down the corridors as he paced them, visiting here, blessing there, promising a future, regretting a past: cushioning his footfall, and his image of himself. But no soft breathings came from Miss Hunter. [He adds, ominously,] . . . he would bring her to it (Weldon 1983, 215–16).

But Miss Hunter continues to refuse, and so will many feminist women. The response of refusal can be recognizably feminist at both an individual and a collective level. It results from understanding the nature of the risks involved— those having to do with the surgical procedures and those related to a potential loss of embodied personal integrity in a patriarchal context. And it results from understanding the conceptual shifts involved in the political technologizing of women's bodies and contextualizing them so that their oppressive consequences are evident precisely as they open up more "choices" to women. "Understanding" and "contextualizing" here mean seeing clearly the ideological biases that frame the material and cultural world in which cosmetic surgeons practice, a world that contains racist, anti-Semitic, eugenicist, and ageist dimensions of oppression, forms of oppression to which current practices in cosmetic surgery often contribute.

The response of refusal also speaks to the collective power of women as consumers to affect market conditions. If refusal is practiced on a large scale, cosmetic surgeons who are busy producing new faces for the "holiday season" and new bellies for the "winter trips to the Caribbean" will find few buyers of their services. Cosmetic surgeons who consider themselves body designers and regard women's skin as a kind of magical fabric to be draped, cut, layered, and designer-labeled may have to forgo the esthetician's ambitions that occasion the remark that "the sculpting of human flesh can never be an exact art" (Silver 1989). They may, instead, (re)turn their expertise to the victims in the intensive burn unit and to the crippled limbs and joints of arthritic women. This might well have the consequence of (re)converting those surgeons into healers.

Although it may be relatively easy for some individual women to refuse cosmetic surgery even when they have access to the means, one deep, morally significant facet of the response of refusal is to try to understand and to care about individual women who do choose to undergo cosmetic surgery. It may well be that one explanation for why a woman is willing to subject herself to surgical procedures, anaesthetic, post-operative drugs, predicted and lengthy pain, and possible "side effects" that might include her own death is that her access to other forms of power and empowerment are or appear to be so limited that cosmetic surgery is the primary domain in which she can experience some semblance of self-determination. . . . Choosing an artificial and technologically designed creation of youthful beauty may not only be necessary to an individual woman's material, economic, and social survival. It may also be the way that she is able to choose, to elect a kind of subjective transcendence against a backdrop of constraint, limitation, and immanence. . . .

As a feminist response, individual and collective refusal may not be easy. As Bartky, I, and others have tried to argue, it is crucial to understand the central role that socially sanctioned and socially constructed femininity plays in a male supremacist, heterosexist society. And it is essential not to underestimate the gender-constituting and identity-confirming role that femininity plays in bringing woman-as-subject into existence while simultaneously creating her as patriarchally defined object (Bartky 1988; Morgan 1986). In these circumstances, refusal may be akin to a kind of death, to a kind of renunciation of the only kind of life-conferring choices and competencies to which a woman may have access. And, under those circumstances, it may not be possible for her to register her resistance in the form of refusal. The best one can hope for is a heightened sense of the nature of the multiple double-binds and compromises that permeate the lives of virtually all women and are accentuated by the cosmetic surgery culture. As a final comment, it is worth remarking that although the response of refusal has a kind of purity to recommend it, it is unlikely to have much impact in the current ideological and cultural climate. . . .

The Response of Appropriation

Rather than viewing the womanly/technologized body as a site of political refusal, the response of appropriation views it as the site for feminist action through transformation, appropriation, parody, and protest. This response grows out of that historical and often radical feminist tradition that regards deliberate mimicry, alternative valorization, hyperbolic appropriation, street theater, counterguerrilla tactics, destabilization, and redeployment as legitimate feminist politics. Here I am proposing a version of what Judith Butler regards as "Femininity Politics" and what she calls "Gender Performatives." . . .

Rather than agreeing that participation in cosmetic surgery and its ruling ideology will necessarily result in further colonization and victimization of women, this feminist strategy advocates appropriating the expertise and technology for feminist ends. One advantage of the response of appropriation is that it does not recommend involvement in forms of technology that clearly have disabling and dire outcomes for the deeper feminist project of engaging "in the historical, political, and theoretical process of constituting ourselves as subjects as well as objects of history" (Hartsock 1990, 170).[7] Women who are increasingly immobilized bodily through physical weakness, passivity, withdrawal, and domestic sequestration in situations of hysteria, agoraphobia, and anorexia cannot possibly engage in radical gender performatives of an active public sort or in other acts by which the feminist subject is robustly constituted. In contrast, healthy women who have a feminist understanding of cosmetic surgery are in a situation to deploy cosmetic surgery in the name of its feminist potential for parody and protest. . . .

As Butler correctly observes, parody "by itself is not subversive" (1990, 139) since it always runs the risk of becoming "domesticated and recirculated as instruments of cultural hegemony." She then goes on to ask, in relation to gender identity and sexuality, what words or performances would

> compel a reconsideration of the *place* and stability of the masculine and the feminine? And what kind of gender performance will enact and reveal the performativity of gender itself in a way that destabilizes the naturalized categories of identity and desire? (Butler 1990, 139)

We might, in parallel fashion, ask what sorts of performances would sufficiently destabilize the norms of femininity, what sorts of performances will sufficiently expose the truth of the slogan "Beauty is always made, not born." In response I suggest two performance-oriented forms of revolt.

The first form of revolt involves revalorizing the domain of the "ugly" and all that is associated with it. Although one might argue that the notion of the "ugly" is parasitic on that of "beauty," this is not entirely true since the ugly is also contrasted with the plain and the ordinary, so that we are not even at the outset constrained by binary oppositions. The ugly, even in a beauty-oriented culture, has always held its own fascination, its own particular kind of splendor. Feminists can use that and explore it in ways that might be integrated with a revalorization of being old, thus simultaneously attacking the ageist dimension of the reigning ideology. Rather than being the "culturally enmired subjects" of Butler's analysis, women might constitute themselves as culturally liberated subjects through public participation in Ms. Ugly Canada/America/Universe/Cosmos pageants *and use the technology of cosmetic surgery to do so.*

Contemplating this form of revolt as a kind of imaginary model of political action is one thing; actually altering our bodies is another matter altogether. And the reader may well share the sentiments of one reviewer of this paper who asked: "Having oneself surgically mutilated in order to prove a point? Isn't this going too far?" I don't know the answer to that question. If we cringe from contemplating this alternative, this may, in fact, testify (so to speak) to the hold that the beauty imperative has on our imagination and our bodies. If we recoil from *lived* alteration of the contours of our bodies and regard it as "mutilation," then so, too, ought we to shrink from contemplation of cosmetic surgeons who de-skin and alter the contours of women's bodies so that we become more and more like athletic or emaciated (depending on what's in vogue) mannequins with large breasts in the shop windows of modern patriarchal culture. In what sense are these not equivalent mutilations?

What this feminist performative would require would be not only genuine celebration of but *actual* participation in the fleshly mutations needed to produce what the culture constitutes as "ugly" so as to destabilize the "beautiful" and expose its technologically and culturally constitutive origin and its political consequences. Bleaching one's hair white and applying wrinkle-inducing "wrinkle creams," having one's face and breasts surgically pulled down (rather than lifted), and having wrinkles sewn and carved into one's skin might also be seen as destabilizing actions with respect to aging. And analogous actions might be taken to undermine the "lighter is better" aspect of racist norms of feminine appearance as they affect women of color.

A second performative form of revolt could involve exploring the commodification aspect of cosmetic surgery. One might, for example, envision a set of "Beautiful Body Boutique" franchises, responsive to the particular "needs" of a given community. Here one could advertise and sell a whole range of bodily contours; a variety of metric containers of freeze-dried fat cells for fat implantation and transplant; "body configuration" software for computers; sewing kits of needles, knives, and painkillers; and "skin-Velcro" that could be matched to fit and drape the consumer's body; variously-sized sets of magnetically attachable breasts complete with discrete nipple pumps; and other inflation devices carefully modulated according to bodily aroma and state of arousal. Parallel to the current marketing strategies for cosmetic breast surgeries, commercial protest booths, complete with "before and after" surgical make-over displays for penises, entitled "The Penis You Were Always Meant to Have" could be set up at various medical conventions and health fairs; demonstrations could take place outside the clinics, hotels, and spas of particularly eminent cosmetic surgeons—the possibilities here are endless. Again, if this ghoulish array offends, angers, or shocks the reader, this may well be an indication of the extent to which the ideology of compulsory beauty has anesthetized our sensibility in the reverse direction, resulting in the domesticating of the procedures and products of the cosmetic surgery industry.

In appropriating these forms of revolt, women might well accomplish the following: acquire expertise (either in fact or in symbolic form) of cosmetic surgery to challenge the coercive norms of youth and beauty, undermine the power dynamic built into the dependence on surgical experts who define themselves as aestheticians of women's bodies, demonstrate the radical malleability of the cultural commodification of women's bodies, and make publicly explicit the political role that technology can play in the construction of the feminine in women's flesh.

Conclusion

I have characterized both these feminist forms of response as utopian in nature. What I mean by "utopian" is that these responses are unlikely to occur on a large scale even though they may have a kind of ideal desirability. In any culture that defines femininity in terms of submission to men, that makes the achievement of femininity (however culturally specific) in appearance, gesture, movement, voice, bodily contours, aspirations, values, and political behavior obligatory of any woman who will be allowed to be loved or hired or promoted or elected or simply allowed to live, and in any culture that increasingly requires women to purchase femininity through submission to cosmetic surgeons and their magic knives, refusal and revolt exact a high price. I live in such a culture.

Notes

Many thanks to the members of the Canadian Society for Women in Philosophy for their critical feedback, especially my commentator, Karen Weisbaum, who pointed out how strongly visualist the cosmetic surgery culture is. I am particularly grateful to Sarah Lucia Hoagland, keynote speaker at the 1990 C-SWIP conference, who remarked at my session, "I think this is all wrong." Her comment sent me back to the text to rethink it in a serious way. . . .

1. I say "virtually all women" because there is now a nascent literature on the subject of fat oppression and body image as it affects lesbians. For a perceptive article on this subject, see Dworkin (1989). I am, of course, not suggesting that compulsory heterosexuality and obligatory maternity affect all women equally. Clearly women who are regarded as "deviant" in some respect or other—because they are lesbian or women with disabilities or "too old" or poor or of the "wrong race"—are under enormous pressure from the dominant culture *not* to bear children, but this, too, is an aspect of patriarchal pronatalism.

2. I view this as a recognizably *political* metamorphosis because forensic cosmetic surgeons and social archaeologists will be needed to determine the actual age and earlier appearance of women in cases where identification is called for on the basis of existing carnal data. See Griffin's (1978) poignant description in "The Anatomy Lesson" for a reconstruction of the life and circumstances of a dead mother from just such carnal evidence. As we more and more profoundly artifactualize our own bodies, we become more sophisticated archaeological repositories and records that both signify and symbolize our culture.

3. I intend to use "given" here in a relative and political sense. I don't believe that the notion that biology is somehow "given" and culture is just "added" is a tenable one. I believe that we are intimately and inextricably encultured and embodied, so that a reductionist move in either direction is doomed to failure. For a persuasive analysis of this thesis, see Lowe (1982) and Haraway (1978, 1989). For a variety of political analyses of the "given" as primitive, see Marge Piercy's poem "Right to Life" (1980), Morgan (1989), and Murphy (1984).

4. The extent to which ableist bias is at work in this area was brought home to me by two quotations cited by a woman with a disability. She discusses two guests on a television show. One was "a poised, intelligent young woman who'd been rejected as a contestant for the Miss Toronto title. She is a paraplegic. The organizers' excuse for disqualifying her: 'We couldn't fit the choreography around you.' Another guest was a former executive of the Miss Universe contest. He declared,

'Her participation in a beauty contest would be like having a blind man compete in a shooting match' " (Matthews 1985).

5. It is important here to guard against facile and ethnocentric assumptions about beauty rituals and mutilation. See Lakoff and Scherr (1984) for an analysis of the relativity of these labels and for important insights about the fact that use of the term "mutilation" almost always signals a distancing from and reinforcement of a sense of cultural superiority in the speaker who uses it to denounce what other cultures do in contrast to "our culture."

6. One possible feminist response (that, thankfully, appears to go in *and* out of vogue) is that of feminist fascism, which insists on a certain particular and quite narrow range of embodiment and appearance as the only range that is politically correct for a feminist. Often feminist fascism sanctions the use of informal but very powerful feminist "embodiment police," who feel entitled to identify and denounce various deviations from this normative range. I find this feminist political stance incompatible with any movement I would regard as liberatory for women and here I admit that I side with feminist liberals who say that "the presumption must be on the side of freedom" (Warren 1989) and see that as the lesser of the two evils.

7. In recommending various forms of appropriation of the practices and dominant ideology surrounding cosmetic surgery, I think it important to distinguish this set of disciplinary practices from those forms of simultaneous Retreat-and-Protest that Susan Bordo (1989, 20) so insightfully discusses in "The Body and the Reproduction of Femininity": hysteria, agoraphobia, and anorexia. What cosmetic surgery shares with these gestures is what Bordo remarks upon, namely, the fact that they may be "viewed as a surface on which conventional constructions of femininity are exposed starkly to view, through their inscription in extreme or hyperliteral form." What is different, I suggest, is that although submitting to the procedures of cosmetic surgery involves pain, risks, undesirable side effects, and living with a heightened form of patriarchal anxiety, it is also fairly clear that, most of the time, the pain and risks are relatively short-term. Furthermore, the outcome often appears to be one that generally enhances women's confidence, confers a sense of well-being, contributes to a greater comfortableness in the public domain, and affirms the individual woman as a self-determining and risk-taking individual. All these outcomes are significantly different from what Bordo describes as the "languages of horrible suffering" (Bordo 1989, 20) expressed by women experiencing hysteria, agoraphobia, and anorexia.

References

Barker-Benfield, G. J. 1976. *The Horrors of the Half-Known Life*. New York: Harper and Row.

Bartky, Sandra Lee. 1988. Foucault, femininity, and the modernization of patriarchal power. In *Femininity and Foucault: Reflections on Resistance*, edited by Irene Diamond and Lee Quimby. Boston: Northeastern University Press.

Berger, John. 1972. *Ways of Seeing*. New York: Penguin Books.

Bordo, Susan R. 1989. The body and the reproduction of femininity: A feminist appropriation of Foucault. In *Gender/body/knowledge: Feminist Reconstructions of Being and Knowing*, edited by Alison Jagger and Susan Bordo. New Brunswick, NJ: Rutgers University Press.

Butler, Judith. 1990. *Gender Trouble: Feminism and the Subversion of Identity.* New York: Routledge.

Dworkin, Sari. 1989. Not in man's image. Lesbians and the cultural oppression of body image. *Women and Therapy* 8:27–39.

Foucault, Michel. 1979. *Discipline and Punish: The Birth of the Prison.* Alan Sheridan, trans. New York: Pantheon.

Goodman, Ellen. 1989. A plastic surgeon. *Boston Globe,* September 19.

Griffin, Susan. 1978. *Woman and Nature: The Roaring Inside Her.* New York: Harper and Row.

Haraway, Donna. 1978. Animal sociology and a natural economy of the body politic, Parts I, II. *Signs: Journal of Women in culture and Society* 4:21–60.

———. 1989. *Primate Visions.* New York: Routledge.

Hartsock, Nancy. 1990. Foucault on power: A theory for women? In *Feminism/post-modernism,* edited by Linda Nicholson. New York: Routledge.

Haug, Frigga, ed. 1987. *Female Sexualization: A Collective Work of Memory.* Erica Carter, trans. London: Verso.

Hirshson, Paul. 1987. New wrinkles in plastic surgery: An update on the search for perfection. *Boston Globe Sunday Magazine.* May 24.

Lakoff, Robin Tolmach, and Raquel Scherr. 1984. *Face Value: The Politics of Beauty.* Boston: Routledge and Kegan Paul.

Lowe, Marion. 1982. The dialectic of biology and culture. In *Biological Woman: The Convenient Myth,* edited by Ruth Hubbard, Mary Sue Henifin, and Barbara Fried. Cambridge, MA. Schenkman.

Markovic, Mihailo. 1976. Women's liberation and human emancipation. In *Women and Philosophy: Toward a Theory of Liberation,* edited by Carol Gould and Marx Wartofsky. New York: Capricorn Books.

Matthews, Gwyneth Ferguson. 1985. Mirror, mirror: Self-image and disabled women. *Women and Disability: Resources for Feminist Research* 14:47–50.

Morgan, Kathryn Pauly. 1986. Romantic love, altruism and self-respect: An analysis of Simone De Beauvoir. *Hypatia* 1:117–148.

———. 1989. Of woman born? How old-fashioned! New reproductive technologies and women's oppression. In *The Future of Human Reproduction,* edited by Christine Overall. Toronto: The Women's Press.

Murphy, Julie [Julien S]. 1984. Egg farming and women's future. In *Test-tube Women: What future for Motherhood?,* edited by Rita Arditti, Renate Duelli-Klein, and Shelley Minden. Boston: Pandora Press.

Newsweek. 1985. New bodies for sale. May 27.

Piercy, Marge. 1980. *The Moon is Always Female.* New York: A. Knopf.

Sheboygan Press. 1985. Cosmetic surgery for the holidays. New York Times News Service.

Sherwin, Susan. 1984–85. A feminist approach to ethics. *Dalhousie Review* 64:704–13.

———. 1989. Feminist and medical ethics: Two different approaches to contextual ethics. *Hypatia* 4:57–72.

Silver, Harold. 1989. Liposuction isn't for everyone. *Toronto Star,* October 20.

Toronto Star. 1988. Implants hide tumors in breasts, study says. July 29.

———. 1989a. Changing Faces. May 25.

———. 1989b. Woman, 43, dies after cosmetic surgery. July 7.

———. 1990a. The quest to be a perfect 10. February 1.

———. 1990b. Retouching nature's way: Is cosmetic surgery worth it? February 1.

———. 1990c. Falling in love again. July 23.

———. 1990d. *Madonna passionate about fitness. August 16.*

Warren, Virginia. 1989. Feminist directions in medical ethics. Hypatia 4:73–87.

Weldon, Fay. 1983. *The Life and Loves of a She-Devil.* London: Coronet Books; New York: Pantheon Books.

Williams, John, and Jim Williams. 1990. Say it with liposuction. *Harper's.* August.

12

Medicalization of Racial Features
Asian-American Women and Cosmetic Surgery

Eugenia Kaw

Throughout history and across cultures, humans have decorated, manipulated, and mutilated their bodies for religious reasons, for social prestige, and for beauty (Brain 1979). In the United States, within the last decade, permanent alteration of the body for aesthetic reasons has become increasingly common. By 1988, 2 million Americans, 87% of them female, had undergone cosmetic surgery, a figure that had tripled in two years (Wolf 1991, 218). [In 1994 alone, members of the American Society of Plastic and Reconstructive Surgeons reported performing cosmetic surgery on almost 400,000 Americans, 88% of them female; many other Americans had surgery performed by non-certified physicians.] The cosmetic surgery industry, a $300 million per year industry, has been able to meet an increasingly wide variety of consumer demands. Now men, too, receive services ranging from enlargement of calves and chests to the liposuction of cheeks and necks (Rosenthal 1991). Most noticeably, the ethnic composition of consumers has changed so that in recent years there are more racial and ethnic minorities. In 1994, 14% of cosmetic surgery patients were Latinos, African Americans, and Asian Americans (American Society of Plastic and Reconstructive Surgeons, http://www.plasticsurgery.org). Not surprisingly, within every racial group, women still constitute the overwhelming majority of cosmetic surgery patients, an indication that women are still expected to identify with their bodies in U.S. society today, just as they have across cultures throughout much of human history (Turner 1987, 85).[1]

The types of cosmetic surgery sought by women in the United States are racially specific. Like most white women, Asian women who undergo cosmetic surgery are motivated by the need to look their best as women.

White women, however, usually opt for liposuction, breast augmentation, or wrinkle removal procedures, whereas Asian American women most often request "double-eyelid" surgery, whereby folds of skin are excised from across their upper eyelids to create a crease above each eye that makes the eyes look wider. Also frequently requested is surgical sculpting of the nose tip to create a more chiseled appearance, or the implantation of a silicone or cartilage bridge in the nose for a more prominent appearance. In 1990, national averages compiled by the American Society of Plastic and Reconstructive Surgeons show that liposuction, breast augmentation, and collagen injection were the most common surgical procedures among cosmetic patients, 80% of whom are white. Although national statistics on the types of cosmetic surgery most requested by Asian Americans specifically are not available, data from two of the doctors' offices in my study show that in 1990 eyelid surgery was the most common procedure undergone by Asian-American patients (40% of all procedures on Asian Americans at one doctor's office, 46% at another), followed by nasal implants and nasal tip refinement procedures (15% at the first doctor's office, 23% at the second).[2] While the features that white women primarily seek to alter through cosmetic surgery (i.e., the breasts, fatty areas of the body, and facial wrinkles) do not correspond to conventional markers of racial identity, those features that Asian-American women primarily seek to alter (i.e., "small, narrow" eyes and a "flat" nose) do correspond to such markers.[3]

My research focuses on the cultural and institutional forces that motivate Asian-American women to alter surgically the shape of their eyes and noses. I argue that Asian-American women's decision to undergo cosmetic surgery is an attempt to escape persisting racial prejudice that correlates their stereotyped genetic physical features ("small, slanty" eyes and a "flat" nose) with negative behavioral characteristics, such as passivity, dullness, and a lack of sociability. With the authority of scientific rationality and technological efficiency, medicine is effective in perpetuating these racist notions. The medical system bolsters and benefits from the larger consumer-oriented society not only by maintaining the idea that beauty should be every woman's goal but also by promoting a beauty standard that requires that certain racial features of Asian-American women be modified. Through the subtle and often unconscious manipulation of racial and gender ideologies, medicine, as a producer of norms, and the larger consumer society of which it is a part encourage Asian-American women to mutilate their bodies to conform to an ethnocentric norm.

Social scientific analyses of ethnic relations should include a study of the body. As evident in my research, racial minorities may internalize a body image produced by the dominant culture's racial ideology and, because of it, begin to loathe, mutilate, and revise parts of their bodies. Bodily mutilation and adornment are symbolic mediums most directly and concretely concerned with the construction of the individual as social actor or cultural subject (Turner 1980). Yet social scientists have only recently focused on the body as a central component of social self-identity (Blacking 1977; Brain 1979; Daly 1978; Lock and Scheper-Hughes 1990; O'Neill 1985; Turner 1987).

Moreover, social scientists, and sociocultural anthropologists in particular, have not yet explored the ways in which the body is central to the everyday experience of racial identity.

Method and Description of Subjects

In this article I present findings of an ongoing ethnographic research project in the San Francisco Bay Area begun in April 1991. I draw on data from structured interviews with physicians and patients, medical literature and newspaper articles, and basic medical statistics. The sample of informants for this research is not random in the strictly statistical sense since informants were difficult to locate. In the United States, both clients and their medical practitioners treat the decision to undergo cosmetic surgery as highly confidential, and practitioners do not reveal the names of patients without their consent. In an effort to generate a sample of Asian-American woman informants, I posted fliers and placed advertisements in various local newspapers for a period of at least three months, but I received only one reply. I also asked doctors who had agreed to participate in my study to ask their Asian-American patients if they would agree to be interviewed. The doctors reported that most of the patients preferred not to talk about their operations or about motivations leading up to the operation. Ultimately, I was able to conduct structured, open-ended interviews with eleven Asian-American women, four of whom were referred to me by doctors in the study, six by mutual acquaintances, and one through an advertisement in a local newspaper. Nine have had cosmetic surgery of the eye or the nose; one recently considered a double-eyelid operation; one is considering a double-eyelid operation in the next few years. Nine of the women in the study live in the San Francisco Bay Area, and two in the Los Angeles area. Five had their operations from doctors in my study, while four had theirs in Asia—two in Seoul, Korea, one in Beijing, China, and one in Taipei, Taiwan. Of the eleven women in the study, only two, who received their operations in China and in Taiwan, had not lived in the United States prior to their operations. The two who had surgery in Korea grew up in the United States; they said that they decided to go to Korea for their surgeries because the operations were cheaper there than in the United States and because they felt doctors in Korea are more "experienced" since these types of surgery are more common in Korea than in the United States.[4] The ages of the women in the study range from 18 to 71; one woman was only 15 at the time of her operation.

In addition to interviewing Asian-American women, I conducted structured, open-ended interviews with five plastic surgeons, all of whom practice in the Bay Area. Of the eleven doctors I randomly selected from the phone book, five agreed to be interviewed.

Since the physicians in my study may not be representative of plastic surgeons, I reviewed the plastic surgery literature. To examine more carefully the medical discourse on the nose and eyelid surgeries of Asian-American women,

I examined several medical books and plastic surgery journals dating from the 1950s to 1990. I also reviewed several news releases and informational packets distributed by such national organizations as the American Society of Plastic and Reconstructive Surgeons, an organization that represents 97% of all physicians certified by the American Board of Plastic Surgery.

To examine popular notions of cosmetic surgery and, in particular, of how the phenomenon of Asian-American women receiving double-eyelid and nose-bridge operations is viewed by the public and the media, I referenced relevant newspaper and magazine articles.

For statistical information, I obtained national data on cosmetic surgery from various societies for cosmetic surgeons, including the American Society of Plastic and Reconstructive Surgeons. Data on the specific types of surgery sought by different ethnic groups in the United States, including Asian Americans, are missing from the national statistics. At least one public relations coordinator told me that such data are quite unimportant to plastic surgeons. To compensate for this, I requested doctors in my study to provide me with data from their clinics. One doctor allowed me to review his patient files for basic statistical information. Another doctor allowed his office assistant to give me such information, provided that I paid his assistant for the time she had to work outside of normal work hours reviewing his patient files. Since cosmetic surgery is generally not covered by medical insurance, doctors often do not record their patients' medical information in their computers; therefore, most doctors told me that they have very little data on their cosmetic patients readily available.

Mutilation or a Celebration of the Body?

The decoration, ornamentation, and scarification of the body can be viewed from two perspectives. On the one hand, such practices can be seen as celebrations of the social and individual bodies, as expressions of belonging in society and an affirmation of oneness with the body (Brain 1979; Scheper-Hughes and Lock 1991; Turner 1980). On the other hand, they can be viewed as acts of mutilation, that is, as expressions of alienation in society and a negation of the body induced by unequal power relationships (Bordo 1990; Daly 1978; O'Neill 1985).

Although it is at least possible to imagine race-modification surgery as a *rite de passage* or a bid for incorporation into the body and race norms of the "dominant" culture, my research findings lead me to reject this as a tenable hypothesis. Here I argue that the surgical alteration by many Asian-American women of the shape of their eyes and nose is a potent form of self, body, and society alienation. Mutilation, according to *Webster's*, is the act of maiming, crippling, cutting up, or altering radically so as to damage seriously essential parts of the body. Although the women in my study do not view their cosmetic surgeries as acts of mutilation, an examination of the cultural and institutional forces that influence them to modify their bodies so radically reveals a rejection of their "given" bodies and feelings of marginality. On the one hand, they feel they are exercising their Americanness in their use of the freedom of individual choice. Some deny that they are conforming to any standard—feminine, Western, or otherwise—and others express the idea that they are, in fact, molding their own standards of beauty. Most agreed, however, that their decision to alter their features was primarily a result of their awareness that as women they are expected to look their best and that this meant, in a certain sense, less stereotypically Asian. Even those who stated that their decision to alter their features was personal, based on individual aesthetic preference, also expressed hope that their new appearance would help them in such matters as getting a date, securing a mate, or getting a better job.

For the women in my study, the decision to undergo cosmetic surgery was never purely or mainly for aesthetic purposes, but almost always for improving their social status as women who are racial minorities. Cosmetic surgery is a means by which they hope to acquire "symbolic capital" (Bourdieu 1984 [1979]) in the form of a look that holds more prestige. For example, "Jane," who underwent double-eyelid and nose-bridge procedures at the ages of 16 and 17, said that she thought she should get her surgeries "out of the way" at an early age since as a college student she has to think about careers ahead:

> Especially if you go into business, whatever, you kind of have to have a Western facial type and you have to have like their features and stature—you know, be tall and stuff. In a way you can see it as an investment in your future.

Such a quest for empowerment does not confront the cultural and institutional structures that are the real cause of the women's feelings of distress. Instead, this form of "body praxis" (Scheper-Hughes and Lock 1991) helps to entrench these structures by further confirming the undesirability of "stereotypical" Asian features. Therefore, the alteration by many Asian-American women of their features is a "disciplinary" practice in the Foucauldian sense; it does not so much benignly transform them as it "normalizes" (i.e., qualifies, classifies, judges, and enforces complicity in) the subject (Foucault 1977). The normalization is a double encounter, conforming to patriarchal definitions of femininity and to Caucasian standards of beauty (Bordo 1990).

Gramsci anticipated Foucault in considering subjected peoples' complicity and participation in, as well as reproduction of, their own domination in everyday practice. In examining such phenomena as Asian-American women undergoing cosmetic surgery in the late 20th-century United States, however, one must emphasize, as Foucault does, how mechanisms of domination have become much more insidious, overlapping, and pervasive in everyday life as various forms of "expert" knowledge such as plastic surgery and surgeons have increasingly come to play the role of "traditional" intellectuals (Gramsci 1971) or direct agents of the bourgeois state (Scheper-Hughes 1992, 171) in defining commonsense reality.

Particularly in Western, late capitalist societies (where the decoration, ornamentation, and scarification of the body have lost much meaning for the individual in the existential sense of "Which people do I belong to? What is the meaning of my life?" and have instead become commoditized by the media, corporations, and even medicine in the name of fashion), the normalizing elements of such practices as cosmetic surgery can become obscured. Rather than celebrations of the body, they are mutilations of the body, resulting from a devaluation of the self and induced by historically determined relationships among social groups and between the individual and society.

Internalization of Racial and Gender Stereotypes

The Asian-American women in my study are influenced by a gender ideology that states that beauty should be a primary goal of women. They are conscious that because they are women, they must conform to certain standards of beauty. "Elena," a 20-year-old Korean American, said, "People in society, if they are attractive, are rewarded for their efforts . . . especially girls. If they look pretty and neat, they are paid more attention to. You can't deny that." "Annie," another Korean American who is 18 years old, remarked that as a young woman, her motivation to have cosmetic surgery was "to look better" and "not different from why [other women] put on makeup." In fact, all expressed the idea that cosmetic surgery was a means by which they could escape the task of having to put makeup on every day. As "Jo," a 28-year-old Japanese American who is thinking of enlarging the natural fold above her eyes, said, "I am self-conscious about leaving the house without any makeup on, because I feel just really ugly without it. I feel like it's the mask that enables me to go outside." Beauty, more than character and intelligence, often signifies social and economic success for them as for other women in U.S. society (Lakoff and Scherr 1984; Wolf 1991).

The need to look their best as women motivates the Asian-American women in my study to undergo cosmetic surgery, but the standard of beauty they try to achieve through surgery is motivated by a racial ideology that infers negative behavioral or intellectual characteristics from a group's genetic physical features. All of the women said that they are "proud to be Asian American" and that they "do not want to look white." But the standard of beauty they admire and strive for is a face with larger eyes and a more prominent nose. They all stated that an eyelid without a crease and a nose that does not project indicate a certain "sleepiness," "dullness," and "passivity" in a person's character. "Nellee," a 21-year-old Chinese American, said she seriously considered surgery for double eyelids in high school so that she could "avoid the stereotype of the 'Oriental bookworm' " who is "*dull* and doesn't know how to have fun." Elena, who had double-eyelid surgery two years ago from a doctor in my study, said, "When I look at Asians who have no folds and their eyes are slanted and closed, I think of how they would look better more *awake*." "Carol," a 37-year-old Chinese American who had double-eyelid surgery seven years ago and "Ellen," a 40-year-old Chinese

American who had double-eyelid surgery 20 years ago, both said that they wanted to give their eyes a "more spirited" look. "The drawback of Asian features is the puffy eyes," Ellen said. "Pam," a Chinese American aged 44, who had double-eyelid surgery from another doctor in my study two months earlier, stated, "Yes. Of course. Bigger eyes look prettier. . . . Lots of Asians' eyes are so small they become little lines when the person laughs, making the person look *sleepy.*" Likewise, Annie, who had an implant placed in her nasal dorsum to build up her nose bridge at age 15, said:

> I guess I always wanted that *sharp* look—a look like you are smart. If you have a roundish kind of nose, it's like you don't know what's going on. If you have that sharp look, you know, with black eyebrows, a pointy nose, you look more *alert.* I always thought that was cool. [emphasis added]

Clearly, the Asian-American women in my study seek cosmetic surgery for double eyelids and nose bridges because they associate the features considered characteristic of their race with negative traits.

These associations that Asian-American women make between their features and personality characteristics stem directly from stereotypes created by the dominant culture in the United States and by Western culture in general, which historically has wielded the most power and hegemonic influence over the world. Asians are rarely portrayed in the U.S. popular media and then only in such roles as Charlie Chan, Suzie Wong, and "Lotus Blossom Babies" (a.k.a. China Doll, Geisha Girl, and shy Polynesian beauty). They are depicted as stereotypes with dull, passive, and nonsociable personalities (Kim 1986; Tajima 1989). Subtle depictions by the media of individuals' minutest gestures in everyday social situations can socialize viewers to confirm certain hypotheses about their own natures (Goffman 1979). At present, the stereotypes of Asians as a "model minority" serve a similar purpose. In the model minority stereotype, the concepts of dullness, passivity, and stoicism are elaborated to refer to a person who is hard-working and technically skilled but desperately lacking in creativity and sociability (Takaki 1989, 477).

Similar stereotypes of the stoic Asian also exist in East and Southeast Asia, and since many Asian Americans are immigrants or children of recent immigrants from Asia, they are likely to be influenced by these stereotypes as well. U.S. magazines and films have been increasingly available in many parts of Asia since World War II. Also, multinational corporations in Southeast Asian countries consider their work force of Asian women to be biologically suited for the most monotonous industrial labor because the "Oriental girl" is "diligent" and has "nimble fingers" and a "slow wit" (Ong 1987, 151). Racial stereotypes of Asians as docile, passive, slow witted, and unemotional are internalized by many Asian-American women, causing them to consider the facial features associated with these negative traits as defiling.

Undergoing cosmetic surgery, then, becomes a means by which the women can attempt to permanently acquire not only a feminine look considered more attractive by society, but also a certain set of racial features considered more prestigious. For them, the daily task of beautification entails creating the illusion of features they, as members of a racial minority, do not have. Nellee, who has not yet undergone double-eyelid surgery, said that at present she has to apply makeup every day "to give my eyes an illusion of a crease. When I don't wear makeup I feel my eyes are small." Likewise, Elena said that before her double-eyelid surgery she checked almost every morning in the mirror when she woke up to see if a fold had formed above her right eye to match the more prominent fold above her left eye: "[on certain mornings] it was like any other day when you wake up and don't feel so hot, you know. My eye had no definite folds, because when Asians sleep their folds change in and out—it's not definite." The enormous constraints the women in my study feel with regard to their Asian features are apparent in the meticulous detail with which they describe their discontent, as apparent in a quote from Jo who already has natural folds but wants to enlarge them: "I want to make an even bigger eyelid [fold] so that it doesn't look slanted. I think in Asian eyes this inside corner fold [she was drawing on my notebook] goes down too much."

The women expressed hope that the results of cosmetic surgery would win them better acceptance by society. Ellen said that she does not think her double-eyelid surgery "makes me look too different," but she nonetheless expressed the feeling that now her features will "make a better impression on people because I got rid of that sleepy look." She says that she will encourage her daughter, who is only 12 years old, to have double-eyelid surgery as she did, because "I think having less-sleepy-looking eyes would help her in the future with getting jobs." The aesthetic results of surgery are not an end in themselves but rather a means for these women as racial minorities to attain better socioeconomic status. Clearly, their decisions to undergo cosmetic surgery do not stem from a celebration of their bodies.

Medicalization of Racial Features

Having already been influenced by the larger society's negative valuation of their natural "given" features, Asian-American women go to see plastic surgeons in half-hour consultation sessions. Once inside the clinic, they do not have to have the doctor's social and medical views "thrust" on them, since to a great extent, they, like their doctors, have already entered into a more general social consensus (Scheper-Hughes 1992, 199). Nonetheless, the Western medical system is a most effective promoter of the racial stereotypes that influence Asian-American women, since medical knowledge is legitimized by scientific rationality and technical efficiency, both of which hold prestige in the West and increasingly all over the world. Access to a scientific body of knowledge has given Western medicine considerable social power in defining reality (Turner 1987, 11). According to my Asian American informants who had undergone cosmetic surgery, their plastic surgeons used several medical terms to problematize the shape of their eyes so as to define it as a medical condition. For instance, many patients were told that they had "excess fat" on their eyelids and that it was "normal" for them to feel dissatisfied with the way they looked. "Lots of Asians have the same puffiness over their eyelid, and they often feel better about themselves after the operation," the doctors would assure their Asian-American patients.

The doctors whom I interviewed shared a similar opinion of Asian facial features with many of the doctors of the patients in my study. Their descriptions of Asian features verged on ideological racism, as clearly seen in the following quote from "Dr. Smith."

> The social reasons [for Asian Americans to want double eyelids and nose bridges] are undoubtedly continued exposure to Western culture and the realization that the upper eyelid *without* a fold tends to give a *sleepy* appearance, and therefore a more *dull* look to the patient. Likewise, the *flat* nasal bridge and *lack of* nasal projection can signify *weakness* in one's personality and by *lack of* extension, a *lack of force* in one's character. [emphasis added]

By using words like "without," "lack of," "flat," "dull," and "sleepy" in his description of Asian features, Dr. Smith perpetuates the notion that Asian features are inadequate. Likewise, "Dr. Khoo" said that many Asians should have surgery for double eyelids since "the eye is the window to your soul and having a more open appearance make you look a bit brighter, more inviting." "Dr. Gee" agreed:

> I would say 90% of people look better with double eyelids. It makes the eye look more spiritually alive. . . . With a single eyelid frequently they would have a little fat pad underneath [which] can half bury the eye and so the eye looks small and unenergetic.

Such powerful associations of Asian features with negative personality traits by physicians during consultations can become a medical affirmation of Asian-American women's sense of disdain toward their own features.

Medical books and journals as early as the 1950s and as recent as 1990 abound with similar metaphors of abnormality in describing Asian features. The texts that were published before 1970 contain more explicit associations of Asian features with dullness and passivity. In an article published in 1954 in the *American Journal of Ophthalmology*, the author, a doctor in the Philippines armed forces, wrote the following about a man on whom he performed double-eyelid surgery:

> [He] was born with mere slits for his eyes. Everyone teased him about his eyes with the comment that as he looked constantly sleepy, so his business too was just as sleepy. For this reason, he underwent the plastic operation and, now that his eyes are wider, he has lost the sleepy look. His business, too, has picked up. [Sayoc 1954, 556]

The doctor clearly saw a causal link between the shape of his patient's eyes and his patient's intellectual and behavioral capacity to succeed in life. In 1964 a white American military surgeon who performed double-eyelid surgeries on Koreans in Korea during the American military occupation of that country wrote in the same journal: "The absence of the palpebral fold produces a passive expression which seems to epitomize the stoical and unemotional manner of the Oriental" (Millard 1964, 647). Medical texts published after 1970 are more careful about associating Asian features with negative behavioral or intellectual characteristics, but they still describe Asian features with metaphors of inadequacy or excess. For instance, in the introductory chapter to a 1990 book devoted solely to medical techniques for cosmetic surgery of the Asian face, a white American plastic surgeon begins by cautioning his audience not to stereotype the physical traits of Asians.

> Westerners tend to have a stereotyped conception of the physical traits of Asians: yellow skin pigmentation . . . a flat face with high cheek bones; a broad, flat nose; and narrow slit-like eyes showing characteristic epicanthal folds. While this stereotype may loosely apply to central Asian groups (i.e., Chinese, Koreans, and Japanese), the facial plastic surgeon should appreciate that considerable variation exists in all of these physical traits (McCurdy 1990, 1).

Yet, on the same page, he writes that the medicalization of Asian features is valid because Asians usually have eyes that are too narrow and a nose that is too flat.

> However, given an appreciation of the physical diversity of the Asian population, certain facial features do form a distinct basis for surgical intervention. . . . These facial features typically include the upper eyelid, characterized by an absent or poorly defined superior palpebral fold . . . and a flattened nose with poor lobular definition (McCurdy 1990, 1).

Thus, in published texts, doctors write about Asians' eyes and noses as abnormal even when they are careful not to associate negative personality traits with these features. In the privacy of their clinics, they freely incorporate both metaphors of abnormality and the association of Asian features with negative characteristics into medical discourse, which has an enormous impact on the Asian-American patients being served.

The doctors' scientific discourse is made more convincing by the seemingly objective manner in which they behave and present themselves in front of their patients in the clinical setting. They examine their patients as a technician diagnosing ways to improve a mechanical object. With a cotton swab, they help their patients to stretch and measure how high they might want their eyelids to be and show them in a mirror what could be done surgically to reduce the puffy look above their eyes. The doctors in my study also use slides and Polaroid pictures to come to an agreement with their patients on what the technical goals of the operation should be. The sterile appearance of their clinics, with white walls and plenty of medical instruments, as well as the symbolism of the doctor's white coat with its many positive connotations (e.g., purity, life, unaroused sexuality, superhuman power, and candor) reinforce in the patient the doctor's role as technician and thus his sense of objectivity (Blumhagen 1979). One of my informants, Elena, said that, sitting in front of her doctor in his office, she felt sure that she needed eyelid surgery: "[Dr. Smith] made quite an impression on me. I thought he was more than qualified—that he knew what he was talking about."

With its authority of scientific rationality and technical efficiency, medicine effectively "normalizes" not only the negative feelings of Asian-American women about their features but also their ultimate decision to undergo cosmetic surgery. For example, "Dr. Jones" does not want to make her patients feel "strange" or "abnormal" for wanting cosmetic surgery. All the doctors in my study agreed that their role as doctor is to provide the best technical skills possible for whatever service their patients demand, not to question the motivation of their patients. Her goal, Dr. Jones said, is "like that of a psychiatrist in that I try to make patients feel better about themselves." She feels that surgeons have an advantage over psychiatrists in treating cosmetic surgery patients because "we . . . help someone to change the way they look . . . psychiatrists are always trying to figure out why a person wants to do what they want to do." By changing the patients' bodies the way they would like them, she feels she provides them with an immediate and concrete solution to their feelings of inadequacy.

Dr. Jones and the other doctors say that they only turn patients away when patients expect results that are technically impossible, given such factors as the thickness of the patient's skin and the bone structure. "I turn very few patients away," said Dr. Khoo. And "Dr. Kwan" notes:

> I saw a young girl [a while back] whose eyes were beautiful but she wanted a crease. . . . She was gorgeous! Wonderful! But somehow she didn't see it that way. But you know, I'm not going to tell a patient every standard I have of what's beautiful. If they want certain things and it's doable, and if it is consistent with a reasonable look in the end, then I don't stop them. I don't really discuss it with them.

Like the other doctors in my study, Dr. Kwan sees himself primarily as a technician whose main role is to correct his patient's features in a way that he thinks would best contribute to the patient's satisfaction. It does not bother him that he must expose an individual, whom he already sees as pretty and not in need of surgery, to an operation that is at least an hour long, entails the administering of local anesthesia with sedation, and involves the following risks: "bleeding," "hematoma," "hemorrhage," formation of a "gaping wound," "discoloration," "scarring," and "asymmetry in lid fold" (Sayoc 1974, 162–66). He finds no need to try to change his patients' minds. Likewise, Dr. Smith said of Asian-American women who used to come to him to receive really large double eyelids: "I respect their ethnic background. I don't want to change them drastically." Yet he would not refuse them the surgery "as long as it was something I can accomplish. Provided I make them aware of what the appearance might be with the changes."

Though most of my Asian-American woman informants who underwent cosmetic surgery recovered fully within six months to a year, with only a few minor scars from their surgery, they nonetheless affirmed that the psychologically traumatic aspect of the operation was something their doctors did not stress during consultation. Elena said of her double-eyelid surgery: "I thought it was a simple procedure. He [the doctor] should have known better. It took at least an hour and a half. . . . And no matter how minor the surgery was, I bruised! I was swollen." Likewise, Annie could remember well her fear during nose surgery. Under local anesthesia, she said that she was able to witness and hear some of the procedures.

> I closed my eyes. I didn't want to look. I didn't want to see like the knives or anything. I could hear the snapping of scissors and I was aware when they were putting that thing [implant] up my nose. I was kind of grossed out.

By focusing on technique and subordinating human emotions and motivations to technical ends, medicine is capable of normalizing Asian-American women's decision to undergo cosmetic surgery.

Mutual Reinforcement: Medicine and the Consumer-Oriented Society

The medical system bolsters and benefits from the larger consumer-oriented society by perpetuating the idea that beauty is central to women's sense of self and also by promoting a beauty standard for Asian-American women that requires the alteration of features specific to Asian-American racial identity. All of the doctors in my study stated that a "practical" benefit for Asian-American women undergoing surgery to create or enlarge their eyelid folds is that they can put eye makeup on more appropriately. Dr. Gee said that after double-eyelid surgery it is "easier" for Asian-American women to put makeup on because "they now have two instead of just one plane on which to apply makeup." Dr. Jones agreed that after eyelid surgery Asian-American women "can do more dramatic things with eye makeup." The doctors imply that Asian-American women cannot usually put on makeup adequately, and thus, they have not been able to look as beautiful as they can be with makeup. By promoting the idea that a beautiful woman is one who can put makeup on adequately, they further the idea that a woman's identity should be closely connected with her body and, particularly, with the representational problems of the self. By reinforcing the makeup industry, they buttress the cosmetic surgery industry of which they are a part. A double-eyelid surgery costs patients $1,000 to $3,000.

The medical system also bolsters and benefits from the larger consumer society by appealing to the values of American individualism and by individualizing the social problems of racial inequality. Dr. Smith remarked that so many Asian-American women are not opting for cosmetic surgery procedures largely because of their newly gained rights as women and as racial minorities:

> Asians are more affluent than they were 15 years ago. They are more knowledge-able and Americanized, and their women are more liberated. I think in the past many Asian women were like Arab women. The men had their foot on top of them. Now Asian women do pretty much what they want to do. So if they want to do surgery, they do it.

Such comments by doctors encourage Asian-American women to believe that undergoing cosmetic surgery is merely a way of beautifying themselves and that it signifies their ability to exercise individual freedom.

Ignoring the fact that the Asian-American women's decision to undergo cosmetic surgery has anything to do with the larger society's racial prejudice, the doctors state that their Asian-American women patients come to cosmetic surgeons to mold their own standards of beauty. The doctors point out that the specific width and shape the women want their creases to be or the specific shape of nose bridges they want are a matter of personal style and individual choice. Dr. Smith explains:

> We would like to individualize every procedure. There is no standard nose we stamp on everybody so that each patient's need is addressed individually. My goal is to make that individual very happy and very satisfied.

Dr. Kwan also remarked, "I think people recognize what's beautiful in their own way." In fact, the doctors point out that both they and their Asian-American patients are increasingly getting more sophisticated about what the patients want. As evidence, they point to the fact that as early as a decade ago, doctors used to provide very wide creases to every Asian-American patient who came for double eyelids, not knowing that not every Asian wanted to look exactly Caucasian. The doctors point out that today many Asian-American cosmetic surgery patients explicitly request that their noses and eyelids not be made to look too Caucasian.

Recent plastic surgery literature echoes these doctors' observations. A 1991 press release from the American Academy of Cosmetic Surgery quotes a prominent member as saying, "The procedures they [minorities, including Asian Americans] seek are not so much to look 'Western' but to refine their features to attain facial harmony." The double-eyelid surgery, he says, is to give Asian eyes "a more open appearance," not a Western look. Likewise, McCurdy (1990, 8) points out in his book that double-eyelid procedures should vary in accordance with whether or not the patient actually requests a Western eyelid.

> In patients who desire a small "double-eyelid," the incision is placed 6–7 mm. above the ciliary margin: in those patients desiring a medium-sized lid, the incision is placed 8 mm. above the ciliary margin; in patients who request

westernization of the eyelid, the incision is placed 9–10 mm. above the ciliary margin.

Fifty percent of all Asians in the world do have a natural crease on their eyelids, and thus it can be argued that those Asians who undergo surgery for double eyelids are aiming for Asian looks, that they are not necessarily conforming to a Western standard. Yet, by focusing on technique, that is, by focusing on how many millimeters above the eyes their Asian-American patients want their fold to be or how long across the eyelid they want their fold to be drawn, the doctors do not fully recognize that the trend in Asian-American cosmetic surgery is still toward larger eyes and a more prominent nose. They ignore the fact that the very valuation attached to eyes with " a more open appearance" may be a consequence of society's racial prejudice. If the types of cosmetic surgery Asian Americans opt for are truly individual choices, one would expect to see a number of Asians who admire and desire eyes without a crease or a nose without a bridge. Yet the doctors can refer to no cases involving Asian Americans who wanted to get rid of their creases or who wanted to flatten their noses. Moreover, there are numerous cases of Asian Americans, such as many Southeast Asians, who already have a natural eyelid crease but feel the need to widen it even more for a less puffy appearance.[5] Clearly there is a pattern in the requests of Asian-American cosmetic surgery patients.

In saying that their Asian-American women patients are merely exercising their freedom to choose a personal style or look, the doctors promote the idea that human beings have an infinite variety of needs that technology can endlessly fulfill, an idea at the heart of today's U.S. capitalism. As Susan Bordo explains, the United States has increasingly become a "plastic" culture, characterized by a "disdain for material limits, and intoxication with freedom, change, and self-determination" (Bordo 1990, 654). She points out that many consumer products that could be considered derogatory to women and racial minorities are thought by the vast majority of Americans to be only some in an array of consumer choices to which every individual has a right. She explains:

> Any different self would do, it is implied. Closely connected to this is the construction of all cosmetic changes as the same: perms for white women, corn rows on Bo Derek, tanning, makeup, changing hair styles, blue contacts for black women. [Bordo 1990, 659]

Conclusion

Cosmetic surgery on Asian-American women for nose bridges and double eyelids is very much influenced by gender and racial ideologies. My research has shown that by the conscious or unconscious manipulation of gender and racial stereotypes, the American medical system, along with the larger consumer-oriented society of which it is a part, influences Asian-American women to alter their features through surgery. With the authority of scientific rationality and technological efficiency, medicine is effectively able to maintain a gender ideology that validates women's monetary and time investment in beauty even if this means making their bodies vulnerable to harmful and risky procedures such as plastic surgery. Medicine is also able to perpetuate a racial ideology that states that Asian features signify "dullness," "passivity," and "lack of emotions" in the Asian person. The medicalization of racial features, which reinforces and normalizes Asian-American women's feelings of inadequacy, as well as their decision to undergo surgery, helps to bolster the consumer-oriented society of which medicine is a part and from which medicine benefits.

Given the authority with which fields of "expert" knowledge such as biomedicine have come to define the commonsense reality today, racism and sexism no longer need to rely primarily on physical coercion to legal authority. Racial stereotypes influence Asian-American women to seek cosmetic surgery. Yet, through its highly specialized and validating forms of discourse and practices, medicine, along with a culture based on endless self-fashioning, is able to motivate women to view their feelings of inadequacy as individually motivated, as opposed to socially induced, phenomena, thereby effectively convincing them to participate in the production and reproduction of the larger structural inequalities that continue to oppress them.

Notes

I would like to thank Nancy Scheper-Hughes, Aihwa Ong, and Cecilia de Mello for their help, insight, and inspiration from the inception of this research project. This research was funded by the Edward H. Heller Endowment and a President's Undergraduate Fellowship, University of California, Berkeley.

1. In a 1989 study of 80 men and women, men reported many more positive thoughts about their bodies than did women (Goleman 1991).

    According to the American Society of Plastic Surgeons, 87% of all cosmetic surgery patients in 1990 were women. In my study, in one of the two doctors' offices from which I received statistical data on Asian-American patients, 65% of Asian-American cosmetic surgery patients in 1990 were women; in the other, 62%.

2. At the first doctor's office, the doctor's assistant examined every file from 1990. In all, 121 cosmetic procedures were performed, 81 on white patients, 20 on Asian-American patients. Closely following national data, the most common procedure among white patients was liposuction (58% of all cosmetic surgeries performed on white patients).

    The second doctor allowed me to survey his patient files. I examined the 1990 files for all patients with last names beginning with the letters A through L. Of these files, all the cosmetic patients were Asian American. Thus, I do not have data on white patients from this office.

    It is important to note that at the first doctor's office, where data on white cosmetic surgery patients were available, the patients were older on average than the Asian-American cosmetic surgery patients at the same clinic. Of the Asian-American patients, 65% were in the age range of 19 to 34 years, compared with

14.8% of whites. Only 20% of Asian American cosmetic surgery patients were in the age group of 35–64 years, however, compared with 80.2% of white cosmetic surgery patients. All the other doctors in my study confirmed a similar trend in their practices. They stated that this trend results from the tendency of whites to seek cosmetic procedures to remove fat and sagging skin that results from aging, in contrast to Asian Americans, who usually are not concerned with "correcting" signs of aging.

3. The shapes of eyes and noses of Asians are not meant in this article to be interpreted as categories that define an objective category called Asians. Categories of racial groups are arbitrarily defined by society. Likewise, the physical traits by which people are recognized as belonging to a racial group have been determined to be arbitrary (Molnar 1983).

Also, I use the term "Asian-American" to collectively name the women in this study who have undergone or are thinking of undergoing cosmetic surgery. Although I realize their ethnic diversity, people of Asian ancestry in the United States share similar experiences in that they are subject to many of the same racial stereotypes (Takaki 1989).

4. Cosmetic surgery for double eyelids, nasal-tip refinement, and nose bridges is not limited to Asians in the United States. Asians in East and Southeast Asia have requested such surgeries since the early 1950s, when U.S. military forces began long-term occupation of such countries as Korea and the Philippines (Harahap 1982; Kristof 1991; Millard 1964; and Sayoc 1954).

I do not mean to imply, however, that the situation within which Asian women develop a perspective on the value and meaning of their facial features is identical in Asia and the United States, where Asian women belong to a minority group. The situation in Asia would require further studies. My observations are limited to the United States.

5. Dr. Smith informed me that numerous Vietnamese, Thai, and Indonesian women come to him to widen their eyelid creases. I was allowed to see their before-and-after surgery photographs.

References

Blacking, John. 1977. *The Anthropology of the Body*. London: Academic Press.

Blumhagen, Dan. 1979. The doctor's white coat: The image of the physician in modern America. *Annals of Internal Medicine* 91:111–16.

Bordo, Susan. 1990. Material girl: The effacements of postmodern culture. *Michigan Quarterly Review* 29:635–76.

Bourdieu, Pierre. 1984. *Distinction: A Social Critique of the Judgment of Taste*. R. Nice, trans. Cambridge, MA: Harvard University Press.

Brain, Robert. 1979. *The Decorated Body*. New York: Harper and Row.

Daly, Mary. 1978. *Gyn/Ecology: The Metaethics of Radical Feminism*. Boston: Beacon Press.

Foucault, Michel. 1977. *Discipline and Punish: The Birth of the Prison*. A. Sheridan, trans. New York: Vintage Books.

Goffman, Erving. 1979. *Gender Advertisements*. Cambridge, MA: Harvard University Press.

Goleman, Daniel. 1991. When ugliness is only in the patient's eye, body image can reflect a mental disorder. *New York Times* 2 October:B9.

Gramsci, Antonio. 1971. *Selections from the Prison Notebooks of Antonio Gramsci.* New York: International.

Harahap, Marwali. 1982. Oriental cosmetic blepharoplasty. In *Cosmetic Surgery for Non-White Patients,* edited by Harold Pierce. New York: Grune and Stratton.

Kim, Elaine. 1986. Asian Americans and American popular culture. In *Dictionary of Asian American History,* edited by Hyung-Chan Kim. New York: Greenwood Press.

Kristof, Nicholas. 1991. More Chinese look "West." *San Francisco Chronicle,* 7 July: Sunday Punch 6.

Lakoff, Robin Tolmach, and Raquel L. Scherr. 1984. *Face Value: The Politics of Beauty.* Boston: Routledge and Kegan Paul.

Lock, Margaret, and Nancy Scheper-Hughes. 1990. A critical-interpretive approach in medical anthropology: Rituals and routines of discipline and dissent. In *Medical Anthropology: Contemporary Theory and Method,* edited by Thomas M. Johnson and Carolyn F. Sargent. New York: Praeger.

McCurdy, John A. 1990. *Cosmetic Surgery of the Asian Face.* New York: Thieme Medical Publications.

Millard, Ralph, Jr. 1964. The Oriental eyelid and its surgical revision. *American Journal of Ophthalmology* 57:646–49.

Molnar, Stephen. 1983. *Human Variation: Races, Types, and Ethnic Groups.* Englewood Cliffs, NJ: Prentice-Hall.

O'Neill, John. 1985. *Five Bodies.* Ithaca, NY: Cornell University Press.

Ong, Aihwa. 1987. *Spirits of Resistance and Capitalist Discipline: Factory Women In Malaysia.* Albany: State University of New York Press.

Rosenthal, Elisabeth. 1991. Cosmetic surgeons seek new frontiers. *New York Times* 24 September:B5-B6.

Sayoc, B. T. 1954. Plastic construction of the superior palpebral fold. *American Journal of Ophthalmology* 38:556–559.

———. 1974. Surgery of the Oriental eyelid. *Clinics in Plastic Surgery* 1:157–71.

Scheper-Hughes, Nancy. 1992. *Death Without Weeping.* Berkeley: University of California Press.

Scheper-Hughes, Nancy, and Margaret M. Lock. 1991. The message in the bottle: Illness and the micropolitics of resistance. *Journal of Psychohistory* 18: 409–32.

Tajima, Renee E. 1989. Lotus blossoms don't bleed: Images of Asian women. In *Making Waves: An Anthology of Writings by and about Asian Women,* edited by Diane Yeh-Mei Wong. Boston: Beacon Press.

Takaki, Ronald. 1989. *Strangers from a Different Shore.* Boston: Little, Brown.

Turner, Bryan. 1987. *Medical Knowledge and Social Power.* London: Sage Publications.

Turner, Terence. 1980. The social skin. In *Not Work Alone,* edited by J. Cherfas and R. Lewin. London: Temple Smith.

Wolf, Naomi. 1991. *The Beauty Myth: How Images of Beauty Are Used Against Women.* New York: William Morrow.

13

Mirror Mirror

Marcia Ann Gillespie

In Toni Morrison's first novel, *The Bluest Eye* (1970), a little dark-skinned girl, her hair short and nappy, looks in the mirror and longs for blue eyes. She is a Black child called ugly to her face and behind her back, devalued, unloved, sexually abused, longing to be physically transformed. Blue eyes symbolize all that she is told she is not, all that she does not have. If she had blue eyes, she'd be thought beautiful, like the dolls with the pretty dresses and bows. Her hair would be long and silky if she had blue eyes. She'd be loved and happy like the children in the storybooks. Were this a fairy tale with one of those they-lived-happily-ever-after endings, the people around her would be transformed, suddenly able to see her beauty and their own. But it is not. Black does not become beautiful, the white goddess of beauty continues to reign, and a little girl is forever lost.

Every time I read *The Bluest Eye*, I weep for that little girl lost in a world of pain and for all the women who carry pieces and parts of that little girl buried somewhere in their spirits. For who among us has not at some point in time succumbed to the propaganda, looked in the mirror and felt ourselves to be wanting? Wanting because our skin was too dark, or our noses too wide, or our hips too large, or because our hair wouldn't grow and never blew in the wind, or just because we never seemed to measure up. And how many of us can honestly say that somewhere, sometime, we, too, have not made a big fuss over one child's "good looks" while ignoring another? How many times have you heard someone—maybe yourself—say, "What a homely child, I hope she grows out of it"? We say "Black is beautiful," or we used to, before we began to war with one another. Funny how we still end up adhering to a standard that too often dips Barbie in light chocolate. And more times than not we take our cues from self-styled arbiters who use a Eurocentric standard, one that by design is meant to leave most women wanting. And most especially those women who look like you and me—whose coloring owes nothing to the sun, tube or bottle, whose hair kinks rather than waves, whose eyes aren't blue.

Mirror, mirror on the wall, who's the fairest of them all? America's mirror screams back Blondie, Rapunzel, Cinderella, Marilyn Monroe, Christie Brinkley, Diane Sawyer, Michelle Pfeiffer. Oh yes, sometimes the look changes as those who are styled arbiters decree brunettes, exotics or ethnics the latest "in" look. But no matter that they may sing the praises of voluptuous this year or dark sultry the next, the objects of beauty are always overwhelmingly white. And as the ambitious so-so singer named Madonna knew when she reached for the bleach and peroxide, blonde is still considered the apogee.

And where America's wordsmiths will rhapsodize over the beauty of the late artist Georgia O'Keefe's wizened face, Barbra Streisand's or Angelica Huston's big nose, Lauren Hutton's gap-toothed smile, and work feverishly if they must to find some attribute to exalt or praise on one of their own, rarely do they see or acknowledge as beauty that which we possess. When they do decree a Black woman beautiful, nine times out of ten she conforms to the white aesthetic. Take a close look at the women who are selected as models. Black but not really black: café au lait, not black coffee; pouty rather than full-lipped; a bit of butt but not too much.

Despite all the talk about the ways in which the American beauty standard automatically negates all who are not European, we get sucked in even when we think we're standing pure. We afrocentrize by wearing dreadlocks, twists, cornrows, but still there's the desire to have shake-your-head hair that moves and flips and flies. So we end up buying hair by the pound in order to achieve the desired effect while being ethnically correct. And yet another generation is programmed to believe that only certain shades of Black are beautiful. Programmed to want hair on the pillow, to become fixed on having long hair, lots of hair to flick and shake in weaves, braids, and instant Afro-Asian dreads. Bushels and bales of hair to meet our ever-increasing demand are shorn from the heads of wrenchingly poor Asian women. Sold American—a perfect study of exploitation all around.

As distorted as the mirror is for us, it's just as bad, and in some ways worse, for Asian, Native-American, and Latina women. To be considered beautiful, must a Chinese woman look like Connie Chung? Brazilians like Sonia Braga? I can't recall the last time I saw an identifiably Chinese, Korean, Puerto Rican, or Mexican woman in a beauty ad or fashion spread or on a national-magazine cover. Have you ever seen one?

Getting my nails done a few months ago while working on this article, I asked several of the young Korean manicurists in the shop to describe the women they considered beautiful. They pulled out American fashion and beauty magazines and pointed out varying models, all of them tall, all with blond or brunette hair, none who looked even vaguely like an Asian woman. Almost to a woman, these young Koreans all spoke about wanting to have bigger breasts.

Wanting. Yeah, that sums up what happens to women in this country when it comes to the beauty thing. "Mirror, mirror on the wall, who's the . . . ?" Most of the time when the question is raised, the answer isn't you. In fact, most women rarely (as in almost never) look in a mirror and are satisfied with what they see. You are either too short or too tall, too fat, or too thin. Your eyes aren't the shape, size or color that is considered beautiful. Your hair doesn't blow in the wind, or drape on your shoulder, or fluff out on the pillow. You have too much butt or too little. You worry because you have skinny legs or thunder thighs, 32A's or 36DD's. You worry about gravity sending nipples downward, about time and wrinkles, stretch marks and cellulite.

But then how do you keep a capitalist consumer culture afloat if people are not kept in a perpetual state of wanting, of feeling insecure? Women—of every ethnic group and color—already programmed to see ourselves as commodities, whose value rises or falls depending on how close or how far we are from some standard of ideal beauty, are the perfect marks. One young woman I worked with—tall, naturally blonde, who wore at best a size 10—talked in casual conversation with a group of us one day about how as a teenager she became obsessed with her weight. Nina talked about looking in the mirror and constantly worrying that she was too fat. "I dieted down to a size 6 and still felt I was fat," she said. "All of my girlfriends wanted to be thin, that was the ideal. When my mother started saying I was too thin and told me to stop dieting, I pretended to go along with her. I'd eat and then go into the bathroom and stick my fingers down my throat. For years I was bulimic, eating, gorging on food, then swallowing laxatives and throwing up right afterward. I finally ended up in a hospital with my stomach a mess."

One of my girlfriends used to constantly chide me when I refused to let her or anyone else pluck my eyebrows by saying "Beauty knows no pain." It's probably what Mandarin mothers told their little daughters as they wept through the pain of having their feet bound ever tighter. "Hush now, don't you want to look pretty?" How many Black women heard those words or something similar as children the first time the hot comb burned, the chemical relaxer set your scalp afire? Women's bodies have long been considered little more than malleable clay to be reshaped to meet whatever the standard of the day, no matter what the risk, discomfort, or pain. At the end of the last century, wealthy white women went so far as to have ribs removed to achieve the perfect wasp waist. Thousands of other women endured the fortunes of the damned by constricting waists and rib cages in corsets meant to be pulled to the breaking point. Fashionable women swooned often back then, which had a lot less to do with delicate "white woman sensibilities" than the fact that their corsets left them oxygen-deprived.

"Beauty knows no pain" is the motto millions of women adhere to as they starve themselves to the point of anorexia or develop bulimia, have noses broken and sawed, teeth pulled, lips surgically thinned or plumped by injections, ribs removed, thighs and stomachs suctioned, breasts reduced or added to, faces lifted and tucked, eyes reshaped, and buy contact lenses not to improve their vision but to have the eye color of their dreams—perhaps in a perfect shade of emerald green.

And for beauty's sake millions of women in this country today walk around with silicone time-bomb breast implants. Women made to feel insecure because their breasts are too small, insecure because they were disfigured by cancer surgery.

Mirror, mirror . . . What price beauty? What beauty do you seek? "She does not see her beauty . . ."—so goes a poem by our laureate Langston Hughes. But can one ever see beauty through a distorted mirror? Like Toni Morrison, I never wanted to see another generation of Black girls grow up longing, feeling and believing themselves not beautiful. I know the struggle those of my forty-something and older generation have gone through trying to "decrud" ourselves, break free.

I am just a few years short of 50, and it has been years since I stood in front of a mirror wanting to look like someone other than myself. But I remember how as a teenager, I, like so many of my girlfriends, longed to look like Dorothy Dandridge. To be Black, but not too Black. I remember longing to have my sister's hazel eyes and lighter skin and hoping that my breasts would continue to grow to the melon-size ideal. I remember every time I got my hair done how disappointed I was that it never looked or moved like that of the white girls touted as beautiful in movies and magazines. No, I never longed for blue eyes, never daydreamed about being white; and yet I wanted to be part of the rarified group considered beautiful.

Today when I look in the mirror I'm perfectly content with what I see, and while swearing to lose weight, I am not overwrought by my hips, thighs or belly. Yet I'm constantly reminded every time I open a fashion or beauty magazine, something I try to do only rarely, on those one-in-a-while times when I tune in to BET, VH1, or MTV, that yet another generation is being brainwashed into believing that beauty is less about what they are than it is about what they are not. Automatically, I search for Black women. And yes, there are more of us than was ever true before, and the women are beautiful. But it remains a beauty narrowly defined. They don't look like Grace Jones or Alfre Woodard, Leontyne Price, Sarah Vaughan or Whoopi Goldberg. Don't reflect our range and depth of beauty.

I watch Black men rhapsodize in song to women more likely beige than chocolate-brown. Women wearing lots of somebody else's hair, women with neat little noses and lips that can be full but not too full, women who remind me of Dorothy Dandridge. And I can't help but wonder what effect these images are having on yet another generation of little girls who are more brown than beige, little girls with full lips and noses, little pigtailed girls whose hair doesn't brush their shoulders or fan in waves.

No matter that we profess shock when we see a Michael Jackson distort his color and features, narrow his nose, thin his lips, reconstruct his face as it becomes ever lighter, ever whiter before our eyes, pushing his stray processed hair out of his face while singing "It don't matter if you're black or white . . ." What message do our kids take away? While we may tell our little girls that Olivia on the *Cosby Show* is beautiful, "but no more beautiful than you," what do they really believe if all the little Black girls who appear on television shows are oohed and aahed over, all seem cast from the same mold? Do our children end up standing in front of a mirror dissatisfied with their reflection, believing that beauty is something other than what they see, wanting to be transformed, longing for the bluest eye?

Reference

Morrison, Toni. 1970. *The Bluest Eye.* New York: Washington Square Press.

14

Jane Fonda, Barbara Bush, and Other Aging Bodies
Femininity and the Limits of Resistance

MYRA DINNERSTEIN AND ROSE WEITZ

Although separated by only half a generation, Jane Fonda and Barbara Bush present us with almost diametrically opposed images of how women can age. Fonda, born in 1937, boasts a "relentlessly improved" body—muscular and nearly fat-free, with dyed hair and surgically enhanced face and breasts. In contrast, Bush, born in 1925, exhibits a "resolutely natural" look, with her matronly figure, white hair, and wrinkled countenance.[1]

The striking contrast between the appearances of these two highly visible women led us to select them for a study of how women manage their aging bodies. Their dissimilar appearances seemed to reflect two different approaches to aging and to the prevailing cultural discourse which equates femininity with a youthful appearance (Freedman 1986, 200; Seid 1989; Sontag 1972; Woodward 1991, 161). Moreover, both describe their behavior and appearance as forms of resistance to these cultural pressures. As we will show, however, their lives testify more to the limits of individual resistance than to its possibilities.

As public figures, with sufficient financial resources to employ all that the beauty and fashion industries can offer, Fonda and Bush differ in important ways from most women. In addition, as white heterosexuals, issues of beauty and aging might have different cultural meanings for them than for many lesbians and minority women. Nevertheless, the narratives of their aging reveal a dilemma that most American women confront as they age: how to handle an aging body in a culture in which aging challenges acceptable notions of femininity. . . .

Agency, Social Control, and the Female Body

Part of the problem women face in resisting cultural definitions of femininity is that these definitions influence us in ways that we do not fully recognize. While many women are aware of the barrage of messages from the media about appropriate feminine appearance, few realize how insidiously these notions have entered our individual psyches or think to question their legitimacy. Newspaper articles might report on studies showing that a high proportion of ten-year-old girls diet and that an epidemic of anorexia and bulimia has swept the country, but few women respond to this evidence of the dire consequences of preoccupation with body size by changing their own attitudes and behaviors.

To illuminate the covert and powerful ways that cultural ideas about femininity shape women's conscious and unconscious attitudes toward their bodies, some feminist scholars have drawn on the work of Michel Foucault (1979, 136). Foucault describes the body in some of his writings as an "object and target of power," a field on which the hierarchies of power are displayed and inscribed, and has shown how various institutions such as the army and the school deploy their power by controlling their members' time, space, and movement. Feminists have elaborated his argument, describing how definitions of femininity act, in Foucault's terms, as a "discipline" regulating women's bodies (Bartky 1988, 63–64; Bordo 1989, 13–14; Foucault 1979, 136–39). As army regulations control a soldier's gestures, walk, and posture, cultural definitions of femininity control female bodies by setting standards that specify what is considered appropriate and "normal" (Bartky 1988, 61–63, 75; Foucault 1979, 136–38, 150–53). These feminist scholars have suggested that women have so internalized the rewards and dictates of femininity that they appear to conform willingly (Bartky 1988). . . .

In contrast, other feminist scholars contend that this argument overstates the power of cultural norms to discipline women. Critics such as McNay (1991) argue that Foucault and his followers see women only as "docile bodies," ignoring the many ways that women historically have resisted societal prescriptions, while even those who emphasize oppression such as Bartky (1988, 82) concede that there are "pockets of resistance" and "oppositional discourses" to normative femininity, such as among radical lesbians and female body builders.

Our analysis of Fonda and Bush joins this discussion by highlighting the interplay between agency and social control in the reactions of heterosexual white women to their aging appearance, demonstrating how Fonda and Bush simultaneously have attempted to resist the dominant discourse on aging and have been constrained by it. Their experiences delineate the difficulties of resistance and underscore the struggle required to establish oppositional discourses.

For this paper, we draw on all articles written about Bush and Fonda in women's magazines (including fashion magazines) indexed in the *Readers'*

Guide to Periodical Literature beginning in 1977, when Fonda turned forty. . . .

Aging Female Bodies: A Brief History

What constitutes a culturally appropriate appearance for aging women has changed considerably over time (Banner 1983; Schwartz 1986; Seid 1989). Until the mid-twentieth century, American society expected older women to have what was termed a "mature figure" and to a wear "mature" fashions. Beginning in the 1950s, however, this demarcation between youthful and aging appearances began to break down. The emphasis on youth accelerated in the 1960s and early 1970s, as both medical and fashion experts, bolstered by the highly visible youth culture, declared the youthful, slim body the standard for all (Seid 1989).

By the late 1970s, as the baby boomers who had fostered the youth culture aged, the struggle to maintain a youthful appearance had fostered a nationwide fitness craze.

The admonition to become slim and fit, which intensified in the 1980s, ignored the biological realities of aging—the typically unavoidable weight gain, increased ratio of fat to muscle, and, for women, thickening waists and sagging breasts (Seid 1989, 265). Instead, both medical and popular experts redefined "mature figures" as symbols of self-indulgence and irresponsibility. Failure to take up the new ethic of fitness became a sign of social or even moral failure, with the unfit deemed the secular equivalent of sinners and the fit promised youth and health (Crawford 1979; Stein 1982, 168–69, 174; Tesh 1988; Turner 1984, 202; Waitzkin 1981; Zola 1972).

This new ethic has had greater repercussions for women than for men, for appearance always has formed a more central aspect of how women evaluate themselves and are evaluated by others (Chernin 1981, 145–61; Bartky 1988, 65). Attractiveness often translates not only into feelings of self-esteem but into success in obtaining heterosexual affiliation and professional jobs (Freedman 1986; Morgan 1991).

The increased cultural focus since the 1970s on controlling women's bodies has led several critics to label it a "backlash" to the rising power and visibility of women. These commentators suggest that keeping women involved with controlling their bodies diverts their energies from striving to achieve more control in the public arena (Bordo 1989, 14; Bordo 1990, 105; Faludi 1991, 203–4; Wolf 1991, 9–12). An analysis of Jane Fonda, who both rode the wave of the new fitness craze and helped to create it, and who promotes women's control of the body as a form of "liberation," illuminates the contradictions of preoccupation with the body.

Managing the Aging Body

Jane Fonda: Relentlessly Improved

Jane Fonda has undergone many metamorphoses in her lifetime, summarized by one magazine writer as "a sex kitten in the 50s, antiwar radical in the late

60s, feminist in the 70s, successful entrepreneur in the 80s," and someone who focused on "personal fulfillment" in the 90s (Ball 1992, 96). Throughout, however, Fonda has worked diligently to maintain a shapely body.

Ever since she turned forty, Fonda has garnered particular attention and admiration as a woman who has aged yet retained her beauty. With each successive year, the women's magazines have marked Jane Fonda's chronological aging by announcing her age and marveling at how well and, specifically, how young she looks (e.g., Andersen 1989, 112; Davis 1990, 165). Fonda fascinates aging women, one journalist suggests, "because she has a great body, an over-40 body that offers hope and promise. Along with each book and tape comes convincing evidence that it's possible . . . to remain beautiful and sexy in midlife" (Levin 1987, 27).

Ironically, for those who recall her 1968 film role as the sex machine "Barbarella" and her pleasure-filled lifestyle as the wife of French film director Roger Vadim, by the 1970s, Fonda had begun describing herself as a feminist role model (e.g., Robbins 1977). Fonda began this new phase of her life—as not only a feminist but also as an anti-Vietnam War activist—at about the time that her marriage to Vadim was ending and shortly before meeting and marrying political activist Tom Hayden (Andersen 1990, 214–65). Looking back on her early years from a feminist perspective, Fonda described to interviewers how she had come to reject the cultural stereotypes that formerly oppressed her. In a 1976 magazine story, for example, Fonda bemoaned how she had spent her twenties wearing falsies and declared herself now free from such constraints. She sat before the interviewer "clutching her breasts to make sure the offensive things weren't still around" (Lear 1976, 145).

In the same article, she described how her feminist awareness had grown when Hayden showed her pictures of Vietnamese women who had plastic surgery to make their eyes round and enlarge their breasts. Fonda was "stunned and I thought my God that same phony Playboy image that made me wear falsies for ten years, that made billions of American women dissatisfied with their own bodies, has been transported thousands of miles to another culture and made these women too hate their bodies, made them willing to mutilate themselves" (Lear 1976, 15).

Fonda and Hayden's political involvement provided the spur for Fonda's emergence as a fitness entrepreneur. To finance their political activities, Fonda in 1979 established her first Workout Studio and in 1982 published her best-selling *Workout Book* and videotape (Andersen 1990, 302–3).

In the 1980s, as Fonda emerged as an exercise guru, she at first extolled the virtues of intervening only minimally in the aging process. At age 47, writing about aging skin and cosmetic surgery in *Women Coming of Age* (1984, 71), her book on midlife, she advised, "The course I prefer: making peace with the growing numbers of fine (and some not so fine) lines you see on your face . . . . Wrinkles are part of who we are, of where we've been. Not to have wrinkles means never having laughed or cried or expressed passion, never having squinted into the sun or felt the bite of winter's wind—never having fully lived!" Similarly, she told an interviewer, "I have a few more wrinkles, a few more gray hairs, and that's okay. I don't obsess about my looks the way I used to" (Kaplan 1985, 374).

Despite this rhetoric, however, most of Fonda's pronouncements even during these years centered on changing and controlling rather than accepting the body. Yet in these statements as well, Fonda used feminist rhetoric such as "freedom" and "liberation" to frame this bodily control as a form of resistance to traditional expectations of female emotional and physical weakness. Bodily control, she has argued, "gives me a sense of freedom" (Kaplan 1987, 417), for "discipline is freedom" (*Mademoiselle* 1980, 38). Similarly, she has described herself as "liberated" from the cultural pressures that led her to engage in binge/purge eating until age 35.

Magazine writers, too, have described Fonda's life in feminist terms. One reporter, for example, comments that "There is a sense she's on the right side, making a political statement in warm-ups and running shoes. On one level, her tapes are about women taking control of their bodies, gaining physical confidence in front of their VCRs, then striding out of their homes to flex their new power" (Kaplan 1987, 417).

As she began to promote her fitness methods, Fonda also argued that working to develop bodily control empowers women by improving their health. Although Fonda acknowledges that "exercise isn't a panacea for everything," she nevertheless argues that "much of what ails us can be lessened by making the heart and lungs really work, getting the blood oxygenated and circulating, and limbering up the body" (*Harper's Bazaar* 1980, 82). Similarly, Fonda sees exercise as a means toward mental health: "Exercise does a tremendous amount for emotional and mental stability. . . . That is what satisfies me most, . . . the people who come up after a week or two of classes and say, 'Hey, I'm not depressed anymore' " (*Harper's Bazaar* 1980, 82).

Given the prevailing discourse on femininity and on aging, it is not surprising that Fonda and her admirers have characterized her as feminist. In a culture which characterizes women as weak, Fonda's goal of strengthening the body offers an alternative to fragile womanhood. It also disputes the idea that the aging body is a rundown machine (Martin 1987, 40–46). Fonda demonstrates vigorously that her body—and thus potentially all aging, female bodies—can work. Moreover, the exercise that Fonda advocates challenges the restricted space to which women are constrained in everyday life. Bodies, arms, legs move and extend this space, allowing women to experience a freer use of the body, which many experience as liberating.

The benefits of a reasonable exercise program as a way to enhance emotional and physical health, maintain a healthy body weight, and protect against osteorporosis and heart disease have been well established and should not be minimized. What Fonda and her admirers have overlooked, however, in their litany of the benefits of exercise, is the contrast between the obsessive and punitive self-control and self-surveillance implicit in the exercise and beauty regimens she advocates and the liberation she claims to derive from them. In the same quote in which she encourages women to accept wrinkles, for example, she also urges "doing your best through nutrition, exercise, proper cleansing, moisturizing, sleep, and healthy living habits to avoid aggravated and premature wrinkles" (Fonda 1984, 71). This lengthy list of tasks suggests the level of work needed to age "properly" and not "prematurely."

Similarly, since her twenties, Fonda has controlled her shape through daily exercise. Only recently has she allowed herself to skip exercise for even a few days (Ball 1992, 97, 143). In one interviewer's words, Fonda is "an exercise addict, like few others" (Levin 1987, 28). Her language of war, struggle, and labor indicate the amount of effort and self-surveillance she devotes to bodily control: "I have a constant weight problem. . . . It's just a constant struggle" (*Mademoiselle* 1980, 40). Similarly: "I constantly fight against weight, and I don't necessarily have a good figure. I have to work for it, and I do work for it" (Harrison 1978, 40).

Moreover, in the same way that she compulsively exercises, she continues to watch her food intake. At luncheon with a reporter, "there's one tense moment when the waiter places a pat of butter on her [Jane's] bread dish. 'No, no, take it away, she demands, flustered' " (Levin 1987, 25–26).

It seems, then, that Fonda's desire for a culturally appropriate body has tyrannized rather than liberated her. Fonda's life demonstrates that maintaining an "acceptable" body requires constant vigilance. As feminist critics have pointed out, such constant demands for self-surveillance keep women in line (Faludi 1991; Wolf 1991).

At the same time, Fonda's insistence on the importance of bodily self-control can lead to denigrating those who appear to lack control. In Fonda's worldview, care of the body is not only a personal responsibility but also a moral one. Bodily control signifies self-control, and hence moral superiority. This belief, which permeates the health and fitness movement, has been labeled a "new asceticism" or "new Puritanism" (Kilwein 1989, 9–10; Turner 1984). If in the past individuals disciplined the body to control their passions and submit to God, nowadays individuals discipline the body to extend their lives and increase their pleasures (Turner 1984, 156, 161–63, 172.) Yet the value placed on self-discipline continues to resonate with its religious origins, for a fit body still announces a good character.

In Fonda's secularized world, personal "salvation" (of the character and body, if not the soul) is possible through self-abnegation—denying oneself food and exercising even to the point of pain (cf., Bordo 1990, 83). She has waxed lyrical about the physical benefits of denying herself food: "Going to bed on an empty stomach and waking up hungry is the greatest thing you can do for yourself. If you go to bed hungry and wake up hungry, you've got unbelievable energy" (*Mademoiselle* 1980, 40). She speaks in similarly positive tones about the benefits of fasting (*Mademoiselle* 1980, 38–40). In both her exercise and eating regimens, then, the body becomes a locus of work, something to be subdued.

Fonda explicitly rejects the notion that the ability to control one's body might depend upon such factors as genetics, leisure time, or financial resources. When, for example, a reporter suggested in 1980 that Fonda might have inherited her father's slimness, Fonda bristled and replied, "I don't have my father's body at all. He has absolutely no ass. I like to think a lot of my body is my own doing and my own blood and guts. It's my responsibility" (*Mademoiselle* 1980, 40).

By extension, those who do not take responsibility for their bodies have only themselves to blame for their problems. In pressing this philosophy, Fonda both reflects and contributes to the prevailing discourse of the health and fitness movement, which stresses individual accountability for healthy behavior and harshly condemns those who do not take responsibility for their bodies (Crawford 1979; Nichter and Nichter 1991, 253; Tesh 1988). Despite Fonda's rhetoric of empowerment, therefore, her emphasis on self-control disheartens and disempowers more women than it empowers.

A similar disempowerment results from Fonda's stance on sexuality. Fonda appears to be rescuing aging women from their usual portrayal as asexual by arguing that is possible for aging women to remain active, sexual beings. "I think," she says, "that when you're healthy, no matter what age you are, you have more sexual stamina and desire and flexibility and the things that go into an active sex life" (Orth 1984, 416). In Fonda's worldview, however, a woman can retain sexuality only by retaining a youthful body. No alternative vision of aging sexuality is presented or considered. All that remains is the impossible goal of remaining young.

An emphasis on youth is not the only drawback to Fonda's ideal of femininity. Despite her emphasis on fitness, Fonda has not created a new and liberating model of femininity so much as she has adopted a model that unrealistically combines sterotypically masculine and feminine elements. Fonda began her fitness quest by arguing for the virtues of a muscled and virtually fat-free body. When asked why she added bodybuilding exercises, Fonda remarked "I didn't have any muscles. I like to see muscle, I like to see sinews, and after taking this class, I could see definition in my arms, shoulders and back. There's no fat anywhere, not anywhere" (*Mademoiselle* 1980, 38). This near-fatless ideal corresponds to an archetypical male body. More recently, as her relationship with Hayden faded, Fonda additionally has strived to achieve the archetypical female hallmark—large breasts—by submitting to cosmetic surgery (Andersen 1990, 327–28; Ball 1992, 97). Since her marriage to cable television owner Ted Turner in 1991, she is now, one magazine writer notes, "playing the part of the glamorous wife—blond, bejeweled and dressed to kill" (Messina 1993, 65).

Fonda's body thus has come to symbolize the duality of current femininity: tight muscles but with large breasts. The desire for a more masculine body, Bordo argues, appeals to some women because it symbolizes power in the public arena and a revolt against maternity and restrictive definitions of femininity (Bordo 1990, 105). Simultaneously, the inflated breasts serve as a reminder that a woman's body is there for male desires. Mainstream American culture idealizes women who are both supermen (in their muscles) and superwomen (in their breasts). These women, their bodies suggest, won't be dependent but will continue to seek the "male gaze" to affirm themselves. Fonda's enthusiastic embrace of this dual-function body represents not resistance but submission to the demands of femininity.

Fonda's use of cosmetic surgery (which did not end with her breast implants) suggests that the value she places on having a culturally acceptable body overrides any philosophical commitment to achieving a fit body through hard work. As one magazine asked rhetorically, "Doesn't cosmetic surgery contradict everything she advocates?" (Messina 1993, 65). As Fonda now argues, "If you're trying to buy yourself a few years, especially if you're in the business of looks the way an actress is, then why not? . . . What the hell is the big deal, as long it's done carefully and with thought?" (Ball 1992, 97). In making these decisions, Fonda turns her body into a commodity that can be used, in her words, to "buy" her a few years.

The image of Fonda passively lying on a table while receiving breast implants appears to contradict her active and aggressive advocacy of exercise as a means of achieving self-improvement. Yet all her efforts are really of one piece, aimed at maintaining a youthful and culturally acceptable appearance.

Fonda's struggles to control her inevitably aging body find resonance in many women's lives as they face a culture that rejects the aging female. As one writer said sympathetically about Fonda's "fanatical" physical fitness, "Wasn't it really just the panic of an aging actress with a terror of growing old? Children of Hollywood probably know more than the rest of us what extra wrinkles and pounds mean—and the rest of us know plenty" (Davis 1990, 165).

Fonda's marriage to Turner and use of cosmetic surgery seemed to signify still another shift in her persona. Despite this shift, however, the persistent thread in Fonda's life—her devotion to maintaining a youthful, fit body—remains. In the nineties, Fonda has developed a new exercise video, *Jane Fonda's Lower Body Solution*, and remains "her own best advertisement" (Ball 1992, 96). But Fonda seemed to be backing off from being a role model for other women (Davis 1993, 55). One interviewer, commenting on her new, luxurious lifestyle with Turner, observed to Fonda that those who had thought of her as a feminist symbol might now be dismayed. Fonda, retreating from her earlier stance, replied, "I never asked to be a role model. . . . I'm not Eleanor Roosevelt." In the end, Fonda admitted, "I don't pretend to be different from any other woman. I'm subject to the same foibles and pressures and ups and downs" (Ball 1992, 97, 145).

Over the years, Fonda has expressed the desire to construct a new image for aging women, saying "You can be big and still be in proportion and well-toned" (Bachrach 1989, 82) and that the point is to be the best you can be (Messina 1993, 65). Ultimately, however, she has not done so. Her fit and muscled body and her unwrinkled face offer a standard that few women can attain, suggesting that only by remaining young and fit can women be sexual, strong, and good. As one writer observed, Fonda "at every age . . . has managed to sell her youth. And, most important, we have bought it" (Bachrach 1989). . . .

Barbara Bush: Resolutely "Natural"

In contrast to Jane Fonda, Barbara Bush at least appears to resist and reject the cultural ideal of femininity that valorizes youthfulness. Bush's white hair and wrinkles seem to challenge the prevailing feminine ideal and signal her rejection of technological "fixes" for aging (Morgan 1991, 28).

Even more than Fonda, Bush frames her appearance as resistance to cultural strictures about women's bodies. In Bush's worldview, her unwillingness to change her appearance beyond dressing well, using light makeup, and exercising regularly and moderately underscores her interest in focusing on what she considers important rather than frivolous and narcissistic concerns. She thus draws on a spiritual tradition that disregards the body and looks to the state of the soul for moral value (Turner 1984, 164).

To emphasize this philosophy, Bush often and not very subtly contrasts herself with Nancy Reagan, her ulta-stylish predecessor. Bush told one interviewer that while she "admires" Reagan's "perfectionism," she herself is "more interested in people than in perfection" (Cook 1990, 229). At the same time, her press secretary let writers know that "Mrs. Bush never, but never, borrows designer gowns"; the comparison to Nancy Reagan is obvious. Similarly, Bush distinguished herself from those who dye their hair by saying that "people who worry about their hair all the time are boring" (Avery 1989, 192). She, on the other hand, has other priorities, presumably of a superior nature—"I can exercise, play tennis. I don't have to say to George, 'I can't do that, I just got my hair done'" (Avery 1989, 192). Thus Bush appears not only to present aging positively but also to scorn and mock those who seem more concerned about their looks.

Bush appears to counterpose the value of "naturalness" against the contrivances of anti-aging technology. "What you see is what you get" (*Vogue* 1988, 442) is one of her favorite self-descriptions, implying that her relative lack of artifice in appearance means that she stands revealed for who she is without the "disguises" of cosmetics, plastic surgery, or even a diet-improved shape. One writer quotes her remark that all she owes to the public is "to look nice and have a clean mind and a clean head of hair" (Adams 1988, 151).

Bush's discourse reflects an older view of aging that made allowances for the weight gain and other changes that can accompany aging and that excused women above a certain age from the burdens of maintaining sexual attractiveness (Banner 1983; Schwartz 1986; Seid 1989). Despite Bush's rhetoric, however, a close reading of her interviews reveals the great efforts she makes to meet standards of feminine attractiveness and to show herself as reasonably concerned about her appearance. In doing so she reveals her exquisite awareness of the demands of femininity and of her need at least partially to comply. She wears contact lenses and her well-known three strands of false pearls because, she says, she's "too vain" to wear glasses and needs to cover her "sagging neck" (Avery 1989, 191). Moreover, although she does not engage in the kind of obsessive exercising Fonda does, Bush regularly walks and rides a stationary bicycle to maintain her weight (Avery 1989, 192).

Bush also pays attention to her wardrobe, wearing fashionable designer clothes. As Judith Viorst astutely noted, "though Barbara Bush seems to define herself publicly as a slightly schlumpy Everywoman, she is considerably more than that. . . . Her grooming, from well-coiffed white hair to well-shod toe, is what anyone would call 'impeccable' " (Viorst 1991, 40), an observation repeated by other magazine writers (*Vogue* 1988, 444; Cook 1990, 230). As one points out, "Her hairdresser attends her regularly, sometimes as often as three times a day" (McClellan 1992, 191).

Bush's use of self-deprecating humor further indicates her felt need to explain her deviation from cultural expectations. Self-deprecating humor, in which individuals mock themselves for not meeting social expectations, allows individuals both to demonstrate their commitment to those expectations and to frame their deviations as humorous rather than serious flaws (Coser 1960; Goffman 1963, 100–101; Haig 1988; Koller 1988; Ungar 1984; Walker 1988). As a result, such humor is most common among relatively powerless groups.

Despite her high status, however, it is this form of humor which Barbara Bush seems to rely upon most often. For example, after photos appeared showing her in a matronly swimsuit, one interviewer reported that Bush "jokingly pleaded with photographers not to take any more: 'My children are complaining' " (Avery 1989, 294). She often explains why she does not dye her hair (e.g., Adams 1988, 150) by joking about the time the heat caused her hair dye to run all over her during a campaign trip, and she frequently comments that "fat ladies everywhere" love her (e.g., Reed 1989, 314). Or, speaking of her wardrobe, she comments: "One of the myths is that I don't dress well. I dress very well—I just don't look so good" (Cook 1990, 230).

It seems, then, that Bush, like many women, uses self-deprecating humor to try to turn her departures from appearance norms into an unimportant, humorous matter. At least one reporter has recognized this, describing her humor as "a preemptive strike" (Cook 1990, 230), in which Bush makes comments about her appearance before interviewers can. Thus, Bush is not, despite her protests, rejecting femininity standards, but is acknowledging their power and her failure to meet them.

Bush's statements about her sexuality also reveal the limits of her resistance. In her self-descriptions, she often desexualizes herself, referring to herself not merely as a grandmother but as "everybody's grandmother." She uses this exceptional status to place herself outside the bounds of femininity. "I mean," she says, "kissing me is like kissing your grandmother" (Reed 1989, 314).

Bush's depiction of herself as outside the definition of normative femininity does not help to construct a positive, alternative model of female aging. Rather, she has escaped the bonds of cultural standards only by forfeiting claims to sexuality—a high price to pay. Thus her model is a bleak one, which denies the sensual possibilities of the aging female body.

Bush's treatment by women's magazines demonstrates the reaction women can expect when, like Bush, their aging appearance seems not to conform to cultural dictates on normative femininity. When Bush first appeared on the scene in the late 1980s, the magazines, whose pages are filled with articles devoted to personal improvement and whose income derives largely from advertisements for fashions, diet aids, and cosmetics, were at a loss. How could they deal with a woman who seemed to transgress ideas about what was acceptably feminine and whose stance seemed to challenge the economic structure which supports and defends their version of femininity, particularly when their readers seemed to like and admire her? Bush's appearance was something that the magazines felt had to be explained.

To "normalize" Bush's appearance, the magazines, like Bush, have stressed her grandmotherly qualities, labeling her "every American's favorite grandmother" (Mower 1992) and an honorific grandmother of us all. They have focused on her work with children and her role as the matriarch of the large Bush clan (Reed 1989, 314). In this role as super-grandmother, the magazines allow Bush to remain outside the normal discipline of femininity, a disembodied maternal archetype.

The magazines also deal with Bush's appearance, as she does herself, by highlighting and praising her apparent "naturalness." For example, in an article entitled "The Natural," the headline notes that "Barbara Bush Remains Doggedly Herself" (Reed 1989, 312), while another article proclaims "Barbara Bush is real" (*Vogue* 1988, 218). Like Bush, the magazines assume that such an entity as a "natural body" exists and disregard the considerable role that culture plays in the construction of this "naturalness." Focusing on her "naturalness" as indicative of a praiseworthy inner self allows the magazines to downplay her body, while underscoring for readers how very noteworthy and thus unnatural it is.

Despite these efforts to normalize Bush's appearance, the magazines continue to demonstrate considerable ambivalence toward her looks. For example, in an article published in *Ladies Home Journal* (Avery 1989), the author praises Bush for her apparent acceptance of aging but suggests that other women should hesitate before adopting Bush as a role model, citing the numerous studies that show that attractive women do better in the job market. The writer concludes with the admonition that even "exceptional women" like Bush need to recognize the benefits of attractiveness, and predicts that "perhaps after she's had a year or two squarely in the public eye, we'll begin to notice subtle changes—a wrinkle smoothed here, a pound or two dieted off there." Bush, in other words, will see the light and conform to cultural standards of femininity.

The author and magazine reveal their real attitudes in two full-length pictures of Bush which dominate the article's first two pages (Avery 1989, 120–21). On the first page is the actual Barbara Bush. Attached to various parts of her in balloon-like fashion are boxes advising her how to deal with her wrinkes, her clothes, and her shape. On the opposite page stands a retouched Bush with all the suggestions put into practice: slimmer, with fluffed out hair, wrinkles surgically removed, wearing cosmetics, and fashionable clothes. It is the ultimate make-over! This desire to change Bush so that she fits in with prevailing notions of femininity is a frequent theme in women's magazines.

Women's Power and Women's Bodies

The treatment of Jane Fonda and Barbara Bush by women's magazines explicates the discourse on femininity and illustrates the difficulties women face in resisting cultural dictates regarding their aging bodies. Women's magazines praise Fonda only because she conforms to cultural ideals. The magazines' more ambivalent attitude toward Bush reflects their consternation and ultimate disapproval of those who do not appear to comply with appearance norms, even when such individuals in various ways acknowledge their deviance. . . .

The pressures to conform to cultural standards of femininity disempower women in insidious ways—insidious because we have internalized them in ways we are hardly aware of and at costs we have not calculated. Cultural standards encourage women's sense of inadequacy and promote frantic use of expensive, time-consuming, and sometimes dangerous technologies in a futile effort to check aging and increase one's "femininity." Furthermore, such a focus on the body as a privatistic concern turns people away from focusing on social issues (Stein 1982, 176–77). This is particularly relevant during this current period of backlash to the feminist movement in which many women now find it easier to focus on their individual selves than to continue struggling for the social betterment of women. As Fonda herself admits about exercising, "in a world that is increasingly out of control, it's something you can control" (Ball 1992, 143). Thus an emphasis on the self diverts women from resisting current power relations.

Moreover, as women get older and attempt to move into senior ranks in business, government, and the professions, their employers, clients, and colleagues expect them to maintain norms of femininity. These norms create barriers to advancement for aging women. While on men, gray hair, wrinkles, even a widening waist signify experience, wisdom, maturity, and sometimes sexiness (as in the cases of Clint Eastwood and Sean Connery, for example), on women they denote decline and asexuality. Women's power is diminished, therefore, at the very moment when they might otherwise begin to move into more powerful positions.

Given the difficulties of contesting the discourse on women's bodies, many of which are explicated in the experiences of Fonda and Bush, can we still conclude that effective resistance is possible? We would argue, perhaps optimistically, that it is, but only if women become more aware of the insidious, internalized ways that the discipline of femininity disempowers women and join together to fight it. . . .

Changing cultural standards of femininity will not be easy, and we concur with Bordo that it would be a mistake to minimize the power that the discourse on femininity has to regulate women's lives. To do so is to underestimate the amount of struggle that is required for change and to minimize the difficulty women experience when they try to accomplish change (Bordo 1989, 13). Yet, as the history of women has shown, it would also be a mistake to dismiss the possibility of resistance. While the experiences of Barbara Bush and Jane Fonda demonstrate how difficult it is for any woman, struggling alone, no matter how visible, respected, and in some ways powerful, to fight against entrenched cultural notions, the history of women has taught us that, even in the face of seemingly implacable hegemonic discourses, women can make change when they join together. Perhaps now, with the graying of the feminist movement, feminists will begin to devote more energy to challenging the cultural construction of women's aging bodies. At the same time, the increasing if slow movement of women in their forties and above into positions of power may help a new cultural construction to evolve.

Making changes in our attitudes toward our bodies will not be easy, but it will surely be an important step in empowering women. In such a world, Jane Fonda might be able to moderate her painful and obsessive regimens and Barbara Bush would not have to be so defensive about her appearance.

Note

1. We have borrowed the terms "resolutely natural" and "relentlessly improved" from an article by Avery (1989) on Barbara Bush. Bush is referred to as "resolutely natural" while, in this article, it is Cher and not Jane Fonda who is referred to as "relentlessly improved."

References

Adams, Cindy. October 1988. Talking with the new first lady. *Ladies Home Journal.*

Andersen, Christopher. 1990. *Citizen Jane.* New York: Henry Holt.

Andersen, Christopher P. October 1989. Jane Fonda: I'm stronger than ever. *Ladies Home Journal.*

Avery, Caryl S. June 1989. How good should you look? *Ladies Home Journal.*

Bachrach, Judy. October 1989. Feel the burn. *Savvy Woman.*

Ball, Aimee Lee. March 1992. How does Jane do it? *McCall's.*

Banner, Lois W. 1983. *American Beauty.* New York: Alfred A. Knopf.

Bartky, Sandra Lee. 1988. Foucault, femininity, and the modernization of patriarchal power. In *Feminism and Foucault: Reflections on Resistance*, edited by Irene Diamond and Lee Quinby. Boston: Northeastern University Press.

Bordo, Susan. 1989. The body and the reproduction of femininity: A feminist appropriation of Foucault. In *Gender/Body/Knowledge,* edited by Alison M. Jaggar and Susan R. Bordo. New Brunswick, NJ: Rutgers University Press.

————. 1990. Reading the slender body. In *Body/Politics: Women and the Discourses of Science*, edited by Mary Jacobus, Evelyn Fox Keller, and Sally Shuttleworth. New York: Routledge.

Chernin, Kim. 1981. *The Obsession: Reflections on the Tyranny of Slenderness*. New York: Harper & Row.

Cook, Alison. March 1990. At home with Barbara Bush. *Ladies Home Journal*.

Coser, Rose Loeb. 1960. Laughter among colleagues. *Psychiatry* 23:81–95.

Crawford, Robert. 1979. Individual responsibility and health politics. In *Health Care in America: Essays in Social History*, edited by Susan Reverby and David Rosner. Philadelphia: Temple University Press.

Davis, Sally Ogle. January 1990. Jane Fonda bounces back. *Cosmopolitan*.

————. March 1993. Hollywood marriages: The good, the bad, and the disasters. *Ladies Home Journal*.

Faludi, Susan. 1991. *Backlash: The Undeclared War Against American Women*. New York: Crown.

Fonda, Jane. 1984. *Women Coming of Age*. New York: Simon and Schuster.

————. 1986. *Jane Fonda's Workout Book*. New York: Simon and Schuster.

Foucault, Michel. 1979. *Discipline and Punish*. New York: Vintage Books.

Freedman, Rita. 1986. *Beauty Bound*. New York: D. C. Heath and Company.

Goffman, Erving. 1963. *Stigma: Notes on the Management of Spoiled Identity*. Englewood Cliffs, NJ: Prentice-Hall.

Haig, Robin A. 1988. *Anatomy of Humor*. Springfield, IL: Charles C. Thomas.

Harper's Bazaar. January 1980. The California workout.

Harrison, Barbara Grizzuti. April 1978. Jane Fonda: Trying to be everywoman. *Ladies Home Journal*.

Kaplan, Janice. February 1985. Fonda on: Fit after forty. *Vogue*.

————. November 1987. The fitness queen. *Vogue*.

Kilwein, John H. 1989. No pain, no gain: A Puritan legacy. *Health Education Quarterly* 16:9–12.

Koller, Marvin R. 1988. *Humor and Society: Explorations in the Sociology of Humor*. Houston: Cap and Gown Press, Inc.

Lear, Martha Weinman. June 1976. Jane Fonda: A long way from yesterday. *Redbook*.

Levin, Susanna. December 1987. Jane Fonda: From Barbarella to barbells. *Women's Sports and Fitness*.

Mademoiselle. March 1980. Fitness.

Martin, Emily. 1987. *The Woman in the Body*. Boston: Beacon Press.

McClellan, Diana. October 1992. Barbara Bush: The final battle. *Ladies Home Journal*.

McNay, Lois. 1991. The Foucauldian body and the exclusion of experience. *Hypatia* 6:125–39.

Messina, Andrea. January 12, 1993. Fonda's workouts that work. *Family Circle*.

Morgan, Kathryn Pauly. 1991. Women and the knife: Cosmetic surgery and the colonization of women's bodies. *Hypatia* 6:25–53.

Mower, Joan. September 1992. What kind of First Lady do we really want? *McCall's*.

Nichter, Mark, and Mimi Nichter. 1991. Hype and weight. *Medical Anthropology* 13:249–84.

Orth, Maureen. February 1984. Fonda: Driving passions. *Vogue*.

Reed, Julia. August 1989. The Natural. *Vogue*.

Robbins, Fred. November 1977. Jane Fonda, the woman. *Vogue*.

Schwartz, Hillel. 1986. *Never Satisfied: A Cultural History of Diets, Fantasies, and Fat.* New York: Free Press.

Seid, Roberta Pollack. 1989. *Never Too Thin.* New York: Prentice-Hall.

Sontag, Susan. October 1972. The double standard of aging. *Saturday Review.*

Stein, Howard F. 1982. Neo-Darwinism and survival through fitness in Reagan's America. *The Journal of Psychohistory* 10:163–87.

Tesh, Sylvia. 1988. *Hidden Arguments: Political Ideology and Disease Prevention Policy.* New Brunswick, NJ: Rutgers University Press.

Turner, Bryan S. 1984. *The Body and Society: Explorations in Social Theory.* New York: Basil Blackwell.

Ungar, Sheldon. 1984. Self-mockery: An alternative form of self-presentation. *Symbolic Interaction* 7:121–33.

Viorst, Judith. May 1991. It's time to bring back the family. *Redbook.*

Vogue. October 1988. First Ladies, first impressions.

———. November 1988. Winning style: Kitty Dukakis and Barbara Bush on first lady dressing.

Waitzkin, Howard. 1981. The social origins of illness: A neglected history. *International Journal of Health Services* 11:77–103.

Walker, Nancy A. 1988. *A Very Serious Thing: Women's Humor and American Culture.* Minneapolis: University of Minnesota.

Wolf, Naomi. 1991. *The Beauty Myth.* New York: William Morrow.

Woodward, Kathleen. 1991. *Aging and Its Discontents.* Bloomington, IN: Indiana University Press.

Zola, Irving K. 1972. Medicine as an institution of social control. *Sociological Review* 20:487–504.

IV

BODIES, BEHAVIOR, AND POLITICS

The final section of this volume looks at various critical issues in which ideas about women's behavior are linked to ideas about women's bodies in ways that—whether intentionally or not—have the effect of limiting women's power and women's lives. As such, these issues hark back to the readings on the social construction of women's bodies. As those earlier readings demonstrated, how we define women's bodies can directly affect women's lives.

In "Till Death Us Do Part," Margo Wilson and Martin Daly examine the underpinnings of wife battering. They show how the concept of women as men's property underlies the actions of men who beat their wives. This concept allows men to respond with violence whenever their wives behave in ways that the men perceive as threatening their "property interests," such as changing a hairstyle without their husband's approval (thus "devaluing" the men's property) or smiling at other men (thus tempting others to "steal" the men'a property).

In "Premenstrual Syndrome, Work Discipline, and Anger," Emily Martin contrasts medical understandings of premenstrual syndrome with women's understandings of the changes they experience premenstrually. She shows how by defining women's anger at the disciplines in their lives—a common premenstrual "symptom"—as a sign of illness, doctors preclude the possibility that women have reasonable grounds for that anger. Simultaneously, doctors ignore the feelings of creativity that many women report experiencing premenstrually. By encouraging women to ignore their anger and their creativity, and by encouraging men not to take seriously women's anger or creativity, doctors have helped to limit women's power.

In "Meno-Boomers and Moral Guardians: An Exploration of the Cultural Construction of Menopause," Joy Webster Barbre examines how Victorian doctors argued that women would suffer greatly at menopause if they read novels, danced, expressed anger, and so on, whereas modern doctors argue that menopausal women will lose their femininity and health if they do not seek medical treatment. As she demonstrates, the content of medical and popular ideas about menopause changed dramatically over time, but in both these eras, ideas about menopause served as a form of social control that restricted women's lives.

The last three articles look at issues of reproduction and reproductive rights. In "Morality and Personhood: A Feminist Perspective," Rosalind Pollack Petchesky demonstrates how those who fight for and against abortion rights recognize that without those rights, women will be unable to achieve social equality. The next article, "The Future of Reproductive Choice for Poor Women and Women of Color" by Dorothy E. Roberts, looks more specifically at how reproductive rights have been limited for these most vulnerable segments of the female population, and at the impact of those limitations on their lives. Finally, in "Fetal Rights: A New Assault on Feminism," Katha Pollitt examines how recent legal decisions in this area have served more to punish women for nontraditional behavior than to protect their children. Her article illustrates how separating the rights of fetuses from those of pregnant women, and privileging the former over the latter, turns women's bodies into public property and defines women's wishes as trivial.

15

Till Death Us Do Part

Margo Wilson and Martin Daly

The revelation of wifely infidelity is a provocation so extreme that a "reasonable man" is apt to respond with lethal violence. This impulse is so strong and so natural that the homicidal cuckold [a man whose wife has had an affair] cannot be held fully responsible for his dreadful deed. So says the common law.

Other spousal misbehavior—snoring or burning supper or mismanaging the family finances—cannot be invoked as provocation. Reasonable men do not react violently to their wives' profligacy or stupidity or sloth or insults. In fact, the *only* provocations other than a wife's adultery that are invested with the same power to mitigate a killer's criminal responsibility are physical assaults upon himself or a relative (e.g., Dressler 1982).

The law of provocation reflects a folk theory of the male mind, for which the apprehension of female infidelity allegedly constitutes a uniquely powerful impetus to violence. This folk theory is not peculiar to Western societies but is extremely widespread. Does it match reality?

Provocation and the "Reasonable Man"

Despite the contemporary scourges of serial killers, rape-murders, and homicides in the course of robbery, most murdered women are killed by their mates.

A small proportion of the men who kill their wives are found "unfit to stand trial" or "not guilty by reason of insanity." Such men are often deemed to be suffering from a psychiatric condition called "morbid jealousy" (Mowat 1966), diagnosed on the basis of an obsessive concern about suspected infidelity and a tendency to invoke bizarre "evidence" in support of the suspicion. But most men who kill in jealous rage are not considered insane. Not only is jealousy "normal," but so, it seems, is violent jealousy, at least if perpetrated by a man and in the heat of passion.

Reprinted with permission from Martin Daly and Margo Wilson, *Homicide* (New York: Aldine de Gruyter). Copyright © 1988 Aldine de Gruyter.

The English common law relies heavily upon a conception of the way in which a "reasonable man" could be expected to behave. This hypothetical creature embodies the judiciary's assumptions about the natural order of marital relationships and men's passion, assumptions that are laid bare in this legal scholar's summary characterization: "The judges have gone a considerable way toward establishing—so far as the law of provocation is concerned—a standard portrayal of the makeup and reactions of the reasonable man. They say he is not impotent and he is not normally drunk. He does not lose his self-control on hearing a mere confession of adultery, but he becomes unbalanced at the sight of adultery provided, of course, that he is married to the adulteress" (Edwards 1954, 900).

The "reasonable man" may strike the reader as a quaintly English invention, but he is more than that. Solon's law gave the same right to Greek cuckolds, while Roman law excused the homicidal cuckold only if the adultery occurred in his house. Various such provisions remain in effect in continental Europe today.

Until 1974, it was the law in Texas that homicide is justified—not a criminal act, and therefore subject to no penalty whatever—"when committed by the husband upon the person of anyone taken in the act of adultery with the wife, provided the killing takes place before the parties to the act of adultery have separated" (Texas Penal Code 1925, article 1220). Elsewhere, this is the "unwritten law," and cases both in Texas and in other states with analogous practices based on precedent have considered the justification to extend to lethal assaults upon the errant wife, the rival, or both. (The factors that are predictive of the likelihood that a violent cuckold will assault his wife versus his rival have yet to be elucidated.)

Many other legal traditions quite different from our own address this question of the "victimized" husband's legitimate response in similar fashion. More than merely entitling the wronged husband to material compensation, adultery is widely construed to justify his resorting to violence that would in other circumstances be deemed criminal. Among the Melanesian Islanders of Wogeo, for example, the principal subject of law and morality is adultery, and "the rage of the husband who has been wronged" is considered predictable and excusable; the Wogeans say, "he is like a man whose pig has been stolen," only much angrier (Hogbin 1938, 236–37). Among the Nuer of East Africa, "it is commonly recognized that a man caught in adultery runs the risk of serious injury or even death at the hands of the woman's husband" (Howell 1954, 156). Having caught his wife in flagrante delicto [the act of sexual intercourse], the Yapese cuckold "had the right to kill her and the adulterer or to burn them in the house" (Muller 1917, 229). Among the Toba-Batak of Sumatra, "the injured husband had the right to kill the man caught in adultery as he would kill a pig in a rice field" (Vergouwen 1964, 266). In general, the ethnographic record suggests that the violent rages of cuckolds are universally considered predictable and widely considered legitimate.

Male Sexual Proprietariness

Men exhibit a tendency to think of women as sexual and reproductive "property" that they can own and exchange. To call men sexually "proprietary" is conceptually similar to calling them sexually "jealous" but lacks certain constraining implications of the latter term, such as the sometime connotation of jealousy as excessive or socially undesirable. Proprietariness implies a more encompassing mind-set, referring not just to the emotional force of one's own feelings of entitlement but to a more pervasive attitude toward social relationships. Proprietary entitlements in people have been conceived and institutionalized as identical to proprietary entitlements in land, chattels, and other economic resources. Historically and cross-culturally, the owners of slaves, servants, wives, and children have been entitled to enjoy the benefits of ownership without interference, to modify their property, and to buy and sell, while the property had little or no legal or political status in "its" own right (e.g., Dobash and Dobash 1979; Russell 1982; Sachs and Wilson 1978).

That men take a proprietary view of female sexuality and reproductive capacity is manifested in various cultural practices (Wilson 1987; Wilson and Daly 1992). Anglo-American law is replete with examples of men's proprietary entitlement over the sexuality and reproductive capacity of wives and daughters. Since before the time of William the Conqueror there has been a continual elaboration of legal devices enabling men to seek monetary redress for the theft and damage of their women's sexuality and reproductive capacity. These torts, all of which have been sexually asymmetrical until very recently, include "loss of consortium," "enticement," "criminal conversation," "alienation of affection," "seduction," and "abduction" (Attenborough 1963; Backhouse 1986; Brett 1955; Sinclair 1987; Wilson and Daly 1992). In all of these tort actions the person entitled to seek redress was the owner of the woman, whose virtue or chastity was fundamental; those holding proprietary entitlements in prostitutes and other women of dubious reputation had no legal cause. Furthermore, the woman's consent did not mitigate the wrong.

Throughout human history and around the world, powerful men have tended to accumulate as many women of fertile age as they could manage and have invested substantial efforts and resources in attempting to sequester them from other men (Betzig 1986). A wide range of "claustration" practices, including veiling, foot-binding, and incarceration in women's quarters, as well as such mechanical and surgical interventions as chastity belts and infibulation, have been employed by proprietary men in their efforts to retain sexual and reproductive exclusivity (Dickemann 1979, 1981; Hosken 1979). The bride-price paid in many patrilineal societies by the groom and his family to the bride's father (e.g., Comaroff 1980; Borgerhoff Mulder 1988) is really a child-price that may even be due in installments after each birth. Barrenness is often a grounds for male-initiated divorce with refund of the bride-price (Stephens 1963). The acquisition of rights to a woman's reproductive capacity entails rights to the labor and other value of the children she produces and the right to sire those children. Husbands are almost invariably entitled to exercise control over their wives' sex lives, and that almost always means retaining sexual access for themselves. Sexually asymmetrical adultery laws that make sexual intercourse with a married woman an offense against her husband are characteristic of the indigenous legal codes of all the world's civilizations (Daly, Wilson, and Weghorst 1982).

Not only have husbands been entitled to exclusive sexual access to their wives, but they have been entitled to use force to get it. The criminalization of rape within marriage, and hence the wife's legal entitlement to refuse sex, has been established only recently (Edwards 1981; Russell 1982). English husbands have been entitled to place disobedient wives under restraint, and it was not until 1973 that a husband was convicted of kidnaping for restraining a wife intending to leave him for another man (Atkins and Hoggett 1984). The expression "rule of thumb" derives from the judicial ruling that a husband was entitled to use only a stick no thicker than his thumb to control an overly independent wife (Edwards 1985).

Homicide and Sexual Proprietariness

Granting that men wish to control their wives and are prepared to use force to do so, the question remains why they kill them. Paradoxical though it may appear, there is compelling evidence that uxoricide [wife murder] is a manifestation of proprietariness.

Most studies of homicide "motives" have depended upon summary police files and have been limited by the sparse, special purpose information recorded there. The two leading motive categories in Marvin Wolfgang's (1958) trend-setting study of Philadelphia homicides, for example, were "altercation of relatively trivial origin" and "domestic quarrel." Neither of these category labels tells us much. "Jealousy" ranked third and was thus the leading substantive issue on Wolfgang's list, as it has proved to be in many studies.

In Canada, the investigating police file a report on every homicide with the federal agency Statistics Canada, using a standardized multiple-choice form. The police are offered a choice of 12 motives, one of which is "jealousy." Between 1974 and 1983, Canadian police made an attribution of motive for 1,006 out of 1,060 spousal homicides (Daly and Wilson 1988). Of these, 214 (21.3 percent) were attributed to jealousy: 195 of 812 homicides committed by husbands and 19 of 248 perpetrated by wives. But this is surely a gross underestimate of the role played by jealousy, since the great majority of cases were not linked to any substantive source of conflict: the police attributed 513 cases simply to "argument or quarrel," and another 106 to "anger or hatred." These motive categories reflect detectives' and prosecutors' concern with the question of premeditation versus impulsive reaction, but they tell us nothing about the substance of marital conflict. Any of these cases might have been provoked by the suspicion or discovery of infidelity.

Our claim that the Statistics Canada motive data underestimate the importance of adultery and jealousy in spousal conflict is more than just a conjecture. Catherine Carlson's (1984) study of the spousal homicides investigated by one Ontario police force provides clear evidence on this point. Carlson examined the police files on 36 spousal homicides for which the motive category reported to Statistics Canada was noted in the file. Only four had been labeled "jealousy" cases by the police, and yet sexual proprietariness was clearly relevant to several others. Here, for example, is a statement made to police by an unemployed 53-year-old man who shot his 42-year-old estranged wife:

> I know she was fuckin' around. I had been waiting for approximately five minutes and seen her pull up in a taxi and I drove over and pulled up behind her car. I said, "Did you enjoy your weekend?" She said, "You're fuckin' right I did. I will have a lot more of them too." I said, "Oh no you won't. You have been bullshitting me long enough. I can take no more." I kept asking her if she would come back to me. She told me to get out of her life. I said, "No way. If I get out of this it's going to be both of us" (Carlson 1984, 7–8).

In reporting to Statistics Canada, the police classified this case under the motive category "mentally ill, retarded."

In another case classified under "anger or hatred" (the most popular category with this police force, accounting for 11 of the 36 spousal homicides), a 31-year-old man stabbed his 20-year-old common-law wife after a six-month temporary separation. In his statement to police, the accused gave this account of the fatal argument:

> Then she said that since she came back in April she had fucked this other man about ten times. I told her how can you talk love and marriage and you been fucking with this other man. I was really mad. I went to the kitchen and got the knife. I went back to our room and said were you serious when you told me that. She said yes. We fought on the bed, I was stabbing her and her grandfather came up and tried to take the knife out of my hand. I told him to call the cops for me. I don't know why I killed the woman, I loved her (Carlson 1984, 9).

Police synopses and government statistics are obviously not ideal sources of information on homicide motives. Fortunately, there have been at least a few intensive studies in which the researchers have interviewed the killers themselves about the sources of the conflicts that culminated in spousal homicide. Such studies are unanimous in confirming that male sexual proprietariness constitutes *the* dangerous issue in marriage regardless of whether it is the husband or the wife who is finally slain.

Accused killers are commonly obliged to undergo a psychiatric examination to determine whether they are "fit to stand trial." In 1955, Manfred Guttmacher, the fitness examiner for the city of Baltimore, published a report summarizing his examinations of 31 people who had killed their spouses, 24 men and 7 women. These represented all such killers among 36 consecutive

Baltimore cases of intrafamilial homicide, and Guttmacher tabulated what he called "apparent motivational factors" on the basis of his personal interviews with the perpetrators. While the data are presented a little ambiguously (some cases were tabulated under more than one motive), it appears that as many as 25 (81 percent) of the 31 spousal homicides were motivated by sexual proprietariness. Fourteen cases were provoked by the spouse's deserting for a new partner, five by the spouse's "promiscuity," four by "pathological jealousy," one by the discovery of adultery in flagrante delicto, and one by a delusionary suspicion of adultery between the killer's wife and his son-in-law.

A similar report from the Forensic Psychiatry Clinic of the University of Virginia reveals a preponderance of cases of male sexual proprietariness that is even more dramatic than in the Baltimore sample. Showalter, Bonnie, and Roddy (1980) described 17 cases of "killing or seriously wounding" a legal or common-law spouse. Six cases were attributed to psychiatric disorders, but the authors were so impressed with the essential similarity of the remaining 11 that they called their report "The Spousal Homicide Syndrome." All 11 attackers were men, and all professed that they were deeply in love with their victims. Ten of the 11 attacks were precipitated by "an immediate threat of withdrawal," and 8 of 11 victimized wives had left the offender at least once previously, only to return. Moreover, "in all 11 cases, the victim was engaged in an affair with another man or had led the offender to believe that she was being unfaithful to him. In 10 of the cases, the victim made no attempt to conceal her other relationships" (127). Barnard et al. (1982) reported very similar results in a Florida study.

A Canadian study of convicted spouse killers points again to the over-whelming predominance of male sexual jealousy and proprietariness as motives in spousal homicide. Sociologist Peter Chimbos (1978) interviewed an "availability sample" of 34 spouse killers, 29 men and 5 women. The interviews were conducted at an average interval of three years after the homicide; 30 interviewees were in prison, 4 had recently been released. Seventeen had been legally married to their victims and 17 had been living in common-law relationships. In a finding reminiscent of the Virginia "syndrome," 22 of the 34 couples had previously separated owing to infidelity and had later been reconciled.

The most striking result of Chimbos's study is the near unanimity of the killers in identifying the main source of conflict in their ill-fated marriages. Twenty-nine of the 34 (85 percent) pointed to "sexual matters (affairs and refusals)," 3 blamed "excessive drinking," and 2 professed that there was no serious conflict. Remarkably, these few issues exhaust the list. Most of the killers were of low educational and occupational status, but not one pointed to financial problems as the primary source of conflict. Although 28 of the 34 couples had children, no one considered them to be the main source of conflict either. The conflicts were over sexual matters, and that mainly meant adultery.

Unfortunately, Chimbos did not break down the infidelity quarrels according to sex. Nevertheless, it is clear that the wives' adulteries were a far greater bone of contention than the husbands', no matter which party ended up dead. Scattered through the monograph are verbatim quotations from the interviewed killers. Thirteen such quotes from the male offenders included allusions to infidelity, and all 13 were complaints about the faithfulness of the wife. By way of comparison, there were 4 quotes from female killers that made reference to infidelity, but these were not mirror images of the male complaints. All 4 of the women's allusions to adultery concerned their husbands' accusations against themselves; in 1 of the 4, the accusations were mutual.

Chimbos chose 6 cases for detailed narrative description. Four were committed by men, 2 by women. In every one of these 6 cases—selected, according to the author, to represent the full range of conflicts in the entire sample—the husband angrily accused the wife of adultery before the homicide. In 3 cases, the accusations were mutual.

If I Can't Have You, No One Can

Men do not easily let women go. They search out women who have left them, to plead and threaten and sometime to kill. As one Illinois man told his wife six months before she divorced him and seven months before he killed her in her home with a shotgun, "I swear if you ever leave me, I'll follow you to the ends of the earth and kill you" (*People v. Wood*, 391, N.E. 2d 206).

The estranged wife, hunted down and murdered, is a common item in police files. The converse case of a vengeful murder by a jilted wife is an extreme rarity, the popularity of the theme in fiction notwithstanding. In Canada between 1974 and 1983, 117 of 524 (22 percent) of women slain by their registered-marriage husbands were separated from them as compared to 11 of 118 (9 percent) men slain by their registered-marriage wives. Among these estranged couples the ratio of wife victims to husband victims was 10.6 to 1 (117 versus 11), compared with a ratio of 3.8 to 1 (407 versus 107) for co-residing couples (Wilson 1989). And whereas 43 percent of the 117 homicides by estranged husbands were attributed by the police to "jealousy," only 2 of the 11 by estranged wives were so attributed; the rare case of a woman killing her estranged husband is likely to be a case of self-defense against a man who will not let her be. Wallace (1986) found an even stronger association between estrangement and uxoricide in an Australia study: 98 of 217 women slain by their husbands were separated or in the process thereof, compared with just 3 of 79 men slain by their wives.

The homicides that police and criminologists attribute to "jealousy" include a couple of somewhat different sorts of dramas, which might usefully be distinguished. On the one hand we have what some criminologists have referred to as "love triangles": cases in which there is a known or suspected third party. In other killings, it is not clear that any particular third party was involved or even suspected by the jealous individual, who simply could not abide his partner's terminating the relationship. The jealous party is even more often male in such cases than in triangles. In Detroit in 1972, for example, a man was the jealous party in 30 out of 40 "triangle" murders, and in 17 out of 18 cases where the killer simply would not abide being deserted (Daly, Wilson, and Weghorst 1982).

The distinction between a wife's adultery and her departure illustrates two separable but related considerations underlying male jealousy (Daly and Wilson 1988; Wilson and Daly 1992). Only the former places the man at risk of cuckoldry and misdirected parental investment in another man's child, but the risks are partly the same: in either case, the man is at risk of losing control of his wife's reproductive capacity (Wilson 1987). And this reproductive strategic commonality between the two sorts of cases evidently imparts a psychological commonality as well: researchers have tended to lump these together as "jealousy" cases because of the aggressive proprietariness of the husband, who seems to consider adultery and desertion equivalent violations of his rights. The man who hunts down and kills a woman who has left him has surely lapsed into futile spite, acting out his vestigial agenda of dominance to no useful end.

Conjugal Jealousy and Violence Around the World

The phenomena we have been discussing are not peculiar to industrial society. In every society for which we have been able to find a sample of spousal homicides the story is basically the same: most cases arise out of the husband's jealous, proprietary, violent response to his wife's (real or imagined) infidelity or desertion.

Several monographs have been published, for example, on the topic of homicides among various aboriginal peoples in India. These include the Bison-Horn Maria (Elwin 1950), the Munda (Saran 1974), the Oraon (Saran 1974), and the Bhil (Varma 1978). Rates of lethal violence among these tribal horticulturalists are high, and 99 percent of the killings are committed by men. These homicide samples include 20 cases of Bison-Horn Maria wives killed by their husbands, 3 such Munda cases, 3 Oraon, and 8 Bhil. In each of the four societies, the majority of spousal homicides was precipitated either by the man's suspicion or knowledge of wifely infidelity or by the woman's leaving or rejecting her husband. Moreover, in each of these studies, about 20 percent of the much more numerous male-male homicides were expressly due either to rivalry over a woman or to a man's taking offense at sexual advances made to his daughter or another female relative.

Fallers and Fallers (1960) collated information on 98 consecutive homicide cases (that is, 98 victims) between 1947 and 1954 among the Basoga, a patrilineal, polygynous, horticultural tribe in Uganda. Eight of these were apparently accidents, leaving 90 cases. Forty-two were cases in which a man killed a woman, usually his wife, and some sort of motive was imputed in 32 of these: 10 for adultery, 11 for desertion or for refusing sex, and 11 for a diversity of other motives. An additional 5 male-male cases were clear matters of sexual rivalry. Only 2 women were offenders, one taking the life of a man and one a woman; the latter case was the only one evidently arising out of female sexual jealousy or rivalry, as compared with 26 male jealousy cases. (In polygynous societies, co-wives can be fierce rivals, but they still kill one another far less often than do males).

Sohier (1959) reviewed court records on 275 homicides leading to convictions between 1948 and 1957 in what was then the Belgian Congo. Many cases were assigned to no particular motive category, but of those with identified motives, 59 were attributed to male jealousy and only 1 to female jealousy. Sixteen cuckolded husbands killed their adulterous wives or the male adulterer or both. Ten more killed their wives for desertion or for threatening desertion. Three killed an ex-wife after she had obtained a divorce, and 3 more killed an ex-wife's new husband. Another 13 men killed faithless fiancées or mistresses. And so forth. Only 20 spousal cases were not attributed to male jealousy, and their motives were unspecified. The single female jealousy case was one in which a wife killed her husband's mistress.

Are there no exceptions to this dreary record of connubial coercion and violence? Certainly there are societies within which the homicide rate is exceptionally low. But is there even one exotic land in which the men eschew violence, take no proprietary view of their wives' sexuality, and accept consenting extramarital sex as good, clean fun? The short answer is no, although many have sought such a society, and a few have imagined that they found it.

The most popular place to situate the mythical peaceful kingdom is a South Seas island. Margaret Mead (1931, 46), for example, portrayed Samoa in innumerable writings as an idyllic land of free, innocent sexuality and claimed that sexual jealousy was hardly known there.

> Granting that jealousy is undesirable, a festering spot in every personality so afflicted, an ineffective negativistic attitude which is more likely to lose than gain any goal, what are the possibilities if not of eliminating it, at least of excluding it more and more from human life? Samoa has taken one road, by eliminating strong emotion, high stakes, emphasis upon personality, interest in competition. Such a cultural attitude eliminates many of the attitudes which have afflicted mankind, and perhaps jealousy most importantly of all. . . .

Derek Freeman finally exploded Mead's myth in 1983, showing that violent responses to adultery and sexual rivalry are exceptionally frequent in Samoa and have long been endemic to the society.

The factual evidence that Margaret Mead's Samoa was a fantasy had long been available. But the facts were ignored. Scholars who should have looked at the data critically wanted to believe in a tropical island where jealousy and violence were unknown. The prevalent ideology in the social sciences combines the premise that conflict is an evil and harmony a good—fair enough as a moral stance, although of dubious relevance to the scientific study of society—with a sort of "naturalistic fallacy" that makes goodness natural and evil artificial. The upshot is that conflict must be explained as the product of some modern, artificial nastiness (capitalism, say, or patriarchy), while the romantic ideal of the "noble savage" is retained, with nobility fantastically construed to mean an absence of all conflictual motives, including sexual possessiveness.

Part of the confusion about the alleged existence of exotic people devoid of jealousy derives from a failure to distinguish between societal sanctions and the private use of force. In an influential volume entitled *The Family in Cross-Cultural Perspective*, for example, William Stephens (1963, 251) asserted that in 4 societies out of a sample of 39, "there seems to be little if any bar to any sort of non-incestuous adultery." Yet here is one of Stephen's own sources discussing the situation in one of those four societies, namely the Marquesa Islanders: "When a woman undertook to live with a man, she placed herself under his authority. If she cohabited with another man without his permission, she was beaten or, if her husband's jealousy was sufficiently aroused, killed" (Handy 1923, 100). In fact, when one consults Stephens's ethnographic sources, one finds accounts of wife beating as punishment for adultery in every one of the four permissive societies (Daly, Wilson, and Weghorst 1982). What Stephens evidently meant by claiming there was "little if any bar" to adultery was that no criminal sanctions were levied against adulterers by the larger society. Cuckolded husbands took matters into their own hands.

Ford and Beach's classic work *Patterns of Sexual Behavior* (1951) contains an assertion very like Stephens's but even more misleading. These authors claimed to have discovered 7 societies, out of a sample of 139, in which "the customary incest prohibitions appear to be the only major barrier to sexual intercourse outside of mateship. Men and women in these societies are free to engage in sexual liaisons and indeed are expected to do so provided the incest rules are observed" (113). Once again, we can make sense of these assertions only by assuming that Ford and Beach intend "barriers" to refer to legal or quasi-legal sanctions by the larger society. For just as in Stephens's sample, the original ethnographies make it clear that men in every one of the seven societies were apt to respond with extreme violence to their wives' dalliance (Daly, Wilson, and Weghorst 1982). Cuckolded men in these societies sometimes killed their adulterous wives, and they sometimes killed their rivals. If the fear of violent reprisal was not a "major barrier" to "sexual liaisons," it's hard to imagine what would be.

Violence as Coercive Control

In attempting to exert proprietary rights over the sexuality and reproduction of women, men walk a tightrope. The man who actually kills his wife has usually overstepped the bounds of utility, however utility is conceived. Killing provokes retribution by the criminal justice system or the victim's relatives. At the least, murdered wives are costly to replace.

But killing is just the tip of the iceberg. For every murdered wife, hundreds are beaten, coerced, and intimidated. Although homicide probably does not often serve the interest of the perpetrator, it is far from clear that the same can be said of sublethal violence. Men, as we noted earlier, strive to control women, albeit with variable success; women struggle to resist coercion and to maintain their choices. There is brinkmanship and risk of disaster in any such contest, and homicides by spouses of either sex may be considered the slips in this dangerous game.

What we are suggesting is that most spousal homicides are the relatively rare and extreme manifestations of the same basic conflicts that inspire sublethal marital violence on a much larger scale. As in homicide, so too in wife-beating: the predominant issues are adultery, jealousy, and male proprietariness. Whitehurst (1971), for example, attended 100 Canadian court cases involving couples in litigation over the husband's use of violence upon the wife. He reported, without quantification, that "at the core of nearly all the cases . . . the husband responded out of frustration at being unable to control his wife, often accusing her of being a whore or of having an affair" (686). Dobash and Dobash (1984) interviewed 109 battered Scottish wives, and asked them to identify the main source of conflict in a "typical" battering incident. Forty-eight of the women pointed to possessiveness and sexual jealousy on the part of the batterer, making this far and away the leading response; arguments over money ranked second (18 women), and the husband's expectations about domestic work ranked third (17 women). A similar interview study of 31 battered American women in hostels and hospitals obtained similar results: "jealousy was the most frequently mentioned topic that led to violent argument, with 52 percent of the women listing it as the main incitement and 94 percent naming it as a frequent cause" (Rounsaville 1978, 21). Battering husbands seldom make themselves available for interview, but when they do, they tell essentially the same story as their victims. Brisson (1983), for example, asked 122 wife-beaters in Denver to name the "topics around which violence occurred." Jealousy topped the list, with alcohol second and money a distant third.

Although wife beating is often inspired by a suspicion of infidelity, it can be the product of a more generalized proprietariness. Battered women commonly report that their husbands object violently to the continuation of old friendships, even with other women, and indeed to the wives' having any social life whatever. In a study of 60 battered wives who sought help at a clinic in rural North Carolina, Hilberman and Munson (1978, 461) reported that the husbands exhibited "morbid jealousy," such that "leaving the house for any reason invariably resulted in accusations of infidelity which culminated in assault" in an astonishing 57 cases (95 percent). Husbands who refuse to let their wives go to the store unescorted may run the risk, in our society, of being considered psychiatric cases. Yet there are many societies in which such constraints and confinement of women are considered normal and laudable (e.g., Dickemann 1981).

The Epidemiology of Spousal Homicide

The above review suggests that the incidences of wife battering and uxoricide are likely to be exacerbated by anything that makes sexually proprietary husbands perceive their wives as likely to betray or quit the marital relationship.

One such factor is the woman's age. Youth makes a woman more attractive to rival men (Symons 1979). . . .

One might anticipate that demographic and circumstantial factors associated with an elevated risk of divorce will often be associated with an elevated risk of homicide as well, for two reasons. The first is that we consider homicide a sort of "assay" of interpersonal conflict, and divorce is surely another. Moreover, if men assault and kill in circumstances in which they perceive women as likely to desert them, then female-initiated separation and divorce (as well as men's divorcing of adulterous wives) are likely to be relatively frequent in the same sorts of circumstances as uxoricides. . . . These facts indicate that patterns of separation risk and homicide risk are often similar. However, insofar as wife killing is the act of proprietary husbands, its eliciting circumstances are more likely to match those of separation desired and enacted by the wife, and to be distinct from the reasons why men discard wives they no longer value.

Though the motives in wife killing exhibit a dreary consistency across cultures and across centuries—and although the epidemiological patterns of elevated risk to younger women, de facto unions, and so forth, are also robust—it is important to note that the actual rates at which women are slain by husbands are enormously variable. Women in the United States today face a statistical risk of being slain by their husbands that is about five to ten times greater than that faced by their European counterparts, and in the most violent American cities, the risk is five times higher again. It may be the case that men have proprietary inclinations toward their wives everywhere, but they do not everywhere feel equally entitled to act upon them.

References

Atkins, Susan, and Brenda Hoggett. 1984. *Women and the Law*. Oxford: Blackwell.

Attenborough, Frederick L. [1922] 1963. *The Laws of the Earliest English Kings*. New York: Russell and Russell.

Backhouse, Constance. 1986. The tort of seduction: Fathers and daughters in nineteenth-century Canada. *Dalhousie Law Journal* 10:45–80.

Barnard, George W., Hernan Vera, Maria I. Vera, and Gustave Newman. 1982. Till death do us part: A study of spouse murder. *Bulletin of the American Academy of Psychiatry and Law* 10:271–80.

Betzig, Laura L. 1986. *Despotism and Differential Reproduction: A Darwinian View of History*. Hawthorne, NY: Aldine de Gruyter.

Borgerhoff Mulder, Monique. 1988. Kipsigis bridewealth payments. In *Human Reproductive Behaviors: A Darwinian Perspective*, edited by Laura Getzig, Monique Borgerhoff Mulder, and Paul Turke. Cambridge: Cambridge University Press.

Brett, P. 1955. Consortium and servitium: A history and some proposals. *Australian Law Journal* 29:321–28, 389–97, 428–34.

Brisson, Norman J. 1983. Battering husbands: A survey of abusive men. *Victimology* 6:338–44.

Carlson, C. A. 1984. *Intrafamilial Homicide*. Unpublished B.Sc. thesis, McMaster University.

Chimbos, Peter D. 1978. *Marital Violence: A Study of Interspouse Homicide*. San Francisco: R&E Research Associates.

Comaroff, John L. 1980. *The Meaning of Marriage Payments*. New York: Academic Press.

Daly, Martin, and Margo Wilson. 1988. *Homicide*. Hawthorne, N.Y.: Aldine de Gruter.

Daly, Martin, Margo Wilson, and Suzanne J. Weghorst. 1982. Male sexual jealousy. *Ethology and Sociobiology* 3:11–27.

Dickemann, Mildred. 1979. The ecology of mating systems in hypergynous dowry societies. *Social Science Information* 18:163–95.

———. 1981. Paternal confidence and dowry competition: A biocultural analysis of purdah. In *Natural Selection and Social Behavior: Recent Research and New Theory*, edited by Richard D. Alexander and Donald W. Tinkle. New York: Chiron Press.

Dobash, R. Emerson, and Russell P. Dobash. 1979. *Violence against Wives: The Case against the Patriarchy*. New York: Free Press.

———. 1984. The nature and antecedents of violent events. *British Journal of Criminology* 24:269–88.

Dressler, Joshua. 1982. Rethinking heat of passion: A defense in search of a rationale. *Journal of Criminal Law and Criminology* 73:421–70.

Edwards, J. L. J. 1954. Provocation and the reasonable man: Another view. *Criminal Law Review.* 1954:898–906.

Edwards, Susan S. M. 1981. *Female Sexuality and the Law*. Oxford: Martin Robertson.

———. 1985. Male violence against women: Excusatory and explanatory ideologies in law and society. In *Gender, Sex and the Law*, edited by Susan Edwards. London: Croom Helm.

Elwin, V. 1950. *Maria: Murder and Suicide*. 2d ed. Bombay: Oxford University Press.

Fallers, L. A., and M. C. Fallers. 1960. Homicide and suicide in Busoga. In *African Homicide and Suicide*, edited by Paul Bohannan. Princeton, N.J.: Princeton University Press.

Ford, Clelland S., and Frank A. Beach. 1951. *Patterns of Sexual Behavior*. New York: Harper & Row.

Freeman, Derek. 1983. *Margaret Mead and Samoa*. Cambridge, Mass.: Harvard University Press.

Guttmacher, Marvin S. 1955. Criminal responsibility in certain homicide cases involving family members. In *Psychiatry and the Law*, edited by Paul H. Hoch and Joseph Zubin. New York: Grune and Stratton.

Handy, Martin J. L. 1923. *Blood Feuds and the Payment of Blood Money in the Middle East*. Beirut: Catholic Press.

Hilberman, Elaine and Kit Munson. 1978. Sixty battered women. *Victimology: An International Journal* 2:460–70.

Hogbin, H. I. 1938. Social reaction to crime: Law and morals in the Schouten Islands, New Guinea. *Journal of the Anthropological Institute of Great Britain and Ireland* 68:223–62.

Hosken, Frances P. 1979. *The Hosken Report: Genital and Sexual Mutilation of Females.* Lexington, Mass.: Women's International Network News.

Howell, Paul P. 1954. *A Manual of Nuer Law.* London: Oxford University Press.

Mead, Margaret. 1931. *Sex and Temperament.* New York: Morrow.

Mowat, Ronald R. 1996. *Morbid Jealousy and Murder: A Psychiatric Study of Morbidly Jealous Murderers at Broadmoor.* London: Tavistock.

Muller, Wilhelm. 1917. *Yap*, band 2, halbband 1 (HRAF trans.). Hamburg: Friederichsen.

Rounsaville, Bruce J. 1978. Theories in marital violence: Evidence from a study of battered women. *Victimology: An International Journal* 3:11–31.

Russell, Diane E. H. 1982. *Rape in Marriage.* New York: Macmillan.

Sachs, Albie, and Joan Hoff Wilson. 1978. *Sexism and the Law.* Oxford: Martin Robertson.

Saran, Anirudha B. 1974. *Murder and Suicide among the Munda and the Oraon.* Delhi: National Publishing House.

Showalter, C. Robert, Richard J. Bonnie, and Virginia Roddy. 1980. The spousal homicide syndrome. *International Journal of Law and Psychiatry* 3:117–41.

Sinclair, M. B. W. 1987. Seduction and the myth of the ideal woman. *Law and Inequality* 3:33–102.

Sohier, Jean. 1959. *Essai sur la criminalité dans la province de Léopoldville.* Brussels: J. Duculot.

Stephens, William N. 1963. *The Family in Cross-Cultural Perspective.* New York: Holt, Rinehart, and Winston.

Symons, Donald. 1979. *The Evolution of Human Sexuality.* New York: Oxford University Press.

Varma, S. C. 1978. *The Bhil Kills.* Delhi, India: Kunj Publishing House.

Vergouwen, Jacob C. 1964. *The Social Organization and Customary Law of the Toba-Batak of Northern Sumatra.* The Hague: Martinus Nijhoff.

Wallace, Alison. 1986. *Homicide: The Social Reality.* Sydney: New South Wales Bureau of Crime Statistics and Research.

Whitehurst, Robert N. 1971. Violence potential in extramarital sexual responses. *Journal of Marriage and the Family* 33:683–91.

Wilson, Margo. 1987. Impacts of the uncertainty of paternity on family law. *University of Toronto Faculty of Law Review* 45:216–42.

———. 1989. Marital conflict and homicide in evolutionary perspective. In *Sociobiology and the Social Sciences*, edited by R. W. Bell and N. J. Bell. Lubbock, TX: Texas Tech University Press.

Wilson, Margo, and Martin Daly. 1992. The man who mistook his wife for a chattle. In *The Adapted Mind*, edited by J. Barkow, L. Cosmides, and J. Tooby. Oxford: Oxford University Press.

Wolfgang, Marvin E. 1958. *Patterns in Criminal Homicide.* Philadelphia: University of Pennsylvania Press.

16

Premenstrual Syndrome, Work Discipline, and Anger

Emily Martin

There are so many roots to the tree of anger that sometimes the branches shatter before they bear.

Audre Lorde, from "Who Said It Was Simple," in
Chosen Poems Old and New, 1982

Looming over the whole current scene in England and the United States is the enormous outpouring of interest—the publishing of magazine and newspaper articles, popular books, and pamphlets, the opening of clinics, the marketing of remedies—devoted to premenstrual syndrome.

The dominant model for premenstrual syndrome (PMS) is the physiological/medical model. In this model, PMS manifests itself as a variety of physical, emotional, and behavioral "symptoms" which women "suffer." The list of such symptoms varies but is uniformly negative, and indeed worthy of the term "suffer." Judy Lever's list in her popular handbook (1981, 108) serves as an example (Table I). Other examples of uniformly negative symptomatology are [found in the writings of] Halbreich and Endicott (1982) and Dalton (1983).

The syndrome of which this list is a manifestation is a "genuine illness" (Lever 1981, 1), a "real physical problem" (ad in *Dance* magazine, January 1984, 55) whose cause is at base a physical one.[1] Although psychological factors may be involved as a symptom, or even as one cause, "the root cause of

PMT [short for premenstrual tension, another term for PMS], no matter how it was originally triggered, is physical and can be treated" (Lever 1981, 47). This physical cause comes from "a malfunction in the production of hormones during the menstrual cycle, in particular the female hormone, progesterone. This upsets the normal working of the menstrual cycle and produces the unpleasant symptoms of PMT." Astonishingly, we are told that "more than three quarters of all women suffer from symptoms of PMT" (Lever 1981, 2). Other estimates are "up to 75%" (Southam and Gonzaga 1965, 154) and 40% (Robinson, Huntington, and Wallace 1977, 784). In other words, a clear majority of all women are afflicted with a physically abnormal hormonal cycle.

Various "treatments" are described that can compensate a woman for her lack of progesterone or her excess of estrogen or prolactin. Among the benefits of this approach are that psychological and physical states that many women experience as extremely distressing or painful can be alleviated, a problem that had no name or known cause can be named and grasped, and some of the blaming of women for their premenstrual condition by both doctors and

TABLE 1:
A List of the Symptoms of Premenstrual Syndrome from a Popular Handbook

Complete Checklist of Symptoms

Physical Changes		
Weight gain	Epilepsy	Spontaneous bruising
Skin disorders	Dizziness, faintness	Headache, migraine
Painful breasts	Cold sweats	Backache
Swelling	Nausea, sickness	General aches and pain
Eye diseases	Hot flashes	
Asthma	Blurring vision	

Concentration		
Sleeplessness	Lowered judgment	Lack of coordination
Forgetfulness	Difficulty concentrating	Accidents
Confusion		

Behavior Changes		
Lowered school or work performance	Avoid social activities	Drinking too much alcohol
Lethargy	Decreased efficiency	
	Food cravings	Taking too many pills

Mood Changes		
Mood swings	Restlessness	Tension
Crying, depression	Irritability	Loss of sex drive
Anxiety	Aggression	

Source: Judy Lever with Michael G. Brush, *Pre-menstrual Tension*, 1981 by Bantam Books; reproduced by permission.

family members can be stopped. It seems probable that this view of PMS has led to an improvement over the common dismissals "it's all in your mind," "grin and bear it," or "pull yourself together." Yet, entailed also in this view of PMS are a series of assumptions about the nature of time and of society and about the necessary roles of women and men.

Let us begin by returning to the nineteenth century, when . . . menstruation began to be regarded as a pathological process. Because of ideas prevailing among doctors that a woman's reproductive organs held complete sway over her between puberty and menopause, women were warned not to divert needed energy away from the uterus and ovaries. In puberty, especially, the limited amount of energy in a woman's body was essential for the proper development of her female organs.

> Indeed physicians routinely used this energy theory to sanction attacks upon any behavior they considered unfeminine; education, factory work, religious or charitable activities, indeed virtually any interests outside the home during puberty were deplored (Smith-Rosenberg 1974, 27).

The attacks must have been difficult to withstand. One doctor constructed a dialogue with a mother, who brought her fifteen-year-old daughter to see him, dull and moping, pale and thin. He urged the mother to take the daughter out of school, keep her home, and teach her "domestic administration." *"I should much prefer to have a daughter healthy, sweet-tempered, sensible, and beautiful, without Latin, and algebra, and grammar, than to have one ever so advanced in her humanities, with her health ruined, or, perhaps, lying under a marble urn at Laurel Hill."* The hypothetical mother replied, "Why, doctor, you shock me!" and was told, "I wish to shock you; I wish you to learn that, unless you change the treatment, you will lose her. She will die, madam!" (Meigs 1854, 381)

This view of women's limited energies ran very quickly up against one of the realities of nineteenth-century America: many young girls and women worked exceedingly long and arduous hours in factories, shops, and other people's homes. The "cult of invalidism" with its months and even years of inactivity and bed rest, which was urged on upper-class women, was manifestly not possible for the poor. This contradiction was resolved in numerous ways: by detailing the "weakness, degeneration, and disease" suffered by female clerks and operatives who "strive to emulate the males by unremitting labor" (Clarke 1873, 130) while callously disregarding the very poor health conditions of those workers; or by focusing on the greater toll that brain work, as opposed to manual work, was thought to take on female bodies. According to Edward Clarke's influential *Sex in Education* (1873), female operatives suffer less than schoolgirls because they "work their brain less. . . . Hence they have stronger bodies, a reproductive apparatus more normally constructed, and a catamenial [menstrual] function less readily disturbed by effort, than their student sisters."

If men like Clarke were trying to argue that women (except working-class women) should stay home because of their bodily functions, feminists were trying to show how women could function in the world outside the home in spite of their bodily functions. Indeed, it is conceivable that the opinions of Clarke and others were in the first place a response to the threat posed by the first wave of feminism. . . .

It is obvious that the relationship between menstruation and women's capacity to work was a central issue in the nineteenth century. When the focus shifted from menstruation itself to include the few days before menstruation, whether women could work outside the home was still a key issue. It is generally acknowledged that the first person to name and describe the symptoms of premenstrual syndrome was Robert T. Frank in 1931. Two aspects of Frank's discussion of what he called "premenstrual tension" deserve careful attention. The first is that he carried forward the idea, which flourished in the nineteenth century, that women were swayed by the tides of their ovaries. A woman's ovaries were known to produce female sex hormones, and these were the culprit behind premenstrual tension. His remedy was simple and to the point: "It was decided to tone down the ovarian activity by roentgen [x-ray] treatment directed against the ovaries" (1931, 1054). . . .

It strikes me as exceedingly significant that Frank was writing immediately after the Depression at a time when the gains women had made in the paid labor market because of World War I were slipping away. Pressure was placed on women from many sides to give up waged work and allow men to take the jobs (Kessler-Harris 1982).

Can it be accidental that many other studies (Seward 1934; McCance et al. 1937; Billings 1934; Brush 1938) were published during the interwar years that showed the debilitating effects of menstruation on women? Given this pattern of research finding women debilitated by menstruation when they pose an obstacle to full employment for men, it is hardly surprising that after the start of World War II a rash of studies found that menstruation was not a liability after all (Altmann 1941; Anderson 1941; Brinton 1943; Novak 1941; Percival 1943). "Any activity that may be performed with impunity at other times may be performed with equal impunity during menstruation," wrote Seward in 1944, reversing her own earlier finding in 1934 that menstruation was a debility. Some of the evidence amassed for this conclusion seems astoundingly ad hoc: Seward (1944, 95) argues that when women miss work because of menstrual complaints they are indulging in "a bit of socially acceptable malingering by taking advantage of the popular stereotype of menstrual incapacitation." Her evidence? That when a large life insurance company discontinued pay for menstrual absenteeism after a limited time allowance, menstrual absenteeism markedly declined! She missed the point that if people need their wages and have used up their sick leave, they will go to work, even in considerable discomfort.

After World War II, just as after World War I, women were displaced from many of the paid jobs they had taken on (Kessler-Harris 1982, 295).

The pattern seems almost too obvious to have been overlooked so long, but as we know there was a spate of menstrual research after the Second World War that found, just as after the first, that women were indeed disabled by their hormones. Research done by Katharina Dalton in the 1940s was published in the *British Medical Journal* in 1953 (Dalton and Greene 1953), marking the beginning of her push to promote information about the seriousness of premenstrual syndrome. As we will see, one of her overriding concerns was the effect on women's performance at school and work and the cost to national economies of women's inability to work premenstrually.

Although Dalton's research fit in nicely with the postwar edging of women out of the paid work force, it was not until the mid to late 1970s that the most dramatic explosion of interest in PMS took place. This time there were no returning veterans to demand jobs for which women were suddenly "unqualified"; instead, women had made greater incursions into the paid work force for the first time without the aid of a major war.

> First single women, then wives, and then mothers of school-aged children were, in a sense, freed from social constraints against work outside the home. For each of these groups, wage labor was at one time controversial and debatable, but eventually employment became a socially acceptable and even expected act (Weiner 1985, 118).

Many factors were responsible for women's emergence in the paid work force: the second wave of feminism and stronger convictions about women's right to work, a lower birth rate, legislative support barring sex discrimination, increasing urbanization, and growth in educational opportunities for women (Kessler-Harris 1982, 311–16; Weiner 1985, 89–97, 112–18). It goes without saying that women's move toward center stage in the paid work force (as far away as equality still remains) is threatening to some women and men and has given rise to a variety of maneuvers designed to return women to their homes (Kessler-Harris 1982, 316–18). Laws (1983, 25) has suggested that the recent burgeoning of emphasis on PMS is a "response to the second wave of feminism." I think this is a plausible suggestion, made even more convincing by the conjunction between periods of our recent history when women's participation in the labor force was seen as a threat, and, simultaneously, menstruation was seen as a liability.[2]

Turning to the premenstrual symptoms women themselves report, what views of the world of work are represented in their words? An overriding theme in the changes women articulate is a loss of ability to carry on activities involving mental or physical discipline. For example, from Lever's list (Table 1): "difficulty concentrating," "confusion," "forgetfulness," "lowered judgment," "lack of coordination," "decreased efficiency," "lowered school or work performance." Others report "an inability to string words together correctly" (Birke and Gardner 1982, ii) or increased tendency to "fail examinations, absent themselves from work" (Robinson et al. 1977, 784). One book advises that if women find their ability to perform some aspects of work impaired premenstrually, they might organize their work so that "more routine work, for example, might be carried out during this time, and work requiring more concentration and care might be kept for other times when they feel more capable of it" (Birke and Gardner 1982, 24). Competitive tennis players say their reaction times can be slower and professional singers say they lose voice control (Dalton 1983, 102; Lever 1981, 91).

It is no doubt completely understandable that in a society where most people work at jobs that require and reward discipline of mind and body, loss of discipline would be perceived negatively. Marx showed long ago that in a system in which an owner's profit is based on how much value can be squeezed out of laborers' work, the amount of time laborers would have to work and what they did (down to the precise movements of their hands and bodies) would be controlled by factory owners. Indeed, historically, when legislation forced a shortening of the working day, owners found it necessary to intensify labor during the hours remaining: "Machinery becomes in the hands of capital the objective means, systematically employed for squeezing out more labor in a given time. This is effected in two ways: by increasing the speed of the machinery, and by giving the workman more machinery to tend" (Marx 1967, 412).

Braverman and others have recently shown how scientific management, introduced in the late nineteenth century, has contributed to the deskilling and degradation of work: creative, innovative, planning aspects of the work process are separated from routine manual tasks which are then extremely subject to finely tuned managerial control (Braverman 1974; Melman 1983). [See Edwards (1979, 98–104) for factors that limited the impact of scientific management in industry.] We are perhaps accustomed to the notion that assembly line factory work entails a bending of workers' bodies in time and space according to the demands of "productivity" and "efficiency," but we are less accustomed to realize that deskilling, leading to monotony, routine, and repetition, has increasingly affected not just clerical occupations and the enormous service industry (Braverman 1974, Part 4) but the professions as well. Natalie Sokolov (1984) has shown that the lower edges of the medical and legal professions, edges into which women crowd, hardly have the independence, creativity, and opportunity for growth that we associate with professional work. Allied health workers, legal assistants, and lawyers who work in legal clinics may have to do tedious, boring work requiring minimum skills and little opportunity for advancement in knowledge or position.

With respect to work, then, the vast majority of the population and all but a very few women are subjected to physical and mental discipline, one manifestation of what Foucault (1979, 139) calls a "micro-physics of power," "small acts of cunning" in the total enterprise of producing "docile bodies." What many women seem to report is that they are, during premenstrual days, less willing or able to tolerate such discipline.

An obvious next question is whether the incidence of PMS is higher among women subjected to greater work discipline. [Mullings (1984, 131) points to the higher frequency of these hazards among minority and working-class women.] One would also like to know whether there is any correlation between the experience of PMS symptoms (as well as the reporting of them) and factors such as class and race. Unfortunately, the PMS literature is nearly deaf to these kinds of questions. Although the incidence of PMS in relation to age, parity, and the existence of a male living partner has been examined (and is generally found to increase with each) (Debrovner 1982, 11), these are very crude indicators of the whole working and living environment of particular women. My own interviews, not directed toward women with PMS, turned up only four women out of 165 who described themselves as experiencing it, so I cannot speak to whatever patterns there may be.

Perhaps part of the reason a more sophisticated sociological analysis has not been done is that those who comment on and minister to these women do not see that women's mental and physical state gives them trouble only because of the way work is organized in our industrialized society. Women are perceived as malfunctioning and their hormones out of balance, rather than the organization of society and work perceived as in need of a transformation to demand less constant discipline and productivity.

Many PMS symptoms seem to focus on intolerance for the kind of work discipline required by late industrial societies. But what about women who find that they become clumsy? Surely this experience would be a liability in any kind of social setting. Perhaps so, and yet it is interesting that most complaints about clumsiness seem to focus on difficulty carrying out the mundane tasks of keeping house: "You may find you suddenly seem to drop things more often or bump into furniture around the house. Many women find they tend to burn themselves while cooking or cut themselves more frequently" (Lever 1981, 20). "It's almost funny. I'll be washing the dishes or putting them away and suddenly a glass will just jump out of my hands. I must break a glass every month. But that's when I know I'm entering my premenstrual phase" (Witt 1984, 129). Is there something about housework that makes it problematic if one's usual capacity for discipline relaxes?

On the one hand, for the numbers of women who work a double day (hold down a regular job in the paid work force and come home to do most of the cooking, cleaning, and child care), such juggling of diverse responsibilities can only come at the cost of supreme and unremitting effort. On the other hand, for the full-time homemaker, recent changes in the organization of housework must be taken into account. Despite the introduction of "labor-saving" machines, time required by the job has increased as a result of decline in the availability of servants, rise in the standards of household cleanliness, and elaboration of the enterprise of childbearing (Cowan 1983, 208; Scott 1980; Vanek 1974).

To this increase in expectations placed on homemakers I would add the sense of how desirable it is to be "efficient" and "productive" at home, much as it is in the workplace. "Heloise's Hints" and similar columns in newspapers and magazines are full of tips on how to make every moment count, with clever ways of meeting perfectionist standards in the multitude of roles played by a homemaker. . . .

Perhaps the need for discipline in housework comes from a combination of the desire for efficiency and a sense of its endlessness, a sense described by Simone de Beauvoir (1952, 425) as "like the torture of Sisyphus . . . with its endless repetition: the clean becomes soiled, the soiled is made clean, over and over, day after day. The housewife wears herself out marking time: she makes nothing, simply perpetuates the present."

. . . Here is Katharina Dalton's example (1983, 80) of how a premenstrual woman reacts to this routine:

> Then quite suddenly you feel as if you can't cope anymore—everything seems too much trouble, the endless household chores, the everlasting planning of meals. For no apparent reason you rebel: "Why should I do everything?" you ask yourself defiantly. "I didn't have to do this before I was married. Why should I do it now?" . . . As on other mornings you get up and cook breakfast while your husband is in the bathroom. You climb wearily out of bed and trudge down the stairs, a vague feeling of resentment growing within you. The sound of cheerful whistling from upstairs only makes you feel a little more cross. Without any warning the toast starts to scorch and the sausages instead of happily sizzling in the pan start spitting and spluttering furiously. Aghast you rescue the toast which by this time is beyond resurrection and fit only for the trash. The sausages are charred relics of their former selves and you throw those out too. Your unsuspecting husband opens the kitchen door expecting to find his breakfast ready and waiting, only to see a smoky atmosphere and a thoroughly overwrought wife. You are so dismayed at him finding you in such chaos that you just burst helplessly into tears.

Needless to say, by the terms of the medical model in which Dalton operates (1983, 82), the solution for this situation is to seek medical advice and obtain treatment (usually progesterone). The content of the woman's remarks, the substance of what she objects to, escapes notice.

A woman who drops things, cuts or burns herself or the food in this kind of environment has to adjust to an altogether different level of demand on her time and energy than, say, Beng women in the Ivory Coast. There, albeit menstrually instead of premenstrually, women specifically must not enter the forest and do the usual work of their days—farming, chopping wood, and carrying water. Instead, keeping to the village, they are free to indulge in things they usually have no time for, such as cooking a special dish made of palm nuts. This dish, highly prized for its taste, takes hours of slow tending and cooking and is normally eaten only by menstruating women and their close friends and kinswomen (Gottlieb 1982, 44). Whatever the differing demands on Beng as opposed to Western women, Beng social convention requires a cyclic change in women's usual activities. Perhaps Beng women have fewer burned fingers.

For the most part, women quoted in the popular health literature do not treat the cyclic change they experience as legitimate enough to alter the structure of work time. However, several of the women I interviewed did have this thought. One woman expressed this as a wish, while reinterpreting what she had heard about menstrual huts (places of seclusion used by women in some societies when they are menstruating):

> [Does menstruation have any spiritual or religious significance for you?] I like the idea of menstrual huts a great deal. They intrigue me. My understanding is it's a mysterious thing in some ways. It infuriates me that we don't know more about it. Here are all these women—apparently when you get your period you go off to this hut and you hang around. [Because you're unclean?] That's what I feel is probably bull, that's the masculine interpretation of what's going on passed on generally by men to male anthropologists, whereas the women probably say, "Oh, yeah, we're unclean, we're unclean see ya later." And then they race off to the menstrual hut and have a good time. (Meg O'Hara)

Another got right to the heart of the matter with simplicity:

> Some women have cramps so severe that their whole attitude changes; maybe they need time to themselves and maybe if people would understand that they need time off, not the whole time, maybe a couple of days. When I first come on I sleep in bed a lot. I don't feel like doing anything. Maybe if people could understand more. Women's bodies change. (Linda Matthews)

Still another woman foresaw some of the impediments to change, which might include the attitudes of other women:

> [What would you change if you could reorganize things to make life easier?] On that day I would just tell my TA's, "Well, listen, it's the first day of my period and that's why I wasn't in section and that's why I didn't hand in my paper." And that would be an acceptable thing, because really it can keep me from going to class, keep me from handing in a paper, even if I worked on the paper really long and hard. But it's interesting, a lot of times male TA's are much more understanding than female TA's. There are women who don't get it. So you're just like all this BS, you had your period. Guys, they don't really know what it is so they'll just take you on faith that it was really horrible and you couldn't deal with anything. (Anna Perdoni)

These women are carrying on what amounts to a twin resistance: to science and the way it is used in our society to reduce discontent to biological malfunction and to the integrity of separate spheres which are maintained to keep women in one while ruling them out of the other.

Given that periodic changes in activity in accord with the menstrual cycle are not built into the structure of work in our society, what does happen to women's work during their periods? Much recent research has attempted to discover whether women's actual performance declines premenstrually. The overwhelming impression one gets from reading the popular literature on the subject is that performance in almost every respect does decline. According to Dalton's influential account (1983, 100), women's grades drop, they are more likely to commit crimes and suicide, and they "cost British industry 3% of its total wage bill, which may be compared with 3% in Italy, 5% in Sweden and 8% in America." These figures are still being cited in major newspapers (Watkins 1986). Yet other accounts make powerful criticisms of the research on which these conclusions are based: they lack adequate controls, fail to report negative findings, and fail to report overall levels of women's performance in comparison to men's (Parlee 1973, 461–62). Still other studies find either increased performance or no difference in performance at all (Golub 1976; Sommer 1973; Witt 1984, 160–62). . . .

What we see from the list of PMS symptoms in Table I is not so much a list of traits that would be unfortunate in any circumstance but traits that happen to be unfortunate in our particular social and economic system, with the kind of work it requires. This consideration gives rise to the question of whether the decreases reported by women in their ability to concentrate or discipline their attention are accompanied by gains in complementary areas. Does loss of ability to concentrate mean a greater ability to free-associate? Loss of muscle control, a gain in ability to relax? Decreased efficiency, increased attention to a smaller number of tasks?

Here and there in the literature on PMS one can find hints of such increased abilities. Women report:

No real distress except melancholy which I actually enjoy. It's a quiet reflective time for me.

My skin breaks out around both ovulation and my period. My temper is short; I am near tears, I am depressed. One fantastic thing—I have just discovered that I write poetry just before my period is due. I feel very creative at that time. (Both quoted in Weideger 1977, 48).

Others find they "dream more than usual, and may feel sexier than at other times of the cycle" (Birke and Gardner 1982, 23).

A sculptor described her special abilities when she is premenstrual. "There is a quality to my work and to my visions which just isn't there the rest of the month. I look forward to being premenstrual for its effect on my creativity although some of the other symptoms create strains with my family." Another woman, prone to depression, described in the journal she kept, "When I am premenstrual I can write with such clarity and depth that after I get my period I don't recognize that those were my thoughts or that I could have written anything so profound" (Harrison 1984, 16–17).

I don't know what it is, but I'll wake up one morning with an urge to bake bread. I can hardly wait to get home from work and start mixing the flour, kneading the dough, smelling the yeast. It's almost sensual and very satisfying. Maybe it's the earth-mother in me coming out. I don't know. But I do enjoy my premenstrual time (Witt 1984, 150).

I have heard that many women cry before their period. Well, I do too. Sometimes I'll cry at the drop of a hat, but it's a good crying. I'll be watching something tender on TV or my children will do something dear, and my eyes fill up. My heart is flooded with feelings of love for them or for my husband, for the world, for humanity, all the joy and all the suffering. Sometimes I could just cry and cry. But it strengthens me. It makes me feel a part of the earth, of the life-giving force (Witt 1984, 151).

And from my interviews:

I dream very differently during my period; my dreams are very, very vivid and sometimes it seems that I hear voices and conversations. My dreams are very vivid and the colors are not brighter but bolder, like blues and reds and that's also very interesting. The last three days I feel more creative. Things seem a little more colorful, it's just that feeling of exhilaration during the last few days. I feel really great. (Alice Larrick)

I like being by myself, it gives me time to forget about what people are thinking. I like the time I don't have to worry about talking to anybody or being around anybody. It's nice to be by yourself. Time alone. (Kristin Lassiter)

Amid the losses on which most accounts of PMS focus, these women seem to be glimpsing increased capacities of other kinds. If these capacities are there, they are certainly not ones that would be given a chance to flourish or would even be an advantage in the ordinary dual workday of most women. Only the exception—a sculptor or writer—would be able to put these greater emotional and associative capacities to work in her regular environment. Perhaps it is the creative writing tasks present in most academic jobs that lead to the result researchers find puzzling: if premenstrual women cannot concentrate as well, then why are women academics' work performance and concentration better than usual during the premenstrual phase (Bernstein 1977; Birke and Gardner 1982, 25)? The answer may be that there are different kinds of concentration: some requiring discipline inimical to body and soul that women reject premenstrually and some allowing expression of the depth within oneself that women have greater access to premenstrually. . . .

A common premenstrual feeling women describe is anger, and the way this anger is felt by women and described by the medical profession tells a lot about the niche women are expected to occupy in society. An ad in the *Baltimore City Paper* (April 20, 1984, p. 39) for psychotherapeutic support groups asks: "Do you have PMS? Depression—irritability—panic attacks—food cravings—lethargy—dizziness—headache—backache—anger. How are other women coping with this syndrome? Learn new coping mechanisms;

get support from others who are managing their lives." Anger is listed as a symptom in a syndrome, or illness, that afflicts only women. In fuller accounts we find that the reason anger expressed by women is problematic in our society is that anger (and allied feelings such as irritability) makes it hard for a woman to carry out her expected role of maintaining harmonious relationships within the family.

> Serious problems can arise—a woman might become excessively irritable with her children (for which she may feel guilty afterwards), she may be unable to cope with her work, or she may spend days crying for no apparent reason. Life, in other words, becomes intolerable for a short while, both for the sufferer and for those people with whom she lives . . . PMT is often referred to as a potential disrupter of family life. Women suffering from premenstrual irritability often take it out on children, sometimes violently . . . Obviously an anxious and irritable mother is not likely to promote harmony within the family (Birke and Gardner 1982, 25).

This entire account is premised on the unexamined cultural assumption that it is primarily a woman's job to see that social relationships work smoothly in the family. Her own anger, however substantial the basis for it, must not be allowed to make life hard on those around her. If she has an anger she cannot control, she is considered hormonally unbalanced and should seek medical treatment for her malfunction. If she goes on subjecting her family to such feelings, disastrous consequences—construed as a woman's fault in the PMS literature—may follow. For example, Lever (1981, 61) writes, "Doctor Dalton tells the story of a salesman whose commissions dropped severely once a month, putting a financial strain on the family and worrying him a great deal. Doctor Dalton charted his wife's menstrual cycle and found that she suffered from severe PMS. This affected her husband, who became anxious and distracted and so less efficient at his job. The drop in his commissions coincided with her premenstrual days. Doctor Dalton treated his wife and cured the salesman!"

Not only can a man's failure at work be laid at the doorstep of a woman's PMS, so also can a man's violence. Although the PMS literature acknowledges that many battered women do nothing to provoke the violence they suffer from men, it is at times prone to suggest that women may themselves bring on battering if the man has a "short fuse": "[The woman's] own violent feelings and actions while suffering from PMT could supply the spark that causes him to blow up" (Lever 1981, 63). Or consider this account, in which the woman is truly seen as a mere spark to the man's blaze:

> One night she was screaming at him, pounding his chest with her fists, when in her hysteria she grabbed the collar of his shirt and ripped so hard that the buttons flew, pinging the toaster and the microwave oven. But before Susan could understand what she had done, she was knocked against the kitchen wall. Richard had smacked her across the face with the back of his hand. It was a

forceful blow that cracked two teeth and dislocated her jaw. She had also bitten her tongue and blood was flowing from her mouth. . . . [Richard took her to the emergency room that night and moved out the next morning.] He was afraid he might hit her again because *she was so uncontrollable* when she was in a rage (Lauersen and Stukane 1983, 18). [Emphasis added.]

In this incident, who was most uncontrollable when in a rage—Richard or Susan? Without condoning Susan's actions, we must see that her violence was not likely to damage her husband bodily. A woman's fists usually do not do great harm when pounding a man's chest, and in this case they evidently did not. Ripping his clothes, however unfortunate, is not on the same scale as his inflicting multiple (some of them irreversible!) bodily injuries that required her to be treated in a hospital emergency room. The point is not that she was unable to injure him because of her (presumed) smaller size and lesser strength. After all she could have kicked him in the groin or stabbed him with a knife. The point is, she chose relatively symbolic means of expressing her anger and he did not. Yet in the PMS literature she is the one cited as uncontrollable, and responsible for his actions. The problems of men in these accounts are caused by outside circumstances and other people (women). The problems of women are caused by their own internal failure, a biological "malfunction." What is missing in these accounts is any consideration of why, in Anglo and American societies, women might feel extreme rage at a time when their usual emotional controls are reduced.

That their rage is extreme cannot be doubted. Many women in fact describe their premenstrual selves as being "possessed." One's self-image as a woman (and behind this the cultural construction of what it is to be a woman) simply does not allow a woman to recognize herself in the angry, loud, sometimes violent "creature" she becomes once a month.

> I feel it is not me that is in possession of my body. My whole personality changes, making it very difficult for the people I live and work with. I've tried. Every month I say, "This month it's going to be different, I'm not going to let it get hold of me." But when it actually comes to it, something chemical happens to me. I can't control it, it just happens (Lever 1981, 25).

> Something seems to snap in my head. I go from a normal state of mind to anger, when I'm really nasty. Usually I'm very even tempered, but in these times it is as if someone else, not me, is doing all this, and it is very frightening (Lever 1981, 28).

> It is something that is wound up inside, you know, like a great spring. And as soon as anything triggers it off, I'm away. It is very frightening. Like being possessed, I suppose (Lever 1981, 68).

> I try so hard to be a good mother. But when I feel this way, it's as if there's a monster inside me that I can't control (Angier and Witzleben 1983, 119).

> I just get enraged and sometimes I would like to throw bookshelves through windows, barely feeling that I have control . . . these feelings of fury when there's nothing around that would make that necessary. Life is basically going on as before, but suddenly I'm furious about it. (Meg O'Hara)

> I was verbally abusive toward my husband, but I would really thrash out at the kids. When I had these outbursts I tended to observe myself. I felt like a third party, looking at what I was doing. There was nothing I could do about it. I was not in control of my actions. It's like somebody else is taking over (Lauersen and Stukane 1983, 80).

> Once a month for the last 25 years this wonderful woman (my wife) has turned into a [picture of a devil drawn here] (Letter in *PMS Connection* 1982, 1:3. Reprinted by permission of PMS Action, Inc., Irvine, CA.).

It is an anthropological commonplace that spirit possession in traditional societies can be a means for those who are subordinated by formal political institutions (often women) to express discontent and manipulate their superiors (Lewis 1971, 116). But in these societies it is clear that propitiation of the possessing spirit or accusation of the living person who is behind the affliction involves the women and their social groups in setting social relations right. In our own topsy-turvy version of these elements, women say they feel "possessed," but what the society sees behind their trouble is really their own malfunctioning bodies. Redress for women may mean attention focused on the symptoms but not on the social environment in which the "possession" arose. The anger was not really the woman's fault, but neither was it to be taken seriously. Indeed, one of women's common complaints is that men treat their moods casually:

> Sometimes if I am in a bad mood, my husband will not take me seriously if I am close to my period. He felt if it was "that time of the month" any complaints I had were only periodic. A few weeks ago I told him that until I am fifty-five he will have taken me seriously only half the time. After that he will blame it on menopause (Weideger 1977, 10).

Or if husbands cannot ignore moods, perhaps the moods, instead of whatever concrete circumstances from which they arise, can be treated.

> The husband of a woman who came for help described their problem as follows, "My wife is fine for two weeks out of the month. She's friendly and a good wife. The house is clean. Then she ovulates and suddenly she's not happy about her life. She wants a job. Then her period comes and she is all right again." He wanted her to be medicated so she would be a "good wife" all month (Harrison 1984, 50).

Marilyn Frye, in discussing the range of territory a woman's anger can claim, suggests: "So long as a woman is operating squarely within a realm which is generally recognized as a woman's realm, labeled as such by stereotypes of women and of certain activities, her anger will quite likely be tolerated, at least not thought crazy." And she adds, in a note that applies precisely to the anger of PMS, "If the woman insists persistently enough on her anger being taken seriously, she may begin to seem mad, for she will seem to have her values all mixed up and distorted" (Frye 1983, 91).

What are the sources of women's anger, so powerful that women think of it as a kind of possessing spirit? A common characteristic of premenstrual anger is that women often feel it has no immediate identifiable cause: "It never occurred to me or my husband that my totally unreasonable behavior toward my husband and family over the years could have been caused by anything but basic viciousness in me" (Lever 1981, 61).

Women often experience the depression or anger of premenstrual syndrome as quite different from the depression or anger of other life situations. As one woman described this difference: "Being angry when I know I'm right makes me feel good, but being angry when I know it's just me makes me feel sick inside" (Harrison 1984, 36).

Anger experienced in this way (as a result solely of a woman's intrinsic badness) cannot help but lead to guilt. And it seems possible that the sources of this diffuse anger could well come from women's perception, however inarticulate, of their oppression in society—of their lower wage scales, lesser opportunities for advancement into high ranks, tacit omission from the language, coercion into roles inside the family and out that demand constant nurturance and self-denial, and many other ills. Adrienne Rich (1976, 285) asks:

> What woman, in the solitary confinement[3] of a life at home enclosed with young children, or in the struggle to mother them while providing for them single-handedly, or in the conflict of weighing her own personhood against the dogma that says she is a mother, first, last, and always—what woman has not dreamed of "going over the edge," of simply letting go, relinquishing what is termed her sanity, so that she can be taken care of for once, or can simply find a way to take care of herself? The mothers: collecting their children at school; sitting in rows at the parent-teacher meeting; placating weary infants in supermarket carriages; straggling home to make dinner, do laundry, and tend children after a day at work; fighting to get decent care and livable schoolrooms for their children; waiting for child support checks while the landlord threatens eviction . . . —the mothers, if we could look into their fantasies—their daydreams and imaginary experiences— we would see the embodiment of rage, of tragedy, of the overcharged energy of love, of inventive desperation, we would see the machinery of institutional violence wrenching at the experience of motherhood.

Rich acknowledges the "embodiment of rage" in women's fantasies and daydreams. Perhaps premenstrually many women's fantasies become reality, as they experience their own violence wrenching at all of society's institutions, not just motherhood as in Rich's discussion.

Coming out of a tradition of psychoanalysis, Shuttle and Redgrove suggest that a woman's period may be "a moment of truth which will not sustain lies." Whereas during most of the month a woman may keep quiet about things that bother her, "maybe at the paramenstruum, the truth flares into her consciousness: this is an intolerable habit, she is discriminated against as a woman, she is forced to underachieve if she wants love, this examination question set by male teachers is unintelligently phrased, I will not be a punchball to my loved ones, this child must learn that I am not the supernatural never-failing source of maternal sympathy" (Shuttle and Redgrove 1978, 58, 59). In this rare analysis, some of the systematic social causes of women's second-class status, instead of the usual biological causes, are being named and identified as possible sources of suppressed anger.

If *these* kinds of causes are at the root of the unnamed anger that seems to afflict women, and if they could be named and known, maybe a cleaner, more productive anger would arise from within women, tying them together as a common oppressed group instead of sending them individually to the doctor as patients to be fixed.

> And so her anger grew. It swept through her like a fire. She was more than shaken. She thought she was consumed. But she was illuminated with her rage; she was bright with fury. And though she still trembled, one day she saw she had survived this blaze. And after a time she came to see this anger-that-was-so-long-denied as a blessing (Griffin 1978, 185).

To see anger as a blessing instead of as an illness, it may be necessary for women to feel that their rage is legitimate. To feel that their rage is legitimate, it may be necessary for women to understand their structural position in society, and this in turn may entail consciousness of themselves as members of a group that is denied full membership in society simply on the basis of gender. Many have tried to describe under what conditions groups of oppressed people will become conscious of their oppressed condition. Gramsci (1971, 333) wrote of a dual "contradictory consciousness, . . . one which is implicit in his [humans'] activity and which in reality unites him with all his fellow workers in the practical transformation of the world; and one, superficially explicit or verbal, which he has inherited from the past and uncritically absorbed." Perhaps the rage women express premenstrually could be seen as an example of consciousness implicit in activity, which in reality unites all women, a consciousness that is combined in a contradictory way with an explicit verbal consciousness, inherited from the past and constantly reinforced in the present, which denies women's rage its truth.

It is well known that the oppression resulting from racism and colonialism engenders a diffused and steady rage in the oppressed population (Fanon 1963; Genovese 1974, 647). Audre Lorde (1981, 98) expresses this with power: "My response to racism is anger. That anger has eaten clefts into my living only when it remained unspoken, useless to anyone. It has also served me in classrooms without light or learning, where the work and history of Black women was less than a vapor. It has served me as fire in the ice zone of uncomprehending eyes of white women who see in my experience and the experience of my people only new reasons for fear or guilt." Alongside anger from the injustice of racism is anger from the injustice of sexism: "Every woman has a well-stocked arsenal of anger potentially useful against those oppressions, personal and institutional, which brought that anger into being."

Can it be accidental that women describing their premenstrual moods often speak of rebelling, resisting, or even feeling "at war" (Dalton 1983, 80; Halbreich and Endicott 1982, 251, 255, 256; Harrison 1984, 17)? It is important not to miss the imagery of rebellion and resistance even when the women themselves excuse their feelings by saying the rebellion is "for no apparent reason" (Dalton 1983, 80) or that the war is with their own bodies! ["Each month I wage a successful battle with my body. But I'm tired of going to war" (PMS *Connection* 1984, 3–4)].

Elizabeth Fox-Genovese (1982, 272–73) writes of the factors that lead women to accept their own oppression: "Women's unequal access to political life and economic participation provided firm foundations for the ideology of gender difference. The dominant representations of gender relations stressed the naturalness and legitimacy of male authority and minimized the role of coercion. Yet coercion, and frequently its violent manifestation, regularly encouraged women to accept their subordinate status." Looking at what has been written about PMS is certainly one way of seeing the "naturalness" of male authority in our society, its invisibility and unexamined, unquestioned nature. Coercion in this context need not consist in the violence of rape or beating: sometimes women's violence is believed to trigger these acts, as we have seen, but other times it is the women who become violent. In a best-selling novel, a psychopathic killer's brutal murders are triggered by her premenstruum (Sanders 1981). In either case, physical coercion consists in focusing on women's bodies as the locus of the operation of power and insisting that rage and rebellion, as well as physical pain, will be cured by the administration of drugs, many of which have known tranquilizing properties (Herrmann and Beach 1978; Witt 1984, 205, 208).

Credence for the medical tactic of treating women's bodies with drugs comes, of course, out of the finding that premenstrual moods and discomfort are regular, predictable, and in accord with a woman's menstrual cycle. Therefore, it is supposed, they must be at least partially caused by the changing hormonal levels known to be a part of the cycle. The next step, according to the logic of scientific medicine, is to try to find a drug that alleviates the unpleasant aspects of premenstrual syndrome for the millions of women that suffer them.

Yet if this were to happen, if women's monthly cycle were to be smoothed out, so to speak, we would do well to at least notice what would have been lost. Men and women alike in our society are familiar with one cycle, dictated by a complex interaction of biological and psychological factors, that happens in accord with cycles in the natural world: we all need to sleep part of every solar revolution, and we all recognize the disastrous consequences of being unable to sleep as well as the rejuvenating results of being able to do so. We also recognize and behave in accord with the socially determined cycle of the week, constructed around the demands of work-discipline in industrial capitalism (Thompson 1967). It has even been found that men structure their moods more strongly in accord with the week than women (Rossi and Rossi 1977). And absenteeism in accord with the weekly cycle—reaching as high as 10 percent at General Motors on Mondays and Fridays, according to Braverman (1974, 32)—is a cause of dismay in American industry but does not lead anyone to think that workers need medication for this problem.

Gloria Steinem (1981, 338) wonders sardonically:

> what would happen if suddenly, magically, men could menstruate and women could not?
>
> Clearly, menstruation would become an enviable, boast-worthy, masculine event:
>
> Men would brag about how long and how much.
>
> Young boys would talk about it as the envied beginning of manhood.
>
> Gifts, religious ceremonies, family dinners, and stag parties would mark the day.
>
> To prevent monthly work loss among the powerful, Congress would fund a National Institute of Dysmenorrhea.

Perhaps we might add to her list that if men menstruated, we would all be expected to alter our activities, monthly as well as daily and weekly, and enter a time and space organized to maximize the special powers released around the time of menstruation while minimizing the discomforts.

PMS adds another facet to the complex round of women's consciousness. Here we find some explicit challenges to the existing structure of work and time, based on women's own experience and awareness of capacities that are stifled by the way work is organized. Here we also find a kind of inchoate rage which women, because of the power of the argument that reduces this rage to biological malfunction, often do not allow to become wrath. In the whole history of PMS there are the makings of a debate whose questions have not been recognized for what they are: Are women, as in the terms of our cultural ideology, relegated by the functions of their bodies to home and family, except when, as second best, they struggle into wartime vacancies? Or are women, drawing on the different concepts of time and human capacities they experience, not only able to function in the world of work but able to mount a challenge that will transform it?

Notes

I am indebted to Thomas Buckley and Alma Gottlieb, who solicited the original version of this essay for their volume *Blood Magic* (1988).

1. Few accounts reject the description of PMS as a disease. One that does is Witt, who prefers the more neutral term "condition" (1984, 11–12). It is also relevant to note that I do not experience severe manifestations of PMS, and there is a possibility that for that reason I do not give sufficient credit to the medical model of PMS. I have, however, experienced many similar manifestations during the first three months of each of my pregnancies, so I have some sense that I know what women with PMS are talking about.
2. I am working on a more extensive study of the literature on menstruation and industrial work from the late nineteenth century to the present, including publications in industrial hygiene as well as medicine and public health.
3. On isolation of housewives, see Gilman ([1903] 1972, 92).

References

Altmann, M. 1941. A psychosomatic study of the sex cycle in women. *Psychosomatic Medicine* 3:199–225.

Anderson, M. 1941. Some health aspects of putting women to work in war industries. *Industrial Hygiene Foundation Seventh Annual Meeting*, p. 165–69.

Angier, Natalie, and Janet Witzleben. 1983. Dr. Jekyll and Ms. Hyde. *Reader's Digest* 43:119–21.

Bernstein, Barbara Elaine. 1977. Effect of menstruation on academic women. *Archives of Sexual Behavior* 6:289–96.

Billings, Edward G. 1934. The occurrence of cyclic variations in motor activity in relation to the menstrual cycle in the human female. *Bulletin of Johns Hopkins Hospital* 54:440–54.

Birke, Lynda, and Katy Gardner. 1982. *Why Suffer? Periods and Their Problems.* London: Virago.

Braverman, Harry. 1974. *Labor and Monopoly Capital.* New York: Monthly Review Press.

Brinton, Hugh P. 1943. Women in industry. In *Manual of Industrial Hygiene and Medical Service in War Industries.* National Institutes of Health, Division of Industrial Hygiene. Philadelphia: W. B. Saunders. Pp. 395–419.

Brush, A. L. 1938. Attitudes, emotional and physical symptoms commonly associated with menstruation in 100 women. *American Journal of Orthopsychiatry* 8:286–301.

Buckley, Thomas, and Alma Gottlieb, eds. 1988. *Blood Magic: Explorations in the Anthropology of Menstruation.* Berkeley: University of California Press.

Clarke, Edward H. 1873. *Sex in Education; or a Fair Chance for the Girls.* Boston: James R. Osgood and Co.

Cowan, Ruth Schwartz. 1983. *More Work for Mother: The Ironies of Household Technologies from the Open Hearth to the Microwave.* New York: Basic Books.

Dalton, Katharina. 1983. *Once a Month.* Claremont, CA: Hunter House.

Dalton, Katharina, and Raymond Greene. 1983. The premenstrual syndrome. *British Medical Journal*, May, 1016–17.

de Beauvoir, Simone. 1952. *The Second Sex.* New York: Knopf.

Debrovner, Charles, ed. 1982. *Premenstrual Tension: A Multidisciplinary Approach.* New York: Grove Press.

Edwards, Richard. 1979. *Contested Terrain: The Transformation of the Workplace in the Twentieth Century.* New York: Basic Books.

Fanon, Frantz. 1963. *The Wretched of the Earth*. New York: Grove Press.

Foucault, Michel. 1979. *Discipline and Punish: The Birth of the Prison*. NewYork: Vintage.

Fox-Genovese, Elizabeth. 1982. Gender, class, and power: Some theoretical considerations. *The History Teacher* 15:255–76.

Frank, Robert T. 1931. The hormonal causes of premenstrual tension. *Archives of Neurology and Psychiatry* 26:1053–57.

Frye, Marilyn. 1983. *The Politics of Reality: Essay in Feminist Theory*. Trumansbrug, NY: The Crossing Press.

Genevose, Eugene D. 1974. *Roll, Jordan, Roll: The World the Slaves Made*. New York: Vintage.

Gilman, Charlotte Perkins. 1972 [1903]. *The Home: Its Work and Influence*. Urbana: University of Illinois Press.

Golub, Sharon. 1976. The effect of premenstrual anxiety and depression on cognitive function. *Journal of Personality and Social Psychology* 34:99–104.

Gottlieb, Alma. 1982. Sex, fertility and menstruation among the Beng of the Ivory Coast: A symbolic analysis. *Africa* 52:34–47.

Gramsci, Antonio. 1971. *Prison Notebooks*. New York: International Publishers.

Griffin, Susan. 1978. *Woman and Nature: The Roaring Inside Her*. New York: Harper and Row.

Halbreich, Uriel, and Jean Endicott. 1982. Classification of premenstrual syndromes. In *Behavior and the Menstrual Cycle*, edited by Richard C. Friedman. New York: Marcel Dekker.

Harrison, Michelle. 1984. *Self-Help for Premenstrual Syndrome*. Cambridge, MA: Matrix Press.

Herrmann, W. M. and R. C. Beach. 1978. Experimental and clinical data indicating the psychotropic properties of progestogens. *Postgraduate Medical Journal* 54:82–87.

Kessler-Harris, Alice. 1982. *Out to Work: A History of Wage-Earning Women in the United States*. New York: Oxford University Press.

Lauersen, Niels H. and Eileen Stukane. 1983. *PMS, Premenstrual Syndrome and You: Next Month Can Be Different*. New York: Simon and Schuster.

Laws, Sophie. 1983. The sexual politics of pre-menstrual tension. *Women's Studies International Forum* 6:19–31.

Lever, Judy, with Dr. Michael G. Brush. 1981. *Pre-menstrual Tension*. New York: Bantam.

Lewis, I. M. 1971. *Ecstatic Religion*. Middlesex, England: Penguin.

Lorde, Audre. 1981. The uses of anger. *Women's Studies Quarterly* 9(3): 7–10.

Marx, Karl. 1967. *Capital: A Critique of Political Economy*, Vol.1. New York: International Publishers.

McCance, R. A., M. C. Luff, and E. E. Widdowson. 1937. Physical and emotional periodicity in women. *Journal of Hygiene* 37:571–614.

Meigs, Charles. 1854. *Females and Their Diseases*. Philadelphia: D. G. Brinton.

Melman, Seymour. 1983. *Profits without Production*. New York: Knopf.

Mullings, Leith. 1984. Minority women, work, and health. In *Double Exposure: Women's Health Hazards on the Job and at Home*, edited by Wendy Chavkin. New York: Monthly Review Press.

Novak, Emil. 1941. Gynecologic problems of adolescence. *Journal of the American Medical Association* 117:1950–53.

Parlee, Mary. 1973. The premenstrual syndrome. *Psychological Bulletin* 80:454–65.

Percival, Eleanor. 1943. Menstrual disturbances as they may affect women in industry. *The Canadian Nurse* 39:335–37.

The PMS Connection. 1982–84. *PMS Connection.* Madison, WI: PMS Action.

Rich, Adrienne. 1976. *Of Woman Born.* New York: Bantam.

Robinson, Kathleen, Kathleen M. Huntington, and M. G. Wallace. 1977. Treatment of the premenstrual syndrome. *British Journal of Obstetrics and Gynecology* 84:784–88.

Rossi, Alice S., and Peter E. Rossi. 1977. Body time and social time: Mood patterns by menstrual cycle phase and day of the week. *Social Science Research* 6:273–308.

Sanders, Lawrence. 1981. *The Third Deadly Sin.* New York: Berkley Books.

Scott, Joan Wallach. 1980. The mechanization of women's work. *Scientific American* March: 167–85.

Seward, G. H. 1934. The female sex rhythm. *Psychological Bulletin* 31:153–92.

———. 1944. Psychological effects of the menstrual cycle on women workers. *Psychological Bulletin* 41:90–102.

Shuttle, Penelope, and Peter Redgrove. 1978. *The Wise Wound: Eve's Curse and Everywoman.* New York: Richard Marek.

Smith-Rosenberg, Carroll. 1974. Puberty to menopause: The cycle of femininity in nineteenth-century America. In *Clio's Consciousness Raised,* edited by Mary Hartman and Lois W. Banner. New York: Harper and Row.

Sokolov, Natalie. 1984. Women in the professions. Lecture in series *Women in History, Culture and Society.* Baltimore, MD.

Sommer, Barbara. 1973. The effect of menstruation on cognitive and perceptual-motor behavior: A review. *Psychosomatic Medicine* 35:515–34.

Southam, Anna L., and Florante P. Gonzaga. 1965. Systemic changes during the menstrual cycle. *American Journal of Obstetrics & Gynecology* 91:142–65.

Steinem, Gloria. 1981. *Outrageous Acts and Everyday Rebellions.* New York: Holt, Rinehart, and Winston.

Thompson, E. P. 1967. Time, work-discipline, and industrial capitalism. *Past and Present* 38:56–97.

Vanek, Joan. 1974. Time spent in housework. *Scientific American* 231(5):116–20.

Watkins, Linda M. 1986. Premenstrual distress gains notice as a chronic issue in the workplace. *Wall Street Journal,* 22 Jan.

Weideger, Paula. 1977. *Menstruation and Menopause: The Physiology and Psychology, the Myth and the Reality.* New York: Delta.

Weiner, Lynn Y. 1985. *From Working Girl to Working Mother: The Female Labor Force in the United States, 1820–1980.* Chapel Hill: University of North Carolina Press.

Witt, Reni L. 1984. *PMS: What Every Woman Should Know about Premenstrual Syndrome.* New York: Stein and Day.

17

Meno-Boomers and Moral Guardians
An Exploration of the Cultural Construction of Menopause

JOY WEBSTER BARBRE

In a recent issue of the *Los Angeles Times*, staff writer Linda Roach Monroe (1989) asserted that the United States is about to experience a "menoboom." According to Monroe, with the aging of more than thirty million baby boom generation women, the number of women affected by menopause in the United States will increase by more than thirty-three percent over the next two decades. As the baby boomers turn into meno-boomers, menopause is likely to receive more and more of this kind of coverage in mainstream American culture. Authenticated by scientific studies and medical evidence, the information presented will probably, like Monroe's article, relate that the difficulties associated with menopause and poor health in old age may be substantially reduced when healthy living, proper medical management, and, according to some, hormone replacement therapy begin early in the premenopausal years.

This current perspective on menopause appears to be very different from perspectives that existed in the past. For instance, one hundred years ago Victorian women were warned that menopause could cause a potpourri of ailments from shingles to insanity. And only thirty years ago our own mothers were told that, because of the "empty nest syndrome," menopause might create psychological problems. Advances in medical and scientific knowledge are often cited as the reason for these changes. While I am aware that our increased understanding of biological processes has significantly altered our

Originally published as Joy Webster Barbre. 1993. "Meno-Boomers and Moral Guardians: An Exploration of the Cultural Construction of the Menopause." pp. 23–35 in Joan C. Callahan (ed.) *Menopause: A Midlife Passage*. Bloomington: Indiana University Press.

ideas about menopause, I do not think that new knowledge alone can fully explain the changes. I believe we must also look at their relationship to broader cultural changes surrounding what it has meant to be a woman in the past and what it means to be a woman today.

Menopause is a biological phenomenon with a set of physiological imperatives that do not change over time. All women who live long enough will experience or have experienced menopause. Therefore, menopause would seem to be a natural biological occurrence, over which culture has little influence. However, menopause does not occur in a vacuum. It, like other events resulting from women's reproductive biology, menstruation and childbirth for instance, is given meaning and value by the culture within which it occurs. In other words, menopause may be a biological event, but the significance attributed to it is cultural. Our perceptions of menopause are tied to the broader culture's underlying assumptions about womanhood, aging, and medicine in general. In this respect, menopause, like gender, can be seen as a cultural construct, a construct which reflects and reinforces broader cultural values and assumptions.

I contend that if we as women are to make informed decisions about the information we receive, it is important for us to recognize the culturally constructed nature of menopause. We must be aware that the model of menopause we are receiving is influenced by our culture's worldview, and we must begin to question how the advice we are offered reflects and reinforces the broader culture's underlying assumptions about women's biology, women's aging, and women's social roles in contemporary American society. In order to illustrate my point, and perhaps begin to bring into focus how the contemporary model of menopause can be seen as a cultural construct, in this essay I will explore the cultural construction of menopause in Victorian America. I have selected this period for my focus because scholars have studied the era's prescriptive literature extensively, and their work has uncovered significant links between Victorian medical advice and cultural assumptions about womanhood in nineteenth-century America (see, for example, Martin 1987; Smith-Rosenberg 1973; Wood 1984).

Victorian Womanhood in America

In nineteenth-century America, the Victorian worldview was one which centered around notions of rationality, individualism, "scientific" thought, and moral authority. For the burgeoning middle class, centers of production had moved from the home to the industrial realm, and concepts of a separation between the public and private spheres were emerging. The ideal Victorian [white] woman was perceived to be inherently intuitive, passive, delicate, affectionate, nurturing, and domestic, attributes which afforded her a dimension of moral superiority. These "innate" qualities made women unfit for the harsh and competitive realities of industrialized society (the public sphere). On the other hand, they were qualities which were best expressed in marriage and motherhood, thereby making women particularly suited to the home (the private sphere). The private sphere was thus perceived as women's domain, the place where they, with their moral superiority, created an atmosphere in which men could revitalize their moral sensibilities after their exposure to corrupting immoral influences in the public sphere. The home was also the place where women's "innate" qualities could be utilized to ensure that children would be reared to responsibly fulfill their moral obligations as adults. In this manner, Victorian women came to be seen as guardians of Victorian morality.

Science, rapidly replacing religion as the realm of discourse that could best explain the universe and guide people's lives, played an important role in the rationalization and justification of these separate sphere conceptions. Though perceived as objective, and therefore the conveyor of "truth," science was in fact a part of the broader culture in which it existed. As such, it reflected and reinforced the broader culture's assumptions about how a well-ordered society should work. Medical and moral realms became intertwined as "scientific" evidence emerged which rationalized the broader culture's moral convictions, and an elaborate body of medical and biological theory explained and justified the culture's conceptions about women's inherent nature and hence their role as moral guardians (Banner 1983; Evans 1989; Gordon 1977; Martin 1987; May 1980; Smith-Rosenberg 1973; Wood 1984).

Nineteenth-Century Medical Theory and Women's Bodies

Mid-nineteenth-century medical theory postulated that the ganglionic nervous system served as a storage for the "vital force" and was the source of all energy. This nervous system was directly connected to the reproductive system and the central nervous system, including the brain. This physiology was not peculiar to women, but because of women's more complex reproductive physiology—puberty, menstruation, childbirth, lactation, menopause—their reproductive organs drew more energy from the ganglionic system, and hence, their storage of "vital force" was always in danger of depletion. Any breakdown in a woman's reproductive organs could cause trauma to her nervous system and through it to other parts of her body. In a like manner, any shock to her nervous system could damage her reproductive organs. In any of these cases, extra demands were placed on her "vital forces," which were already in short supply because of her reproductive biology (Tilt 1882). In effect, this theory rationalized what was already suspected, namely that women and men were suited to different societal realms because of their reproductive organs.

A woman's reproductive organs governed her entire being; they dictated her personality, her abilities and limitations, and hence her social role. As Dr. Charles Meigs (1848, 38) asserted,

> Her reproductive organs, that are peculiar to her; and in her intellect and moral perceptivity and powers, which are feminine as her organs are . . . the strange

and secret influences which her organs, by their nervous constitution, and her functions, by their relation to her whole life-force, whether in sickness or health, are capable of exerting not on the body alone, but on the heart, the mind, and the very soul of woman.

Dr. Edward Dixon argued that reproduction was the end and object of woman's existence, the great object of her being (1857, 5, 101). Perhaps M. L. Holbrook put it most succinctly when he noted that it seemed "as if the Almighty, in creating the female sex, had taken the Uterus and built up a woman around it" (Wood 1984, 223). Nineteenth-century medical theory meshed with moral beliefs to construct a model of female physiology that provided Victorian culture with just the kind of scientific proof it needed to explain women's inherent nature, tie women even closer to their reproductive organs, and justify the social roles ascribed to Victorian women.

With her reproductive system as the central agent for good health, the Victorian woman was admonished to lead a life that protected her ovaries and uterus. The advice given was grounded in scientific theory, but the message presented had decidedly moral overtones, and the imperatives for a healthy life were ones which reinforced Victorian conceptions about women's social roles. Employment; social activism; contraception; excesses in food, dress, or sexuality; novel reading; and education were all activities that could overstimulate a woman's nervous system and thus endanger her reproductive system. Further, birth control was risky because it prevented semen from "bathing the female reproductive organs," an act which neutralized the excessive nervous stimulation built up during sexual excitement. At the same time, excess sexual activity was dangerous because it created nervous exhaustion, thereby depleting the energy sources to the reproductive system (Smith-Rosenberg and Rosenberg 1984, 14–19).

In a like manner, education presented particular peril because it diverted the "vital force" away from the uterus, and to the brain. As one respected doctor reported (Meigs 1848, 352–64),

> I have known many to lose their catamenia [menstruation] by severe application of the mind to studies . . . to rack her brain learning Latin is nonsense. She can't learn it, in the first place. She can only try till it makes her sick . . . they [women] cannot . . . participate in the affairs of nations or municipalities, because by the very nature of their moral and physical constitution, they are bound to the horns of the family altar . . . the only arithmetical calculation she requires is the relation between one dozen eggs at 12 1/2 cents and three dozen at the same rate . . .

Clearly, nineteenth-century conceptions about women's biology were tightly bound to the ideology surrounding women's social roles and promoted woman's position as moral guardian. And when Victorian assumptions about women's aging are also explored, we can begin to see how the era's construction of womanhood shaped the meanings and values ascribed to menopause during this period.

Definitions of Female Old Age in Victorian America

During the nineteenth century, when the uterus was the primary definer of womanhood and menopause signaled the end of the very core of woman's existence, menopause heralded the onset of female old age. (Prior to this period, old age for women was perceived to begin at about 60 years of age; see, for example, Demos 1983; Premo 1983). The very title of Dr. E. J. Tilt's influential nineteenth-century book indicates his stand on the issue: *The Change of Life . . . Women at the Decline of Life*. In his preface, Tilt (1882) reported that he was about to " . . . describe the closing scenes of the life of women" (6). Another doctor described menopause as the "climax of life-force . . . the possessor to decline toward the last term of existence . . . she has now become an old woman . . ." (Meigs 1848, 444). And yet another referred to menopause as " . . . a transition to the closing phase of her exis-tence" (Dixon 1857, 101). By mid-nineteenth century, many women were living well into old age. In 1870 the average life span for women was about sixty-five, women over sixty-five made up three percent of the total popu-lation, and one half of those over sixty-five were women (see, for example, Achenbaum 1978, 91–92; Fisher 1978, 279; Premo 1983, 16). Victorian doctors set the average age for menopause at forty-five (Tilt 1882, 21; Meigs 1848, 453). Thus, while large numbers of nineteenth-century women had many years of life left after menopause, the culture considered them years of old age.

In Victorian culture female old age was often presented as a pleasurable stage of life. Many doctors asserted that, with the debilitating effects of menstruation and childbearing behind them, postmenopausal women not only regained the beauty and health of their younger days, but in fact those qualities were enhanced by the plumpness that resulted from menopause (Meigs 1848, 445; Tilt 1882, 103–105). In addition, because older people were thought to have discovered the code of behavior that ensured a long life, old age was romanticized in the second half of the nineteenth century. As historian Andrew Achenbaum (1978, 15) has noted, "Precisely because most Americans believed that one's mental outlook and personal habits affected chances for living a full life, older men and women . . . demonstrated which lifestyles were more effective than others for promoting healthful longevity." Old women, possessing the natural moral endowment of their sex and the acquired status of an exemplary long life, were doubly romanticized.

This romanticization is clearly evident in the medical literature. Tilt (1882, 103) noted that once menopause had passed,

> love still rules paramount in the breast of women, . . it still engrosses the thoughts, . . crowning the evening of life with unanticipated happiness . . . becoming the guides, the supports, and the mainstays of both sexes in the difficulties of life. Indeed, it would not be too much to say that the discordant elements of society can never be blended without the authority willingly conceded to the combined influence of age and sex.

Dixon (1857, 315) wrote, "The crowning glory of a healthy woman is a large family . . . when faithfully carried out . . . she is adding to her length of years, and the happiness of her old age."

Ideally, for the postmenopausal Victorian woman life was to be a continuation of the nurturing, domestic, and moral aspects of her younger days, but with the added dimensions of improved health and beauty and veneration and respect for her example of right living. Women could enjoy the promise of old age, but not until they had passed through menopause, a period of danger laden with physical risks and hidden cultural significance.

Victorian Perceptions of Menopause

Menopause was the point at which the system that had regulated women's entire lives failed, and the crisis it presented was not to be taken lightly. Doctors asserted that because of the integral connection between women's reproductive organs and their central nervous systems, menopause, when the reproductive organs were in a disturbed state, " . . . is universally admitted to be a critical and dangerous time for her" (Tilt 1882, 15). Chronic ill health, chronic debility, consumption, rheumatism, ulcerated legs, diabetes, urinary tract problems, hemorrhoids, gout, tooth decay, heart disease, shingles, chronic diarrhea and constipation, deafness, and cancer are just a few of the conditions doctors warned could be brought on by menopause (Tilt 1882, 106–224).

Reflecting the culture's emphasis on women's moral superiority, one of the most serious conditions associated with menopause was "moral insanity." E. J. Tilt (1882, 101) explained "moral insanity" by noting that

> During the change of life the nervous system is so unhinged that the management of the mental and moral faculties often taxes the ingenuity of the medical confidant . . . [the disturbance] can cause normally moral women to act without principle . . . be untruthful . . . be peevish . . . even have fits of temper . . . steal . . . leave their families . . . brood in melancholy self-absorption.

The perceived association between menopause and moral insanity was so pervasive that Victorian era court records indicate moral insanity due to menopause was often accepted as a defense in cases of shoplifting (Abelson 1989, 184–87). While the ailments listed above were perceived to be the result of menopause, prescriptions for surviving this dangerous period of life indicate that a woman's behavior determined whether she would have the kind of menopause that caused these conditions.

Packaged as medical advice, the counsel about menopause given to Victorian women stressed the critical nature of the experience, but it also conveyed a warning that the hazards of menopause could be avoided if women held fast to their "innate" nurturing, delicate, and moral nature. The morally questionable acts of novel reading, sexual intercourse, dancing, going to the theater or parties, and displays of temper were all risky because they excited the nervous system and hence endangered the reproductive organs (Tilt 1882, 48, 73, 94–99; Meigs 1848, 464). Emphasizing the delicate and fragile nature of women, most doctors prescribed a quiet life at this time. Tilt recommended long periods of rest and the avoidance of any kind of excitement during this period (1882, 189). Dixon (1857, 105, 108) wrote, "The first caution we would urge upon the female relates to . . . the management of her temper . . . the mind and the uterine system should remain in profound repose." Another advised, " . . . keep the mind not stupefied, certainly, but in a calm and complacent mood" (Meigs 1848, 369). In essence, women were advised to retire from the world, devote themselves to domesticity, and concentrate on their roles as moral guardians.

For the nineteenth-century woman, it was not only her behavior during menopause that determined the kind of old age she would have; the accumulated experiences of her past life were also a contributing factor. Indiscretions in earlier life, as one doctor noted, " . . . will find this period [menopause] a veritable Pandora's box of ills" (Haller 1972, 65). Dr. J. H. Kellogg (1893, 350) asserted that " . . . the grey-haired women who passed their climacteric, who frequent the offices of popular gynecologists . . . are to a large extent victims of sexual transgressions." He also argued that birth control and abortion were " . . . injurious to character and led to the most wretched diseases in women's later years." Mrs. Emma Drake, M.D., advised that women who ignored their physical nature would pay the consequences at menopause. The detrimental effects of dancing, exercise, improper dress, and education might not be felt until menopause but " . . . at the crisis, when a reserve force is needed, they find themselves without it, and go down with the current to days of suffering, if not death itself." On birth control and abortion Drake (1902, 131) warned,

> Women who have lent their souls to heartless work will, if they persist, go to swell the number of those who suffer not only discomfort, but disease and lifelong suffering at the time of and after the menopause. Nature has become so outraged that she can never again adjust the proper working of the physical system.

Charles Meigs (1848, 349–55) asserted that " . . . a badly passed youth will show up in a disastrous menopause," and related the example of a young woman who attempted to delay the onset of her monthly menses by cold baths so that she might attend a dance. Meigs reported that her efforts were successful, but at the change of life she suffered diseases of the womb which were directly related to this one incident. A young girl's decision to neglect the imperatives of her biology in favor of the morally questionable act of dancing doomed her to problems during her menopausal years. In effect, menopause and its signaling of old age became an event of moral reckoning for Victorian women.

For nineteenth-century Victorian women, representations of old age held the promise of comfortable fulfillment and familial and societal reverence.

But the prelude to old age, menopause, was fraught with danger, the point at which previous violations of their moral and delicate nature took their toll. The prescriptive model for surviving those dangers and receiving the rewards of old age was a model based on "objective" scientific evidence, but one that was also decidedly in tune with the definition of womanhood in Victorian America. It was a model which stressed and reinforced the delicate, nurturing, and moral qualities assumed to be a part of Victorian womanhood, whether or not the essential element of reproductive capability was present.

Women, Culture, and Menopause in Contemporary America

Today's model of womanhood appears to bear little resemblance to the nineteenth-century model described above. Reproduction is still a core element in our culture's definition of woman, but giving birth and rearing children comprise only one option in a woman's life, not the very reason for her existence. For modern woman a whole spectrum of choices, experiences, and social roles are available. And yet, it is impossible to open a magazine, watch a television show, or view a movie without receiving our culture's definition of ideal womanhood. No matter what the choices, or age, today's woman is competent and capable in all areas. She is able to succeed in her chosen career, raise perfect children, create the perfect home, and juggle the numerous demands of all three. She is sexually responsive, youthfully attractive, intellectually stimulated, and thus a perfect companion for the man in her life. She keeps up on current affairs, supports the right causes, and knows what foods and behaviors are scientifically proven to be the best for the human body. In her busy schedule she finds time to take care of herself in order to assure that she will be attractive, energetic, physically fit, and healthy well into old age. On this model of womanhood the menopausal woman differs little from her younger sister. Images that reflect the ideal woman smile out at us from the covers of *Lear's* magazine, and Jane Fonda is admired as the exemplary menopausal woman.

However, like our Victorian sisters a century ago, we, the women of today, are also warned that menopause is a crisis. As Dr. Wulf H. Utian (1989, 2) wrote,

> Many women perceive menopause—like menses and pregnancy—as just another physiologic event in the course of female reproduction, and do not seek medical help. . . . We now know that menopausal symptoms must not be ignored. Even 'asymptomatic menopause' may initiate silent, progressive, and ultimately lethal sequelae.

The definition of "sequela" is "a pathological condition resulting from a disease" (*American Heritage Dictionary* 1982). The disease in question here is estrogen deficiency disease, a disease which, we are warned, causes pathological conditions. The cause of this disease is reported to be menopause.

According to numerous medical and scientific experts and commercial drug companies, hormone replacement therapy (HRT) is an important treatment for this disease, and many advise that women begin a program of HRT at or before menopause and continue therapy for the rest of their lives. "The American College of Obstetrics and Gynecology recommends that every woman be considered for HRT . . ." (Monroe 1989, 1). Echoing the sentiments of the majority of this association's conferees at a recent conference on menopause, one speaker stated, "It is becoming increasingly clear that estrogen therapy has an important second purpose, that is, prevention of disease. The second aspect of estrogen therapy should prompt serious consideration of estrogen replacement therapy for every woman at the time of menopause" (Ettinger 1987, 1298). And Robert G. Wells, M.D., director of The Menopause Center, wrote, "With so many benefits and virtually no dangers, it now seems reasonable to recommend that all post-menopausal women—regardless of age or menopausal symptoms—seriously be considered for hormone replacement therapy" (1989, 67).

The assertion that HRT is a reasonable course of treatment for all women is not new. Roughly thirty years ago, when our mothers were being told that the "empty nest syndrome" could cause psychological problems at menopause, Dr. Robert Wilson wrote his best seller, *Feminine Forever*, in which he asserted that, with HRT, "Menopause is curable. . . . menopause is completely preventable. . . . Instead of being condemned to witness the death of their own womanhood . . . [women] will remain fully feminine— physically and emotionally—for as long as they live" (1966, 15–19). In the 1990s, Wilson's rationale for advocating HRT seems chauvinistic and even anachronistic. Few of us view menopause as the death of womanhood. And yet, at that time, on the prevailing model of womanhood as represented by [the TV roles of] June Cleaver, Donna Reed, and Margaret Anderson, femininity was virtually synonymous with motherhood. Wilson's medical advice was shaped and formed by the culture's assumption that menopause presented a psychological crisis in women's lives and, like the Victorian doctors before him, his underlying message reflected and reinforced the era's cultural assumptions about women's social roles and women's biology.

Contemporary proponents of HRT have drawn their conclusions from the evidence provided by "objective" scientific studies. We must remember, however, that today, as in the 1960s and the nineteenth century, science does not stand outside of culture; it is a part of the culture in which it exists, and therefore "objectivity" is, at best, a nebulous term. Scientific evidence in the nineteenth century "proved" that menopause was a physiological crisis with moral overtones. In the early 1960s, scientific thought proposed that HRT could circumvent the psychological crisis menopause caused in women's sense of femininity. Today the scientific evidence once again suggests that menopause is a physiological crisis; but as in the 1960s and the nineteenth century, the unspoken message reinforces and reflects our current model of ideal womanhood. For instance, as previously noted, today's ideal woman, whatever her age, is youthfully attractive and physically fit. Robert G. Wells in 1989 wrote "HRT may not be the elusive 'fountain of youth,' but it surely qualifies as one of its 'springs' " (70). This claim for the benefits of HRT may provide us with a starting point in our search for the ways in which current advice on menopause constructs a model of menopause which is consistent with contemporary cultural assumptions about women's biology, women's social roles, and women's aging.

Definitions of what it means to be a woman have been constructed in different ways at different times throughout America's history. These changing definitions have emerged from changing broader cultural assumptions about how the world works. However, one essential element in all of these definitions has remained constant—woman's physiological ability to reproduce. And yet, the natural biological process of menopause—the end of those reproductive abilities—is an unavoidable experience for most women. It is an event which all definitions of womanhood must somehow accommodate in ways that are consistent with broader definitions of womanhood. Just as the models presented to women in the past must be questioned for the ways in which they were constructed to accomplish this accommodation, we, the women of today, must also question the model we are receiving. We must ask if the current rush to save us from menopause is the result of new "objective" medical and scientific knowledge—a breakthrough in humans' ability to correct nature's mistakes. Or is the perceived need to save women influenced by something more complex—specifically, by current assumptions about women's biology, women's social roles, and women's aging, as well as the broader cultural values that prevail in America today?

References

Abelson, Elaine S. 1989. *When Ladies Go A-Thieving: Middle-Class Shoplifters in the Victorian Department Store.* New York: Oxford University Press.

Achenbaum, W. Andrew. 1978. *Old Age in the New Land: The American Experience Since 1790.* Baltimore: Johns Hopkins University Press.

American Heritage Dictionary. 2nd College Edition. 1982. Boston: Houghton Mifflin.

Banner, Lois W. 1983. *American Beauty.* Chicago: University of Chicago Press.

Demos, John. 1983. Old age in early New England. In *The American Family in Social-Historical Perspective,* edited by Michael Gordon. New York: St. Martin's.

Dixon, Edward Henry. 1857. *Woman and Her Diseases, from the Cradle to the Grave.* New York: A. Ranney.

Drake, Emma F. Angell. 1902. *What a Woman of Forty-Five Ought to Know.* London: Virago.

Ettinger, Bruce. 1987. Overview of the efficacy of hormonal replacement therapy. *American Journal of Obstetrics and Gynecology* 156:1298–1303.

Evans, Sara M. 1989. *Born for Liberty: A History of Women in America.* New York: Free Press.

Fisher, David Hackett. 1978. *Growing Old in America.* New York: Oxford University Press.

Gordon, Linda. 1977. *Woman's Body, Woman's Right*. New York: Penguin.

Haller, John S., Jr. 1972. From maidenhood to menopause: Sex education for women in Victorian America. *Journal of Popular Culture* 6:49–70.

Kellogg, J. H. 1893. *Ladies' Guide in Health and Disease*. Battle Creek, MI: Modern Medicine.

Martin, Emily. 1987. *The Woman in the Body: A Cultural Analysis of Reproduction*. Boston: Beacon.

May, Elaine Tyler. 1980. *Great Expectations: Marriage and Divorce in Post-Victorian America*. Chicago: University of Chicago Press.

Meigs, Charles. 1848. *Females and Their Diseases*. Philadelphia: Lea and Blanchard.

Monroe, Linda Roach. 1989. Menopause: Baby boomers' next step. *Los Angeles Times*, 5 December, E1–3.

Premo, Terri L. 1983. *Women Growing Old in the New Republic: Personal Responses to Old Age, 1785–1835*. Ph.D. Diss., University of Cincinnati.

Smith-Rosenberg, Carroll. 1973. Puberty to menopause: The cycle of femininity in nineteenth century America. *Feminist Studies* 1(3–4):58–72.

Smith-Rosenberg, Carroll, and Charles R. Rosenberg. 1984. The female animal. In *Women and Health in America*, edited by Judith Walzer Leavitt. Madison, WI: University of Wisconsin Press.

Tilt, Edward John. 1882. *The Change of Life in Health and Disease. A Clinical Treatise on the Diseases of the Ganglionic Nervous System Incidental to Women at the Decline of Life*. 4th Ed. New York: Birmingham.

Utian, Wulf H. 1989. Renewing our commitment to the remaining 85%. *Menopause Management* 2(1–2).

Wells, Robert G. 1989. Should all postmenopausal women receive hormone replacement therapy? *Senior Patient* 6:65–70.

Wilson, Robert A. 1966. *Feminine Forever*. New York: M. Evans.

Wood, Ann Douglas. 1984. The fashionable disease: Women's complaints and their treatment in nineteenth-century America. In *Women and Health in America*, edited by Judith Walzer Leavitt. Madison, WI: University of Wisconsin Press.

18

Morality and Personhood
A Feminist Perspective

ROSALIND POLLACK PETCHESKY

I choose to side with women, because they will have the
responsibility for the results of that decision, and I trust their
ability to weigh the alternatives carefully. The "pro-life" side picks
fetuses, because they have little confidence in the moral judgment
of women. These women have, after all, "gotten themselves
pregnant," as one state legislator put it. They have obviously
sinned and are deserving of punishment. A fetus, on the other
hand, is virginal and pure.

MARY KAY BLAKELY, *NEW YORK TIMES*

Feminism as a perspective stands squarely in a humanist philosophical and historical tradition. Because feminists are "defenders and advocates" of women
who live in the real world, their vantage point is necessarily historical as well
as humanist.[1] Generations of earlier feminists subscribed to a set of moral
principles that were abstract and universalist, drawn from the natural rights
doctrine of the Enlightenment or from religious faith. They were arguing for
the application of those principles (including the right of "selfhood") to the
other half of the human race. Yet in practice, they found themselves having to
discard all traditions, all moral "authorities." They had to rewrite the Bible, as
Elizabeth Cady Stanton (1972) did, and to redraft every legal code because
all sources of traditional morality, even enlightened republicanism, originated
in patriarchal power and "maligned" women.

Originally published as *Abortion and Woman's Choice: The State, Sexuality, and Reproductive Freedom* (Revised Edition) by Rosalind Pollack Petchesky. Copyright 1984, 1990 by Rosalind Pollack Petchesky. Reprinted with the permission of Northeastern University Press, Boston.

Thus, even as they drew from a male-dominated culture for the language and perhaps some of the conceptual framework of a feminist moral sensibility, "women's rights" advocates in the past also looked to the actual conditions of women—their work, their marital and sexual relations, their education or lack of it—to determine the elements of a new, antipatriarchal moral vision. Their perspective, in other words, was implicitly *contextual* and *social*, its references being the relations between women and men, women and children. Similarly, many feminists today, locked in the abstract moral language of "prochoice" and "privacy" derived from a male-dominated tradition of liberal individualism and property rights, nevertheless ground their practical morality about abortion in the real relations in which the necessity for abortion arises. This is the often inchoate, unarticulated perspective I refer to as "moral praxis," and it is that perspective that informs the [following] discussion of abortion morality.

My approach to understanding the moral problems of abortion is premised on the conviction that prevailing ideas about morality are inevitably shaped by their historical and cultural contexts. This is as true of the concept of "personhood" as it is of the concepts of "murder" or "maternal duty"; such concepts change historically and across cultures, which is evidence that they are neither biologically rooted nor divinely ordained. Our only reliable source of verification for their rightness or wrongness is their impact on human life and on the welfare and consciousness of human beings. Willis (1981, 207) points out that the distinction between "to kill" and "to murder" is itself understood by most legal and ethical systems, including that of the Catholic church, as relative to particular situations. "It makes no sense to discuss whether abortion is murder without considering why women have abortions and what it means to force women to bear children they don't want." The changing conditions of women are part of the total context of the morality of abortion. No amount of scientific measurement or reading of ancient theological texts can determine the "social, political and moral" meanings either of the act of abortion in a given case or of what it is to be a "person" in today's society: "Nothing outside the practice of a human group can decide or determine its membership, since it is comprised of just those individuals who have reciprocal practical relations with each other" (Manier 1977, 5).

Any serious discussion of the moral and ethical issues of abortion must be prefaced by a clear understanding that the status of the fetus and whether it shall be regarded as a "person" or a "human life" do not exhaust the bases for moral inquiry about abortion. Whether anyone can be compelled to carry and nourish a fetus she does not want is also a moral issue. Philosophers and moralists who assume that the "humanity of the fetus" is the bottom line issue in the "abortion dilemma" close their eyes to the fact that in many cultures and historical periods this way of framing the abortion question (fetus *versus* woman) was unknown. While abortion practices seems to have existed in all recorded times and cultures, the values and sanctions attached to them have been remarkably variable. Devereux's survey of primitive and ancient societies, for example, uncovers a tremendous variety of attitudes toward abortion and the fetus, "[ranging] from mild resignation to deep horror," with a corresponding range of social signs and sanctions expressing approval or disapproval. Burial customs give evidence of such differences; some cultures bury fetuses "like adults," others distinguish between miscarried and aborted fetuses for burial purposes, still others discard them indiscriminately "in the refuse heap," and at least one cannibalizes them "in time of famine" (Devereux 1955, 43–45).

Significantly, in primitive and ancient societies that have regarded abortion as wrong, it is not usually the fetus that is considered the wronged party. On the contrary, sanctions against abortion are invoked more often on behalf of the family, the tribe, the state, or the husband or maternal uncle, depending on the prevailing basis of patriarchal authority. Under Roman law, an imperial decree declared that if a woman obtained an abortion, she should be exiled, "for it may be considered dishonorable for a woman to deprive her husband of children with impunity" (cited in Noonan 1986, 27). Thus, ancient patriarchal law valued the fetus as it valued children, slaves, and wives: as the father's property rather than in its own right.

Most current literature on the morality of abortion and on how pregnant women understand that morality is striking for its historical amnesia. It assumes that moral discourse is static and given rather than socially constructed. [Yet] the major historians of abortion in nineteenth-century England and America find a widespread popular acceptance of the practice prior to "quickening," an assumption that there was no "murder" until then because there was no "child" until then. Abortion "was simply a fact of American life," and if it was thought to raise any moral issues, those had to do with women's "health and safety" rather than the status of the fetus (McLaren 1978, 34–35, 124; Mohr 1978, 73–74). Knowing the particular conditions in which abortion came to be seen as immoral, its association with lapsed "maternal duty," and the instrumental role of physicians in promoting those ideas gives us a historical perspective. It helps us to see that the "moral agonies" and guilt cited by "right-to-lifers" as the *intuitive* effects of abortion are the product of historically distinct cultural norms. Specifically, the idea that abortion is "murder" and you are "killing a baby" is a culturally generated one, not shared by many eras and peoples.

Contemporary moral discourse about abortion is constructed out of "a distinct moral language," one that may be identified with a particularly female regimen of socialization and moral development: "the language of selfishness and responsibility, which defines the moral problem as one of obligation to exercise care and avoid hurt" (Gilligan 1982, 73). This language is recognizable as the discourse of *maternalism*, which women in modern industrial societies, whether they become mothers or not, are trained to internalize and to embody in their behavior toward others (Chodorow 1978). Social historians (e.g., Badinter 1981; Flandrin 1979; Shorter 1975) document that the modern definition of motherhood as total and selfless devotion to one's biological children was not shared by our preindustrial forebears in Western Europe and that the "preciousness" of each child is a modern— and thoroughly ideological—invention. As feminist analysis shows, however, this "modernization" of motherhood, its "civilization" within the property relations of the bourgeois family, may be seen as unqualifiedly "progressive" only if we exclude the vantage point of the mother herself.

Similarly, the idea of "fetal personhood" and of the fetus as the primary protagonist in the abortion conflict is relatively new to secular thought. Where that idea has emerged historically, it has been linked with an attack on the social position and morality of women. Indeed, I argue that the moral construction of the "abortion dilemma" as one that pits the fetus against the woman in an adversarial relationship of two separate "persons" is not only a relatively recent concept but also a distortion of reality. Even within Catholic doctrine, the precise moment when the fetus becomes "animated" with a soul was for centuries the source of some dispute; Catholic moral theologians throughout the early modern period argued for various exceptions and qualifications to the abortion prohibition. Not until the mid-eighteenth century did the papacy, facing a decline in its authority and a rise in the use of birth control and abortion, impose a much stricter doctrine; and not until 1869 was abortion at any stage of pregnancy, for any reason, declared a mortal sin punishable by excommunication (Callahan 1970, 307–8, 413; Noonan 1986, 86–90, 362–65, 404–5). . . .

Fetuses and Persons

> The paramount right to life is vested in each human being from the moment of fertilization without regard to age, health, or conditions of dependency.— Proposed Text, Human Life Amendment

The position that a fetus at any point in a pregnancy, beginning at conception, is a full human person bearing the panoply of rights available to all persons under the Constitution broaches no compromise. It is not a position based on "scientific evidence," but rests crucially on religious, philosophical, and moral premises. Stated in the absolutist terms in which "right-to-lifers" almost invariably couch it, that doctrine has the consequence that every abortion, under any circumstances, is murder, the fetus being regarded in all instances as not merely human but also uniquely "innocent," or, in the more theologically correct formulation, "helpless." Thus, abortion can be nothing other than a wanton form of human killing: "When the mask is lifted from the liberty of abortion, it is seen that the liberty consists in a freedom to knife, poison, starve, or choke a human being differing only in his or her degree of helplessness from the one who kills and the judge whose decree makes the killing possible" (Noonan 1979, 171).

Emotionally charged rhetoric such as this is aimed at reclaiming the terms of moral judgement and righteousness from what are seen as the individualistic, libertarian values of the last two decades. More than a battle to save fetal lives, more even than a battle over the limits of legitimate sexuality, the antiabortion movement must be understood as the battle for *moral hegemony* and control over popular consciousness accompanying a right-wing economic and political resurgence. One surmises that it is not so much the *act* of abortion that "right-to-lifers" and the Catholic church hierarchy are worried about as it is the legitimation and visibility of abortion and the "permissive" sexual morality they seem to uphold. As Blanche Cook observes with regard to homosexuality, it is not the committing of sin but its politicization and public display that are the threat (Scholar and the Feminist Conference 8, Barnard College, April 11, 1981). Abortions, like gay bars, can stay in back alleys. Three constitutive elements in this struggle over morality need to be sorted out if we are to understand the emotional power and ethical fallacies in "right-to-life" ideology: religious symbolism, biological reductionism, and maternal revivalism.

Religious Symbolism

"Right-to-life" spokespeople strenuously oppose the characterization of their movement as primarily religious, despite all the evidence about the centrality of religious personnel and institutions in antiabortion organizing. Many liberal Catholics are sensitive to the charge that the antiabortion cause is led by the church hierarchy, or to the association of the "right-to-life" movement with the church, seeing behind it a veiled expression of anti-Catholic bigotry (e.g., Steinfels 1981). In fact, the argument made again and again about the cross-denominational character of both antiabortion attitudes and antiabortion activism is valid. Yet the emphasis on interdenominationalism obscures the importance of religious symbolism in abortion politics, especially in regard to "fetal personhood." A pluralism of sects does not necessarily mean an absence of doctrinaire religious values and motifs inspiring that idea. It is not religion that is objectionable in "right-to-life" ideology but conservative, antihumanist religion, which contradicts its claim to rest on "science" and reveals its fundamentally narrow, sectarian character. An important part of the struggle for moral hegemony is that being waged *within* the major religious groups (Catholic, Protestant, and Jewish), between their liberal and sometimes feminist tendencies and their orthodox or fundamentalist tendencies.

The religious doctrines underlying antiabortion ideology, taken as a related cluster, are more characteristic of fundamentalist and orthodox sects. These religious doctrines include (1) belief in the existence of an immortal soul; (2) belief that the soul is "implanted" in the fetus from the moment of conception; (3) belief in the doctrine of original sin or the innate sinfulness of human beings, who are "conceived in sin"; (4) belief therefore that souls "killed unbaptized" are lost to eternal salvation and that death before birth is an especially horrible "curse"; (5) belief in divine creation and in the fetus as the "bearer of God's image"; and (6) belief in the doctrine of "stewardship," that human bodies belong neither to themselves nor to their parents nor to society, but to God, their creator, who alone has the right to kill the "innocent" (Callahan 1970; *McRae v. Califano* 1980, 695; Frame 1978; Noonan 1967).[2]

While there is little theological content or consistency to the idea of fetal innocence[3] (which, at least in Roman Catholic theology, contradicts the idea of fetal sin), it is used continually by the antiabortion movement as a symbol to mobilize, not just moral outrage but religious sentiment in an attempt to justify an absolute prohibition against abortion. A polemical device that draws on religious signifiers, the notion of innocence constructs the view of abortion as murder and the fetus as helpless victim. It also implies that the fetus is an object of preference—holier, closer to God, than women and their families. Thus the "absolutist" or "one-dimensional" position of the Catholic church and the "right-to-life" movement on abortion "gives the fetus the overwhelming advantage," making conflicting concerns, such as the health or well-being of pregnant women, negligible (Callahan 1970, 419, 430–31). The church's 1974 Declaration of Abortion, denying that even danger to a woman's life is insufficient justification for abortion, makes this perfectly clear:

> We do not deny these very great difficulties. It may be a serious question of health, sometimes of life or death, for the mother; it may be the burden represented by an additional child, especially if there are good reasons to fear that the child will be abnormal or retarded; it may be the importance attributed in different classes of society to considerations of honor or dishonor, of loss of social standing, and so forth. We proclaim only that none of these reasons can ever objectively confer the right to dispose of another's life, even when that life is only beginning (cited in *McRae v. Califano* 1980, 693).

To a moral tradition that celebrates renunciation and turning away from the human world, the woman who dies in childbirth become the supreme "exemplar" of blessed motherhood and Christian "self-sacrifice" (Noonan 1967, 130–31).

Biological Reductionism

Increasingly, in response to accusations of religious bias and violations of church-state separation, the evidence marshaled by antiabortionists to affirm the personhood of the fetus is not its alleged possession of a soul but its possession of a human body and genotype. In addition, by relying on biological, or genetic, determinism, the "right-to-life" movement asserts a claim to scientific objectivity. Biological determinism grows out of the social Darwinism and eugenics of the nineteenth and early twentieth centuries, which were applied in the service of racism, class domination, and population control. Its essential core is an attempt to explain the meaning and direction of human society, behavior, and values in terms of biochemistry and what we can observe about heredity: "For sociobiologists and believers in natural aristocracies of class and sex, the properties of society are determined by the intrinsic properties of individual human beings, individuals are the expressions of their genes, and genes are nothing but self-replicating molecules" (Lewontin 1983, 34). All human life is reduced to its chemical bits. It is no accident, of course, that the "right-to-life" movement draws on mechanistic biological explanation as well as religion to legitimate its moral and social philosophy. For it does so in a general ideological climate that has seen the revival of genetic "theories" of race and reductionist theories of genetics; the rise of sociobiology in the social sciences; and, as part of the backlash against feminism, the renewed respectability of biological arguments supporting gender distinctions (e.g., Levin 1980).

"Fetal personhood" doctrine draws upon biological determinism in several ways. Its crudest expression is the profusion of antiabortion imagery presenting the fetus as a "baby." It is a propagandistic tour de force to have taken the notion of "personhood" (a metaphysical, moral idea) and translated it into a series of arresting visual images that are utterly physiological and often just plain morbid. Various techniques are used to convey the idea that the fetus is literally a baby from the moment of conception: (1) photographs of fetuses at different stages of development, revealing recognizable physiological features; (2) photographs of aborted (bloody, gory) fetuses, particularly those aborted late; (3) clinical descriptions of fetal development, with special emphasis on the formation of heartbeat, fingerprints, fingers, and toes; (4) juxtaposition or alternation of pictures of fetuses with pictures of live babies, reinforcing the idea of their identity; and (5) the constant use of language referring to fetuses as "babies," "children," or "unborn children."[4]

The fetus as an image of the small, the helpless, and the mortal is made to *embody* one's desire for protection, for the safety of the womb; hence its power as a symbol to manipulate emotions. Through an erroneous attempt to portray the fetus as a miniature replica of you or me, this imagery not only denies the subtle processes of biological development but also seeks to arouse one's sense of identity with the fetus. Indeed, continually stressing the "small fingers and toes" or the capacity of the fetus to "feel pain" excites this kind of identification, through a psychological mechanism that reduces the sense of "humanity" to its most primitive biological and sentimental manifestations. The purpose of shocking, scaring and eliciting morbid fears is connected to the biologistic reduction of the meaning of "human life." "Right-to-life" rhetoric communicates the worst horrors of our age; abortion is "killing babies," clinics are "death camps" and "abortion chambers," clinicians who perform abortions are "death peddlers" and "Nazi murderers." Their emphasis on fetuses "hacked to pieces" or "burned" in saline solution is polemical, since it refers to only 5 percent of all abortions. For people who claim to uphold "life," as critics have frequently noted, "right-to-lifers" are enormously preoccupied, even obsessed, with death and the remnants of aborted fetuses, apotheosizing and even displaying them in public rituals. . . .

The broader problem with the idea that the fetus is a "person" from conception is its concept of personhood, or even humanity, for it either rests on a theological premise—"ensoulment"—or it reduces to a crude, mechanistic biologism. In legal and moral terms, this means that the concept of "person" (moral) is totally collapsed into the concept of "human life" (biological, or genetic).[5] In fact, as Dr. Leon Rosenberg testified in the Senate hearings on S. 158, there is *not* agreement among scientists about the question of "when human life begins," nor any way to determine the answer definitively (Meyer 1981; Sullivan 1981; Weintraub 1981). But I submit that *the beginning of human life is not the issue*, for it can be argued that fetuses, even if they are "human life," are still not human *persons*. It might be conceded that the fetus is a *form* of life insofar as it is alive (as established by EEG readings, heartbeat, and other biological responses) and it is human (in the narrow and morally insignificant sense that it is composed of authentically human genes or DNA, derived from genetically human parents). Yet, agreeing on this reduction of the fetus' identity to its genetic material does not move us one step toward knowing what *value* to give the fetus, what *rights* it has (either as a class or in a particular case), or whether to regard it as a person in the moral and legal sense (which is the only sense there is) (Callahan 1970 377–78, 388–89). . . .

Maternal Revivalism

Like its view of the fetus, the "right-to-life" view of motherhood is a re-markably Victorian mixture of religious and biological-determinist elements. On the one hand, there is the Augustinian image of woman as ordained by God to procreate; the passive receptacle of the male seed, "selfish" and "sinful" if she evades that destiny and directs her sexuality to nonprocreative ends. Abortion, from this view, is a sin against God in defiance of woman's nature, for which she is morally culpable. Hence the message communicated in "right-to-life" literature, demonstrations, and harassment of women at abor-tion clinics. Women who get abortions are "murdering their own children," putting their "selfish desires" before their "own children's lives," and will suffer terrible guilt. But what if the woman does not feel agony or guilt but, like many women after an abortion, feels mainly relief that a difficult problem has been put behind her? One antihumanist, "prolife" writer insists that the woman's feelings have nothing to do with whether or not she *is* guilty, which is determined by her objective relation to the "moral law" and not by "subjective experience." She *"ought* to feel guilty" because she has in fact committed "an evil of incomprehensible dimensions" (Ganz 1978, 30, 33). The fundamentalist doctrine that "man's nature is wholly corrupt" is opposed here to "the humanist tenet that man is basically good." The very idea of human progress and social or moral development or "enrichment" in history is anathema to this doctrine, which asserts "the wickedness of man" (and, assuredly, of woman) as the source of every human (i.e., social) problem. Hence, "why have mothers, in the name of the liberation of womanhood, demanded the death of their own children?" For the antihumanist "prolifer," the answer is quite simple: "human wickedness" (Ganz 1978, 35–36).

The "right-to-life" doctrine of the fetus' "personhood" and the aborting woman's "selfishness" is akin to the antihumanist philosophy of the New Right. Antihumanism, as professed by the "right-to-life" and "profamily" movements, pits itself squarely against every intellectual and philosophical tradition that grew out of the Enlightenment and secularism. Marxism and feminism are of course denounced by the right, but so are all philosophies, including radical Christian movements such as liberation theology, whose central focus is social change on this earth or even human, as opposed to divine or scriptural, ends. When Weyrich (1979, 18) describes the Moral Majority as "a Christian democratic movement rooted in the authentic Gospel, not the social gospel," he is attacking and distinguishing his politics from those Christian movements in the United States and Latin America that ally with the poor to change oppressive social conditions.[6] All social movements, including labor movements, peasant uprisings, anticolonial struggles, civil rights, and antinuclear protests, would thus be categorized by the New Right under "materialistic, atheistic humanism," charged with the sin of making human life and human pleasure on earth the measure of all value. But a particular condemnation is reserved for feminism and the movement for sexual liberation. The New Right associates this branch of humanism most closely with hedonism, equated with "doing whatever feels good," with "moral perversity and total corruption."

By the end of the 1970s, some "right-to-lifers" began to promote the view that women who get abortions are themselves victims—of profiteering doctors or coercion by Planned Parenthood—and should be offered protection and Christian compassion (through such structures as Birthright and pregnancy hotlines, for example). In this view, abortion is depicted as contrary to women's true desires and interests as mothers, invariably a source of anguish and "ambivalence." Yet this profession of "compassion" and support for pregnant women is simply a more paternalistic version of the idea of an innate maternalism, which abortion violates. In a major "right-to-life" propaganda piece, Francis A. Schaeffer, a fundamentalist minister, and C. Everett Koop, U.S. surgeon general and head of the National Institutes of Health under Reagan, refer to women who have had abortion as "aborted mothers" and "bereft mothers" filled with bitterness and "sorrow":

> With many of the women who have had abortion, their "motherliness" is very much present even though the child is gone. . . . One of the facts of being a human being is that in spite of the abnormality of human beings and the cruelty of their actions, there still exist the hopes and fears, the longings and aspirations,

that can be bundled together in the word *motherliness*. To stamp out these feelings is to insure that many women will turn into the kind of hard people they may not want to be (1978, 52).

Like the fundamentalist fire-and-brimstone view, the implication of the "Christian compassionate" view of abortion is the basic precept of all patriarchal ideology: Motherhood—and indeed "motherliness," a *state of being* and not just a social role or relationship—is the primary purpose of a woman's life. Abortion is thus "abnormal," "unnatural"; a woman who undergoes an abortion is subverting her own nature and will surely suffer or become "hardened" (read, unmotherly, *unwomanly*). Whether the "prolife Christian" confronts her "suffering" with pity or hatred, the point is that suffer she must, for procreation and childbearing are woman's "privileged position and purpose in human history" and to renounce them—whether once or for good—is to place herself outside female nature and "human history."

More ancient than the idea of the fetus as person, the primacy and necessity of woman as Mother has been a continuous ideological thread in antiabortion pronouncements since the nineteenth century. Callahan (1970, 421) quotes the Catholic theologian Bernard Häring, writing in 1966 in terms that lay bare the deeper passions underlying "right-to-life" sentiments:

> If it were to become an accepted principle of moral teaching on motherhood to permit a mother whose life was endangered simply to "sacrifice" the life of her child in order to save her own, motherhood would no longer mean absolute dedication to each and every child.

Because the pregnant woman is Mother, she must be ready to die for the fetus. More than survival of the individual fetus, what is ultimately at stake in the abortion struggle, in this view, is the "moral teaching" of motherhood as "absolute dedication." It is the *idea* of woman as Mother, and of the fetus as the tie that binds her to marital chastity and selflessness, that takes precedence over anything else. The woman who has an abortion makes a clear statement about her life and her understanding of her moral and social commitments relative to a potential maternal relationship; she renounces, defies the concept of motherhood as total self-sacrifice for the sake of others. On some level, perhaps, she even asserts her capacity to exercise control over life and death— and this makes her particularly, ineffably dangerous.[7] Thus does antiabortion ideology reveal its association, not only with antifeminism, but with the most primitive traditions of misogyny.

Contemporary opponents of abortion reflect these elements of misogynist thinking in their perpetuation of the myth that women who get abortions do so mostly for reasons of "convenience" and to repudiate motherhood. (Thus, for example, one social scientist refers to abortion as "an easy alternative for women who perceived that having children was no longer one of the attractive feminine roles" (Liu 1977, 147). We have seen that the social reality behind this perception is complex; motherhood has assumed a *different* place in many women's lives during the past decade, interwoven with work and study, deferred but hardly abandoned. What is important here is the tremendous emotionalism and hostility toward women that the perception of change has apparently generated. The cry that women are "killing their children" (you too, it seems to say, might have been an abortion) signals a new wave of "momism" and "motherhood revivalism," a fundamental current of the New Right's moral offensive. This cry touches deep nerves—fears of maternal abandonment, fears that women will no longer mother. The assumption behind it, that woman's purpose is to exemplify "unselfishness" through motherhood, is not often challenged even by those who claim to favor "choice."[8] Recently, a rash of disclaimers and apologies by liberals, leftists, and even some feminists in the popular media, confessing "ambivalence" about abortion, reveal the extent to which "right-to-life" ideology has penetrated the dominant culture and fostered guilt, even without a change in the law. More than ever, we need a feminist morality of abortion, one that addresses the issues that "right-to-lifers" raise in human, social terms and moves well beyond them.

Toward a Feminist Concept of Personhood

The doctrine of fetal personhood is morally offensive from a feminist, socialist, and humanist standpoint because what makes human life distinct is its capacity for consciousness and sociability. To reduce it to genetics, to equate Holocaust victims with aborted fetuses, is to demean human life and the moral value of consciousness. It is, moreover, to demean pregnant women, who are treated in this perspective as the physical vessels for genetic messages rather than responsible moral agents. Motherhood in this sense becomes, not a socially determined relationship, but a physiological function, a "fact of life." At the same time, "right-to-life" ideology equates pregnancy with motherhood as it has been defined in modern Western patriarchal culture—as a moral and social duty. Although pregnant nulliparous women do not usually regard themselves as "mothers," since in their experience there is no "child" with whom they have a relationship, this doctrine tells them they should become instantaneously "motherly" from the moment of conception.

Reducing motherhood to a passive biological state is a way of dehumanizing it, stripping it of dependence on women's consciousness. Oddly enough, however, imposing an absolute maternal duty on pregnant women induces the same deadening passivity. Biological determinism and moral absolutism arrive at the same end. The antiabortionists' charge that women who get abortions are invariably "selfish" and "irresponsible" insults not only women as moral agents but motherhood as a human practice and a conscious, demanding activity. By insisting that the abortion question has only one answer, the "right-to-life" position denies the role of human will and judgment in moral decision making, particularly in decision making about childbirth and sex. It thus denies the full human personhood of women.

What is necessary to personhood, it would seem, is *personality*—the existence of a self, which implies a psychological and a social component beyond mere biological integrity or vitalism, involving some degree of self-awareness in relation to others. What it means to be human involves an irreducible social or relational basis without which the very concept of humanity, or persons as actual or developing moral beings, makes no sense. . . .

Philosophers of diverse persuasions have understood that the preformed, self-sufficient monad—of which the fetus as person is a vulgarization—is not only philosophically but socially (*and biologically*) implausible. The Catholic humanist Jacques Maritain (1958, 6–7, 10, 27, 37) presents a concept of the person that is insistent in its emphasis on not only spirituality but sociability: "The person is a whole, but it is not a closed whole, it is an *open* whole. . . . It tends by its very nature to social life and to communion . . . demands an entrance into relationship with other persons. To state it rigorously, the person cannot be alone." The Marxist humanist Agnes Heller (1976, 46–47) clarifies the necessary interrelationship or "synthesis" between "self-consciousness," or "I-consciousness," and consciousness of being part of a larger whole, a "species-being" in Marx's sense: "The individual is a person who 'synthesizes' in himself the chance uniqueness of his individuality with the universal generality of the species," who has a *consciousness* not only of himself/herself as an end but of "his (her) world. Every person forms his world and thus himself too." "Personhood" or "humanism" in this view is not static, not a set of physical or even intellectual "properties"; rather, it is a *process*, a continual *coming to consciousness*. We *become humanized*, in a never-ending development that involves, as consciousness, rational and "moral" faculties but, more primally, feelings, sensations, the body—and always in a context of *relationship* with others. It is this relationship, this interdependence, that humanizes us; the particular physical, verbal, or intellectual mode of relating is secondary. Seen from this perspective of humanization as a continual process of "movement toward liberation" (Maritain 1958, 27) or greater consciousness, personhood must inevitably involve some differences of degree. Moral philosophy cannot avoid distinguishing "between the human and the 'truly human' " (Steinfels 1981, 661) as for example when we speak of the "inhumanity of man." More important, this theoretical perspective on personhood may help us to formulate a more precise philosophical approach to the meaning of fetuses and infants at different stages of development than . . . the "right-to-life" . . . position allows. . . .

The emergence of a "self"—the psychological process of individuation in which the child begins to acquire a consciousness of itself in relation to, and separate from, others, and thus a consciousness *of* others—occurs, and *can only occur*, in an interactive and social context.

The relationship with others constructs the self in a complex and sometimes protracted process of reciprocal perceptual and later emotional cues, so that the "self" could not possibly be a genetic or inborn property. Thus, the antiabortion argument that "I cannot will that my mother should have had an abortion when she was pregnant with me," so I cannot "consistently deny to others the right to life that I claim myself," is illogical. There was no self, no "me," during my mother's pregnancy with me, with whom my present self is continuous. The fetus has no interest in preserving its body because it has no "self," no consciousness: " . . . while you have interests regarding your body, your body and its parts have no interest of their own, and in its earliest stages a fetus is only a body and not a self at all" (Wertheimer 1977, 130). While the self, the *person*, cannot exist separately from its body and its sensory apparatus, which is the biological precondition for its consciousness, the body predates the self and may survive its extinction (as consciousness).

What, then, of the "preindividuated" infant prior to its development of self-awareness, and of the fetus in its later stages? A social, relational concept of personhood, because it is focused on process rather than some illusory substance or property, allows us the possibility, the only humanist possibility, of encompassing such beings within our moral framework. It gives human control to the otherwise mystical, abstract notion of "potentiality." Human pregnancy, like any other human experience, is never raw biology; its biological dimensions are mediated by the social process of coming into relationship, in this case the earliest, most elemental relationship, which is what humanizes it. "Relationship" means, first, that there is *interdependence;* and, second, that there is *consciousness* of this, even if that consciousness is one-sided for a time. Willis (1981, 208) captures the human reality of pregnancy when she says: "There is no way a pregnant woman can passively let the fetus live; she must create and nurture it with her own body, a symbiosis that is often difficult, sometimes dangerous, uniquely intimate." The idea of a "symbiosis," however, can only refer to a social or cultural construct, a learned response. On the level of "biology alone," the dependence is one-way—the fetus is a parasite.[9] Not only is it not a part of the woman's body, but it contributes nothing to her sustenance. It only draws from her: nutrients, immunological defenses, hormonal secretions, blood, digestive functions, energy. Even the concept of "viability," *whenever* it may occur, is meaningless—a device to protect doctors against lawsuits and to denigrate the role of the pregnant woman in prenatal nurturing. What does it mean to speak of viability in a society that has no intention of providing care for the children of working mothers, much less aborted fetuses? More important, the fetus is never viable insofar as it remains utterly dependent for its survival on the mother or another human caretaker until long after birth.

Yet, pregnancy, like all relationships, is characterized by mutual dependency in a social and moral sense. For the pregnant woman, whether she wants the fetus or not, is caught up irrevocably in a condition of intimacy with and perhaps longing for it as well. The experience of going through a full-term pregnancy, bearing a child, and giving it up for adoption is punitive and traumatic for a woman because the relationship by then is real; it exists. No woman who has ever borne a child needs to be told that its "personality" and certainly its relationship to her begin to emerge well before its birth. It is not surprising that until relatively recently (and perhaps still) the moment of "quickening" was considered by most women the dividing line between the nonexistence and existence of a "child." The movements of the fetus are signs, communications, that denote to the pregnant woman its life and its dependence on and relationship to herself. Certainly up until that time a pregnant woman is in no sense a "mother," for the simple reason that motherhood is a *socially* constructed relationship, not a biological condition alone (the situation of adoption is an obvious example). She is not yet a mother any more than the man who has inseminated a fertile ovum with his sperm become from that moment a "father." With the onset of movement in the uterus, the woman begins to develop her consciousness of interrelatedness. That consciousness, emerging out of reciprocal sensory activity, marks the beginning of the social relationships that are the necessary and sole basis through which the fetus' development of a "self," its *humanization*, is possible.

The point is not that the fetus now has a "subjective" relationship with this particular "mother" but that it has objectively entered the community of human beings through its social interaction with (and not only its physical dependency on) *an* other. Its earliest "socialization" occurs through its body and the interdependence of its body with a conscious human being. The fact that the (post-"quickening") fetus or the early infant is not yet a "self" does not negate this reciprocal quality. Piaget (1952, 108–9), for example, discovered that the three-month-old infant, in the process of "assimilating" visual images (a hand) to motor activity and sucking, engages in imitation of the caretaker's movements, even before there is any recognition "of another's body and his own body. . . ." But of course, the existence of the other and its (her/his) *attentive consciousness* is the necessary precondition for the imitative activity to occur. What is irreducible and indispensable in this humanization process (the formation of the "person") is *the subjectivity of the pregnant woman*, her consciousness of existing in a relationship with the fetus. Short of artificial wombs and Brave New World laboratories (which may be the "final solution" "right-to-lifers" have in mind), there is no getting around this, no eliminating the pregnant woman as active agent of the fetus' "personhood." For it is *her* consciousness that is the condition of its humanization, of its consciousness evolving from the potential to the actual. . . .

Notes

1. The framework for thinking about feminism that I am drawing from here comes from the groundbreaking work of the late Joan Kelly. See especially Kelly (1984) and her unpublished notes on feminist history.
2. I do not mean to suggest that any one of these points, taken by itself, is particular to right-wing fundamentalist sects but that as a chain of interconnected reasoning it reflects their doctrinal position. According to Noonan, there is "no relation" between "the Christian position" on fetal personhood beginning at conception and "theories of infant baptism" (1967, 125). But there is no doubt that this vulgarization of that position is embedded in "right-to-life" ideology.

3. At least in Roman Catholic theology, fetal "innocence" is a heresy or highly contradictory, since it conflicts with the doctrine that all human beings are "conceived in sin." As Dr. Beverly Harrison, author of *Our Right to Choose* (1983), explained to me, it cannot both be true that "personhood" has nothing to do with consciousness or moral awareness and that the fetus is innocent, which implies the capacity for guilt. "Innocence" in this usage must be a metaphorical, polemical, and ultimately "nostalgic" (Harrison's term) use of the notion of "helplessness," the concept preferred by Noonan (1967). My thanks to Beverly Harrison for discussing this question with me, and to Janet Gallagher, who brought the issue to my attention.

4. This synopsis is based on examination of dozens of pieces of antiabortion propaganda material produced between 1975 and 1980 by "prolife" groups and widely available through churches and National Right-to-Life Committee chapters.

5. Thus the legal memorandum (Galebach, 1981) that provided the theoretical ammunition for "prolife" sponsors of S. 158 justifies Congress' authority to override the Supreme Court in *Roe v. Wade* on the unexamined assumption that "if Congress decides that unborn children are human life for the purpose of the fourteenth amendment's protection of life, it follows logically that for this purpose they are persons as well. By common usage of language, any human being must be recognized a person." It by no means "follows logically" nor is it a matter of "common usage" to equate fetuses with persons in this way.

6. Typical of fundamentalist right-wing attacks on "secular humanism" in relation to abortion are Ganz (1978, 26–42) and Schaeffer and Koop (1978). In a like-spirited address before the Institute of Religious Life's Conference in St. Louis, 22 April 1978, Rep. Henry Hyde expressed concern over the rise of left-wing and feminist dissidents within the church who are critical of the church's social policies—a trend he sees as posing "serious problems for the church." The text of this speech is available from Rep. Hyde's office.

7. On the ancient origins and continuities of myths embodying men's fear of women's power over mortality, see de Beauvoir (1961), Rich (1976), and Slater (1968).

8. Callahan, a liberal supporter of women's "right to decide," expresses diffidence toward women who get abortions for what he considers to be "selfish" or not "serious reasons," which turn out to be any reasons not grounded in maternal duty, either to other children or to "the good of mankind" (1970, 429–31). This contradicts the strong arguments he makes later on about women's right to define the abortion situation as they see fit.

9. My thanks to Randy Reiter for helping me to clarify this point.

References

Badinter, Elisabeth. 1981. *Mother Love: Motherhood in Modern History*. New York: Macmillan.

Callahan, Daniel. 1970. *Abortion: Law, Choice, and Morality*. New York: Macmillan.

Chodorow, Nancy. 1978. *The Reproduction of Mothering*. Palo Alto, Calif.: Stanford University Press.

de Beauvoir, Simone. 1961. *The Second Sex*. New York: Bantam.

Devereux, George. 1955. *A Study of Abortion in Primitive Societies: A Typological,*

Distributional, and Dynamic Analysis of the Prevention of Birth in 400 Preindustrial Societies. New York: Julian Press.

Flandrin, Jean Louis. 1979. *Families in Former Times: Kinship, Household, and Sexuality*. Cambridge, UK: Cambridge University Press.

Frame, John M. 1978. Abortion from a Biblical perspective. In *Thou Shalt Not Kill: The Christian Case Against Abortion*, edited by Richard L. Ganz. New Rochelle, N.Y.: Arlington House.

Galebach, Stephen H. 1981. A human life statute. *Congressional Record* 19 (January): 5289.

Ganz, Richard L. 1978. Psychology and abortion: The deception exposed. In *Thou Shalt Not Kill: The Christian Case Against Abortion*, edited by Richard L. Ganz. New Rochelle, N.Y.: Arlington House.

Gilligan, Carol. 1982. *In a Different Voice: Psychological Theory and Women's Development*. Cambridge, Mass.: Harvard University Press.

Harrison, Beverly. 1983. *Our Right to Choose*. Boston: Beacon.

Heller, Agnes. 1976. Marx's theory of revolution and the revolution in everyday life. In *The Humanisation of Socialism: Writings of the Budapest School*, edited by Andras Hegedus, Agnes Heller, Markus, and Vajna. New York: St. Martin's Press.

Kelly, Joan. 1984. Early feminist theory and the querelle des femmes, 1400–1789. In *Women, History, and Theory*, edited by Joan Kelly. Chicago: University of Chicago Press.

Levin, Michael. December 1980. The feminist mystique. *Commentary* 70:25–30.

Lewontin, R. C. 1983. The corpse in the elevator. *New York Review of Books* 20 (January):34–39.

Liu, William T. 1977. Abortion and the social system. In *Abortion: New Directions for Policy Studies*, edited by Edward Manier, William Liu, and David Solomon. Notre Dame: University of Notre Dame Press.

Manier, Edward. 1977. Abortion and public policy in the U.S.: A dialectical examination of expert opinion. In *Abortion: New Directions for Policy Studies*, edited by Edward Manier, William Liu, and David Solomon. Notre Dame: University of Notre Dame Press.

Maritain, Jacques. 1958. *The Rights of Man and Natural Law*. London: Geoffrey Bles.

McLaren, Angus. 1978. *Birth Control in Nineteenth-Century England*. New York: Holmes & Meier.

McRae v. Califano. 1980. 491 F. Supp. 630.

Meyer, Harriet S. 1981. Science and the "Human Life Bill," Commentary. *Journal of the American Medical Association* 246:837–39.

Mohr, James C. 1978. *Abortion in America*. New York: Oxford University Press.

Noonan, John T., Jr. 1967. Abortion and the Catholic church. *Natural Law Forum* 12:85–131.

———. 1979. *A Private Choice: Abortion in America in the Seventies*. New York: Free Press.

———. 1986. *Contraception: A History of Its Treatment by the Catholic Theologians and Canonists*. Cambridge, Mass.: Belknap Press of Harvard University Press.

Piaget, Jean. 1952. *The Origins of Intelligence in Children*. New York: Norton.

Rich, Adrienne. 1976. *Of Woman Born: Motherhood as Experience and Institution*. New York: Norton

Schaeffer, Francis A., and C. Everett Koop. 1978. *Whatever Happened to the Human Race?* Old Tappan, N.J.: Fleming H. Revell.

Shorter, Edward. 1975. *The Making of the Modern Family.* New York: Basic.

Slater, Philip E. 1968. *The Glory of Hera.* Boston: Beacon.

Stanton, Elizabeth Cady. 1972 [c. 1895–98]. *The Woman's Bible.* New York: Arno Press.

Steinfels, Peter. 1981. The search for an alternative. *Commonweal* 108:660–61.

Sullivan, Walter. May 4, 1981. Onset of human life: Answer on crucial moment elusive. *New York Times*, p. B12.

Weintraub, Bernard. April 25, 1981. Senator agrees to extend hearings on abortion bill. *New York Times*, p. A7.

Wertheimer, Roger. 1977. Philosophy on humanity. In *Abortion: New Directions for Policy Studies*, edited by Edward Manier, William Liu, and David Solomon. Notre Dame: University of Notre Dame Press.

Weyrich, Paul. August 1979. Building the Moral Majority. *Conservative Digest* 5:18–19.

Willis, Ellen. 1981. Abortion: Is a woman a person? In *Beginning to See the Light: Pieces of a Decade,* edited by Ellen Willis. New York: Knopf.

19

The Future of Reproductive Choice for Poor Women and Women of Color

Dorothy E. Roberts

In 1893, a former slave named Anna Julia Cooper spoke to the Congress of Representative Women [a group instrumental in convening Chicago's 1893 Columbian Exposition] about the struggle of Black women to protect their daughters from sexual exploitation by white slavemasters. Her words were:

> Yet all through the darkest period of the colored woman's oppression in this country her yet unwritten history is full of heroic struggle, a struggle against fearful and overwhelming odds, that often ended in horrible death, to maintain and protect that which woman holds dearer than life. The painful, patient, and silent toil of mothers to gain a fee simple title to the bodies of their daughters, the despairing fight, as of an entrapped tigress, to keep hallowed their own persons, would furnish material for epics (Loewenberg and Bogin 1976, 329).

To me, Anna Cooper's words capture so incisively the truth that reproductive freedom has historically been the cornerstone of women's control over their lives. She tells us that slavewomen recognized then that reproductive autonomy was a precious right worth struggling for—even dying for.

I have chosen to begin my talk on the future of reproductive freedom for poor women and women of color by looking at the past. Studying the experience of Black women during slavery has taught me lessons about the historical significance of reproductive choice. The slaveowners' oppression of Black women, through the exploitation of their reproductive capacity, exemplifies the intimate connection between reproductive freedom and equality.

Originally published as Dorothy E. Roberts. 1990. "The Future of Reproductive Choice for Poor Women and Women of Color." *Women's Rights Law Reporter* 12(2):59–67. Reprinted with permission of *Women's Rights Law Reporter*.

Female slaves were valuable not only for their labor but also for their capacity to produce more slaves. The slaveholder understood that controlling Black women's reproductive choices was vital to his economic interests. Legislation giving the children of Black women and white men the status of slaves left female slaves vulnerable to sexual violation as a means of financial gain. Black slavewomen were also sexually exploited as a way to subjugate the entire slave community. Even after Emancipation, the Ku Klux Klan's terrorization of the Black community included the rape of Black women. Throughout American history the subordination of women has been tied to their reproductive capacity. This biological difference has been used as an excuse for discrimination against women and their unequal treatment under the law. Women have been denied autonomy over their bodies and over fundamental decisions by restricting their reproductive choices. Without the ability to determine their reproductive destinies, women will never achieve an equal role in social, economic, and political life and will continue to be politically subordinate to and economically dependent on men.

We cannot understand, for example, the danger of a company's policy of excluding all fertile women from employment unless we understand the connection between reproductive freedom and equality. The 7th Circuit recently upheld such a policy of a Milwaukee battery manufacturer because of the possible harm to potential fetuses by lead contamination (*Auto Workers v. Johnson Controls, Inc.* 1989). [This decision was overturned by a higher court.] Is this policy one that simply demonstrates the company's concern for the health of women and their children? Or does it contribute to the subordination of women by denying them the same opportunity as men to work and advance in the company?[1] Does it work to deny women control over their reproductive future by coercing blue collar women who desperately need employment to undergo sterilization so that they can submit the required doctor's affirmation that they are not fertile? Does it, in the long run, diminish the community's health by diverting attention from what *should* be the company's concern—providing a safe workplace for all of its workers?

This connection between denying reproductive choice and oppression will necessarily be the sharpest for poor women and women of color. Because of poverty, these women have fewer real options and are dependent on government funds to realize the decisions they make. Because the government is more involved in their lives, through the use of public facilities and bureaucracies, they are more susceptible to government monitoring and supervision. Because it is harder for them to meet the ideal middle-class standard of what a woman or mother should be, society is more likely to approve of, or overlook, punishing them for making reproductive decisions. Because they have less access to lawyers, the media, and advocacy organizations, and because society has convinced many that they are powerless, they are less likely to challenge government restrictions of their rights. Reproductive freedom is a right that belongs to all women; but its denial is felt the hardest by poor and minority women.

What are the limitations on poor women's reproductive freedom? To answer that question we must first come to an understanding of what reproductive choice means. Supreme Court jurisprudence has definitively recognized only a minimal piece of reproductive rights—the freedom to decide, without active government interference, whether to use contraceptives and whether to terminate a pregnancy. Some commentators have suggested that that is the full extent of a woman's right to control her reproductive health.

Let me suggest a different definition. It involves a broader concept of both the words "reproductive" and "choice." A woman's reproductive life is clearly implicated in more than just the decision to use contraceptives and to have an abortion. Reproduction encompasses a range of events and conditions from the ability to bear children, to conception, to carrying a fetus, to abortion, to delivering a baby, to caring for a child. Each stage in turn involves myriad decisions that the woman must make; her decisions at each stage may be affected by numerous factors—economic, environmental, legal, political, emotional, ethical. Reproductive freedom then must extend, for example, to decisions about sterilization and medical treatment during pregnancy; it must include access to fertilization technologies and to prenatal and perinatal care. I like Kathryn Kolbert's (1988, 8) definition in "Developing a Reproductive Rights Agenda": "Reproductive freedom means the ability to choose whether, when, how, and with whom one will have children."

A choice—at least where fundamental rights are concerned—means more than the abstract ability to reach a decision in one's mind. A true choice means an uncoerced selection of one course of action over another and the ability to follow one's chosen course. An indigent woman may have the legal option to decide that she wants to terminate her pregnancy. She may even feel that an abortion is essential to her economic, physical, and emotional survival. But if the government will pay for her childbirth expenses but not for an abortion, and she has no money for either option, she does not have a choice.

I do not have the time today to discuss in detail all of the ways that the reproductive choices (in the sense I just described) of poor women are limited. Let me instead use the example of a hypothetical young woman in the inner city—Mary—who finds that she is pregnant. What are the conditions that limit her choice?

Perhaps she became pregnant because she lacked information about birth control or contraceptives were not readily available to her. Or the intercourse that caused her pregnancy may have been unwanted in the first place, either because of abuse or pressure from her partner. Maybe she is a crack addict and had sex in exchange for drugs. Or perhaps she felt pressure to become pregnant from a more subtle source: lack of any hope for employment or other personal fulfillment may have led her to seek self-worth in motherhood. If she did receive birth control counseling, she may have been directly advised to be sterilized, or forced, by lack of alternatives, to make sure she has no further pregnancies.[2]

Once pregnant, Mary may have wanted to terminate her pregnancy, but didn't know where to get information about abortion and couldn't afford one anyway.[3] Perhaps she really wanted a baby, but knows she would be solely responsible for its care and can't afford to raise a child on her own.

If Mary decides to keep the baby, it is likely that poor nutrition, indecent housing, and stress have already put her pregnancy at risk. She cannot afford to go to a private doctor for prenatal care and there may be no public prenatal clinic in her community. If she is a drug addict, she has virtually no chance of getting treatment for her drug problem or health care for her pregnancy.[4] If she lives in a jurisdiction where the district attorney has announced a policy to prosecute pregnant drug addicts, she may stay away from any available care to avoid detection. Faced with the threat of jail, she may try to abort the fetus in any way possible. Once the baby is born, she may be tempted to abandon it.

Can we say that Mary has reproductive freedom in any meaningful sense? For her, *Roe v. Wade* is worse than an abstract right; it is a cruel deception.

I see three major legal events in the last two years that signal a frightening future for the reproductive rights of poor women and women of color. They are merely representative decisions among many that are part of what seems to be a growing trend to control women's lives in the name of fetal rights. First, in November 1987, a Washington, D.C., Superior Court judge ordered Angela Carder, a pregnant woman dying of cancer, to undergo a cesarean section against her will. In affirming the trial court decision, the Court of Appeals decided that a physician's tenuous predictions about the viability of an unborn fetus can outweigh a woman's right to bodily integrity and to decide for herself how she wants to give birth to her child. Although the decision was posthumously vacated, the surgery resulted in the premature death of both Angela and the fetus.

Second, a thirty-year-old woman named Brenda Vaughn charged with forging checks was sentenced by a Washington, D.C., judge to several months in jail, despite the prosecutor's recommendation of probation, because she was pregnant and using drugs. The judge stated at sentencing that he wanted to make sure the baby was born in jail in order to protect her from her mother's drug abuse.

Finally, the United States Supreme Court's decision in *Webster v. Reproductive Health Services* handed down in 1989 confirmed the Court's position that poor women have no right effectively to exercise their choice to terminate their pregnancy.

These three decisions say that in America when it comes down to real choices, when it comes down to the nitty-gritty, when it comes down to the knife and drugs and taxpayers' money, women don't matter much and poor women of color don't matter at all.

Let me address the *Webster* decision first. In *Webster* the Supreme Court upheld a Missouri statute that, among other restrictions, banned the use of public employees or facilities for performing abortions not necessary to save the mother's life. Thus, the Court further constricted the availability of abortions to poor women—a course it had begun in prior funding decisions. In *Maher v. Roe*, the court already permitted states to deny welfare payments for nontherapeutic abortions even though they pay for medical expenses related to childbirth. *Harris v. McRae* upheld a version of the Hyde Amendment that withheld from states federal Medicaid funds used to reimburse the costs of abortions. The court reasoned in all these cases that the government is not constitutionally required to commit any resources to facilitate abortions; its failure to fund abortions does not constitute active interference in a woman's choice.

Of course, the reality for poor women is that these decisions do deny them the choice to terminate their pregnancy. The Court has allowed states to make it impossible for an indigent woman to obtain an abortion (at least a safe one) by foreclosing both government reimbursement for private abortions and the use of public hospitals. And by approving a policy of "encouraging childbirth" by providing funds for that option alone, the Court has permitted the government to use financial coercion to influence women's reproductive decisions.

Forced medical procedures—typically cesarean sections and blood transfusions—are one manifestation of a rights theory advanced by some legal scholars and enforced by judges. The argument goes: if a woman chooses to exercise her right to have a baby, rather than have an abortion, she forfeits her right to bodily autonomy. The state's interest in protecting the fetus may therefore outweigh the woman's interest in making decisions about her physical health and lifestyle. This is the only area of the law where a competent adult has been required to compromise her own health and bodily integrity for the sake of another. The trend toward increased state control of pregnant women's decisions will have the greatest effect on poor women of color. This disparate impact has already been demonstrated by empirical evidence. A study of 15 court-ordered cesareans published in 1987 found that 81% involved Black, Hispanic, and Asian women; 24% were not native English speakers (Kolder, Gallagher, and Parsons 1987).

Finally, I want to address what the prosecution of pregnant drug addicts means for the future of reproductive choice for poor women. Across the country, district attorneys have instituted a policy of prosecuting women who use drugs during pregnancy on charges of child abuse and distributing drugs to a minor. Again, the rationale for this decision is protecting the rights of the fetus. The barbarity of this policy can only be comprehended in light of the deplorable status of prenatal care for these women. The lack of adequate prenatal care for poor women already results in a disproportionate number of low birthweight babies and high infant mortality rates. The virtual nonexistence of centers for pregnant drug addicts exacerbates the problem for the women being punished. This policy means that not only does our society tell poor inner-city women that we will not recognize your right to choose to have an abortion, we will not recognize your right to have a healthy pregnancy, but if you are a drug addict, we will punish you for having a baby.

It does not take an expert to figure out that these prosecutions will not result in healthier pregnancies. They will have just the opposite effect: they will deter pregnant drug addicts from seeking help in order to avoid jail. This policy will also divert attention from the critical need for universal prenatal care and drug counseling on demand by convincing some that incarceration is the solution to the problem of unhealthy babies in poor communities.

Last week I saw a program that interviewed women in Pakistan. In that country, a woman who is raped needs the testimony of four men to be believed; otherwise she is likely to be charged with adultery and imprisoned without trial—if she escapes being stoned to death. Women—mostly poor—languish in jail based on the charge of a jealous husband or neighbor under the Zena law that prohibits the slightest indication of a woman's sexual infidelity. Young girls, forced to marry men they do not know, are subjected to regular abuse and then ostracized by their families if they escape to government shelters.

What struck me about the condition of Pakistani women was not just the system's cruelty, but the parallels to the situation in this country. That may seem a far-fetched comparison, but think about the utmost resistance requirement in rape laws that required that a woman be brutalized before she would be believed. Think about women stuck in violent relationships with nowhere to go. To me the most profound parallel was the accepting attitude of many of the women. They were resigned to life in jail or a government shelter or a violent home because that is simply what it means to be a woman. I think too often we accept the limitations that our society places on women's reproductive choices because we have learned that that is what it means to be a woman. We accept the axiom that our biological difference is a natural limitation that means we must make sacrifices that men do not have to make.

I would challenge all of us to question that premise.

Shouldn't every woman be able to walk down a street in her community at night without the fear of being attacked? (I include rape as the denial of reproductive choice.)

Shouldn't every woman be able to make an uncoerced decision whether to carry a pregnancy to term and have the means to carry out her choice?

Shouldn't every woman have access to prenatal care so that she can give birth to a healthy baby?

Shouldn't every woman who is a drug addict and wants to have a healthy baby have a place to go for help without fear she will be prosecuted for a crime?

Shouldn't every woman have the right to decide what medical procedures a doctor may perform on her body, even if she is pregnant?

I realize that these questions can only be answered affirmatively as broader problems of poverty, racism, and sexism are solved. But I think we can begin by expanding our concept of reproductive choice, understanding its connection to women's status in our society, and recognizing the fundamental, inalienable human right of every woman to control her life by controlling her reproductive destiny.

We must continue the tradition of slave mothers who, in the words of Anna Julia Cooper, "struggle[d] against fearful and overwhelming odds . . . to maintain and protect that which woman holds dearer than life . . . to gain a fee simple title to the bodies of their daughters . . . to keep hallowed their own persons."

Notes

The author thanks Nina Loewenstein and Andrea Williams for their research assistance. This paper was originally presented as part of a panel discussion at Rutgers University School of Law on October 5, 1989.

1. Women are typically the victims of fetal protection policies, even though workplace hazards can also cause genetic and other damage to *male* reproductive capacity. Exposure of men to chemicals, radiation, and other hazards may result in sperm mutations and deformities, slow movement of sperm or reduction in sperm numbers, and changes in hormones necessary for reproduction (*New York Times* 1990 and OSHA 1978). The usual response of the government and employers to such male injury has been drastically different from their policy towards women. Proven hazards for men have been banned from the workplace, while women have been excluded from jobs that are suspected to cause fetal harm (Bertin, 1989).

2. Poor women of color have been subjected to sterilization abuse for decades (Nsiah-Jefferson 1989; Levin and Taub 1987; Clarke 1984). This abuse may take the form of blatant coercion and trickery or more subtle influences on women's decisions to be sterilized. In the 1970s, for example, doctors conditioned delivering babies and performing abortions on consent to sterilization. Physicians and other health care providers still urge minority women to consent to sterilization because they view their family size as excessive or believe these women are incapable of effectively using other methods of birth control. Sterilization services are provided by states under the Medicaid program, while information about and access to other contraceptive techniques may not be available.

3. Federal regulations prohibit abortion counseling and referral by family planning clinics that receive funds under Title X of the Public Health Service Act. These regulations mean that poor women who use Title X-funded clinics are unable to obtain information about abortions at the clinic or even learn where such information can be obtained.

4. The needs of pregnant addicts have been virtually ignored by drug treatment programs. Treatment centers either overtly refuse to treat pregnant women or are effectively closed to them because of lengthy waiting lists or lack of child care. (Brotman, Hutson, and Suffet 1985; McNulty 1988). A recent survey of seventy-eight drug treatment programs in New York City conducted by Dr. Wendy Chavkin (1989) revealed that 54 percent denied treatment to pregnant women; 67 percent refused to treat pregnant addicts on Medicaid; and 87 percent excluded pregnant women on Medicaid addicted specifically to crack. Less than half of those programs that did accept pregnant addicts provided prenatal care and only two provided child care (cf. Marriott 1989).

References

Auto Workers v. Johnson Controls, Inc. 1989. 886 F. 2d 871 (7th Cir.) (*en banc*) *cert. granted*, 58 U.S.L.W. 3609 (Mar. 27, 1990).

Bertin, Joan. 1989. Reproductive hazards in the workplace. In *Reproductive Laws for the 1990s: A Briefing Handbook,* edited by Nadine Taub and Sherrill Cohen. Clifton, NJ: Humana Press.

Brotman, R., D. Hutson, and F. Suffet, eds. 1985. *Pregnant Addicts and Their Children: A Comprehensive Care Approach.* New York: New York Medical College.

Chavkin, Wendy. 1989. Help, don't jail, addicted mothers. *New York Times,* 18 July, A21.

Clarke, Adele. 1984. Subtle forms of sterilization abuse: A reproductive rights analysis. In *Test-Tube Women,* edited by Rita Arditti, Renate Duelli Klein, and Shelley Minden. London: Pandora.

Kolbert, Kathryn. 1988. Developing a reproductive rights agenda. In *Reproductive Laws for the 1990s: A Briefing Handbook,* edited by Nadine Taub and Sherrill Cohen. Clifton, NJ: Humana Press.

Kolder, Veronica E. B., Janet Gallagher, and Michael T. Parsons. 1987. Court-ordered obstetrical interventions. *New England Journal of Medicine* 316: 1192–96.

Levin, Judith, and Nadine Taub. 1987. Reproductive rights. In *Women and the Law,* edited by Carol Lefcourt. Deerfield, IL: C. Boardman.

Loewenberg, Bert J., and Ruth Bogin, eds. 1976. *Black Women in Nineteenth-cCntury American Life: Their Words, Their Thoughts, Their Feelings.* University Park: Pennsylvania State University Press.

McNulty, Molly. 1988. Pregnancy police: The health policy and legal implications of punishing pregnant women for harm to their fetuses. *New York University Review of Law and Social Change* 16:277–319.

Marriott, Michel. 1989. Treatment for addicts is as elusive as ever. *New York Times,* 19 July, E5.

New York Times. 1990. Children's cancer tied to a-plant workers. 18 February, A27.

Nsiah-Jefferson, Laurie. 1989. Reproductive laws, women of color, and low-income women. In *Reproductive Laws for the 1990s: A Briefing Handbook,* edited by Nadine Taub and Sherrill Cohen. Clifton, NJ: Humana Press.

OSHA. 1978. *Final Standard for Occupational Exposure to Lead.* 43 Fed. Reg. 52959–60.

20

"Fetal Rights"
A New Assault on Feminism

Katha Pollitt

Some scenes from the way we live now:

§In New York City, a pregnant woman orders a glass of wine with her restaurant meal. A stranger comes over to her table. "Don't you know you're poisoning your baby?" he says angrily, pointing to a city-mandated sign warning women that drinking during pregnancy can cause birth defects.

§In California, Pamela Rae Stewart is advised by her obstetrician to stay off her feet, to eschew sex and "street drugs," and to go to the hospital immediately if she starts to bleed. She fails to follow this advice and delivers a brain-damaged baby who soon dies. She is charged with failing to deliver support to a child under an old criminal statute that was intended to force men to provide for women they have made pregnant.

§In Washington, D.C., a hospital administration asks a court whether it should intervene and perform a caesarean section on Angela Carder, seriously ill with cancer, against her wishes and those of her husband, her parents, and her doctors. Acknowledging that the operation would probably shorten her life without necessarily saving the life of her 25-week-old fetus, the judge nonetheless provides the order. The caesarean is performed immediately, before her lawyers can appeal. Angela Carder dies; so does her unviable fetus. That incident is subsequently dramatized on *L.A. Law*, with postfeminist softy Anne Kelsey for the hospital; on TV the baby lives.

§In the Midwest, the U.S. Court of Appeals for the Seventh Circuit, ruling in *Auto Workers v. Johnson Controls Inc.*, upholds an automotive battery plant's

Originally published as "Fetal Rights: A New Assault on Feminism" by Katha Pollitt, from the 26 March 1990 issue of *The Nation*. Reprinted with permission from *The Nation*. Copyright The Nation Company, L. P.

seven-year-old "fetal protection policy" barring fertile women (in effect, all women) from jobs that would expose them to lead (Marshall 1987). The court discounts testimony about the individual reproductive lives and plans of female employees (many in their late 40s, celibate, and/or with completed families), testimony showing that no child born to female employees had shown ill effects traceable to lead exposure, and testimony showing that lead poses a comparable danger to male reproductive health. The court accepts the testimony that says making the workplace safe would be too expensive.

All over the country, pregnant women who use illegal drugs and/or alcohol are targeted by the criminal justice system. They are "preventively detained" by judges who mete out jail sentences for minor charges that would ordinarily result in probation or a fine; charged with child abuse or neglect (although by law the fetus is not a child) and threatened with manslaughter charges should they miscarry; and placed under court orders not to drink, although drinking is not a crime and does not invariably (or even usually) result in birth defects. While state legislatures ponder bills that would authorize these questionable practices by criminalizing drug use or "excessive" alcohol use during pregnancy (California Senator Pete Wilson is pushing a similar bill at the federal level), mothers are arrested in their hospital beds when their newborns test positive for drugs. Social workers increasingly remove positive-testing babies into foster care on the presumption that even a single use of drugs during pregnancy renders a mother ipso facto an unfit parent.

What's going on here? Right now the hot area in the developing issue of "fetal rights" is the use of drugs and alcohol during pregnancy. We've seen all the nightly news reports of inner-city intensive care units overflowing with crack babies, of Indian reservations where one in four children are said to be born physically and mentally stunted by fetal alcohol syndrome (FAS) or the milder, but still serious, fetal alcohol effect. We've read the front-page stories reporting studies that suggest staggering rates of drug use during pregnancy (11 percent, according to *The New York Times*, or 375,000 women per year) and the dangers of even moderate drinking during pregnancy.

But drugs and alcohol are only the latest focus of a preoccupation with the fetus and its "rights" that has been wandering around the *Zeitgeist* for the past decade. A few years ago, the big issue was forced caesareans. (It was, in fact, largely thanks to the horrific Angela Carder case—one of the few involving a white, middle-class woman—that the American College of Obstetricians and Gynecologists condemned the practice, which nonetheless has not entirely ceased.) If the Supreme Court upholds the *Auto Workers v. Johnson Controls* decision [ed: it did not], the next battleground may be the workplace. The "save the babies" mentality may look like a necessary, if troubling, approach when it's a matter of keeping a drug addict away from a substance that is, after all, illegal. What happens if the same mentality is applied to some 15 million to 20 million highly paid unionized jobs in heavy industry to "protect" fetuses that do not even exist? Or if the list of things women are put on legal notice to avoid expands to match medical findings on the dangers to the fetus posed by junk food, salt, aspirin, air travel, and cigarettes?

Critics of the punitive approach to pregnant drug and alcohol users point out the ironies inherent in treating a public-health concern as a matter for the criminal justice system: the contradiction, for instance, of punishing addicted women when most drug treatment programs refuse to accept pregnant women. Indeed, Jennifer Johnson, a Florida woman who was the first person convicted after giving birth to a baby who tested positive for cocaine, had sought treatment and been turned away. (In her case the charge was delivering drugs to a minor.) The critics point out that threats of jail or the loss of their kids may drive women away from prenatal care and hospital deliveries, and that almost all the women affected so far have been poor and black or Latina, without private doctors to protect them (in Florida, nonwhite women are ten times as likely to be reported for substance abuse as white women, although rates of drug use are actually higher for whites).

These are all important points. But they leave unchallenged the notion of fetal rights itself. What we really ought to be asking is, How have we come to see women as the major threat to the health of their newborns, and the womb as the most dangerous place a child will ever inhabit? Why is our basic model of "innocent" fetuses that would be fine if only presumably "guilty" women refrained from indulging their "whims"? The list of dangers to the fetus is, after all, very long; the list of danger to children even longer. Why does maternal behavior, a relatively small piece of the total picture, seem such an urgent matter, while much more important factors—that one in five pregnant women receive no prenatal care at all, for instance—attract so little attention? Here are some of the strands that make up the current tangle that is fetal rights.

The Assault on the Poor

It would be pleasant to report that the aura of crisis surrounding crack and FAS babies—the urge to do *something*, however unconstitutional or cruel, that suddenly pervades society, from judge's bench to chic dinner party to 7 o'clock news—was part of a massive national campaign to help women have healthy, wanted pregnancies and healthy babies. But significantly, the current wave of concern is not occurring in that context. Judges order pregnant addicts to jail, but they don't order drug treatment programs to accept them, or Medicaid, which pays for heroin treatment, to cover crack addiction—let alone order landlords not to evict them, or obstetricians to take uninsured women as patients, or the federal government to fund fully the Women, Infants, and Children supplemental feeding program, which reaches only two-thirds of those who are eligible. The policies that have underwritten maternal and infant health in most of the industrialized West since World War II—a national health service, paid maternity leave, direct payments to mothers, government-funded day care, home health visitors for new mothers, welfare payments that reflect the cost of living—are still regarded in the United States by even the most liberal as hopeless causes, and by everyone else as budget-breaking giveaways to the undeserving, pie-in-the-sky items from a mad socialist's wish list.

The focus on maternal behavior allows the government to appear to be concerned about babies without having to spend any money, change any priorities, or challenge any vested interests. As with crime, as with poverty, a complicated, multifaceted problem is construed as a matter of freely chosen individual behavior. We have crime because we have lots of bad people, poverty because we have lots of lazy people (Republican version) or lots of pathological people (Democratic version), and tiny, sickly, impaired babies because we have lots of women who just don't give a damn.

Once the problem has been defined as original sin, coercion and punishment start to look like hardheaded and commonsensical answers. Thus, syndicated columnist and *New Republic* intellectual Charles Krauthammer proposes locking up pregnant drug users en masse. Never mind the impracticality of the notion—suddenly the same administration that refuses to pay for drug treatment and prenatal care is supposed to finance all that plus nine months of detention for hundreds of thousands of women a year. Or its disregard of real life—what, for example, about the children those women already have? Do they go to jail, too, like Little Dorrit? Or join the rolls of the notorious foster care system? The satisfactions of the punitive mind-set sweep all such considerations aside. (Nor are liberal pundits immune from its spell. Around the same time Krauthammer was calling for mass incarceration, Mary McGrory was suggesting that we stop wasting resources—*what* resources?—on addicted women and simply put their babies in orphanages. . . .)

Science Marches On

We know a lot more about fetal development than we did twenty years ago. But how much of what we know will we continue to know in ten years? As recently as the early 1970s, pregnant women were harassed by their doctors to keep their weight down. They were urged to take tranquilizers and other prescription drugs, to drink in moderation (liquor was routinely used to stop premature labor), to deliver under anesthesia, and not bother to breast-feed. Then too, studies examined contemporary wisdom and found it good. Today, those precepts seem the obvious expression of social forces: the wish of doctors to control pregnancy and delivery, a lack of respect for women, and a distaste for female physiological processes. It was not the disinterested progress of science that outmoded these practices. It was another set of social forces: the women's movement, the prepared-childbirth movement, and the natural-health movement.

What about today's precepts? At the very least, the history of scientific research into pregnancy and childbirth ought to make us skeptical. Instead, we leap to embrace tentative findings and outright bad science because they fit current social prejudices. Those who argue for total abstinence during pregnancy have made much, for example, of a recent study in *The New England Journal of Medicine* (Frezza et al. 1990) that claimed women are more vulnerable than men to alcohol because they have less of a stomach enzyme that neutralizes it before it enters the bloodstream. Universally unreported, however, was the fact that the study included alcoholics and patients with gastrointestinal disease. It is a basic rule of medical research that results cannot be generalized from the sick to the healthy.

In a 1989 article (Koren et al.) in *The Lancet*, Canadian researchers reported that studies that found a connection between cocaine use and poor pregnancy outcome had a better than even chance of being accepted for presentation at the annual meeting of the Society for Pediatric Research, while studies that found no connection had a negligible chance—although the latter were better designed. While it's hard to imagine that anyone will ever show that heavy drug use or alcohol consumption is good for fetal development, studies like this one suggest that when the dust settles (because the drug war is officially "won"? because someone finally looks at the newborns of Italy, where everyone drinks moderate amounts of wine with food, and finds them to be perfectly fine?) the current scientific wisdom will look alarmist. . . .

The "Pro-life" Movement

Antichoicers have not succeeded in criminalizing abortion but they have made it inaccessible to millions of women (only sixteen states pay for poor women's abortions, and only 18 percent of counties have even one abortion provider) and made it a badge of sin and failure for millions more. In Sweden, where heavy drinking is common, relatively few FAS babies are born, because alcoholic women have ready access to abortion and it is not a stigmatized choice. In America antichoice sentiment makes it impossible to suggest to a homeless, malnourished, venereally diseased crack addict that her first priority ought to be getting well: Get help, then have a baby. While the possibility of coerced abortions is something to be wary of, the current policy of regulation and punishment in the name of the fetus ironically risks the same end. Faced with criminal charges, pregnant women may seek abortions in order to stay out of jail (a Washington, D.C., woman who "miscarried" a few days before sentencing may have done just that).

As lobbyists, antichoicers have sought to bolster their cause by interjecting the fetus-as-person argument into a wide variety of situations that would seem to have nothing to do with abortion. They have fought to exclude pregnant women from proposed legislation recognizing the validity of "living wills" that reject the use of life support systems (coma baby lives!), and have campaigned to classify as homicides assaults on pregnant women that result in fetal death or miscarriage. Arcane as such proposals may seem, they have the effect of broadening little by little the areas of the law in which the fetus is regarded as a person, and in which the woman is regarded as its container.

At a deeper level, the "pro-life" movement has polluted the way we think about pregnancy. It has promoted a model of pregnancy as a condition that by its very nature pits women and fetuses against each other, with the fetus invariably taking precedence, and a model of women as selfish, confused, potentially violent, and incapable of making responsible choices. As the "rights" of the fetus grow and respect for the capacities and rights of women declines, it becomes harder and harder to explain why drug addiction is a crime if it produces an addicted baby, but not if it produces a miscarriage, and why a woman can choose abortion but not vodka. And that is just what the "pro-lifers" want. . . .

The "Duty of Care"

Not everyone who favors legal intervention to protect the fetus is antichoice. Some pro-choicers support the coercion and punishment of addicts and alcoholics—uneasily, like some of my liberal women friends, or gleefully, like Alan Dershowitz, who dismisses as absurd the "slippery slope" argument (crack today, cigarettes tomorrow) he finds so persuasive when applied to First Amendment issues. For some years now biochemists have been fascinated by the doctrine of "duty of care," expounded most rigorously by Margery Shaw and John Robertson. In this view a woman can abort, but once she has decided to bear a child she has a moral, and should have a legal, responsibility to insure a healthy birth. It's an attractive notion because it seems to combine an acceptance of abortion with intuitive feelings shared by just about everyone, including this writer, that pregnancy is a serious undertaking, that society has an interest in the health of babies, that the fetus, although not a person, is also not property.

Whatever its merits as a sentiment, though, the duty of care is a legal disaster. Exactly when, for instance, does the decision to keep a pregnancy take place? For the most desperately addicted—the crack addicts who live on the subway or prostitute themselves for drugs—one may ask if they ever form any idea ordinary people would call a decision, or indeed know they are pregnant until they are practically in labor. Certainly the inaccessibility of abortion denies millions of women the ability to decide.

But for almost all women the decision to carry a pregnancy to term has important, if usually unstated, qualifications. What one owes the fetus is balanced against other considerations, such as serious health risks to oneself (taking chemotherapy or other crucial medication), or the need to feed one's family (keeping a job that may pose risks), or to care for the children one already has (not getting the bed rest the doctor says you need). Why should pregnant women be barred from considering their own interests? It is, after all, what parents do all the time. The model of women's relation to the fetus proposed by the duty of care ethicists is an abstraction that ignores the realities of life even when they affect the fetus itself. In real life, for instance, to quit one's dangerous job means to lose one's health insurance, thus exposing the fetus to another set of risks.

It is also, even as an abstraction, a false picture. Try as she might, a woman cannot insure a healthy newborn; nor can statistical studies of probability (even well-designed ones) be related in an airtight way to individual cases. We know that cigarettes cause lung cancer, but try proving in a court of law that cigarettes and not air pollution, your job, your genes, or causes unknown caused *your* lung cancer.

Yet far from shrinking from the slippery slope, duty of care theorists positively hurl themselves down it. Margery Shaw, for instance, believes that the production of an imperfect newborn should make a woman liable to criminal charges and "wrongful life" suits if she knows, or should have known, the risk involved in her behavior, whether it's drinking when her period is late (she has a duty to keep track of her cycle), delivering at home when her doctor advises her not to (what doctor doesn't?), or failing to abort a genetically damaged fetus (which she has a duty to find out about). So much for that "decision" to bear a child—a woman can't qualify it in her own interests but the state can revoke it for her on eugenic grounds.

As these examples show, there is no way to limit the duty of care to cases of flagrant or illegal misbehavior—duty is duty, and risk is risk. Thus, there is no way to enshrine duty of care in law without creating the sort of Romania-style fetal police state whose possibility Dershowitz, among others, pooh-poohs. For there is no way to define the limits of what a pregnant woman must sacrifice for fetal benefit, or what she "should have known," or at what point a trivial risk becomes significant. My aunt advised me to get rid of my cats while I was pregnant because of the risk of toxoplasmosis. My doctor and I thought this rather extreme, and my husband simply took charge of the litter box. What if my doctor had backed up my aunt instead of me? If the worst had happened (and it always does to someone, somewhere), would I have been charged with the crime of not sending my cats to the Bide-A-Wee?

Although duty of care theorists would impose upon women a virtually limitless obligation to put the fetus first, they impose that responsibility *only* on women. Philosophy being what it is, perhaps it should not surprise us that they place no corresponding duty upon society as a whole. But what about Dad? It's his kid too, after all. His drug and alcohol use, his prescription medications, his workplace exposure and general habits of health not only play a part in determining the quality of his sperm but affect the course of pregnancy as well. Cocaine dust and smoke from crack, marijuana and tobacco present dangers to others who breathe them; his alcoholism often bolsters hers. Does he have a duty of care to make it possible for his pregnant partner to obey those judge's orders and that doctor's advice that now has the force of the law? To quit his job to mind the children so that she can get the bed rest without which her fetus may be harmed? Apparently not.

The sexist bias of duty of care has already had alarming legal consequences. In the Pamela Rae Stewart case cited at the beginning of this article, Stewart's husband, who had heard the doctor's advice, ignored it all and beat his wife into the bargain. Everything she did, he did—they had sex together, smoked pot together, delayed getting to the hospital together—but he was not charged with a crime, not even with wife-beating, although no one can say that his assaults were not a contributing cause of the infant's injury and death. In Tennessee, a husband succeeded in getting a court order forbidding his wife to drink or take drugs, although he himself had lost his driver's license for driving while intoxicated. In Wyoming, a pregnant woman was arrested for drinking when she presented herself at the hospital for treatment of injuries inflicted by her husband. Those charges were dropped (to be reinstated, should her baby be born with defects), but none were instituted against her spouse.

It is interesting to note in this regard that approximately one in twelve women are beaten during pregnancy, a time when many previously nonviolent men become brutal. We do not know how many miscarriages, stillbirths, and damaged newborns are due, or partly due, to male violence—this is itself a comment on the skewed nature of supposedly objective scientific research. But if it ever does come to be an officially recognized factor in fetal health, the duty of care would probably take yet another ironic twist and hold battered women liable for their partner's assaults.

The Broken Cord, Michael Dorris's much-praised (1989) memoir of his adopted FAS child, Adam, is a textbook example of the way in which all these social trends come together—and the largely uncritical attention the book has received shows how seductive a pattern they make. Dorris has nothing but contempt for Adam's birth mother. Perhaps it is asking too much of human nature to expect him to feel much sympathy for her. He has witnessed, in the most intimate and heartbreaking way, the damage her alcoholism did, and seen the ruin of his every hope for Adam, who is deeply retarded. But why is his anger directed only at her? Here was a seriously alcoholic woman, living on an Indian reservation where heavy drinking is a way of life, along with poverty, squalor, violence, despair, and powerlessness, where, one might even say, a kind of racial suicide is taking place, with liquor as the weapon of choice. Adam's mother, in fact, died two years after his birth from drinking antifreeze.

Dorris dismisses any consideration of these facts as bleeding-heart fuzzy-mindedness. Like Hope on *thirtysomething*, Adam's mother "decides" to have a baby; like the martini-sipping pregnant woman Dorris badgers in an airport bar, she "chooses" to drink out of "weakness" and "self-indulgence."

Dorris proposes preventive detention of alcoholic pregnant women and quotes sympathetically a social worker who thinks the real answer is sterilization. Why do alcoholic Indian women have so many children? To up their government checks. (In fact, the Bureau of Indian Affairs hospitals are prohibited by law from performing abortions, even if women can pay for them.) And why, according to Dorris, do they drink so much in the first place? Because of the feminist movement, which has undermined the traditional temperance of reservation women.

The women's movement has had about as much effect on impoverished reservation dwellers as it had on the slum women of eighteenth-century London, whose heavy binge drinking—and stunted babies—appalled contemporary observers. That Dorris pins the blame on such an improbable villain points to what fetal rights is all about—controlling women. It's a reaction to legalized abortion and contraception, which have given women, for the first time in history, real reproductive power. They can have a baby, they can "kill" a baby, they can refuse to conceive at all, without asking permission from anyone. More broadly, it's an index of deep discomfort with the notion of women as self-directed social beings, for whom parenthood is only one aspect of life, as it has always been for men. Never mind that in the real world, women still want children, have children and take care of children, often under the most discouraging circumstances and at tremendous emotional, economic, and physical cost. There is still a vague but powerful cultural fear that one of these days, women will just walk out on the whole business of motherhood and the large helpings of humble pie we have, as a society, built into that task. And *then* where will we be?

Looked at in this light, the inconsistent and fitful nature of our concern about the health of babies forms a pattern. The threat to newborns is interesting when and only when it can, accurately or fancifully, be laid at women's doorstep. Babies "possibly" impaired by maternal drinking? Front-page stories, a national wave of alarm. A *New England Journal of Medicine* report (Needleman et al. 1990) that 16 percent of American children have been mentally and neurologically damaged because of exposure to lead, mostly flaking lead paint in substandard housing? Peter Jennings looks mournful and suggests that "all parents can do" is to have their children tested frequently. If the mother isn't to blame, no one is to blame.

In its various aspects "fetal rights" attacks virtually all the gains of the women's movement. Forced medical treatment attacks women's increased control over pregnancy and delivery by putting doctors back in the driver's seat, with judges to back them up. The *Auto Workers v. Johnson Controls* decision reverses the entry of women into high-paying, unionized, traditionally male jobs. In the female ghetto, where women can hardly be dispensed with, the growing practice of laying off or shifting pregnant women around transforms women, whose rates of labor force participation are approaching those of men, into casual laborers with reduced access to benefits, pensions, seniority, and promotions. In a particularly vicious twist of the knife, "fetal rights" makes legal abortion—which makes all the other gains possible—the trigger for a loss of human rights. Like the divorce court judges who tell middle-aged housewives to go out and get a job, or who favor fathers in custody disputes because to recognize the primary-caretaker role of mothers would be "sexist," protectors of the fetus enlist the rhetoric of feminism to punish women.

There are lots of things wrong with the concept of fetal rights. It posits a world in which women will be held accountable, on sketchy or no evidence, for birth defects; in which all fertile women will be treated as potentially pregnant all the time; in which courts, employers, social workers, and doctors—not to mention nosy neighbors and vengeful male partners—will monitor women's behavior. It imposes responsibilities without giving women the wherewithal to fulfill them, and places upon women alone duties that belong to both parents and to the community.

But the worst thing about fetal rights is that it portrays a woman as having only contingent value. Her work, her health, her choices and needs and beliefs, can all be set aside in an instant because, next to maternity, they are all perceived as trivial. For the middle class, fetal rights is mostly symbolic, the gateway to a view of motherhood as self-sacrifice and endless guilty soul-searching. It ties in neatly with the currently fashionable suspicion of working mothers, day care, and (now that wives are more likely than husbands to sue for it) divorce. For the poor, for whom it means jail and the loss of custody, it becomes a way of saying that women can't even be mothers. They can only be potting soil. . . .

Note

Katha Pollitt would like to express her thanks to Joan E. Bertin and Lynn Paltrow of the American Civil Liberties Union for their generous sharing of time, ideas and information, and to Janet Gallagher, whose article "Prenatal Invasions and Interventions: What's Wrong with Fetal Rights" (1987) brilliantly analyzes the pitfalls of the duty of care ethic.

References

Dorris, Michael. 1989. *The Broken Cord.* New York: Harper & Row.

Frezza, Mario, Carlo di Padova, Gabriele Pozzato, Maddalena Terpin, Enrique Baraona, and Charles S. Lieber. 1990. High blood alcohol levels in women: The role of decreased gastric alcohol dehydrogenase activity and first pass metabolism. *New England Journal of Medicine* 322(2):95–99.

Gallagher, Janet. 1987. Prenatal invasions and interventions: What's wrong with fetal rights. *Harvard Women's Law Journal* 10:9–58.

Koren, Gideon, Heather Shear, Karen Graham, and Tom Einarson. 1989. Bias against the null hypothesis: The reproductive hazards of cocaine. *Lancet* 2(8677):1440–1443.

Marshall, Carolyn. 1987. An excuse for workplace hazards. *The Nation*, April 25.

Needleman, Herbert L., Alan Schell, David Bellinger, and Alan Leviton. 1990. The long-term effects of exposure to low doses of lead in childhood: An 11-year follow-up report. *New England Journal of Medicine* 322(3):83–88.